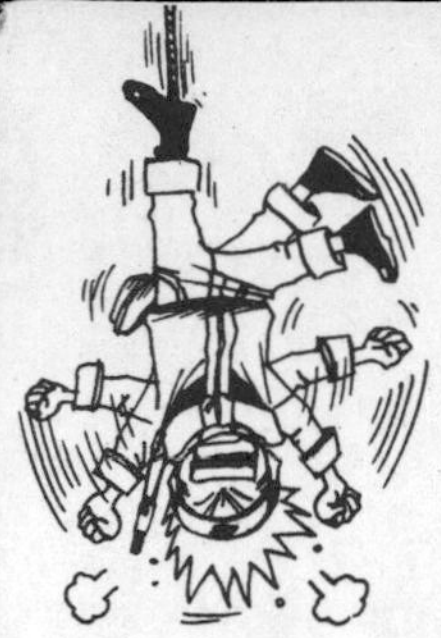

You're Reading in the Wrong Direction!!

Whoops! Guess what? You're starting at the wrong end of the comic!

...It's true! In keeping with the original Japanese format, **Naruto** is meant to be read from right to left, starting in the upper-right corner.

Unlike English, which is read from left to right, Japanese is read from right to left, meaning that action, sound effects and word-balloon order are completely reversed...something which can make readers unfamiliar with Japanese feel pretty backwards themselves. For this reason, manga or Japanese comics published in the U.S. in English have sometimes been published "flopped"—that is, printed in exact reverse order, as though seen from the other side of a mirror.

By flopping pages, U.S. publishers can avoid confusing readers, but the compromise is not without its downside. For one thing, a character in a flopped manga series who once wore in the original Japanese version a T-shirt emblazoned with "M A Y" (as in "the merry month of") now wears one which reads "Y A M"! Additionally, many manga creators in Japan are themselves unhappy with the process, as some feel the mirror-imaging of their art alters their original intentions.

We are proud to bring you Masashi Kishimoto's **Naruto** in the original unflopped format. For now, though, turn to the other side of the book and let the ninjutsu begin...!

—Editor

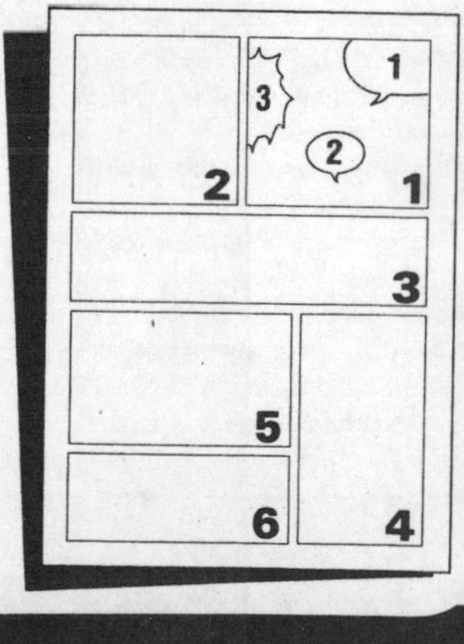
1
3
2
1
2
3
5
4
6

岸本斉史

Greetings. With everyone's support, my first comic has been published. I'm ecstatic. Speaking of ecstatic, the first time I won an award for one of my manga, I was so happy I was flying high. But this time is 10 times better than that. I don't know how to say it, but this is the happiest moment of my life. But I guess I'm happiest knowing that this comic will be read and enjoyed. Yup, that's it!
—*Masashi Kishimoto*, 2000

Author/artist Masashi Kishimoto was born in 1974 in rural Okayama Prefecture, Japan. After spending time in art college, he won the Hop Step Award for new manga artists with his manga **Karakuri** ("mechanism"). Kishimoto decided to base his next story on traditional Japanese culture. His first version of **Naruto**, drawn in 1997, was a one-shot story about fox spirits; his final version, which debuted in **Weekly Shonen Jump** in 1999, quickly became the most popular ninja manga in Japan.

NARUTO VOL. 1
SHONEN JUMP Manga Edition

This graphic novel contains material that was originally published in English in **SHONEN JUMP** #2–5. Artwork in the magazine may have been slightly altered from that presented here.

STORY AND ART BY
MASASHI KISHIMOTO

Translation/Katy Bridges
English Adaptation/Jo Duffy
Touch-Up Art & Lettering/Heidi Szykowny
Cover Design, Graphics & Layout/Sean Lee
Senior Editor/Jason Thompson
Series Editor/Joel Enos

Printed in Canada

Published by VIZ Media, LLC
P.O. Box 77010
San Francisco, CA 94107

36
First printing, July 2003
Thirty-sixth printing, January 2021

VIZ MEDIA
viz.com

ratings.viz.com
RATED T TEEN

SHONEN JUMP

SHONEN JUMP MANGA

NARUTO

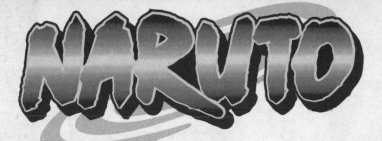

VOL. 1

UZUMAKI NARUTO

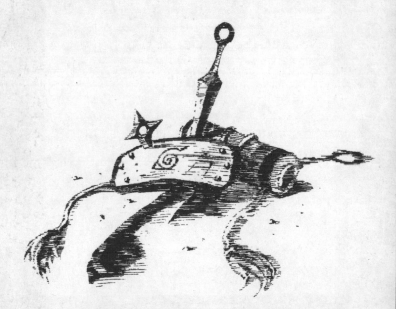

STORY AND ART BY

MASASHI KISHIMOTO

NARUTO

VOL. 1
UZUMAKI NARUTO

CONTENTS

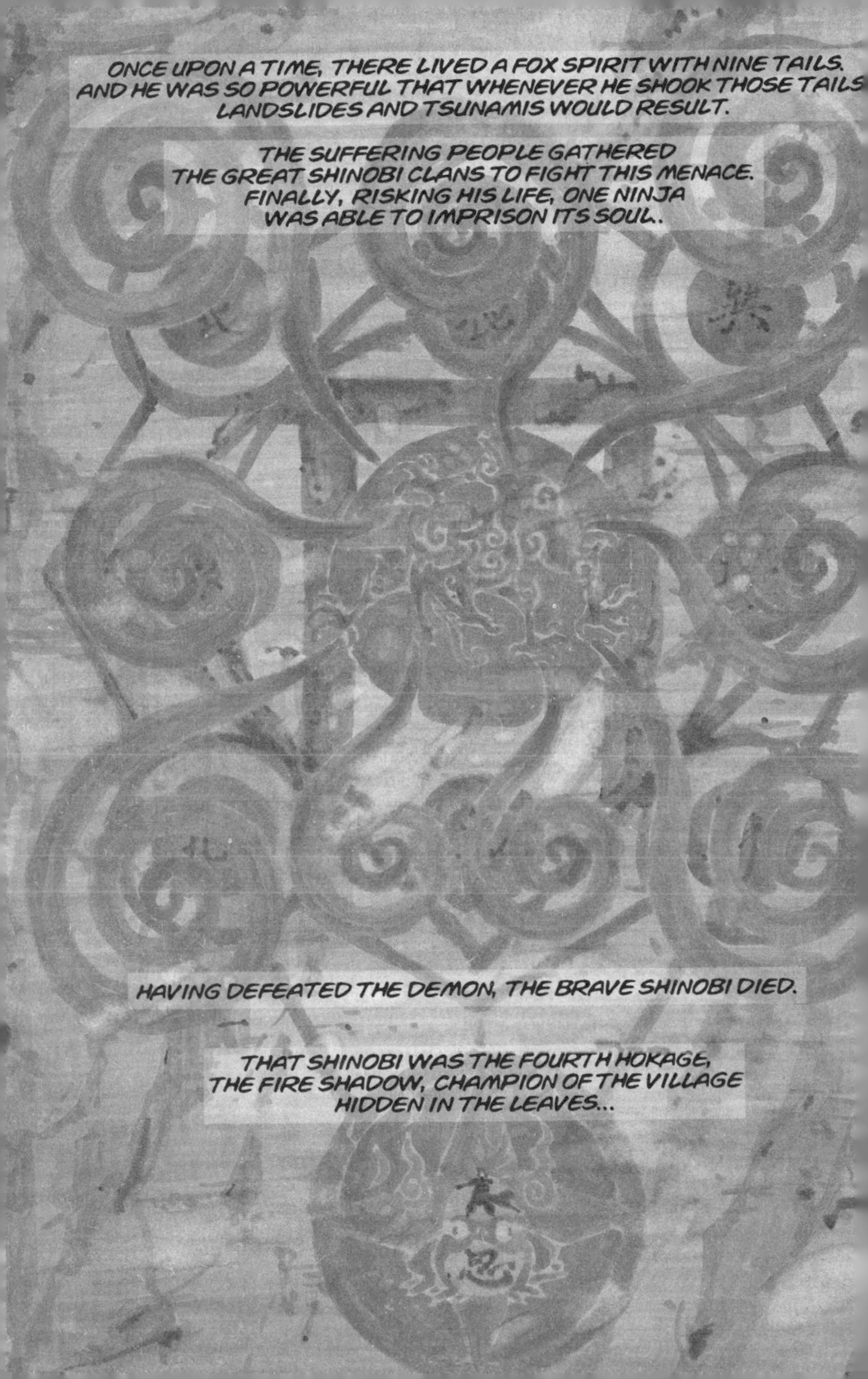
ONCE UPON A TIME, THERE LIVED A FOX SPIRIT WITH NINE TAILS. AND HE WAS SO POWERFUL THAT WHENEVER HE SHOOK THOSE TAILS LANDSLIDES AND TSUNAMIS WOULD RESULT.
THE SUFFERING PEOPLE GATHERED THE GREAT SHINOBI CLANS TO FIGHT THIS MENACE. FINALLY, RISKING HIS LIFE, ONE NINJA WAS ABLE TO IMPRISON ITS SOUL..
HAVING DEFEATED THE DEMON, THE BRAVE SHINOBI DIED.
THAT SHINOBI WAS THE FOURTH HOKAGE, THE FIRE SHADOW, CHAMPION OF THE VILLAGE HIDDEN IN THE LEAVES...

1: Uzumaki Naruto!

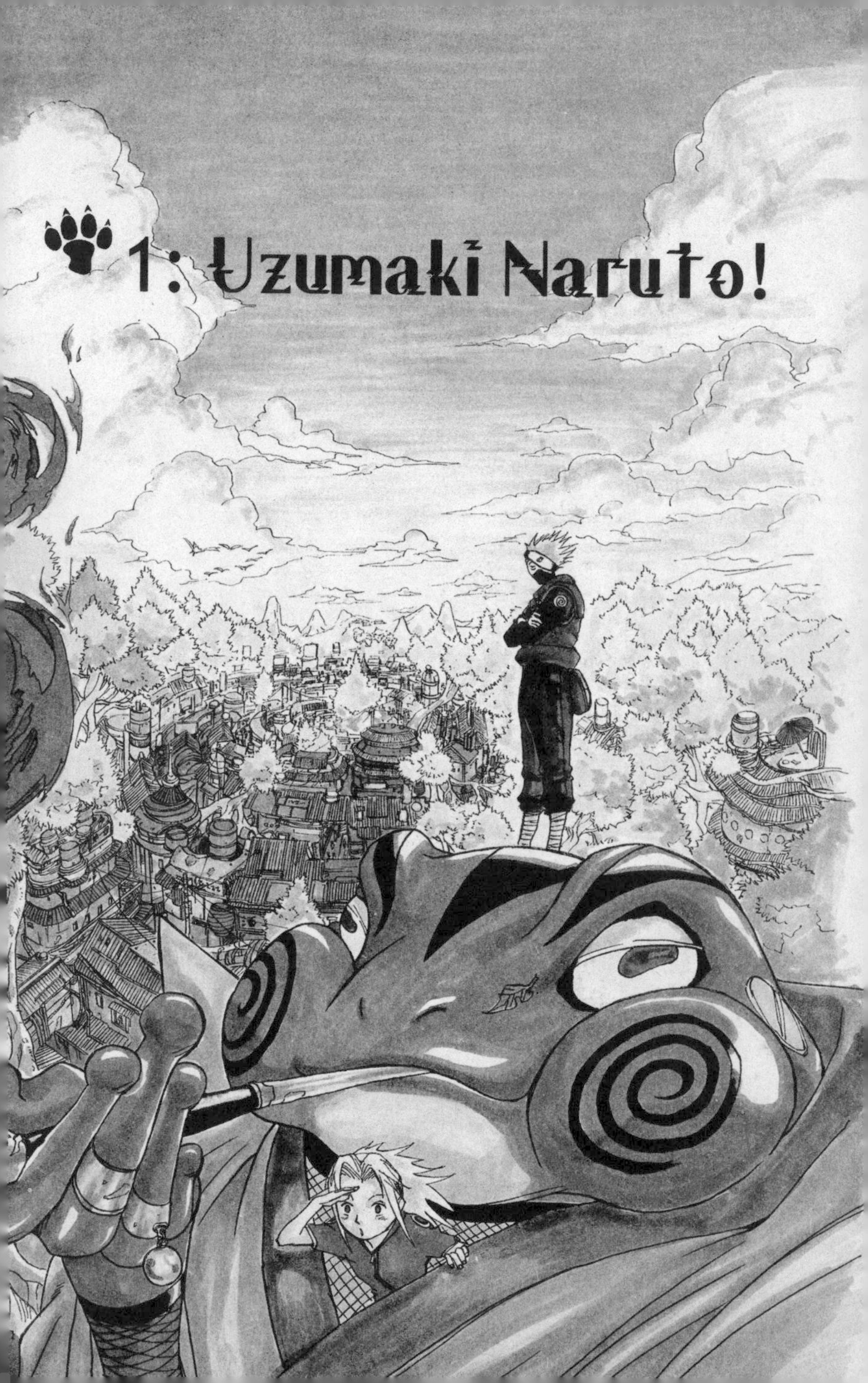

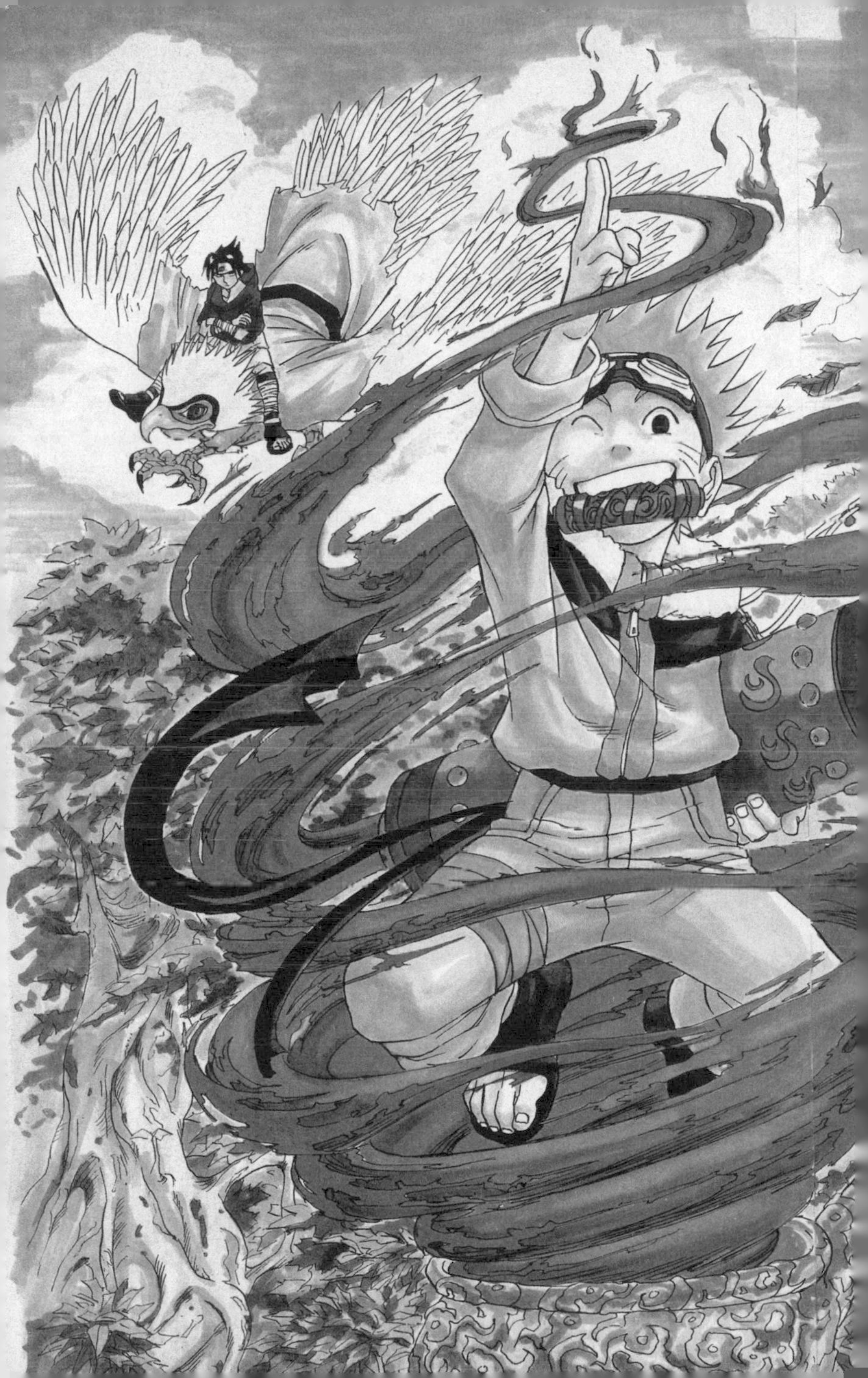

NARUTO

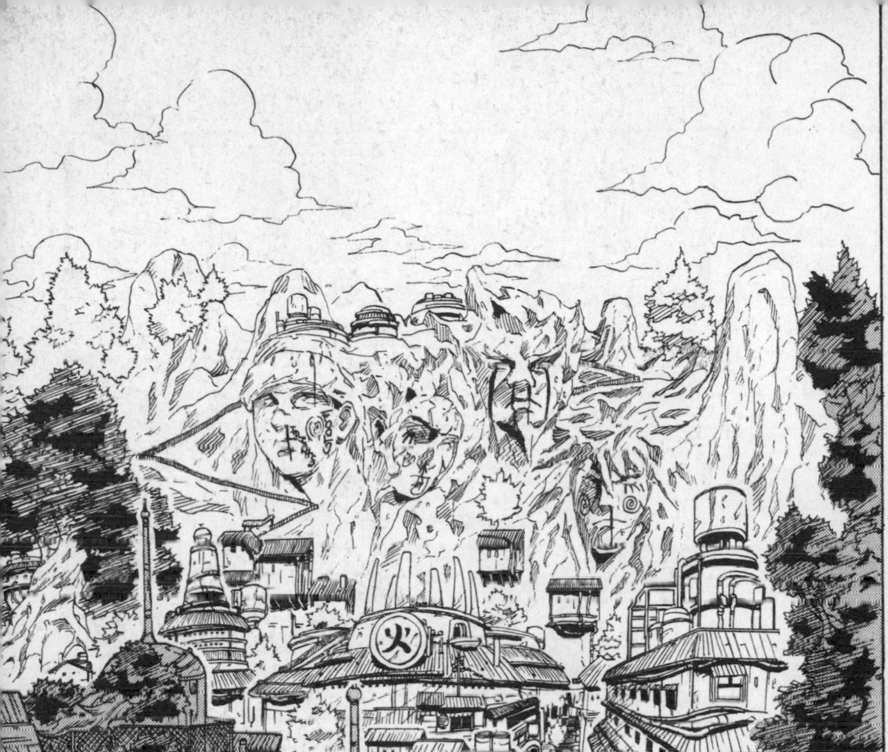

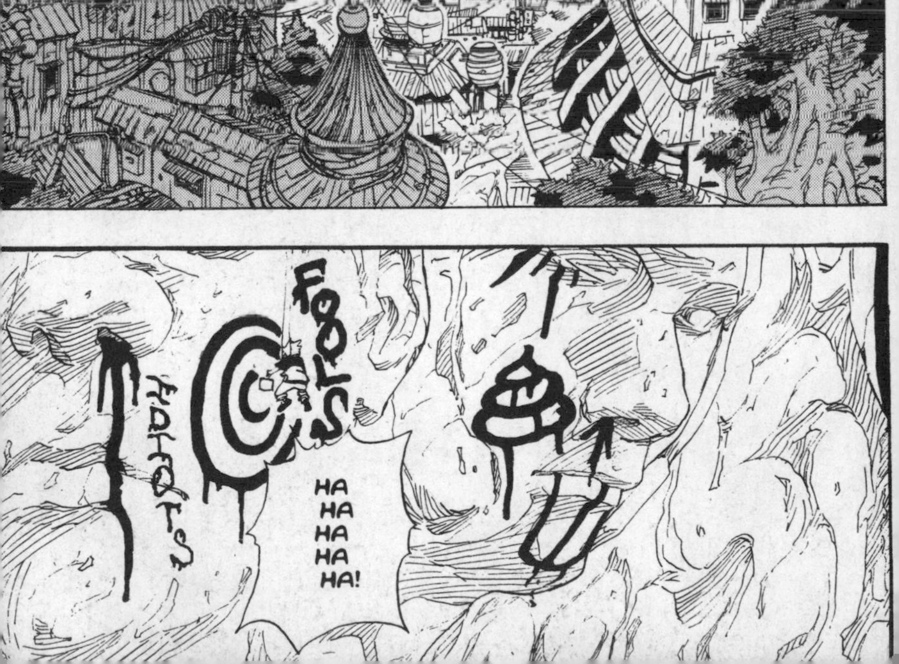
FOOLS
IDIOTS
HA
HA
HA
HA
HA!

READ THIS WAY

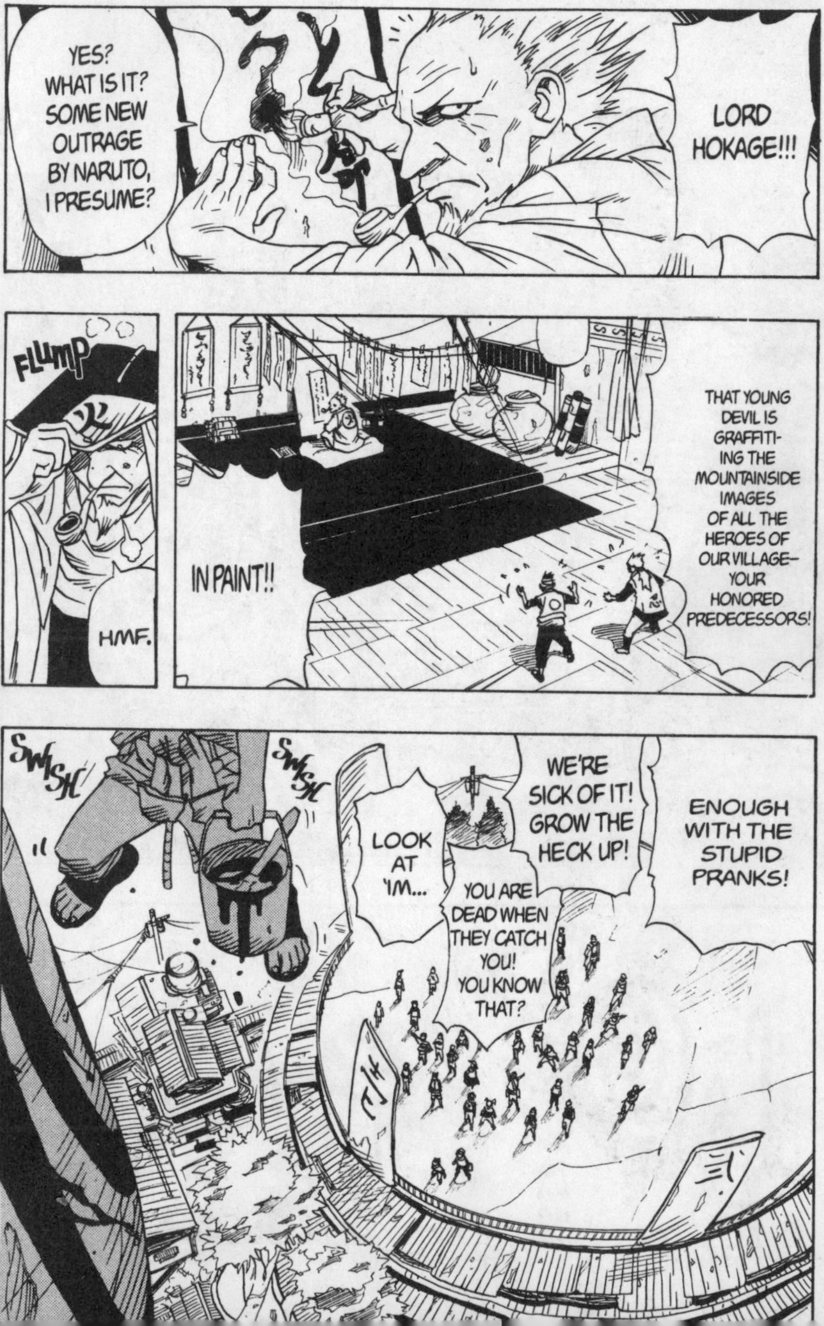
LORD HOKAGE!!!
YES? WHAT IS IT? SOME NEW OUTRAGE BY NARUTO, I PRESUME?
THAT YOUNG DEVIL IS GRAFFITI-ING THE MOUNTAINSIDE IMAGES OF ALL THE HEROES OF OUR VILLAGE— YOUR HONORED PREDECESSORS!
IN PAINT!!
FLUMP
HMF.
ENOUGH WITH THE STUPID PRANKS!
WE'RE SICK OF IT! GROW THE HECK UP!
YOU ARE DEAD WHEN THEY CATCH YOU! YOU KNOW THAT?
LOOK AT 'IM...
SWISH
SWISH

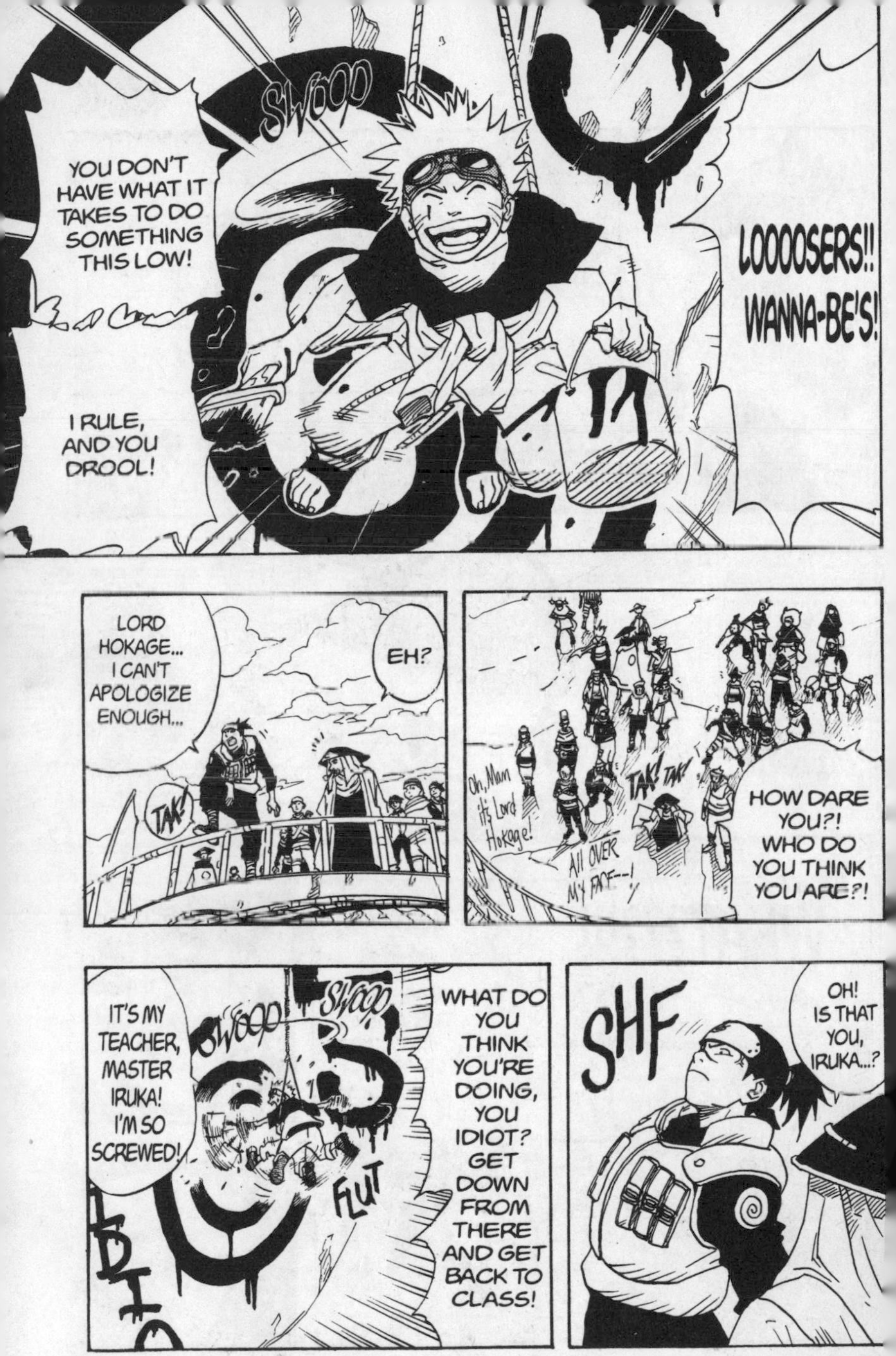
LOOOOSERS!! WANNA-BE'S!
SWOOD
YOU DON'T HAVE WHAT IT TAKES TO DO SOMETHING THIS LOW!
I RULE, AND YOU DROOL!
HOW DARE YOU?! WHO DO YOU THINK YOU ARE?!
TAK! TAK!
Oh, Man it's Lord Hokage!
All over my face---!
EH?
LORD HOKAGE... I CAN'T APOLOGIZE ENOUGH...
TAK!
OH! IS THAT YOU, IRUKA...?
SHF
WHAT DO YOU THINK YOU'RE DOING, YOU IDIOT? GET DOWN FROM THERE AND GET BACK TO CLASS!
SWOOP
SWOOP
IT'S MY TEACHER, MASTER IRUKA! I'M SO SCREWED!
FLUT

READ THIS WAY

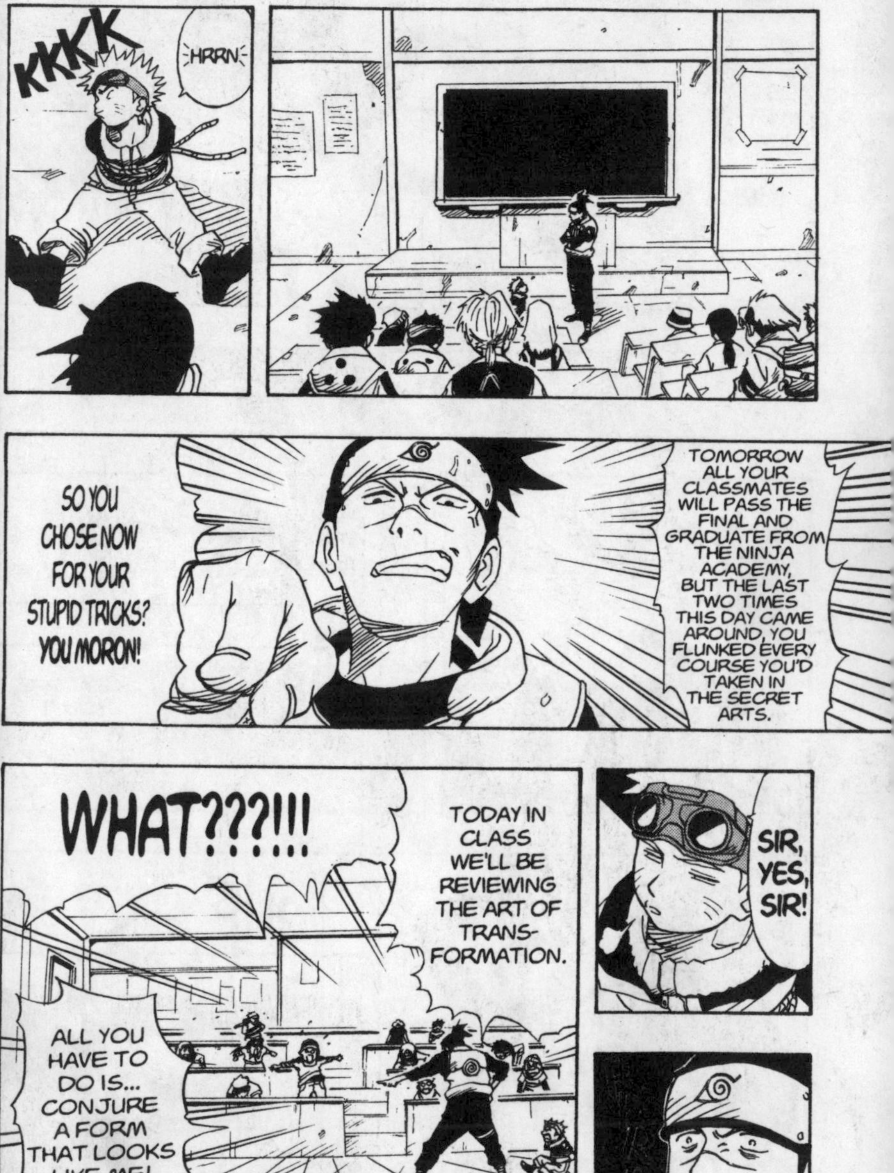
KKKK
HRRN
TOMORROW ALL YOUR CLASSMATES WILL PASS THE FINAL AND GRADUATE FROM THE NINJA ACADEMY, BUT THE LAST TWO TIMES THIS DAY CAME AROUND, YOU FLUNKED EVERY COURSE YOU'D TAKEN IN THE SECRET ARTS.
SO YOU CHOSE NOW FOR YOUR STUPID TRICKS? YOU MORON!
SIR, YES, SIR!
TODAY IN CLASS WE'LL BE REVIEWING THE ART OF TRANS-FORMATION.
WHAT???!!!
ALL YOU HAVE TO DO IS... CONJURE A FORM THAT LOOKS LIKE ME!

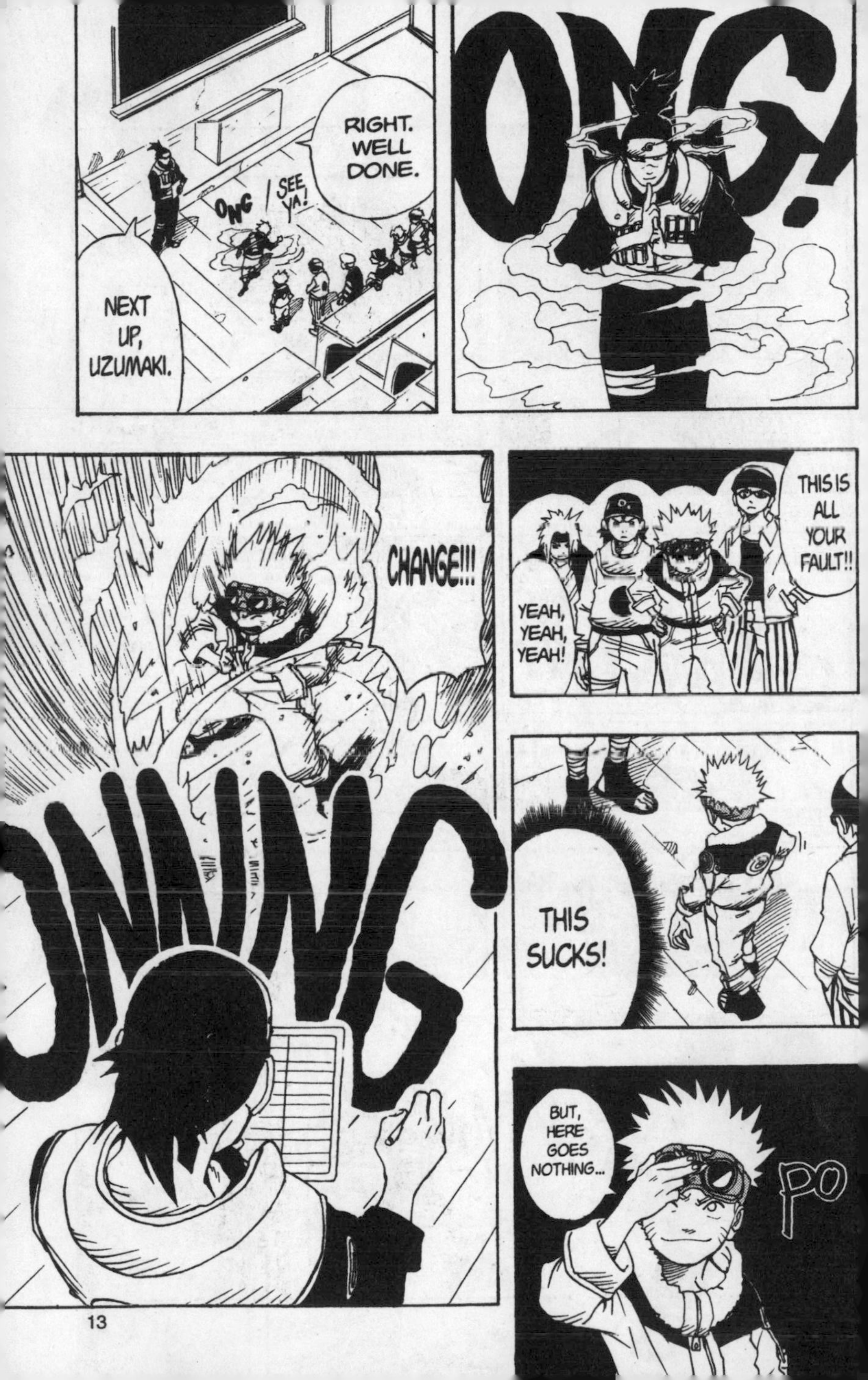
ONG!
RIGHT. WELL DONE.
SEE YA!
ONG
NEXT UP, UZUMAKI.
THIS IS ALL YOUR FAULT!!
YEAH, YEAH, YEAH!
THIS SUCKS!
BUT, HERE GOES NOTHING...
PO
CHANGE!!!

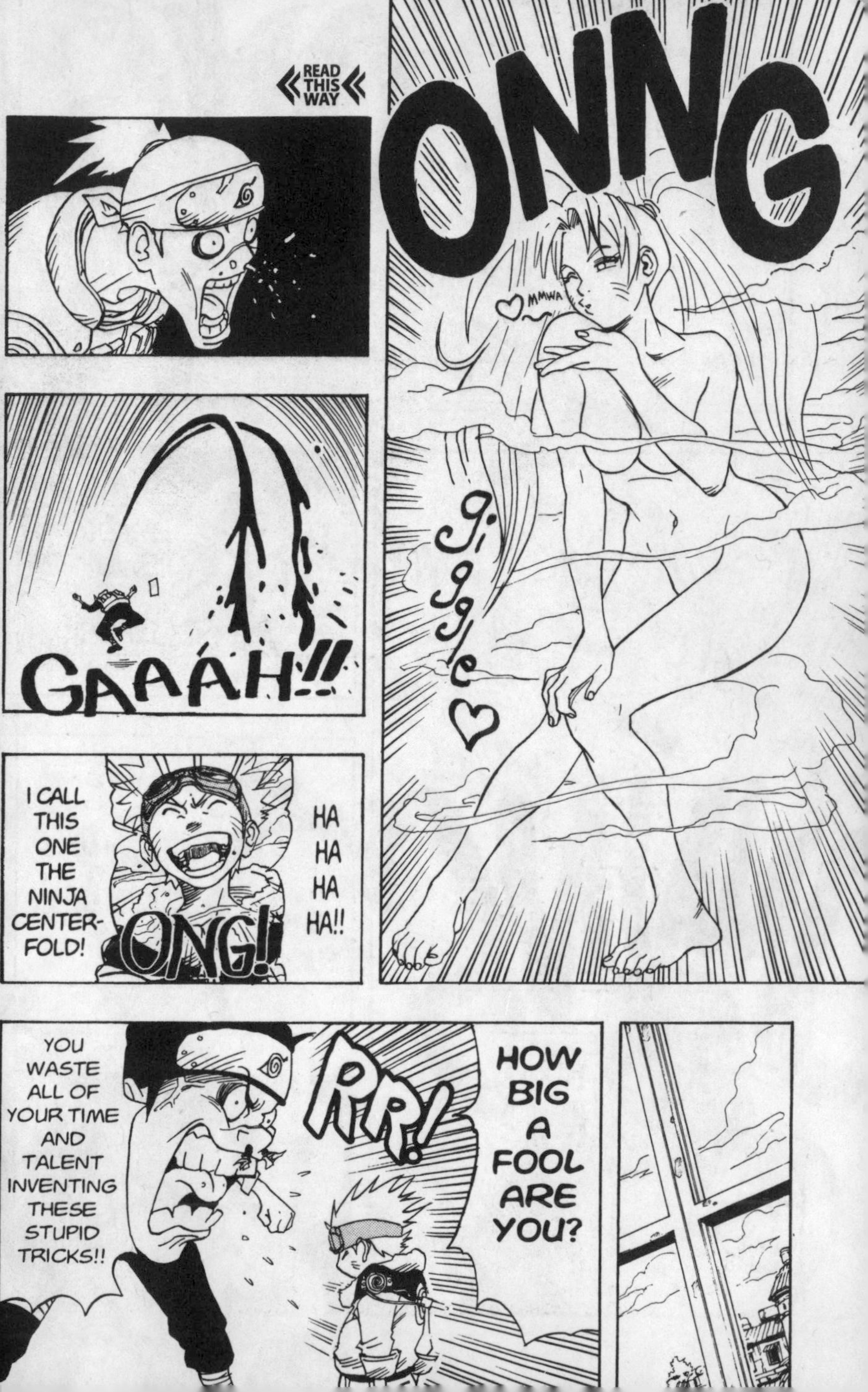
READ THIS WAY
ONNG
MMWA
giggle
GAAAH!!
I CALL THIS ONE THE NINJA CENTER-FOLD!
HA HA HA HA!!
ONG!!
HOW BIG A FOOL ARE YOU?
RRR!
YOU WASTE ALL OF YOUR TIME AND TALENT INVENTING THESE STUPID TRICKS!!

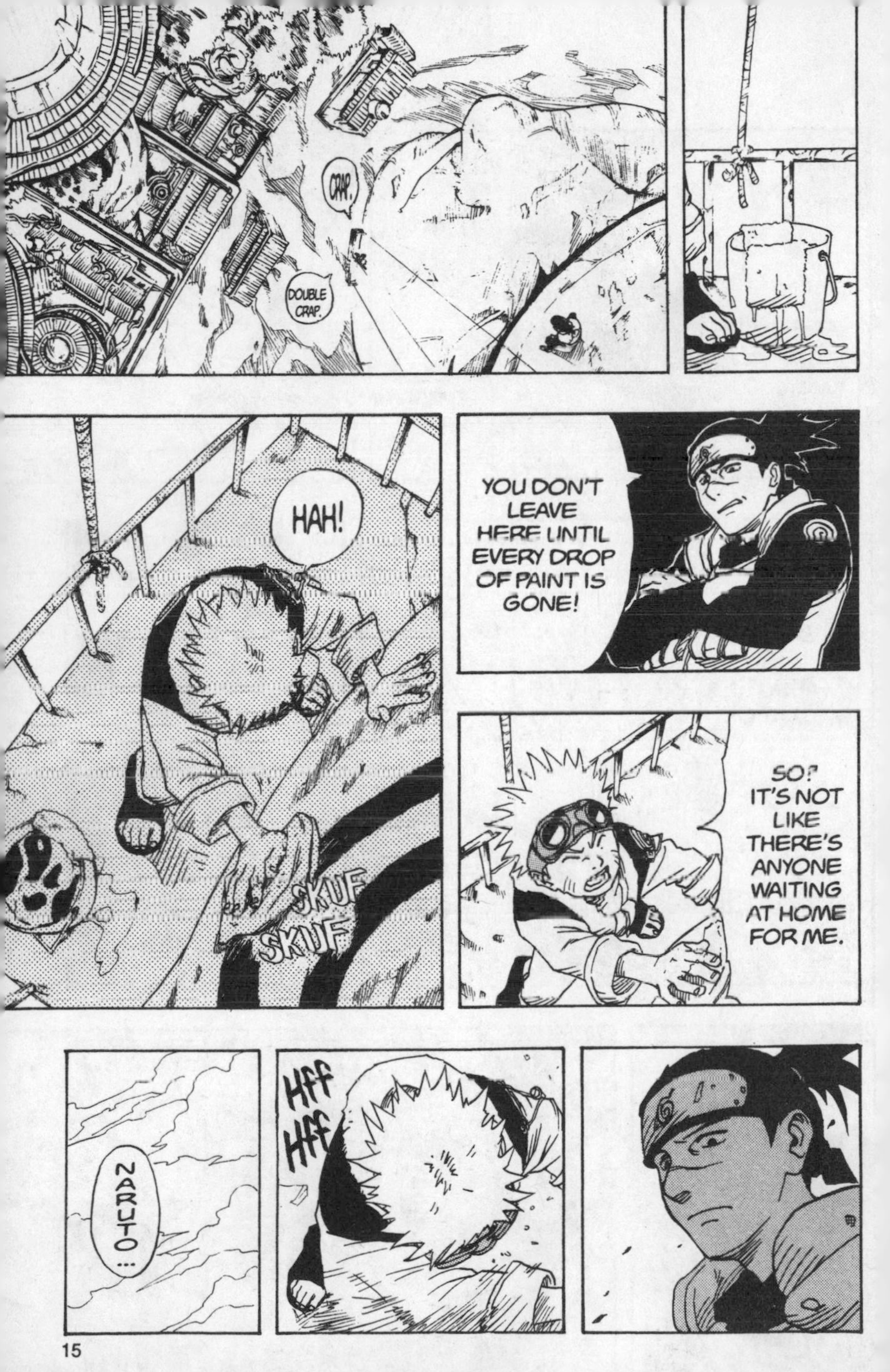
CRAP.
DOUBLE CRAP.
YOU DON'T LEAVE HERE UNTIL EVERY DROP OF PAINT IS GONE!
SO? IT'S NOT LIKE THERE'S ANYONE WAITING AT HOME FOR ME.
HAH!
SKUF
SKUF
Hff
Hff
NARUTO...

READ THIS WAY

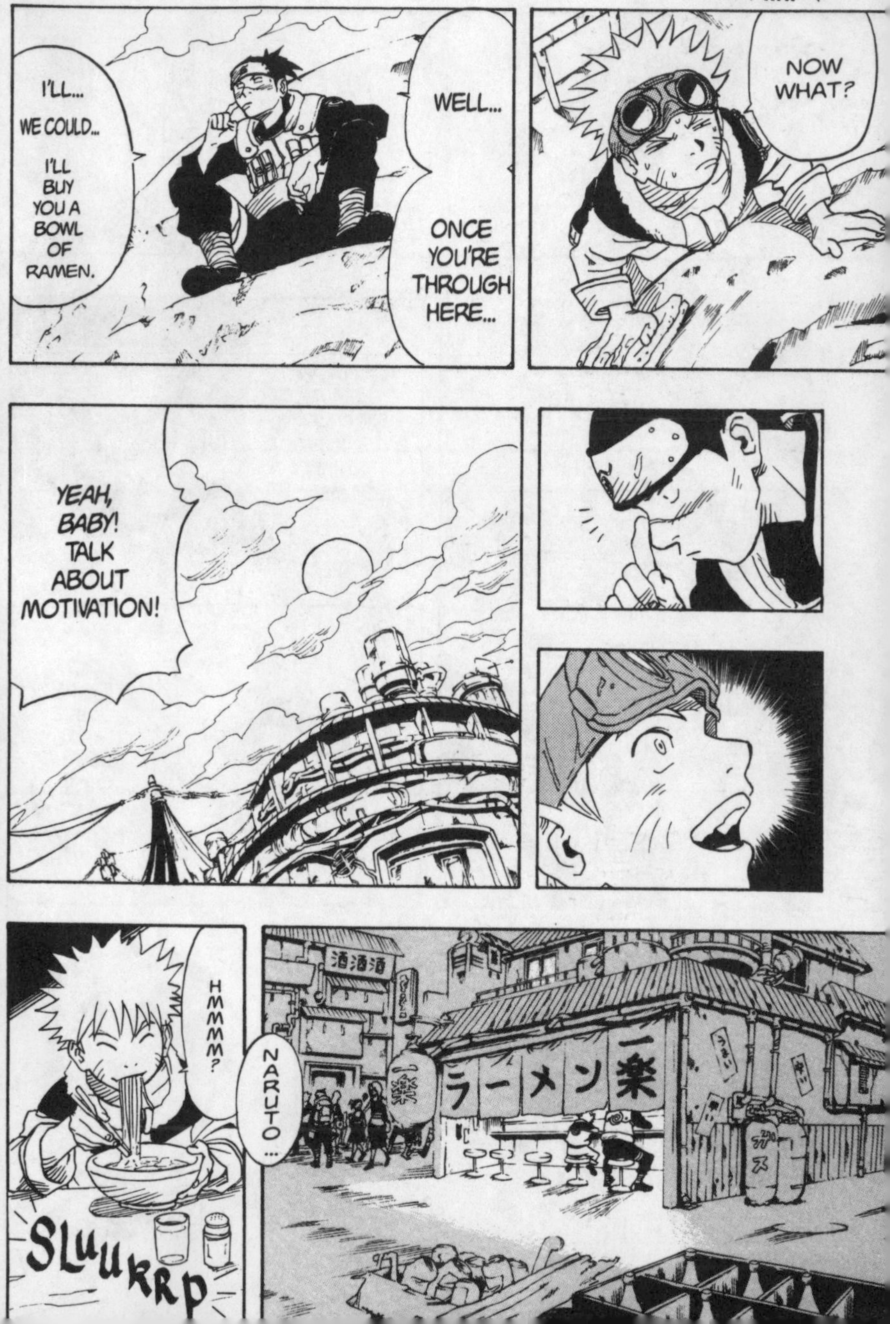
NOW WHAT?
WELL...
ONCE YOU'RE THROUGH HERE...
I'LL...
WE COULD...
I'LL BUY YOU A BOWL OF RAMEN.
YEAH, BABY! TALK ABOUT MOTIVATION!
酒酒酒
一楽
ラーメン
NARUTO...
HMMMMM?
SLUUKRRP

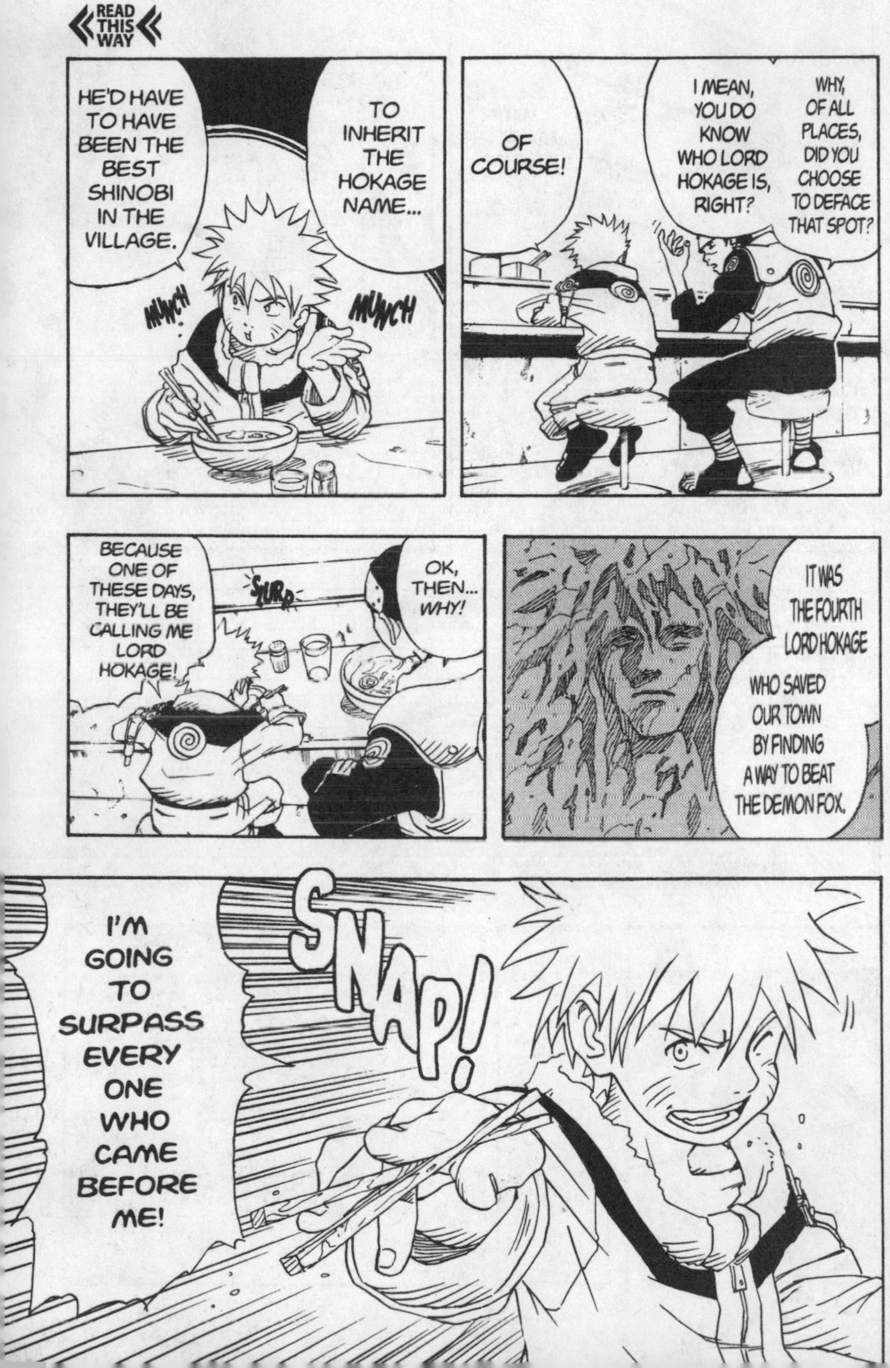
READ THIS WAY
WHY, OF ALL PLACES, DID YOU CHOOSE TO DEFACE THAT SPOT?
I MEAN, YOU DO KNOW WHO LORD HOKAGE IS, RIGHT?
OF COURSE!
TO INHERIT THE HOKAGE NAME...
HE'D HAVE TO HAVE BEEN THE BEST SHINOBI IN THE VILLAGE.
MUNCH
MUNCH
IT WAS THE FOURTH LORD HOKAGE
WHO SAVED OUR TOWN BY FINDING A WAY TO BEAT THE DEMON FOX.
OK, THEN... WHY!
SLURP
BECAUSE ONE OF THESE DAYS, THEY'LL BE CALLING ME LORD HOKAGE!
SNAP!
I'M GOING TO SURPASS EVERY ONE WHO CAME BEFORE ME!

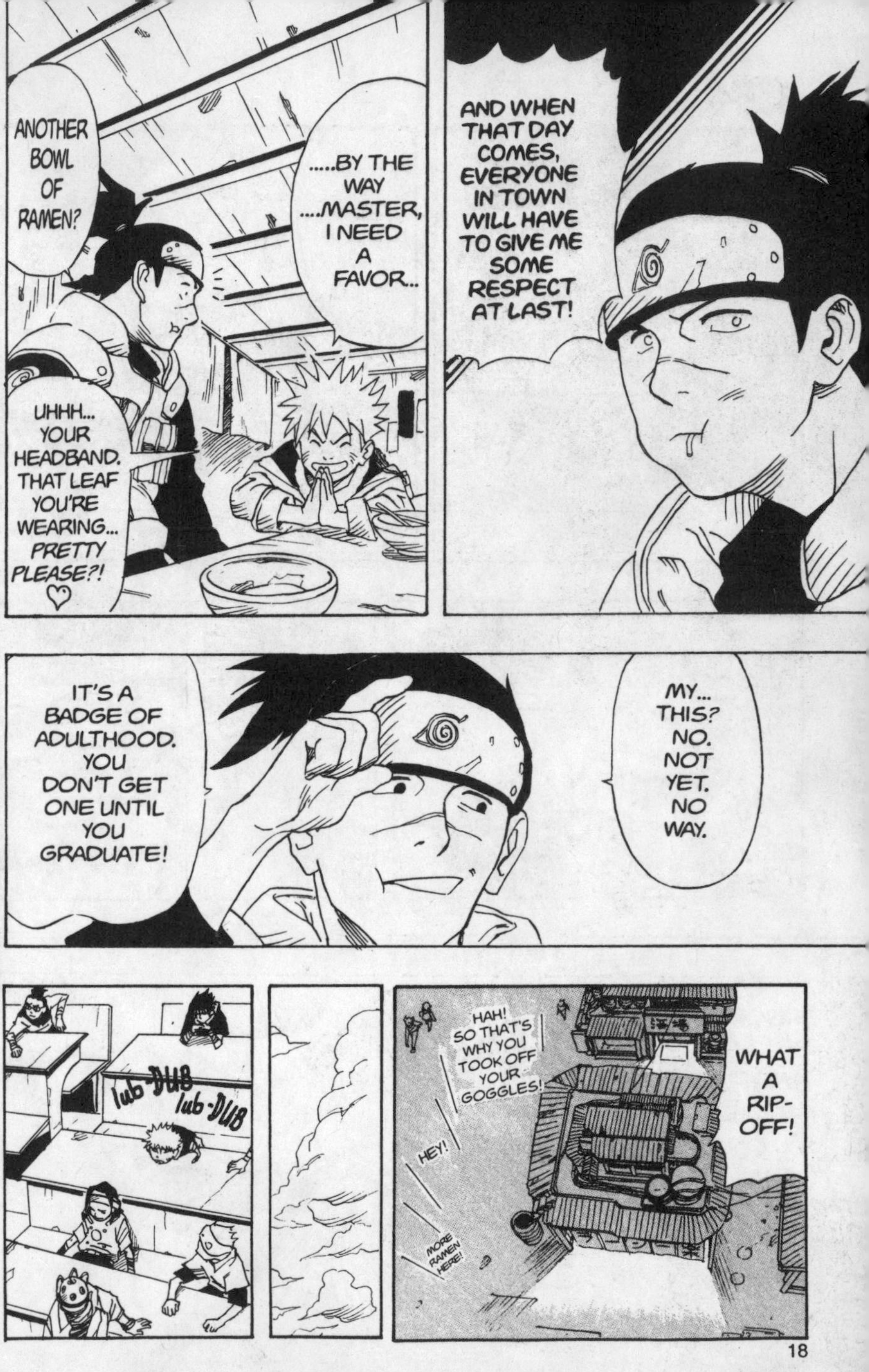
AND WHEN THAT DAY COMES, EVERYONE IN TOWN WILL HAVE TO GIVE ME SOME RESPECT AT LAST!
.....BY THE WAY ....MASTER, I NEED A FAVOR...
ANOTHER BOWL OF RAMEN?
UHHH... YOUR HEADBAND. THAT LEAF YOU'RE WEARING... PRETTY PLEASE?! ♡
MY... THIS? NO. NOT YET. NO WAY.
IT'S A BADGE OF ADULTHOOD. YOU DON'T GET ONE UNTIL YOU GRADUATE!
WHAT A RIP-OFF!
HAH! SO THAT'S WHY YOU TOOK OFF YOUR GOGGLES!
HEY!
MORE RAMEN HERE!
lub-DUB lub-DUB

READ THIS WAY

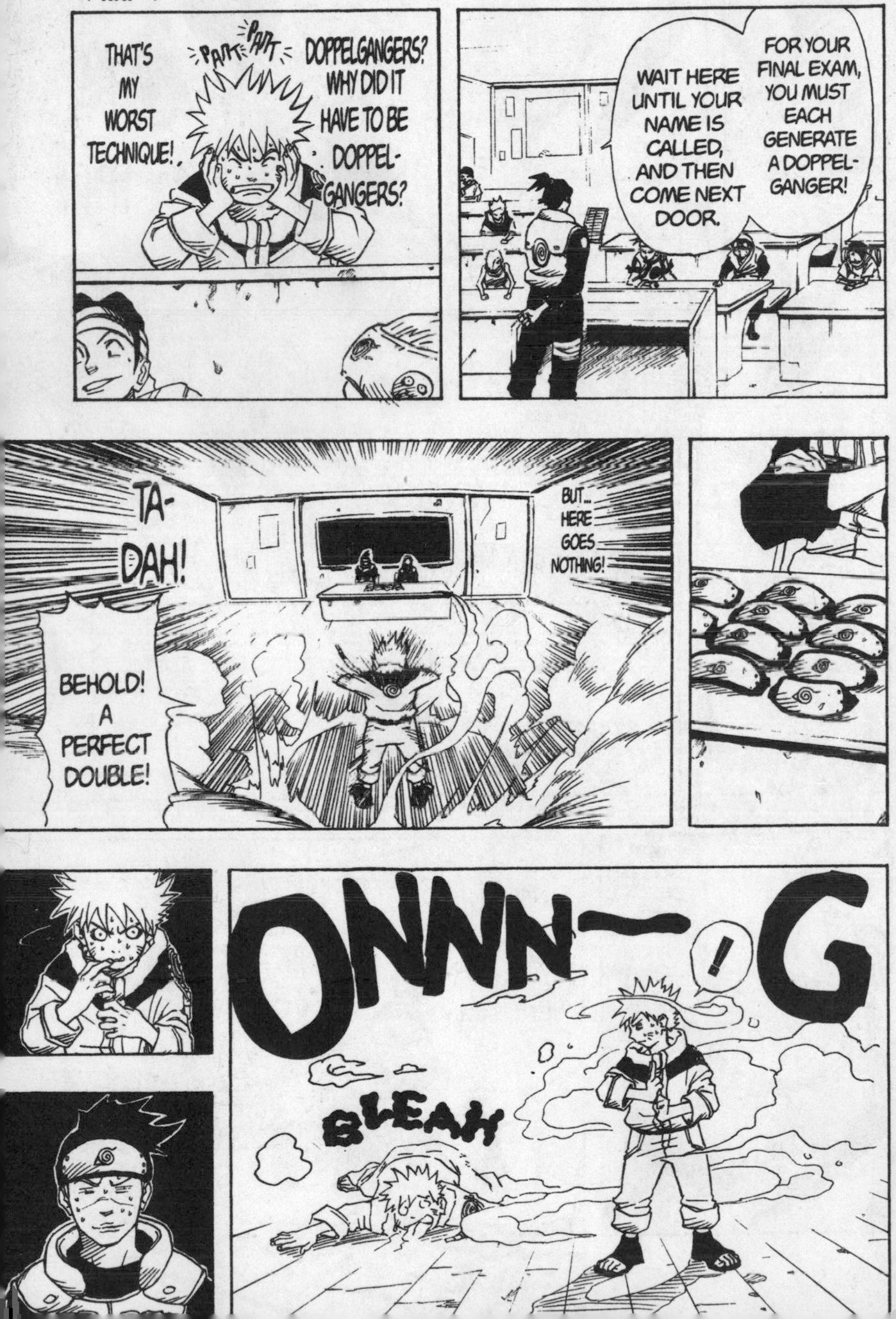
FOR YOUR FINAL EXAM, YOU MUST EACH GENERATE A DOPPEL-GANGER!
WAIT HERE UNTIL YOUR NAME IS CALLED, AND THEN COME NEXT DOOR.
DOPPELGANGERS? WHY DID IT HAVE TO BE DOPPEL-GANGERS?
PANT PANT
THAT'S MY WORST TECHNIQUE!
BUT... HERE GOES NOTHING!
TA-DAH!
BEHOLD! A PERFECT DOUBLE!
ONNN—G
!
BLEAH

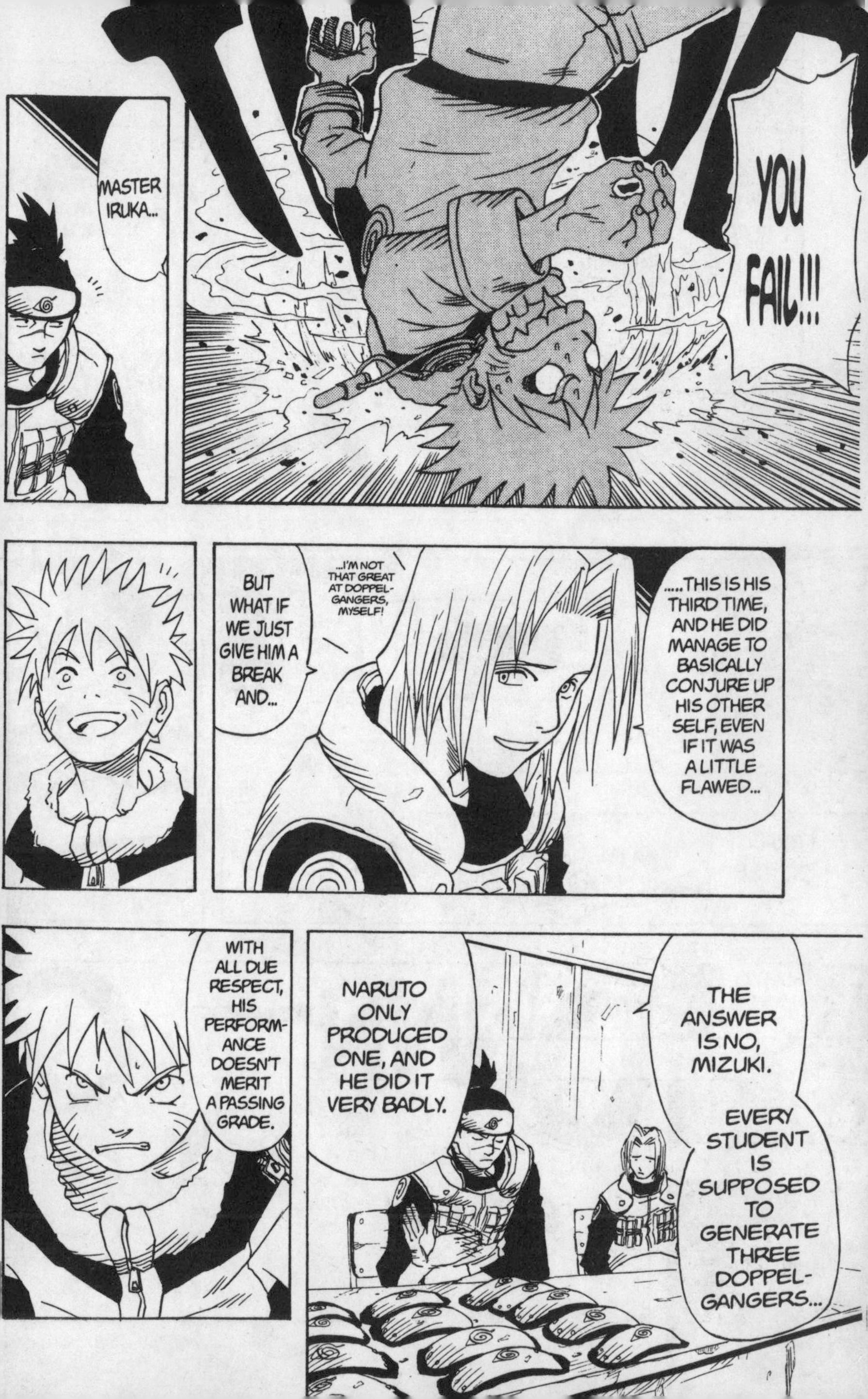
YOU FAIL!!!
MASTER IRUKA...
.....THIS IS HIS THIRD TIME, AND HE DID MANAGE TO BASICALLY CONJURE UP HIS OTHER SELF, EVEN IF IT WAS A LITTLE FLAWED...
...I'M NOT THAT GREAT AT DOPPELGANGERS, MYSELF!
BUT WHAT IF WE JUST GIVE HIM A BREAK AND...
THE ANSWER IS NO, MIZUKI.
EVERY STUDENT IS SUPPOSED TO GENERATE THREE DOPPELGANGERS...
NARUTO ONLY PRODUCED ONE, AND HE DID IT VERY BADLY.
WITH ALL DUE RESPECT, HIS PERFORMANCE DOESN'T MERIT A PASSING GRADE.

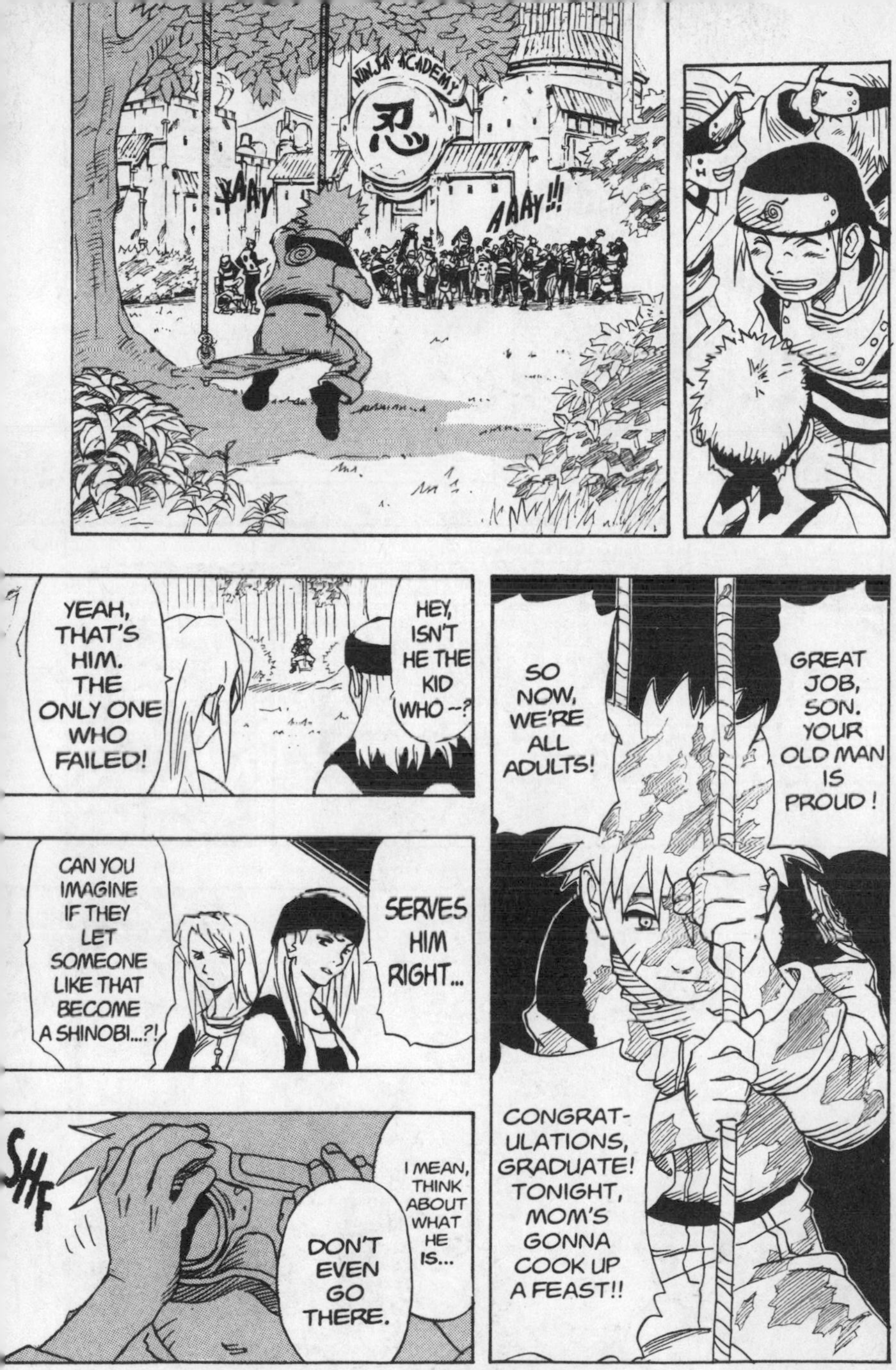
NINJA ACADEMY
忍
AAAY!!!
YAAY
GREAT JOB, SON. YOUR OLD MAN IS PROUD!
SO NOW, WE'RE ALL ADULTS!
CONGRATULATIONS, GRADUATE! TONIGHT, MOM'S GONNA COOK UP A FEAST!!
HEY, ISN'T HE THE KID WHO--?
YEAH, THAT'S HIM. THE ONLY ONE WHO FAILED!
SERVES HIM RIGHT...
CAN YOU IMAGINE IF THEY LET SOMEONE LIKE THAT BECOME A SHINOBI...?!
I MEAN, THINK ABOUT WHAT HE IS...
DON'T EVEN GO THERE.
SHF

READ THIS WAY

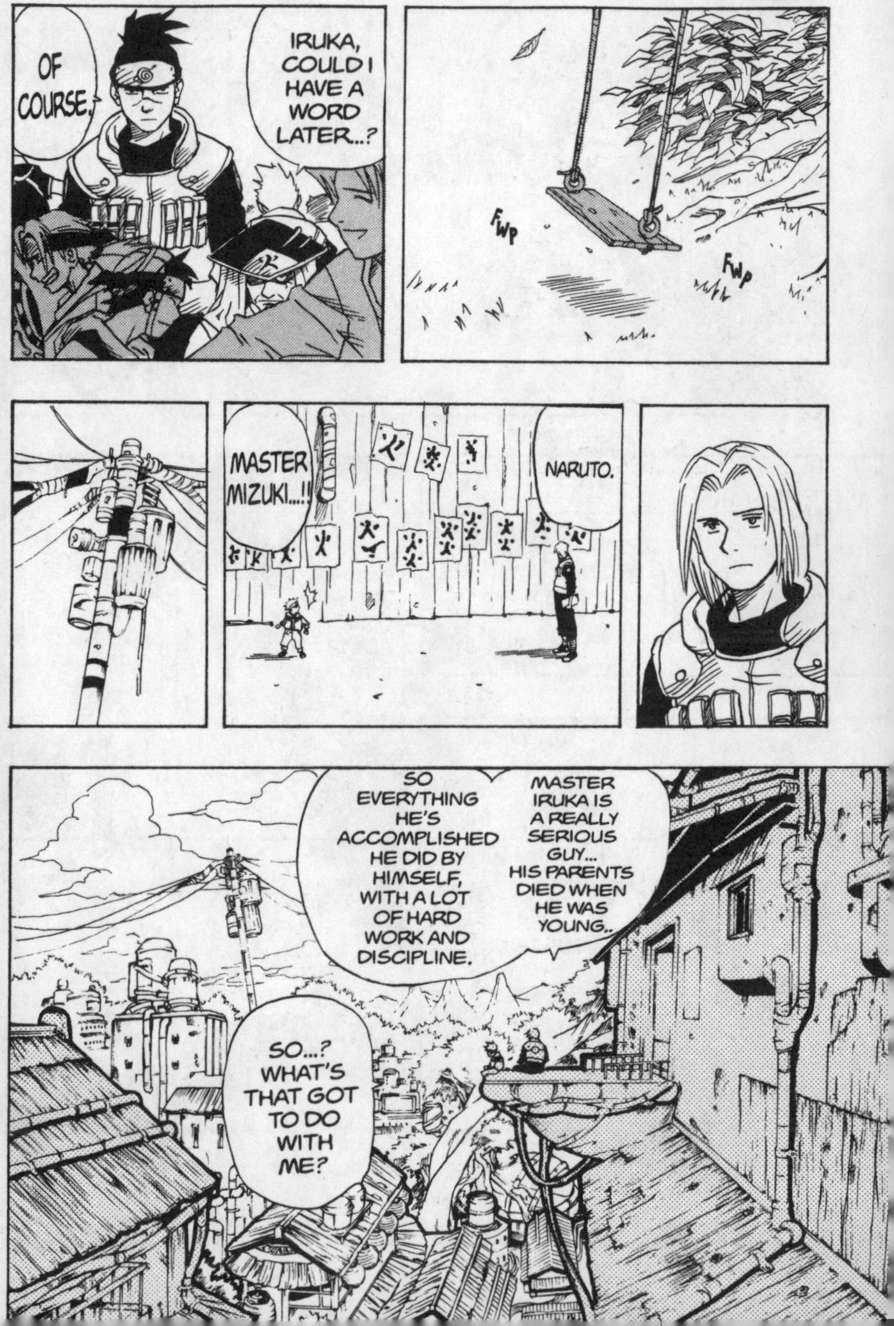
FWP
FWP
IRUKA, COULD I HAVE A WORD LATER...?
OF COURSE.
NARUTO.
MASTER MIZUKI...!!
MASTER IRUKA IS A REALLY SERIOUS GUY... HIS PARENTS DIED WHEN HE WAS YOUNG..
SO EVERYTHING HE'S ACCOMPLISHED HE DID BY HIMSELF, WITH A LOT OF HARD WORK AND DISCIPLINE.
SO...? WHAT'S THAT GOT TO DO WITH ME?

READ THIS WAY

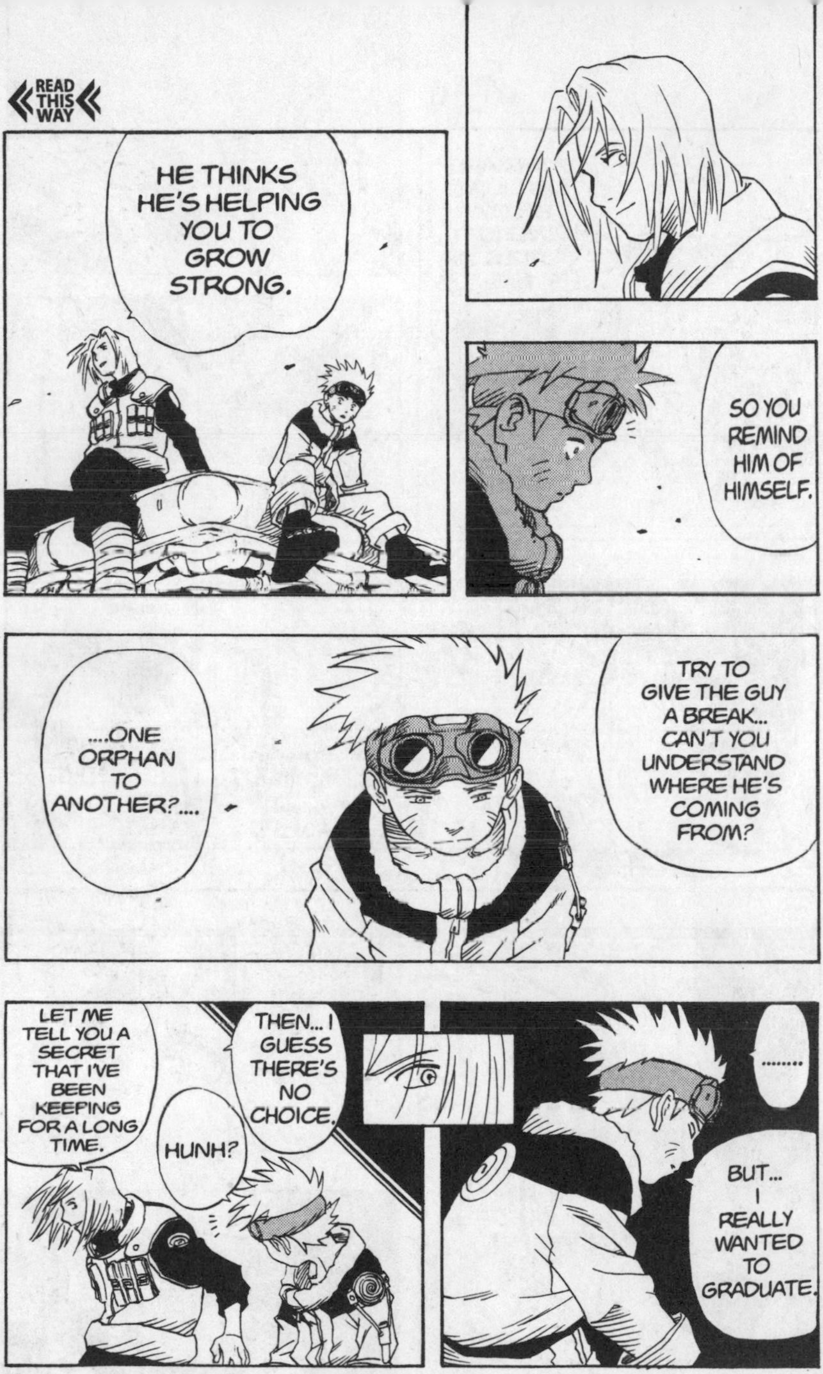
SO YOU REMIND HIM OF HIMSELF.
HE THINKS HE'S HELPING YOU TO GROW STRONG.
TRY TO GIVE THE GUY A BREAK... CAN'T YOU UNDERSTAND WHERE HE'S COMING FROM?
....ONE ORPHAN TO ANOTHER?....
....
BUT... I REALLY WANTED TO GRADUATE.
THEN... I GUESS THERE'S NO CHOICE.
LET ME TELL YOU A SECRET THAT I'VE BEEN KEEPING FOR A LONG TIME.
HUNH?

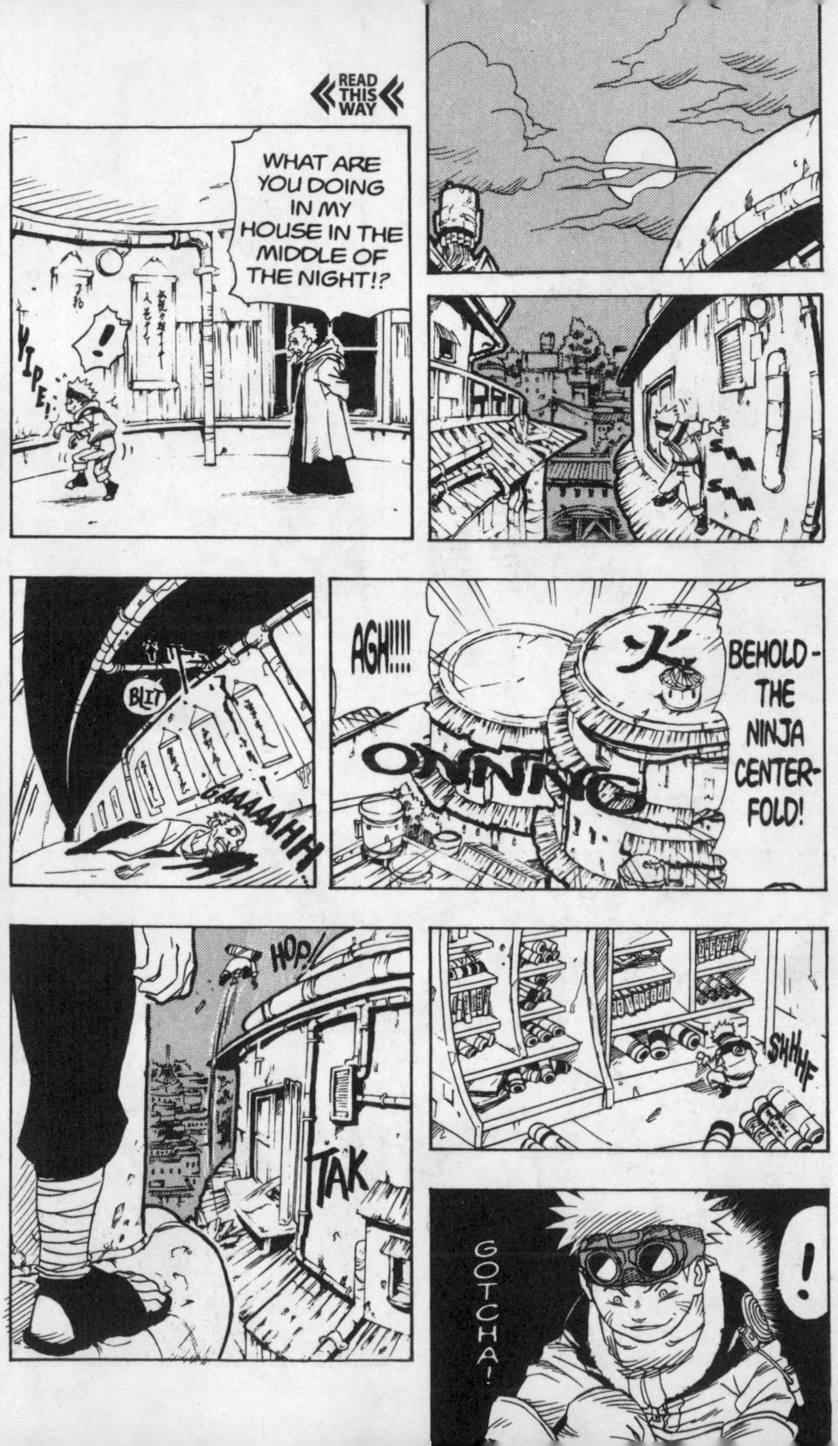
READ THIS WAY
SWA
SWA
WHAT ARE YOU DOING IN MY HOUSE IN THE MIDDLE OF THE NIGHT!?
!
YIPE!
BEHOLD- THE NINJA CENTER-FOLD!
ONNNG
AGH!!!!
BLIT
GAAAAAHH
SHHHF
!
GOTCHA!
HOP!
TAK

READ THIS WAY

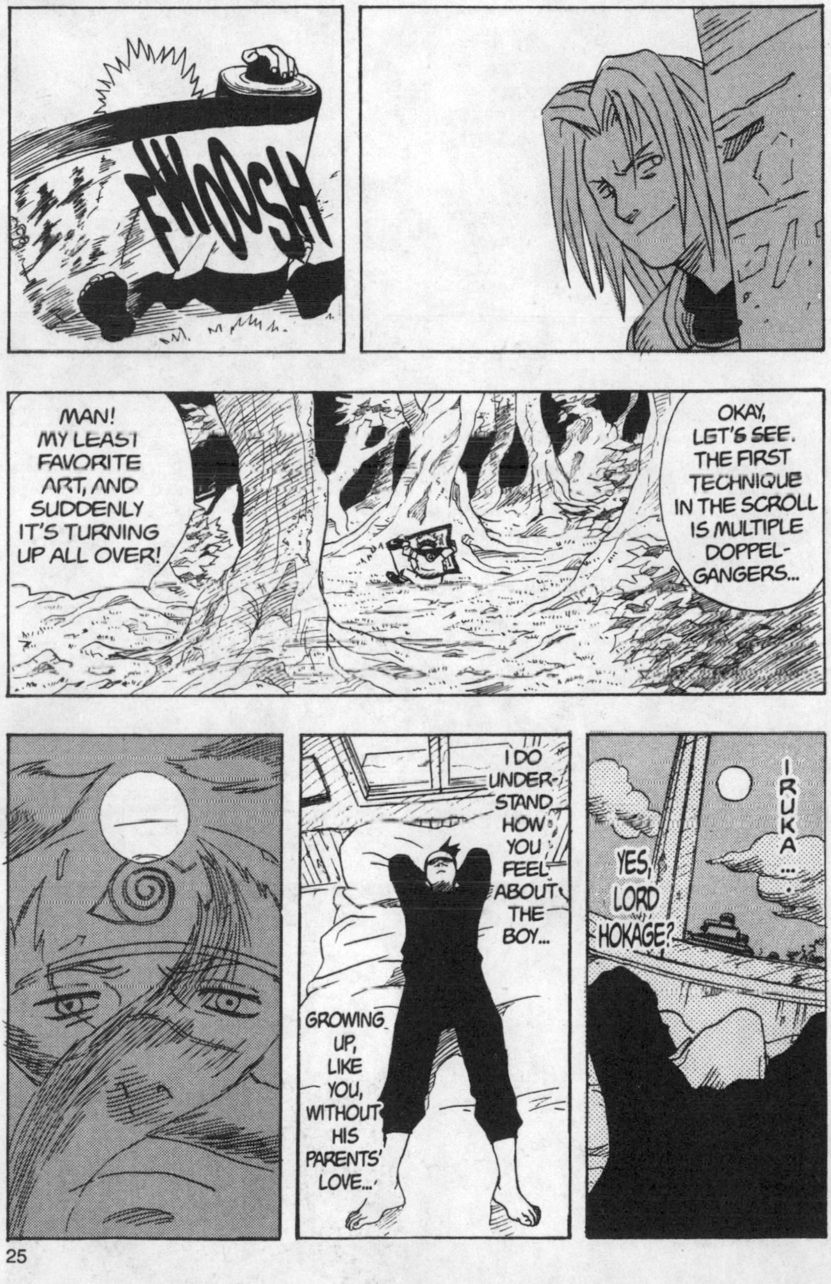
FWOOSH
OKAY, LET'S SEE. THE FIRST TECHNIQUE IN THE SCROLL IS MULTIPLE DOPPELGANGERS...
MAN! MY LEAST FAVORITE ART, AND SUDDENLY IT'S TURNING UP ALL OVER!
IRUKA...
YES, LORD HOKAGE?
I DO UNDERSTAND HOW YOU FEEL ABOUT THE BOY...
GROWING UP, LIKE YOU, WITHOUT HIS PARENTS' LOVE...

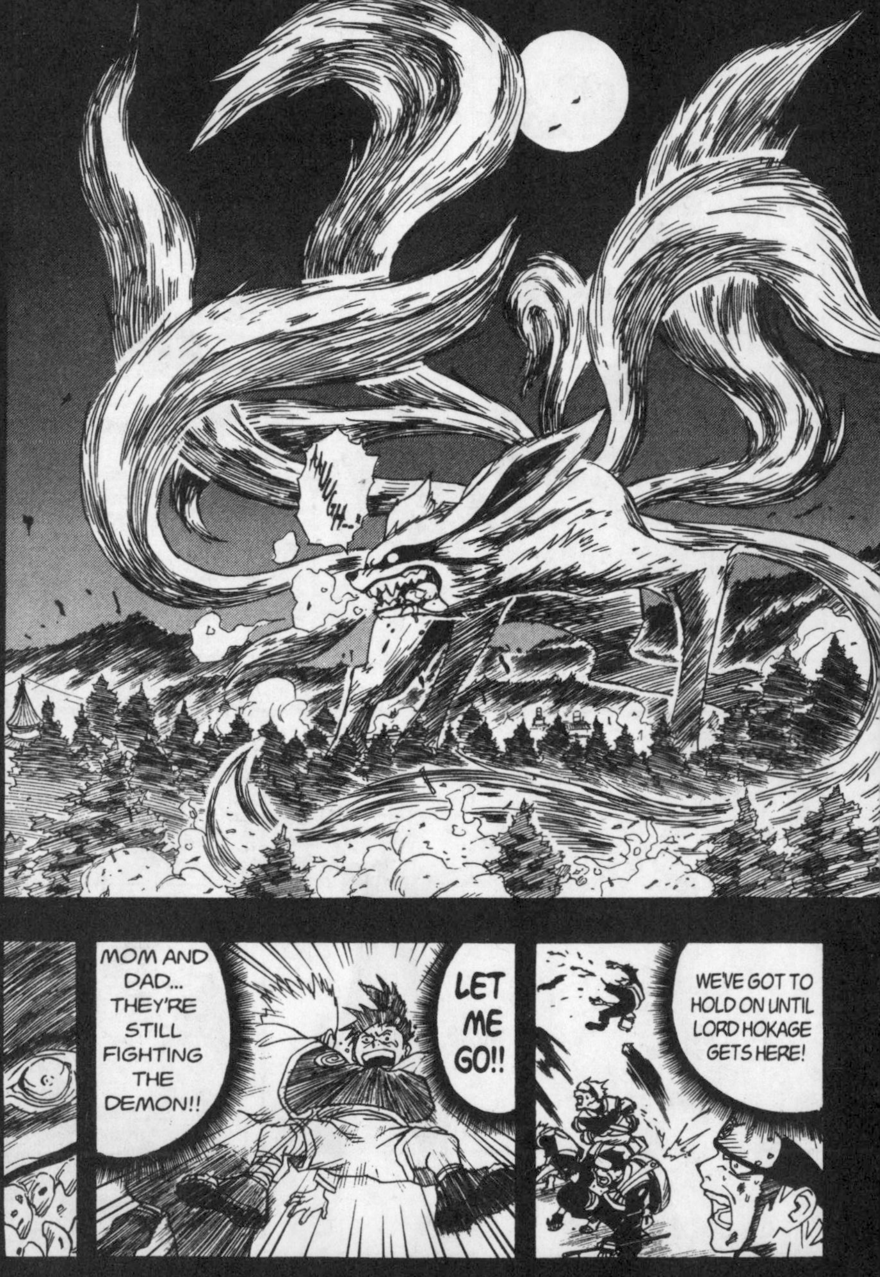

AHUUGH...
WE'VE GOT TO HOLD ON UNTIL LORD HOKAGE GETS HERE!
LET ME GO!!
MOM AND DAD... THEY'RE STILL FIGHTING THE DEMON!!

READ THIS WAY

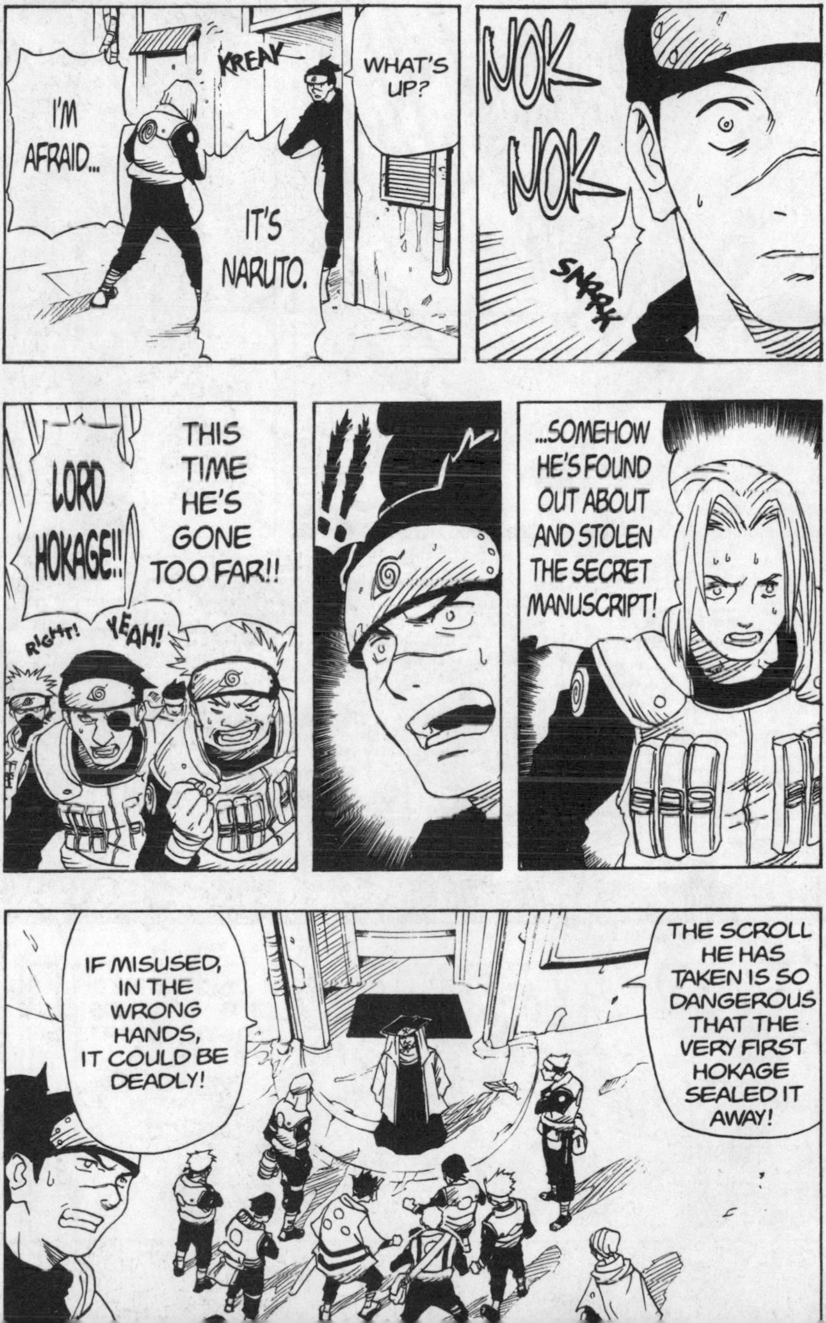
NOK NOK
SNORK
KREAK
WHAT'S UP?
I'M AFRAID...
IT'S NARUTO.
...SOMEHOW HE'S FOUND OUT ABOUT AND STOLEN THE SECRET MANUSCRIPT!
!!
THIS TIME HE'S GONE TOO FAR!!
LORD HOKAGE!!
YEAH!
RIGHT!
THE SCROLL HE HAS TAKEN IS SO DANGEROUS THAT THE VERY FIRST HOKAGE SEALED IT AWAY!
IF MISUSED, IN THE WRONG HANDS, IT COULD BE DEADLY!

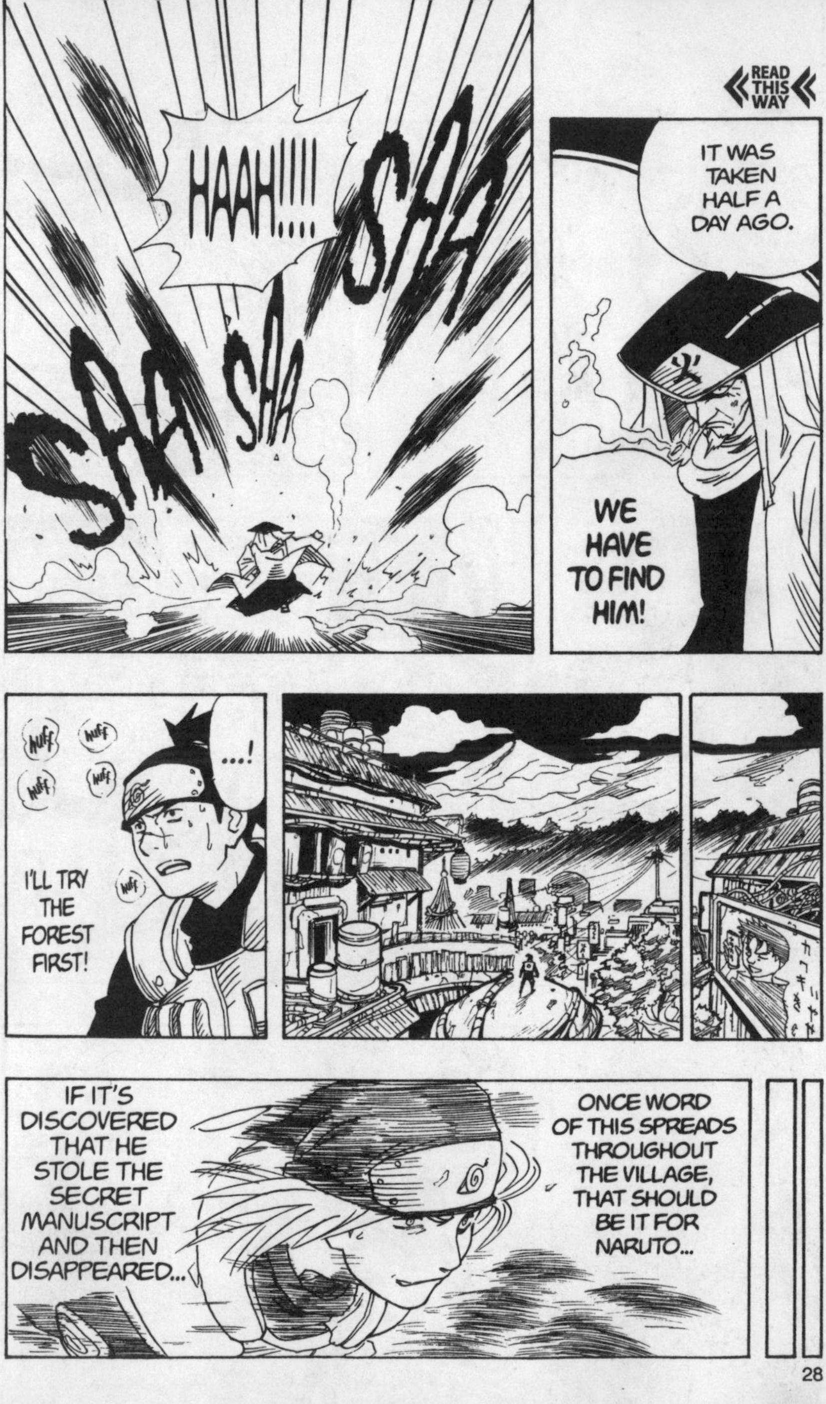
READ THIS WAY
IT WAS TAKEN HALF A DAY AGO.
WE HAVE TO FIND HIM!
HAAH!!!!
SAA
SAA
SAA
SAA
...!
huff
huff
huff
huff
huff
I'LL TRY THE FOREST FIRST!
ONCE WORD OF THIS SPREADS THROUGHOUT THE VILLAGE, THAT SHOULD BE IT FOR NARUTO...
IF IT'S DISCOVERED THAT HE STOLE THE SECRET MANUSCRIPT AND THEN DISAPPEARED...

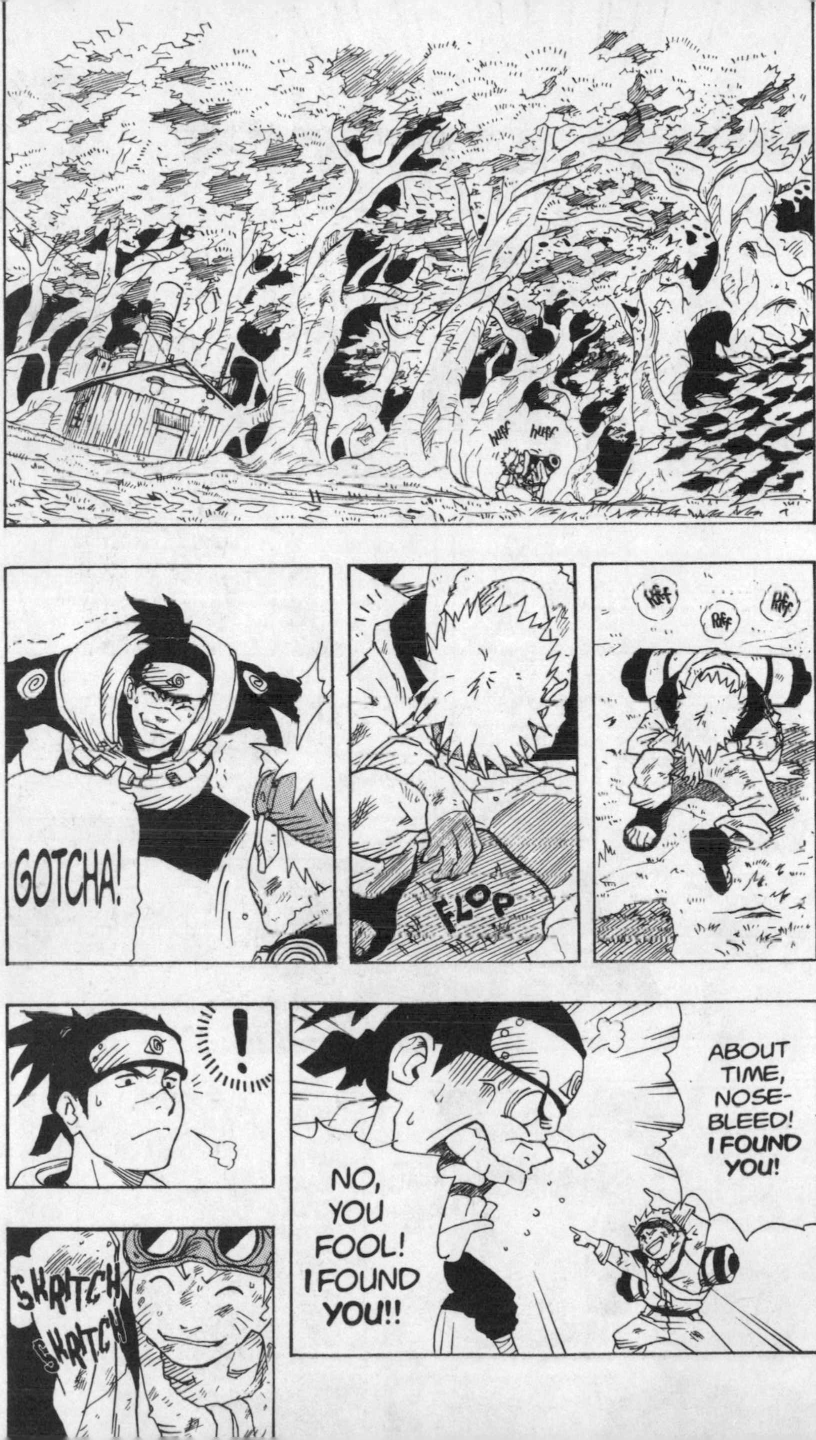
huff
huff
FLOP
GOTCHA!
ABOUT TIME, NOSE-BLEED! I FOUND YOU!
NO, YOU FOOL! I FOUND YOU!!
!
SKRITCH
SKRITCH

READ THIS WAY

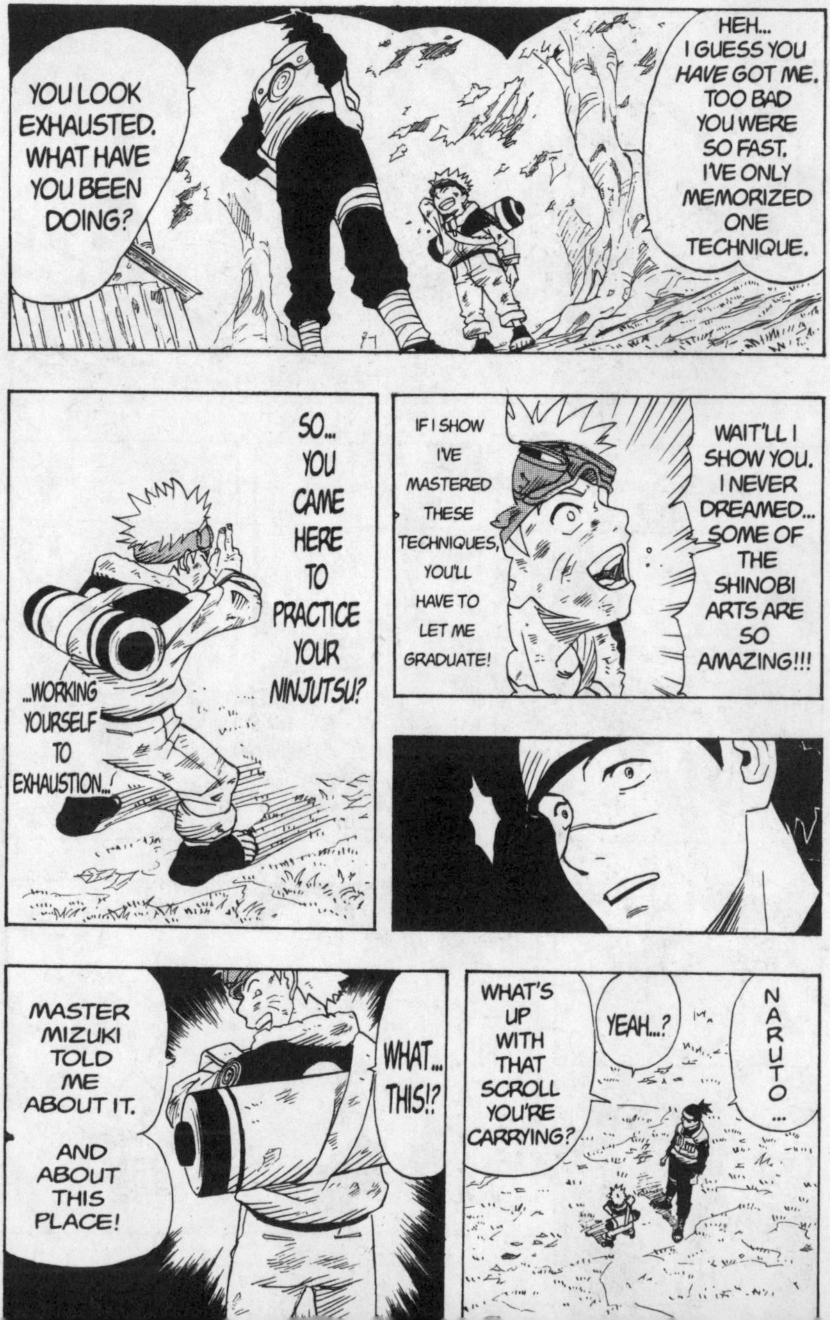
HEH... I GUESS YOU HAVE GOT ME. TOO BAD YOU WERE SO FAST. I'VE ONLY MEMORIZED ONE TECHNIQUE.
YOU LOOK EXHAUSTED. WHAT HAVE YOU BEEN DOING?
WAIT'LL I SHOW YOU. I NEVER DREAMED... SOME OF THE SHINOBI ARTS ARE SO AMAZING!!!
IF I SHOW I'VE MASTERED THESE TECHNIQUES, YOU'LL HAVE TO LET ME GRADUATE!
SO... YOU CAME HERE TO PRACTICE YOUR NINJUTSU?
...WORKING YOURSELF TO EXHAUSTION...!
NARUTO...
YEAH...?
WHAT'S UP WITH THAT SCROLL YOU'RE CARRYING?
WHAT... THIS!?
MASTER MIZUKI TOLD ME ABOUT IT.
AND ABOUT THIS PLACE!

READ THIS WAY

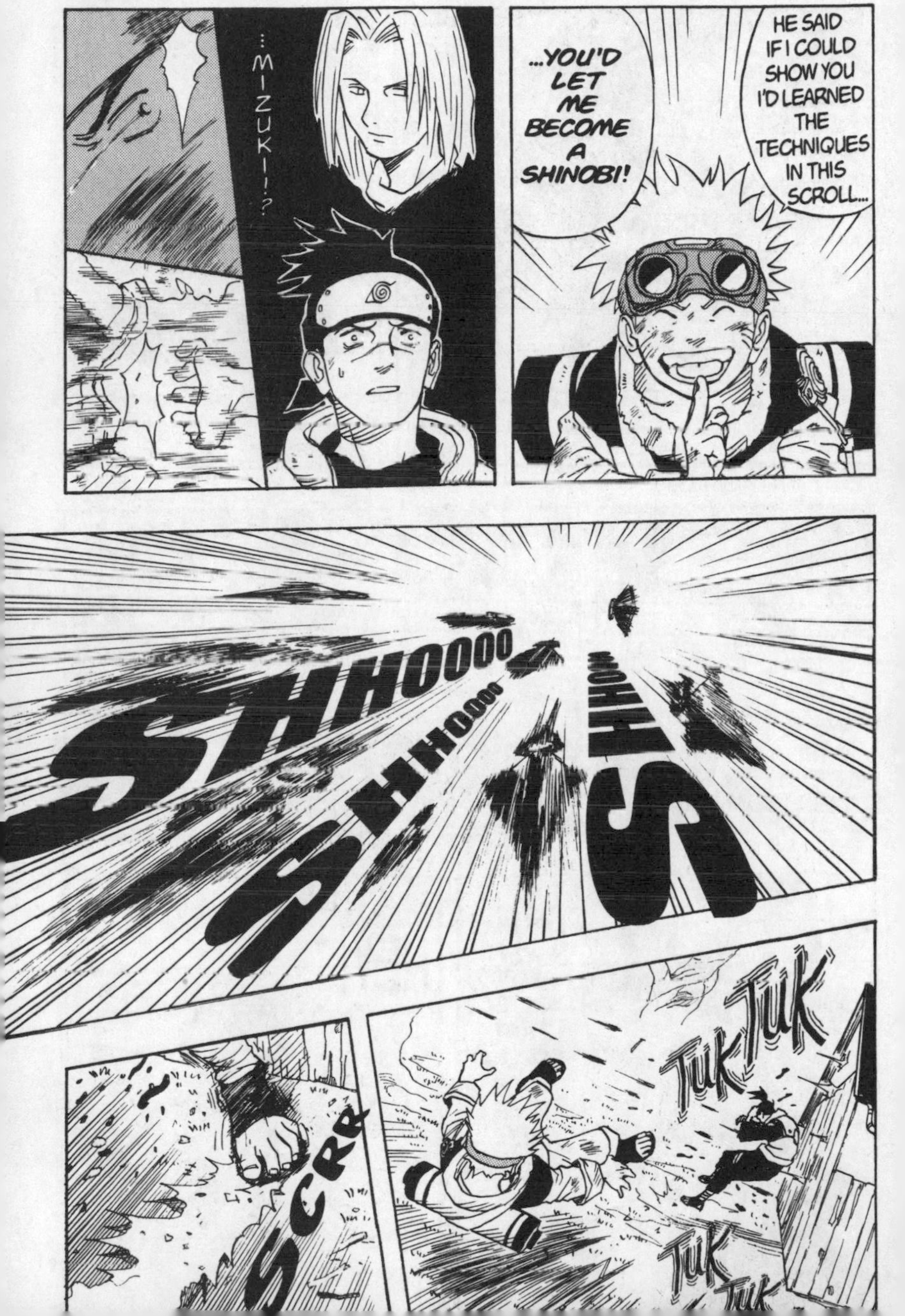
HE SAID IF I COULD SHOW YOU I'D LEARNED THE TECHNIQUES IN THIS SCROLL...
...YOU'D LET ME BECOME A SHINOBI!
...MIZUKI!?
SHHOOOO
SHHOOOO
SHHOOOO
TUK TUK
TUK TUK
SCRR

READ THIS WAY

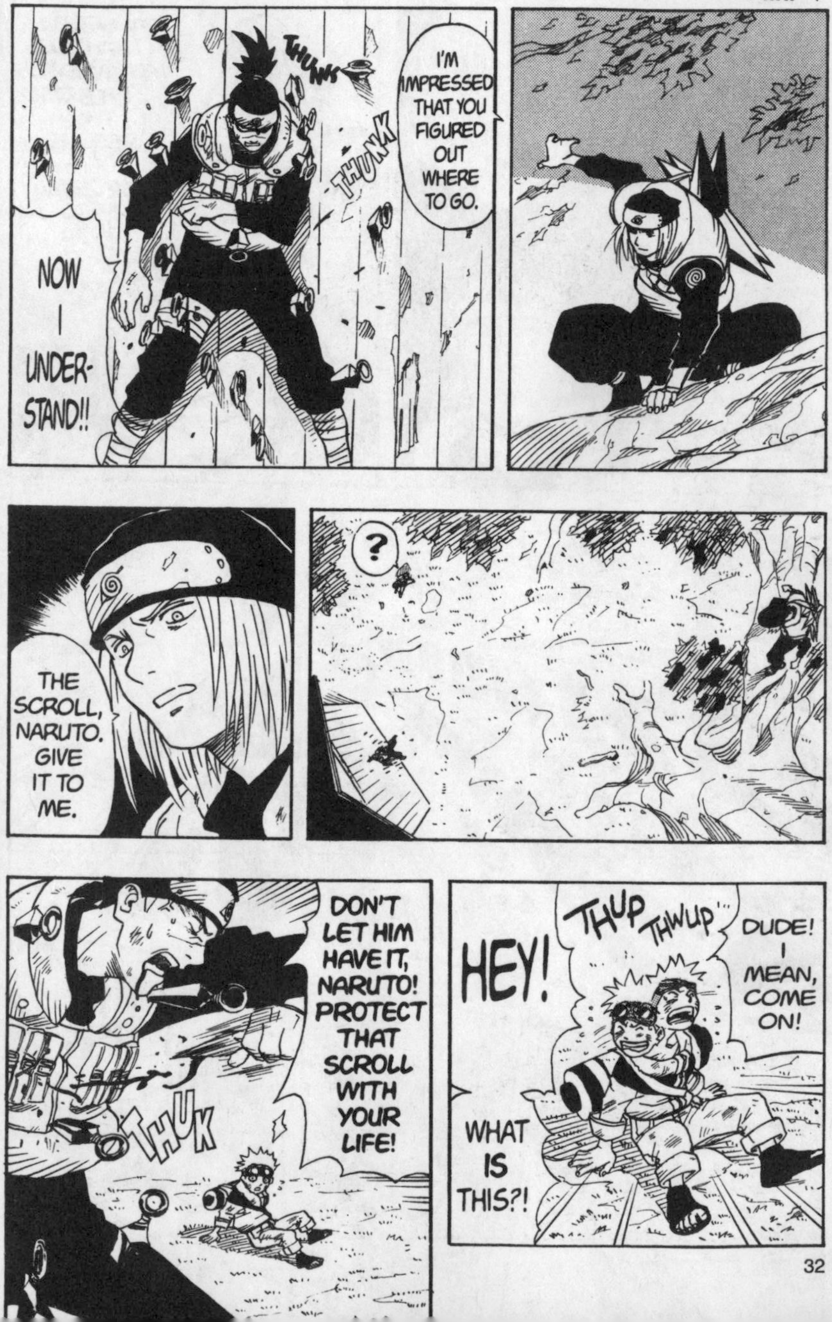
I'M IMPRESSED THAT YOU FIGURED OUT WHERE TO GO.
THUNK
THUNK
NOW I UNDERSTAND!!
?
THE SCROLL, NARUTO. GIVE IT TO ME.
DUDE! I MEAN, COME ON!
THUP THWUP
HEY!
WHAT IS THIS?!
DON'T LET HIM HAVE IT, NARUTO! PROTECT THAT SCROLL WITH YOUR LIFE!
THUK

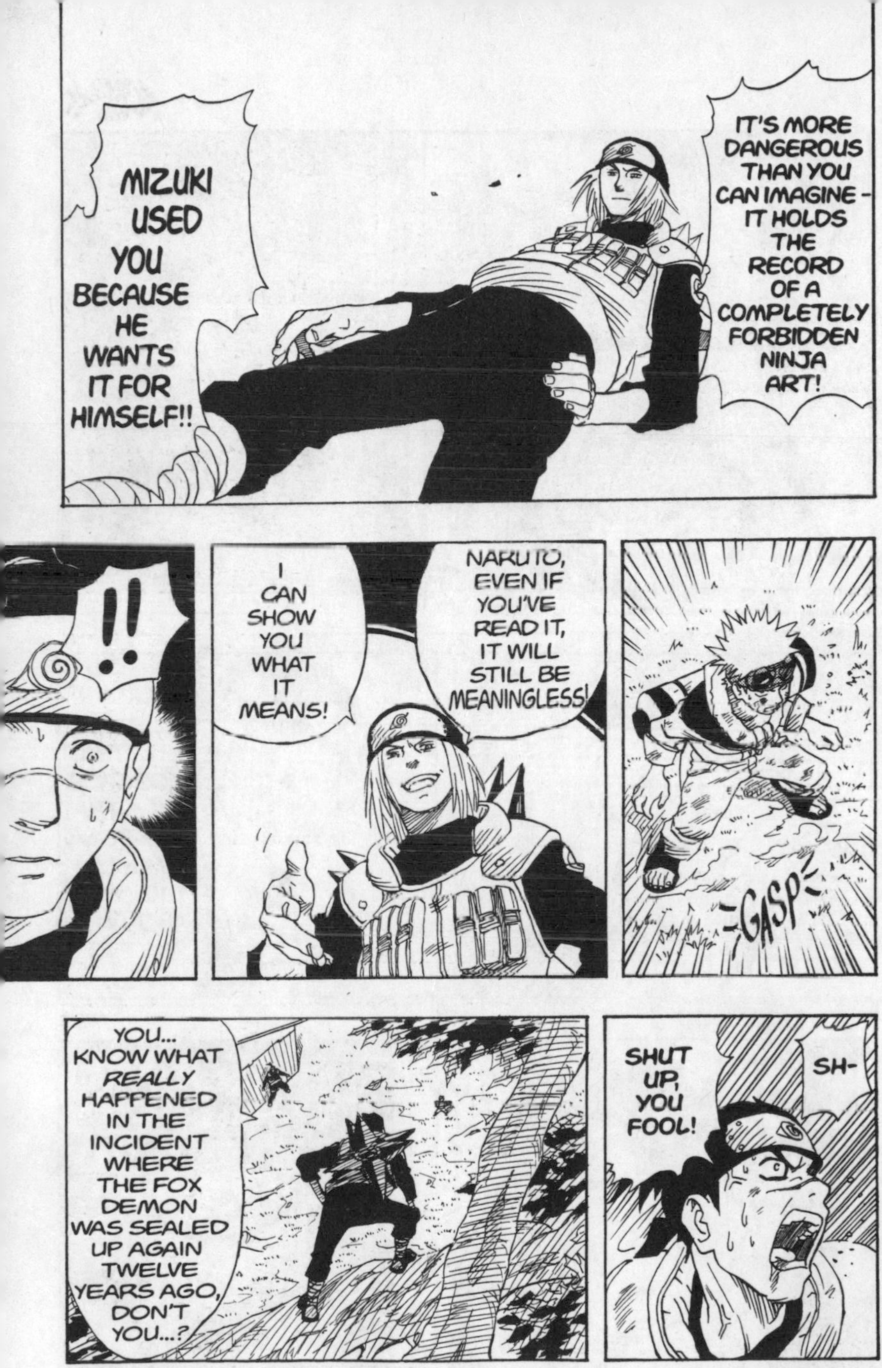
IT'S MORE DANGEROUS THAN YOU CAN IMAGINE - IT HOLDS THE RECORD OF A COMPLETELY FORBIDDEN NINJA ART!
MIZUKI USED YOU BECAUSE HE WANTS IT FOR HIMSELF!!
GASP
NARUTO, EVEN IF YOU'VE READ IT, IT WILL STILL BE MEANINGLESS!
I CAN SHOW YOU WHAT IT MEANS!
!!
SH-
SHUT UP, YOU FOOL!
YOU... KNOW WHAT *REALLY* HAPPENED IN THE INCIDENT WHERE THE FOX DEMON WAS SEALED UP AGAIN TWELVE YEARS AGO, DON'T YOU...?

READ THIS WAY

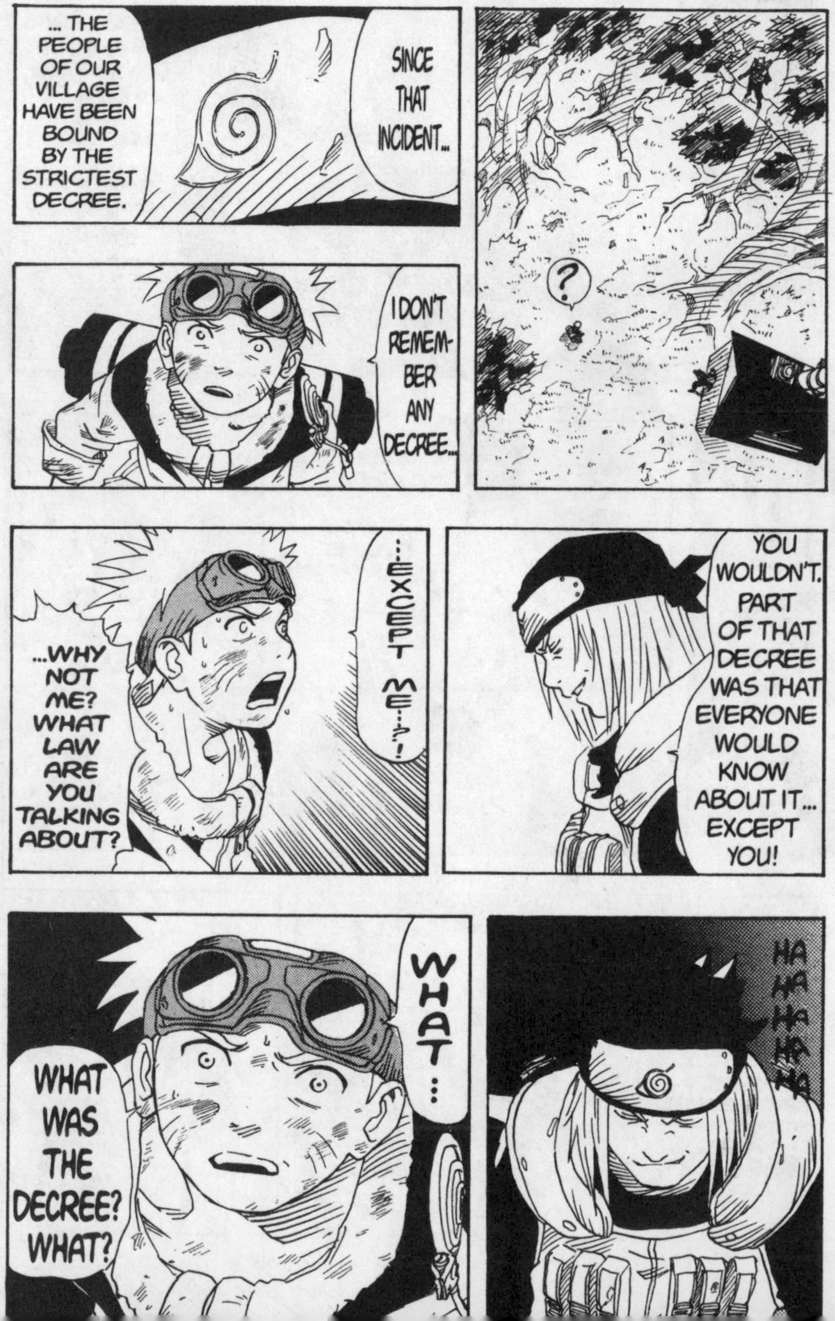
?
SINCE THAT INCIDENT...
... THE PEOPLE OF OUR VILLAGE HAVE BEEN BOUND BY THE STRICTEST DECREE.
I DON'T REMEMBER ANY DECREE...
YOU WOULDN'T. PART OF THAT DECREE WAS THAT EVERYONE WOULD KNOW ABOUT IT... EXCEPT YOU!
...EXCEPT ME...?!
...WHY NOT ME? WHAT LAW ARE YOU TALKING ABOUT?
HA HA HA HA HA
WHAT...
WHAT WAS THE DECREE? WHAT?

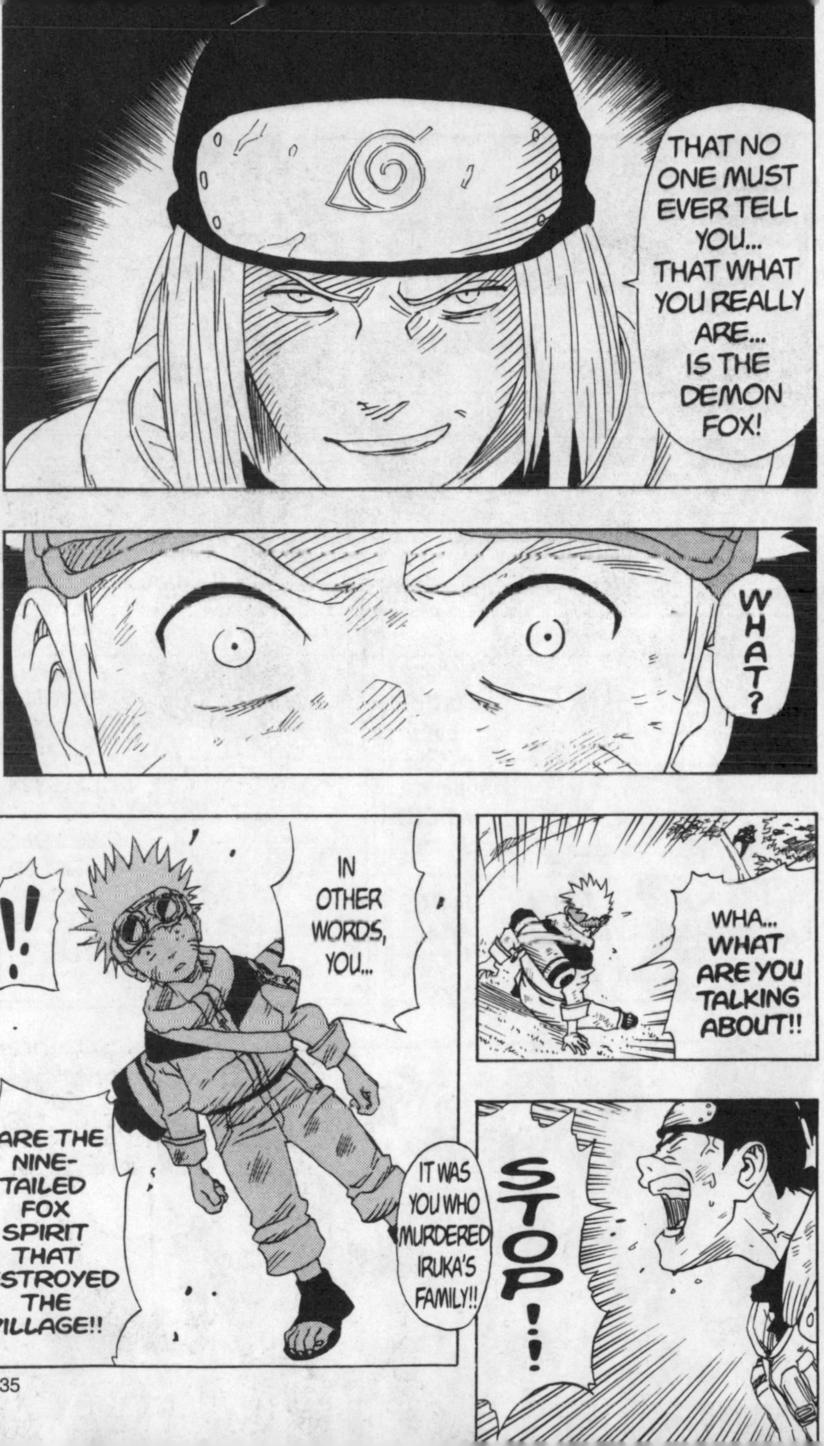
THAT NO ONE MUST EVER TELL YOU... THAT WHAT YOU REALLY ARE... IS THE DEMON FOX!
WHAT?
WHA... WHAT ARE YOU TALKING ABOUT!!
STOP!!
IN OTHER WORDS, YOU...
!!
...ARE THE NINE-TAILED FOX SPIRIT THAT DESTROYED THE VILLAGE!!
IT WAS YOU WHO MURDERED IRUKA'S FAMILY!!

READ THIS WAY

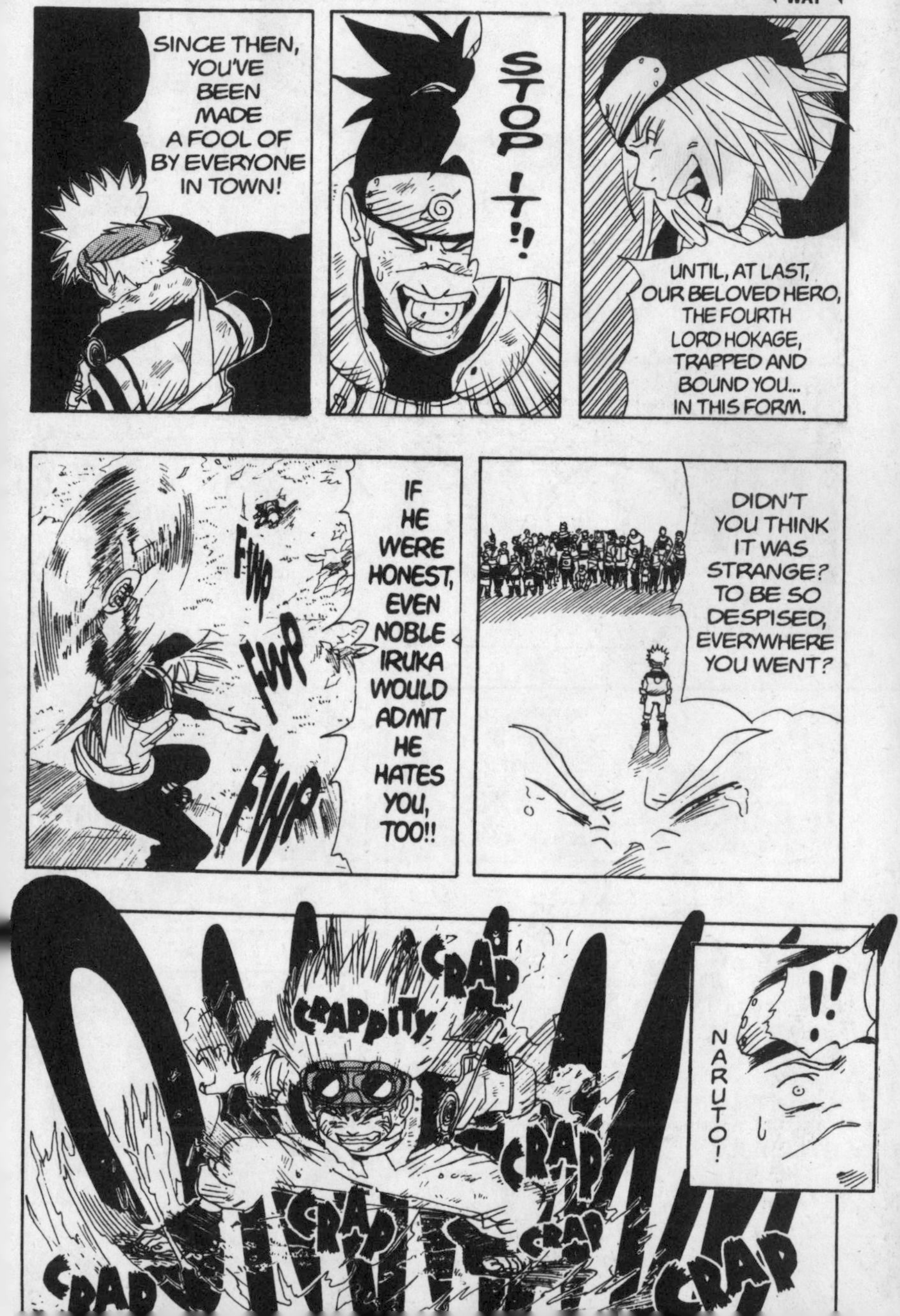
UNTIL, AT LAST, OUR BELOVED HERO, THE FOURTH LORD HOKAGE, TRAPPED AND BOUND YOU... IN THIS FORM.
STOP IT!!
SINCE THEN, YOU'VE BEEN MADE A FOOL OF BY EVERYONE IN TOWN!
DIDN'T YOU THINK IT WAS STRANGE? TO BE SO DESPISED, EVERYWHERE YOU WENT?
IF HE WERE HONEST, EVEN NOBLE IRUKA WOULD ADMIT HE HATES YOU, TOO!!
FWP
FWP
FWP
!!
NARUTO!
CRAP
CRAPPITY
CRAP
CRAP
CRAP
CRAP
CRAP
CRAP

READ THIS WAY

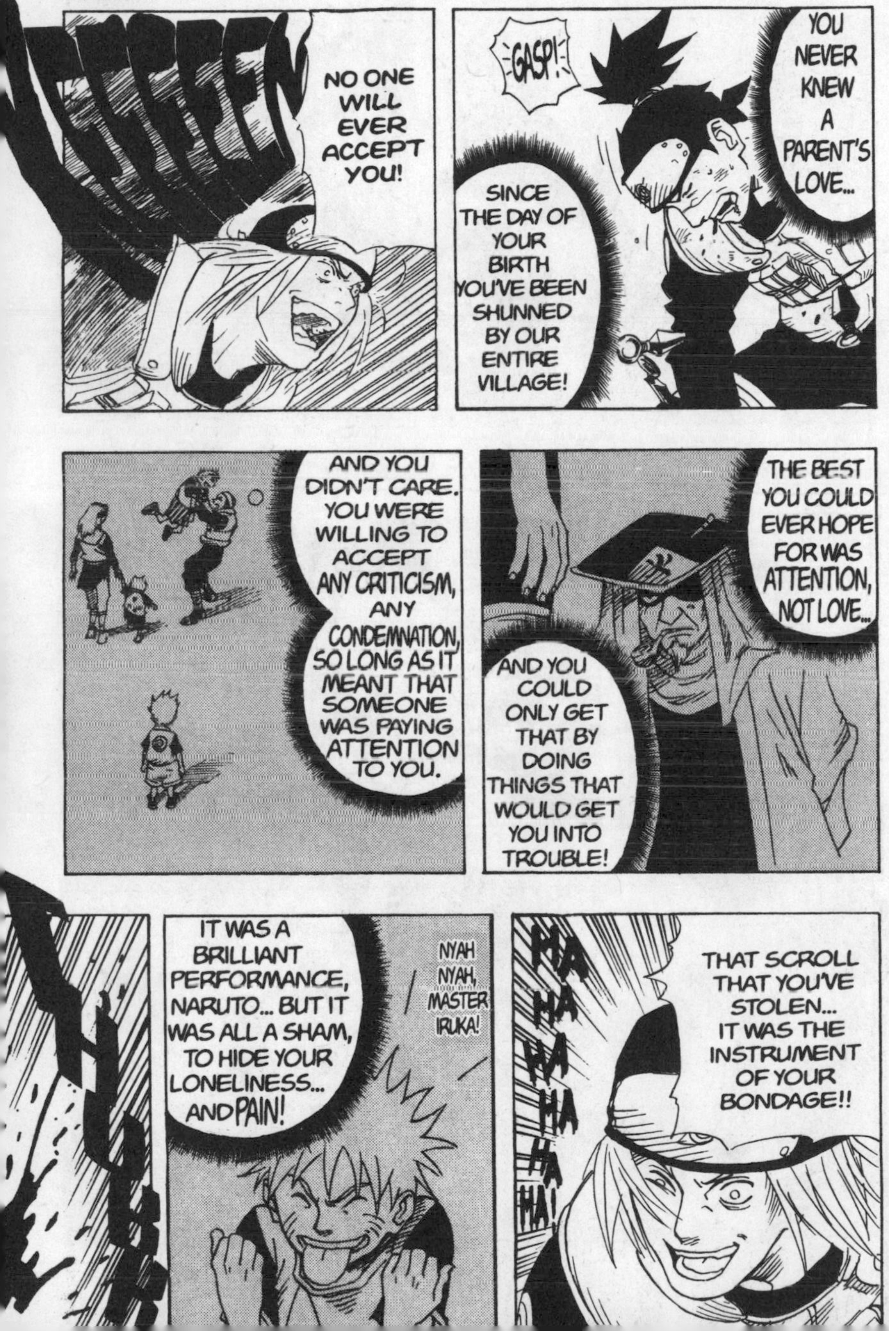
YOU NEVER KNEW A PARENT'S LOVE...
GASP!
SINCE THE DAY OF YOUR BIRTH YOU'VE BEEN SHUNNED BY OUR ENTIRE VILLAGE!
NO ONE WILL EVER ACCEPT YOU!
THE BEST YOU COULD EVER HOPE FOR WAS ATTENTION, NOT LOVE...
AND YOU COULD ONLY GET THAT BY DOING THINGS THAT WOULD GET YOU INTO TROUBLE!
AND YOU DIDN'T CARE. YOU WERE WILLING TO ACCEPT ANY CRITICISM, ANY CONDEMNATION, SO LONG AS IT MEANT THAT SOMEONE WAS PAYING ATTENTION TO YOU.
THAT SCROLL THAT YOU'VE STOLEN... IT WAS THE INSTRUMENT OF YOUR BONDAGE!!
HA HA HA HA HA HA HA HA!
NYAH NYAH, MASTER IRUKA!
IT WAS A BRILLIANT PERFORMANCE, NARUTO... BUT IT WAS ALL A SHAM, TO HIDE YOUR LONELINESS... AND PAIN!

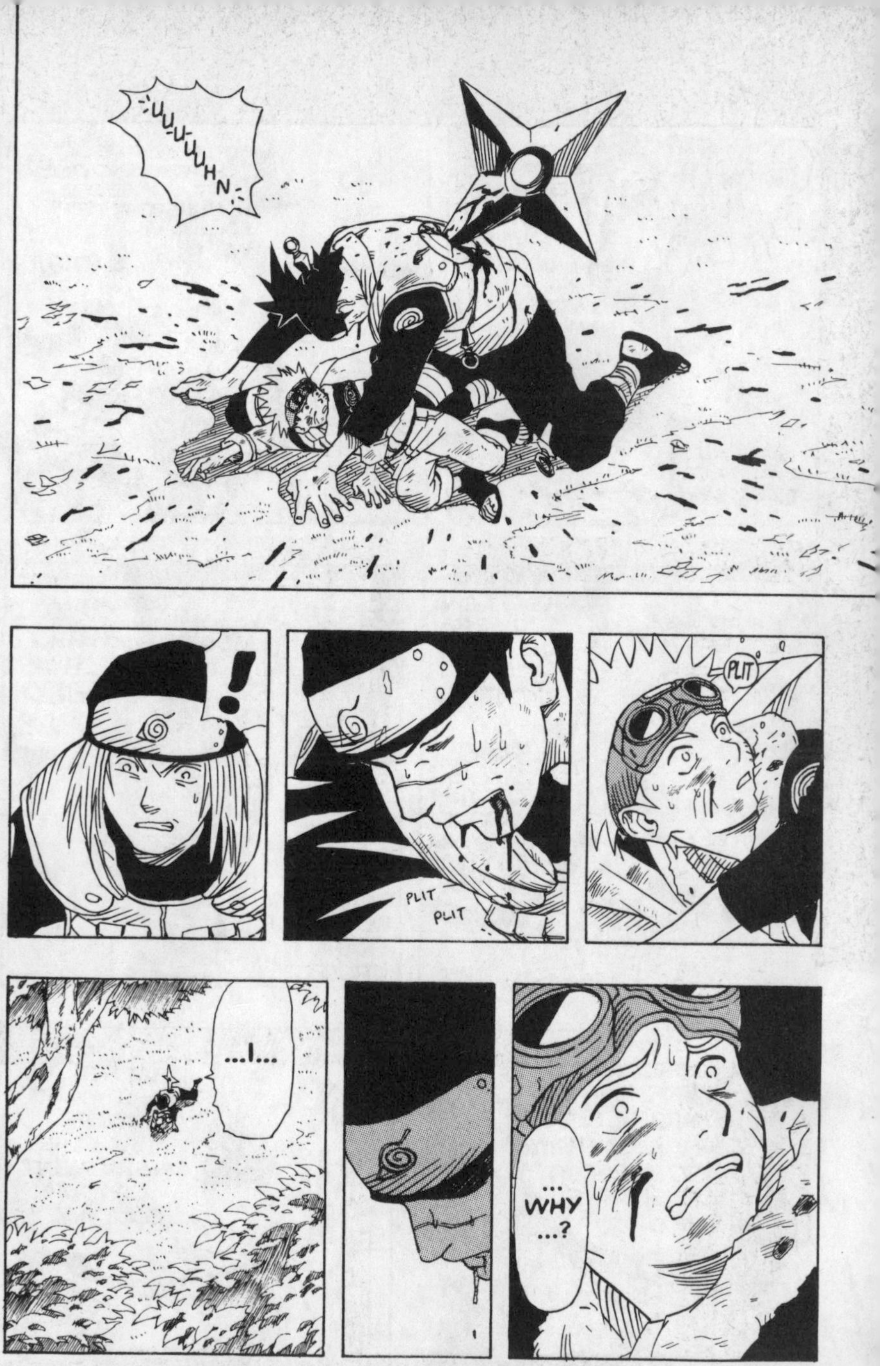
UU-U-UUHN
PLIT
PLIT
PLIT
!
... WHY ...?
...I...

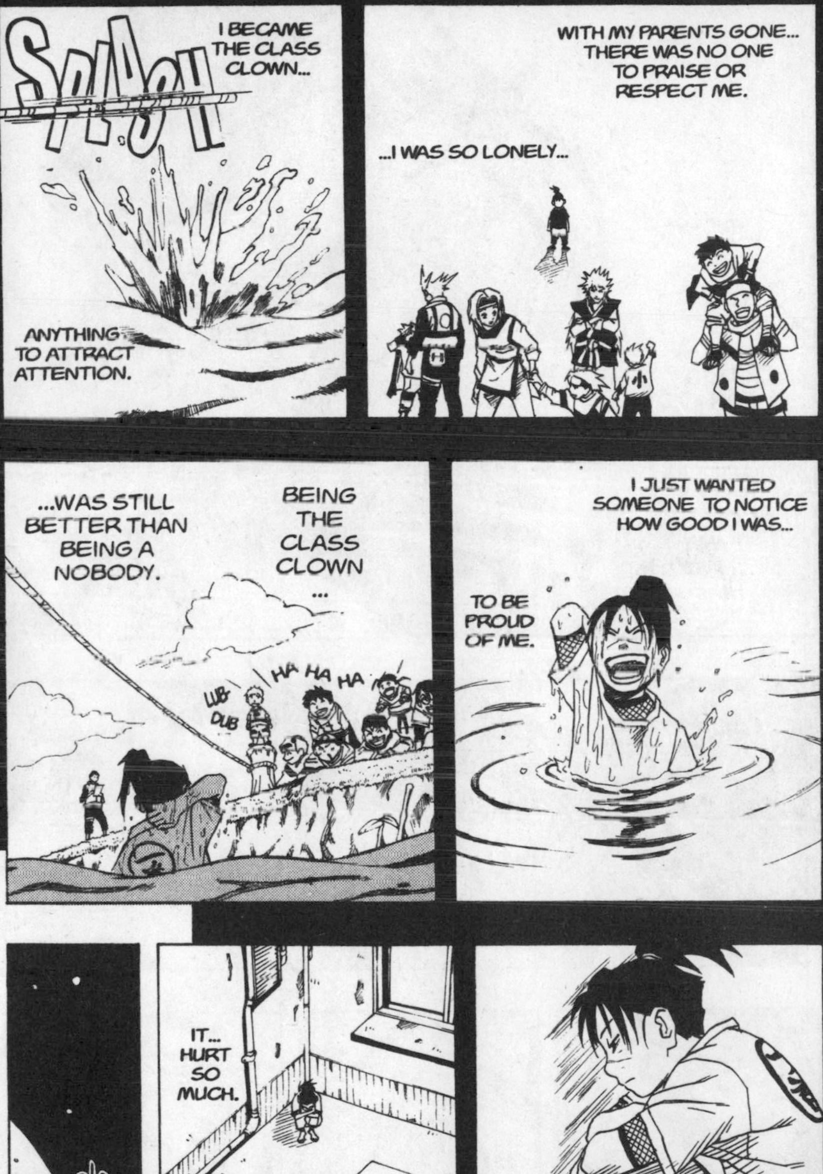
WITH MY PARENTS GONE... THERE WAS NO ONE TO PRAISE OR RESPECT ME.
...I WAS SO LONELY...
SPLASH
I BECAME THE CLASS CLOWN...
ANYTHING TO ATTRACT ATTENTION.
I JUST WANTED SOMEONE TO NOTICE HOW GOOD I WAS...
TO BE PROUD OF ME.
BEING THE CLASS CLOWN ...
...WAS STILL BETTER THAN BEING A NOBODY.
HA HA HA
LUB DUB
IT... HURT SO MUCH.
PLIT

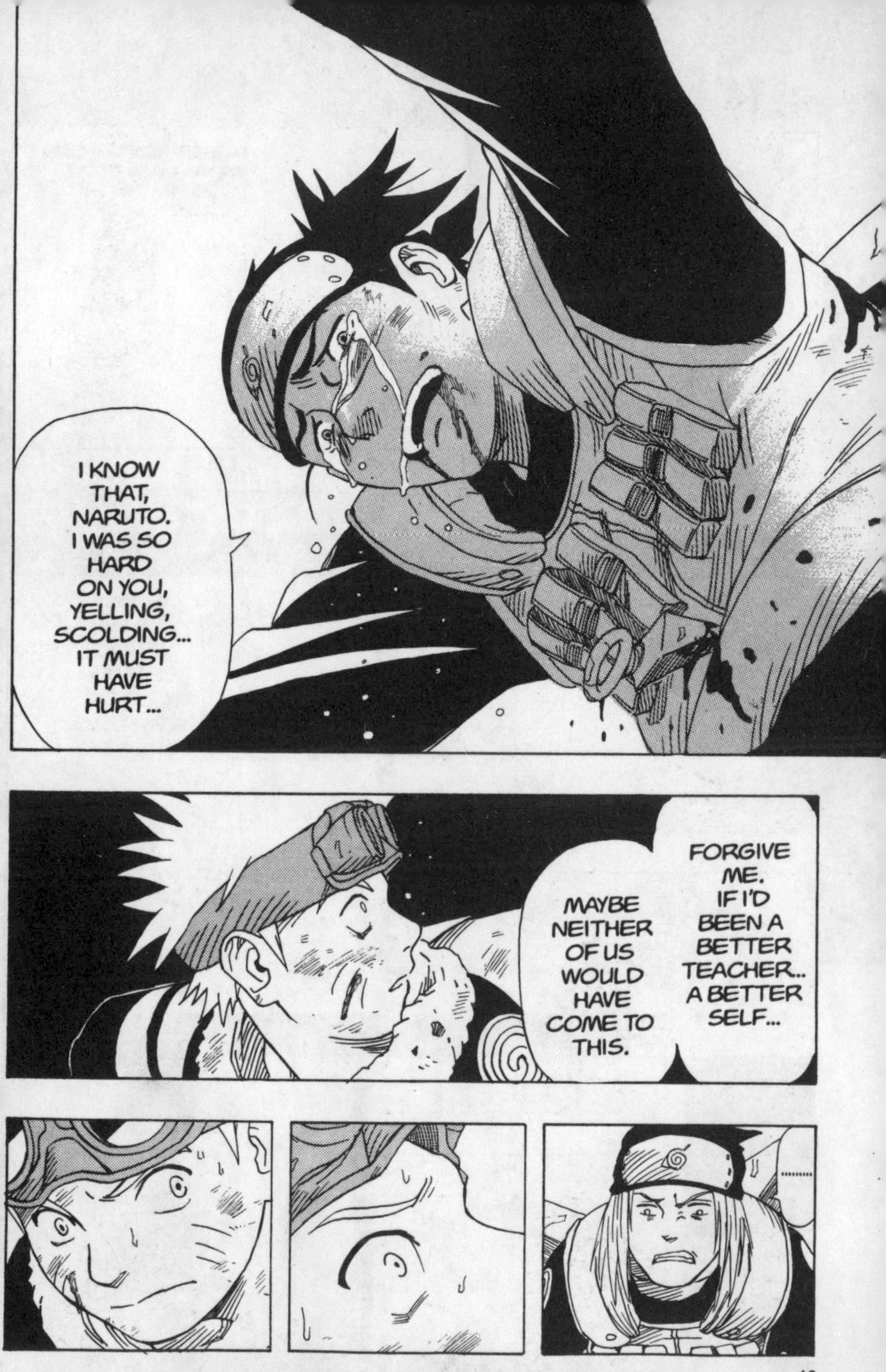
I KNOW THAT, NARUTO. I WAS SO HARD ON YOU, YELLING, SCOLDING... IT MUST HAVE HURT...
FORGIVE ME. IF I'D BEEN A BETTER TEACHER... A BETTER SELF...
MAYBE NEITHER OF US WOULD HAVE COME TO THIS.
....

READ THIS WAY

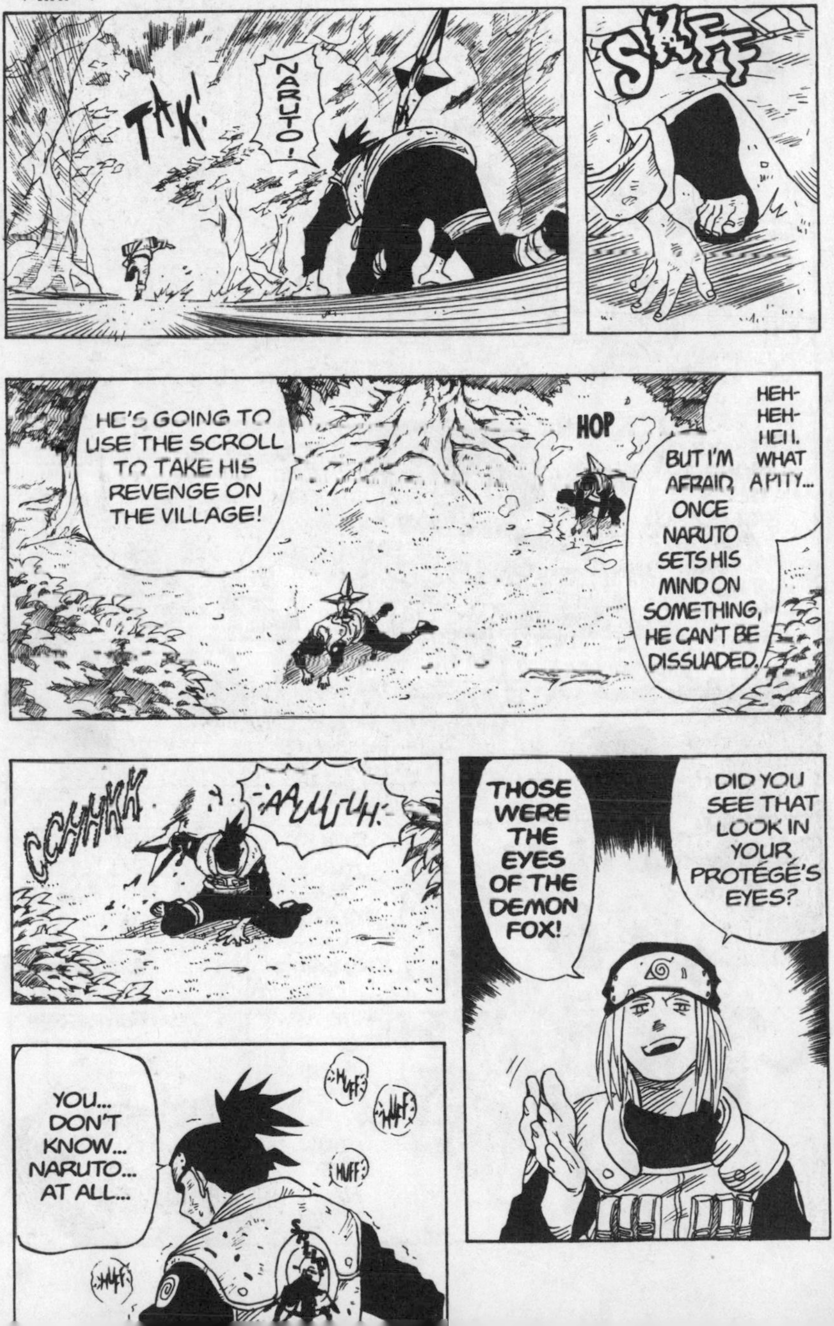
SKFF
TAK!
NARUTO!
HEH-HEH-HEH. WHAT A PITY...
BUT I'M AFRAID, ONCE NARUTO SETS HIS MIND ON SOMETHING, HE CAN'T BE DISSUADED.
HOP
HE'S GOING TO USE THE SCROLL TO TAKE HIS REVENGE ON THE VILLAGE!
DID YOU SEE THAT LOOK IN YOUR PROTÉGÉ'S EYES?
THOSE WERE THE EYES OF THE DEMON FOX!
AAUU-UH
CCHHKK
HUFF
HUFF
YOU... DON'T KNOW... NARUTO... AT ALL...
HUFF
HUFF

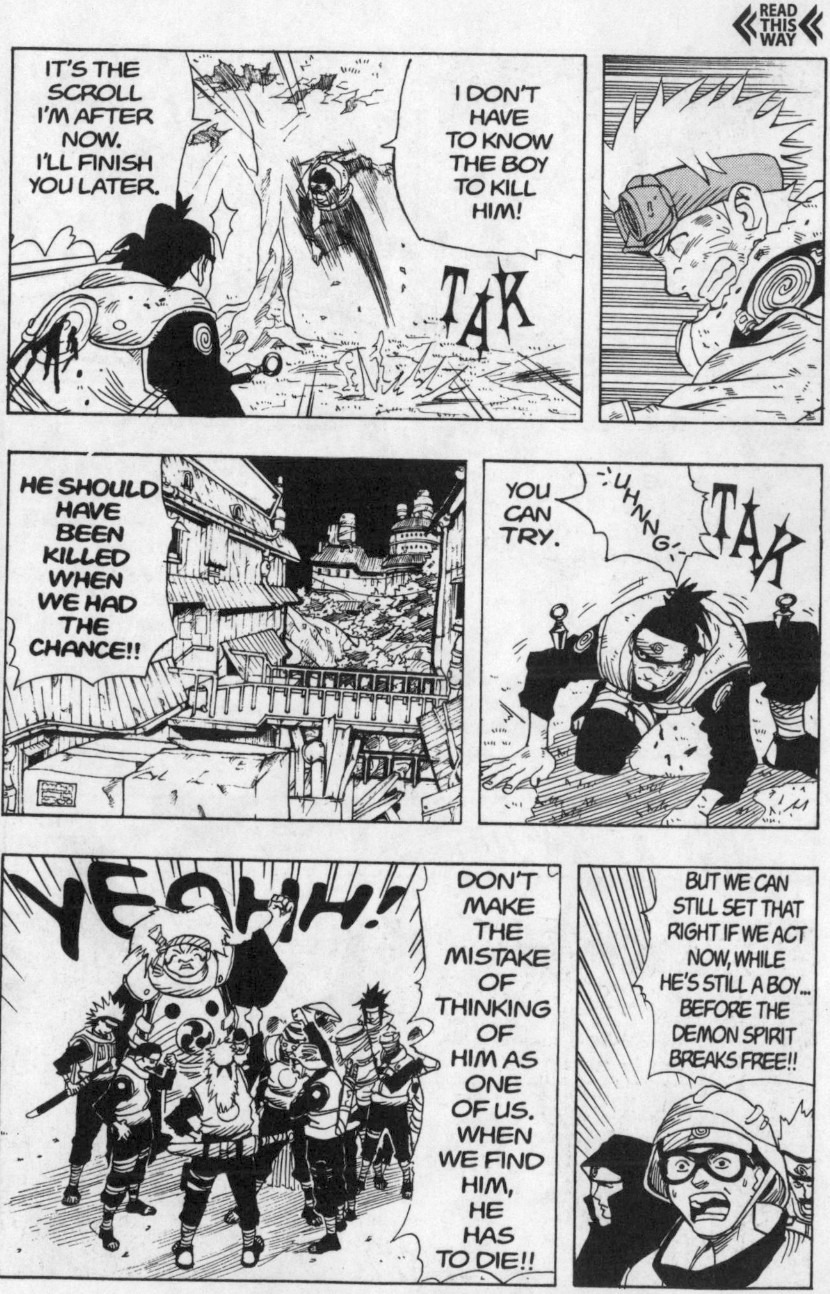
READ THIS WAY
I DON'T HAVE TO KNOW THE BOY TO KILL HIM!
IT'S THE SCROLL I'M AFTER NOW. I'LL FINISH YOU LATER.
TAK
TAK
UHNNG
YOU CAN TRY.
HE SHOULD HAVE BEEN KILLED WHEN WE HAD THE CHANCE!!
BUT WE CAN STILL SET THAT RIGHT IF WE ACT NOW, WHILE HE'S STILL A BOY... BEFORE THE DEMON SPIRIT BREAKS FREE!!
DON'T MAKE THE MISTAKE OF THINKING OF HIM AS ONE OF US. WHEN WE FIND HIM, HE HAS TO DIE!!
YEOHH!

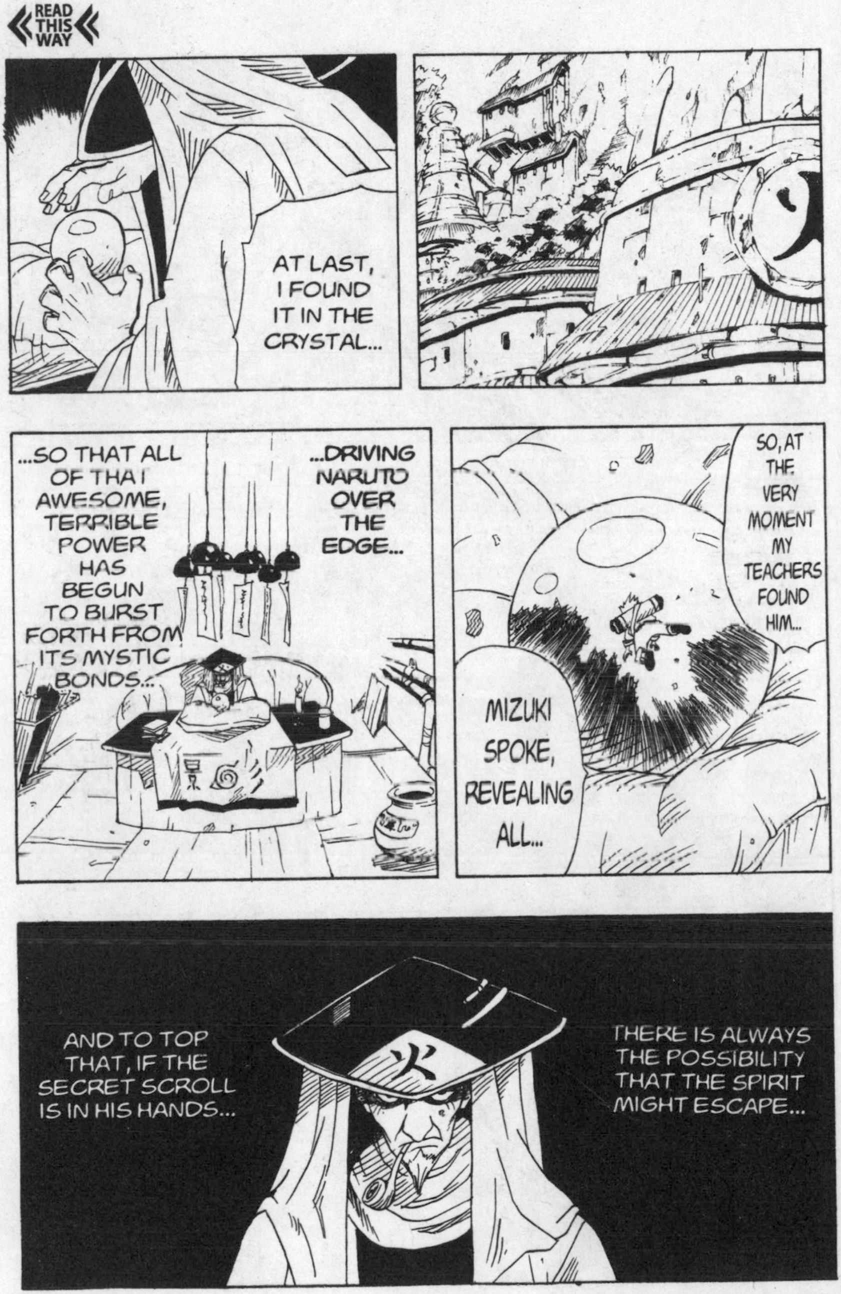
READ THIS WAY
AT LAST, I FOUND IT IN THE CRYSTAL...
SO, AT THE VERY MOMENT MY TEACHERS FOUND HIM...
MIZUKI SPOKE, REVEALING ALL...
...DRIVING NARUTO OVER THE EDGE...
...SO THAT ALL OF THAT AWESOME, TERRIBLE POWER HAS BEGUN TO BURST FORTH FROM ITS MYSTIC BONDS...
THERE IS ALWAYS THE POSSIBILITY THAT THE SPIRIT MIGHT ESCAPE...
AND TO TOP THAT, IF THE SECRET SCROLL IS IN HIS HANDS...

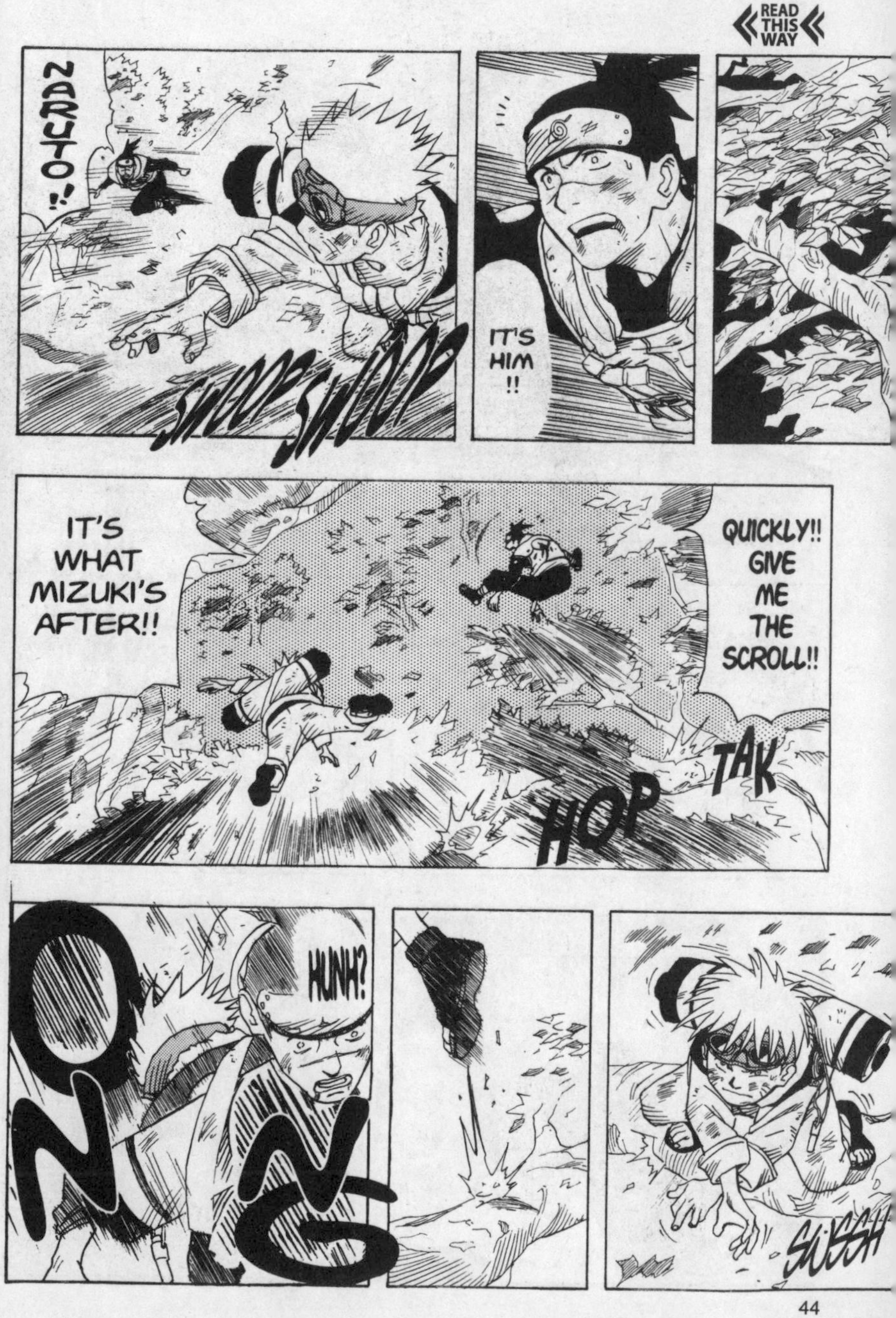
READ THIS WAY
IT'S HIM !!
NARUTO !!
SWOOP SWOOP
QUICKLY!! GIVE ME THE SCROLL!!
IT'S WHAT MIZUKI'S AFTER!!
TAK
HOP
SUSSH
HUNH?

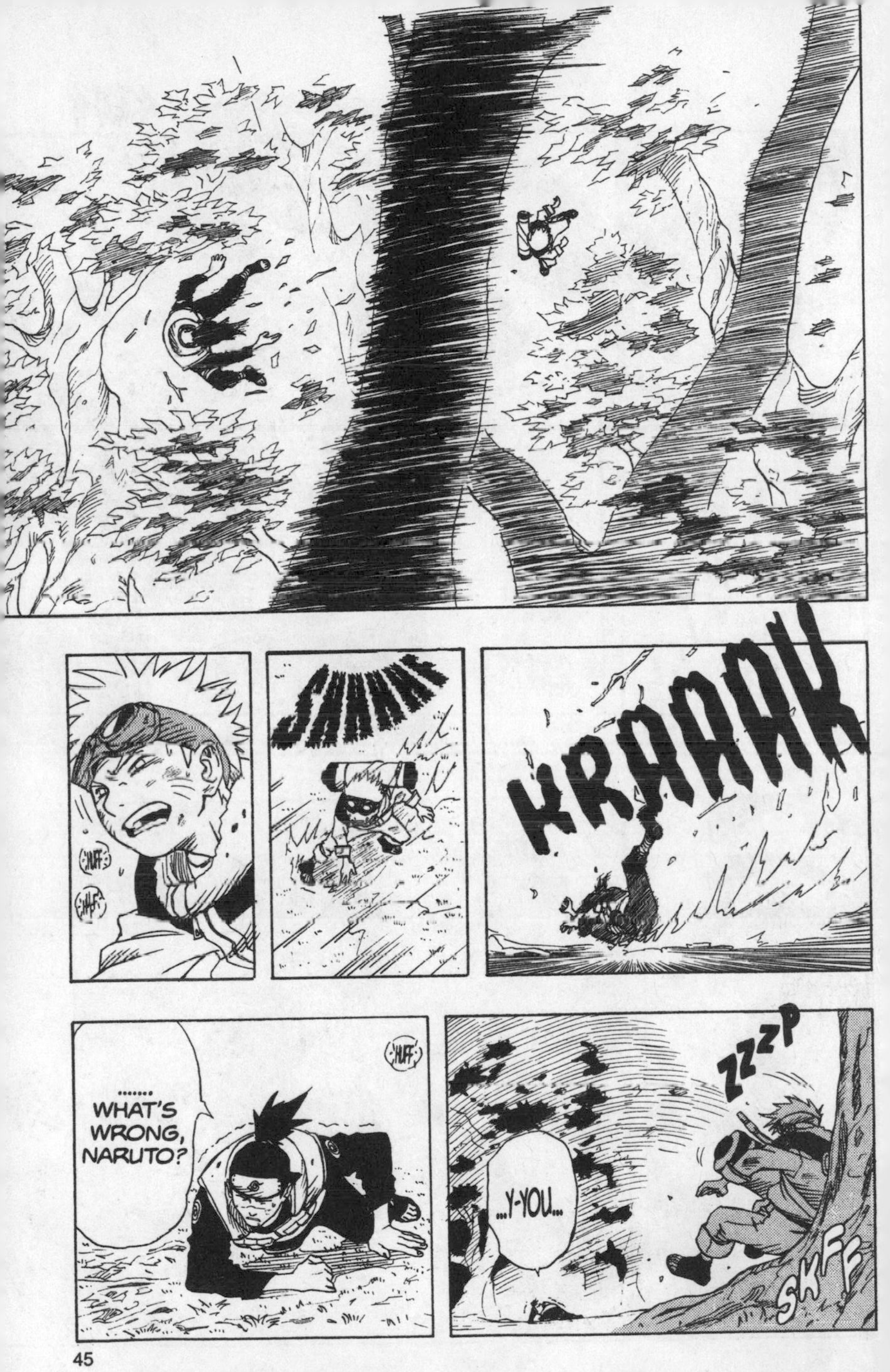
KRAAAK
SHAAAK
HUFF
HUFF
ZZZZP
...Y-YOU...
SKFF
HUFF
......WHAT'S WRONG, NARUTO?

READ THIS WAY

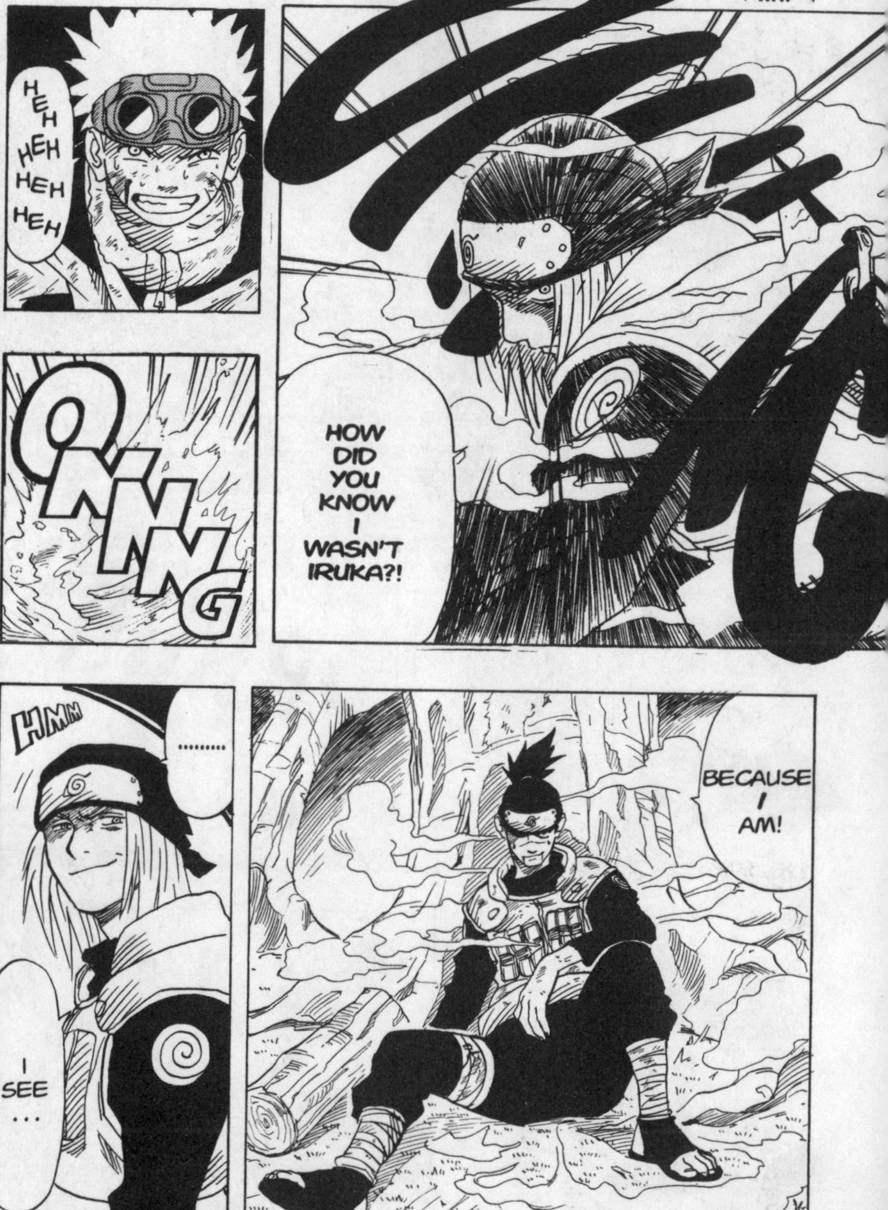
HOW DID YOU KNOW I WASN'T IRUKA?!
HEH HEH HEH HEH
ONNNG
BECAUSE I AM!
....
HMM
I SEE ...

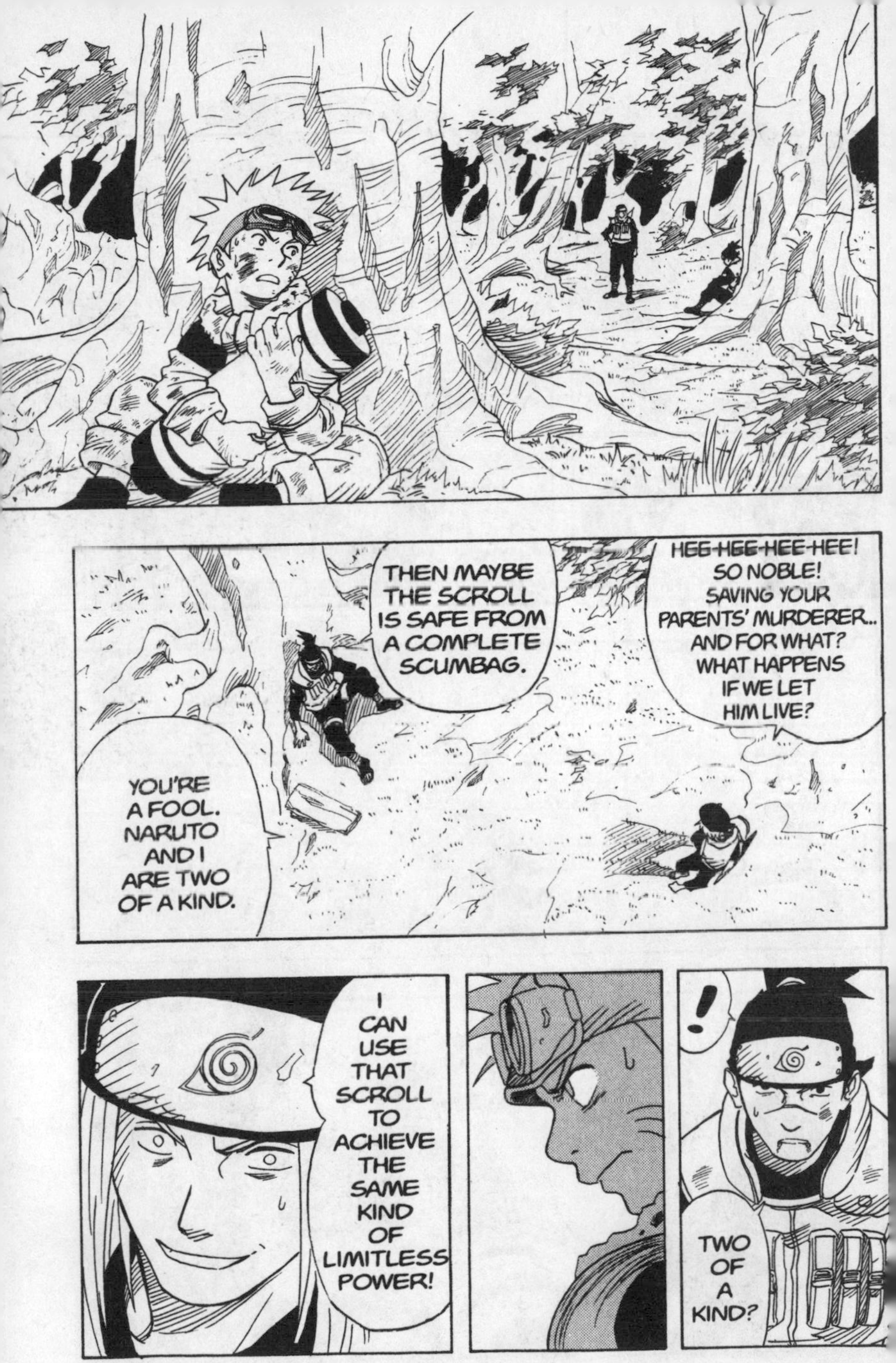
HEE-HEE-HEE-HEE! SO NOBLE! SAVING YOUR PARENTS' MURDERER... AND FOR WHAT? WHAT HAPPENS IF WE LET HIM LIVE?
THEN MAYBE THE SCROLL IS SAFE FROM A COMPLETE SCUMBAG.
YOU'RE A FOOL. NARUTO AND I ARE TWO OF A KIND.
!
TWO OF A KIND?
I CAN USE THAT SCROLL TO ACHIEVE THE SAME KIND OF LIMITLESS POWER!

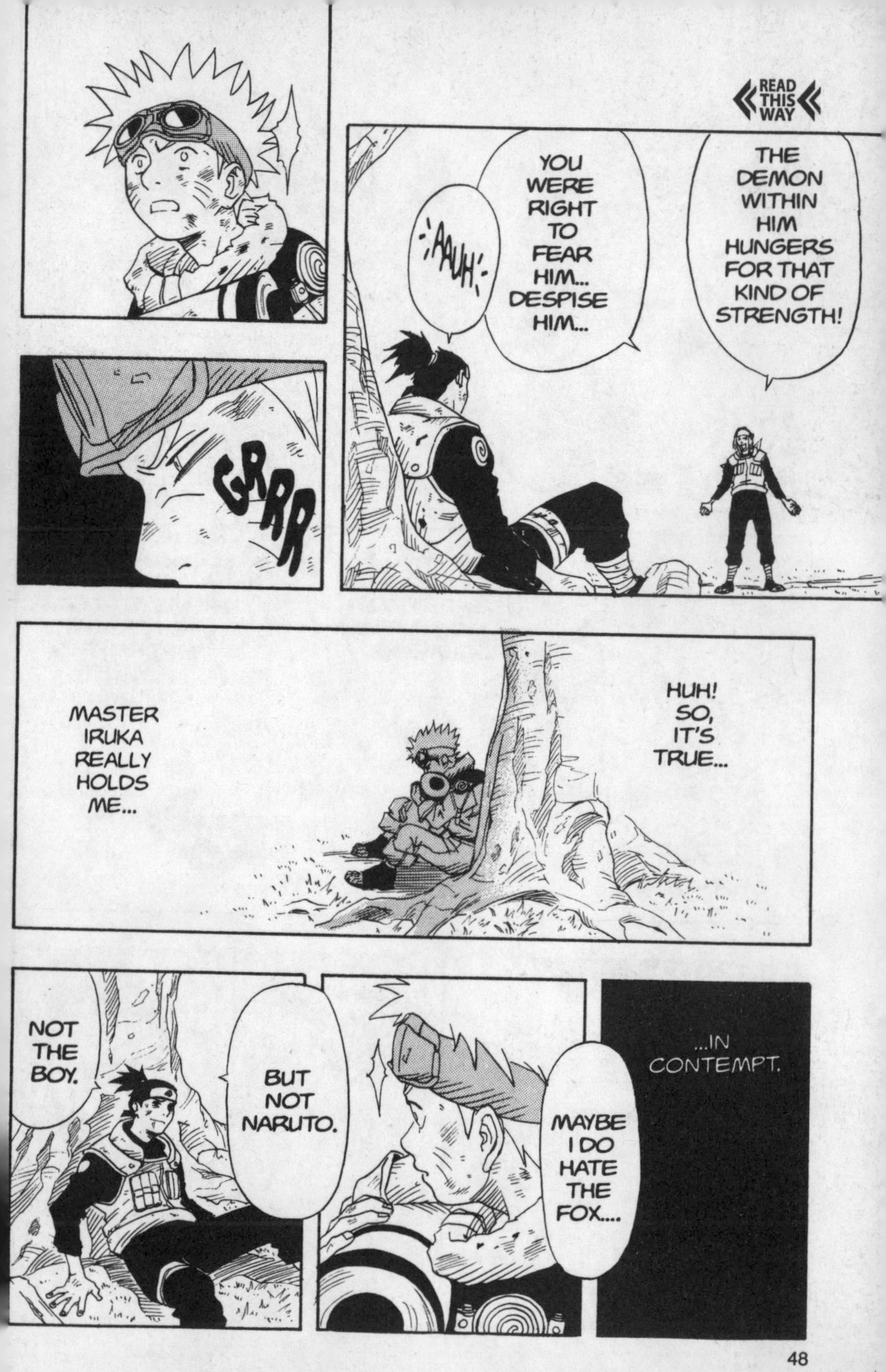
READ THIS WAY
THE DEMON WITHIN HIM HUNGERS FOR THAT KIND OF STRENGTH!
YOU WERE RIGHT TO FEAR HIM... DESPISE HIM...
AAUH!
GRRR
HUH! SO, IT'S TRUE...
MASTER IRUKA REALLY HOLDS ME...
...IN CONTEMPT.
MAYBE I DO HATE THE FOX....
BUT NOT NARUTO.
NOT THE BOY.

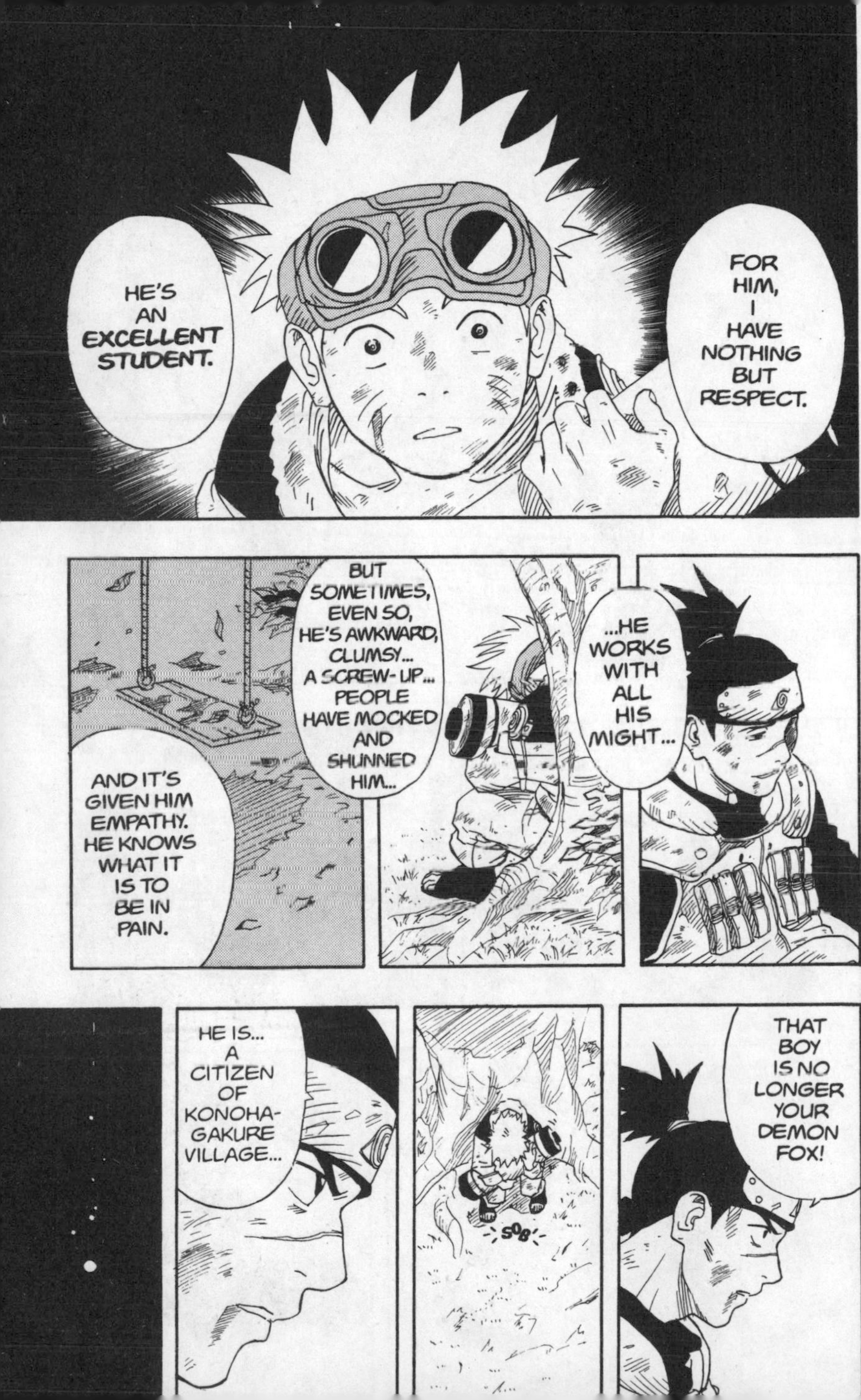
FOR HIM, I HAVE NOTHING BUT RESPECT.
HE'S AN EXCELLENT STUDENT.
...HE WORKS WITH ALL HIS MIGHT...
BUT SOMETIMES, EVEN SO, HE'S AWKWARD, CLUMSY... A SCREW-UP... PEOPLE HAVE MOCKED AND SHUNNED HIM...
AND IT'S GIVEN HIM EMPATHY. HE KNOWS WHAT IT IS TO BE IN PAIN.
THAT BOY IS NO LONGER YOUR DEMON FOX!
SOB
HE IS... A CITIZEN OF KONOHA-GAKURE VILLAGE...

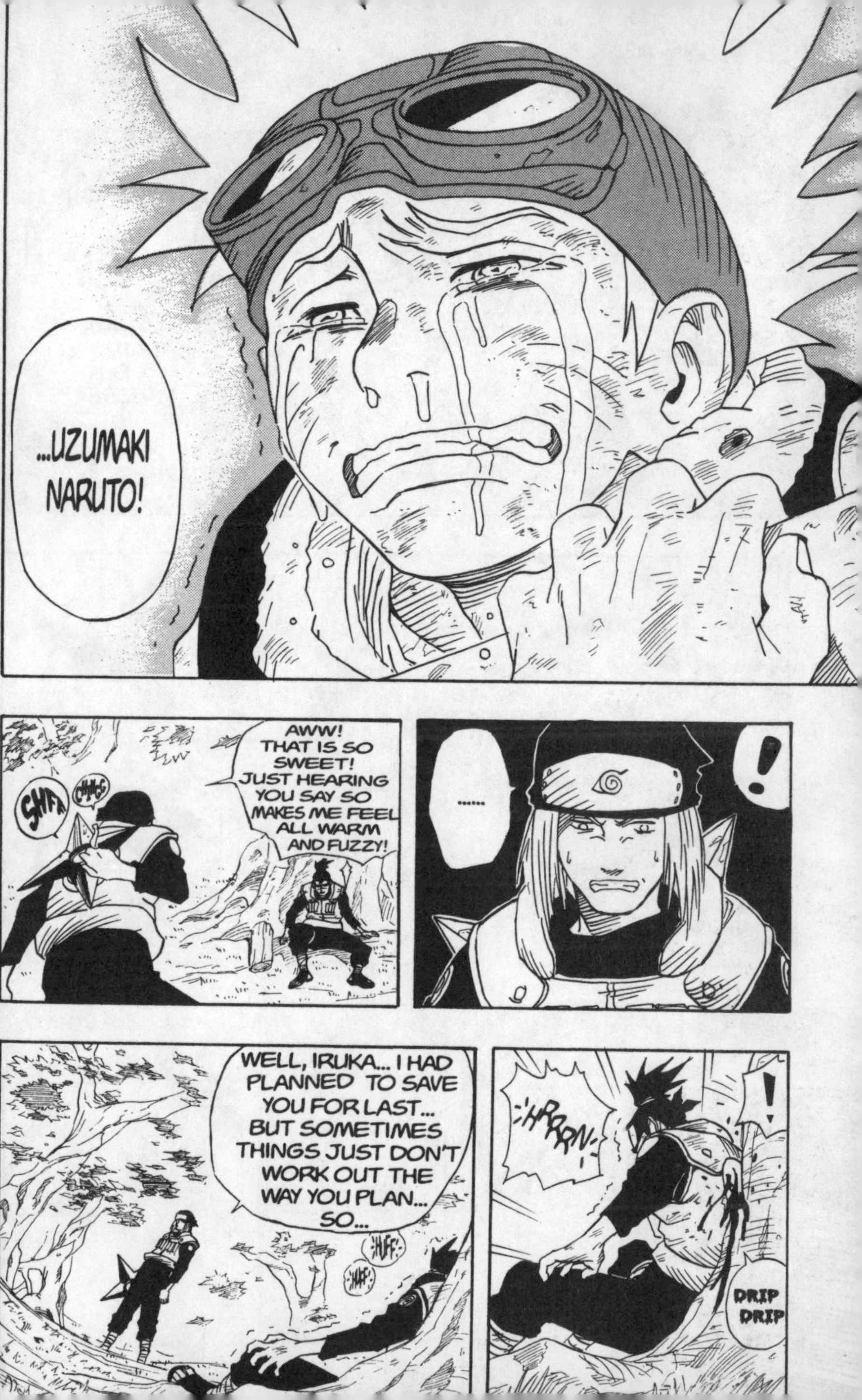

...UZUMAKI NARUTO!
......
!
AWW! THAT IS SO SWEET! JUST HEARING YOU SAY SO MAKES ME FEEL ALL WARM AND FUZZY!
SHFA
CHING
HRRRN
!
DRIP DRIP
WELL, IRUKA... I HAD PLANNED TO SAVE YOU FOR LAST... BUT SOMETIMES THINGS JUST DON'T WORK OUT THE WAY YOU PLAN... SO...
HUFF
HUFF

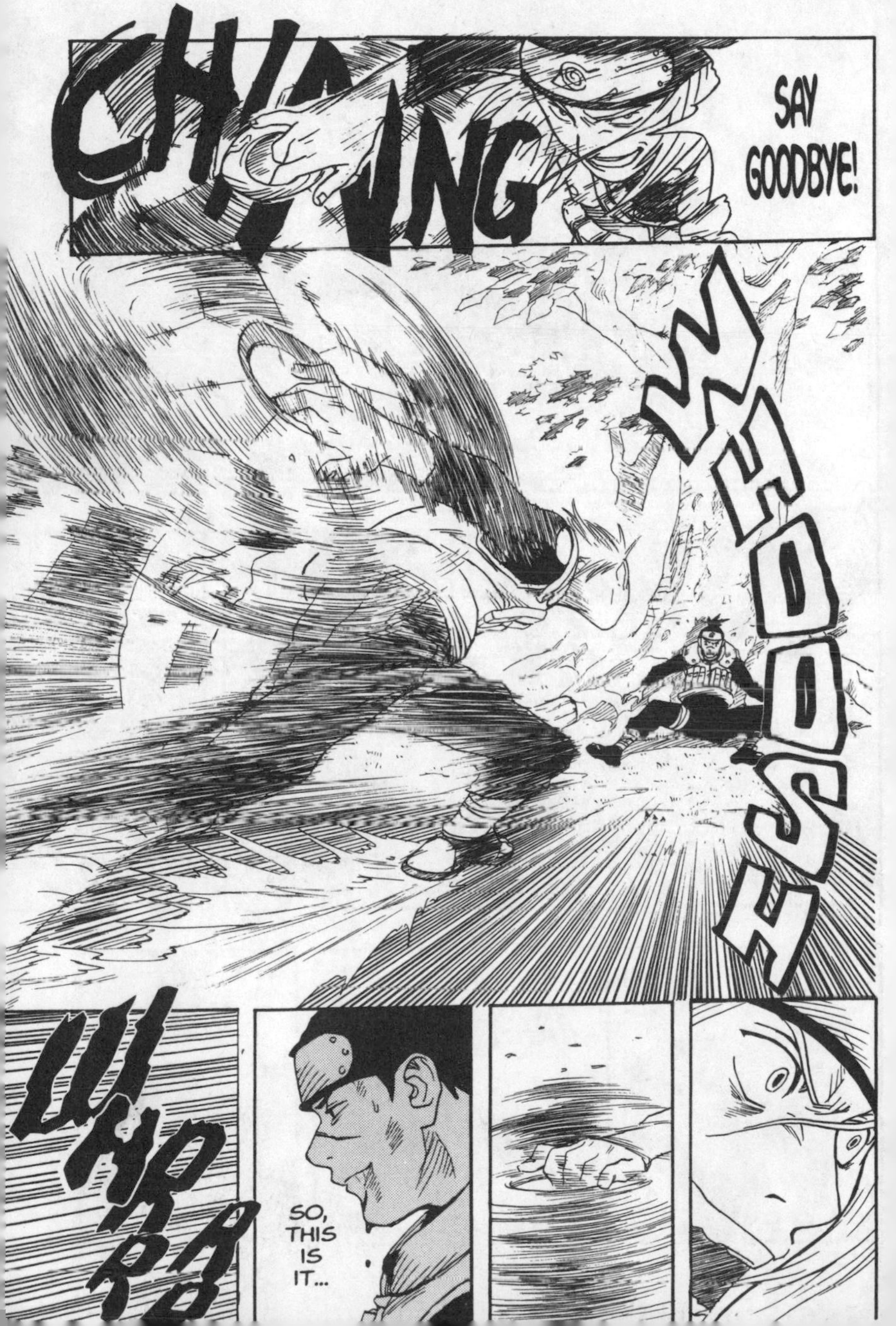
SAY GOODBYE!
WHOOSH
SO, THIS IS IT...

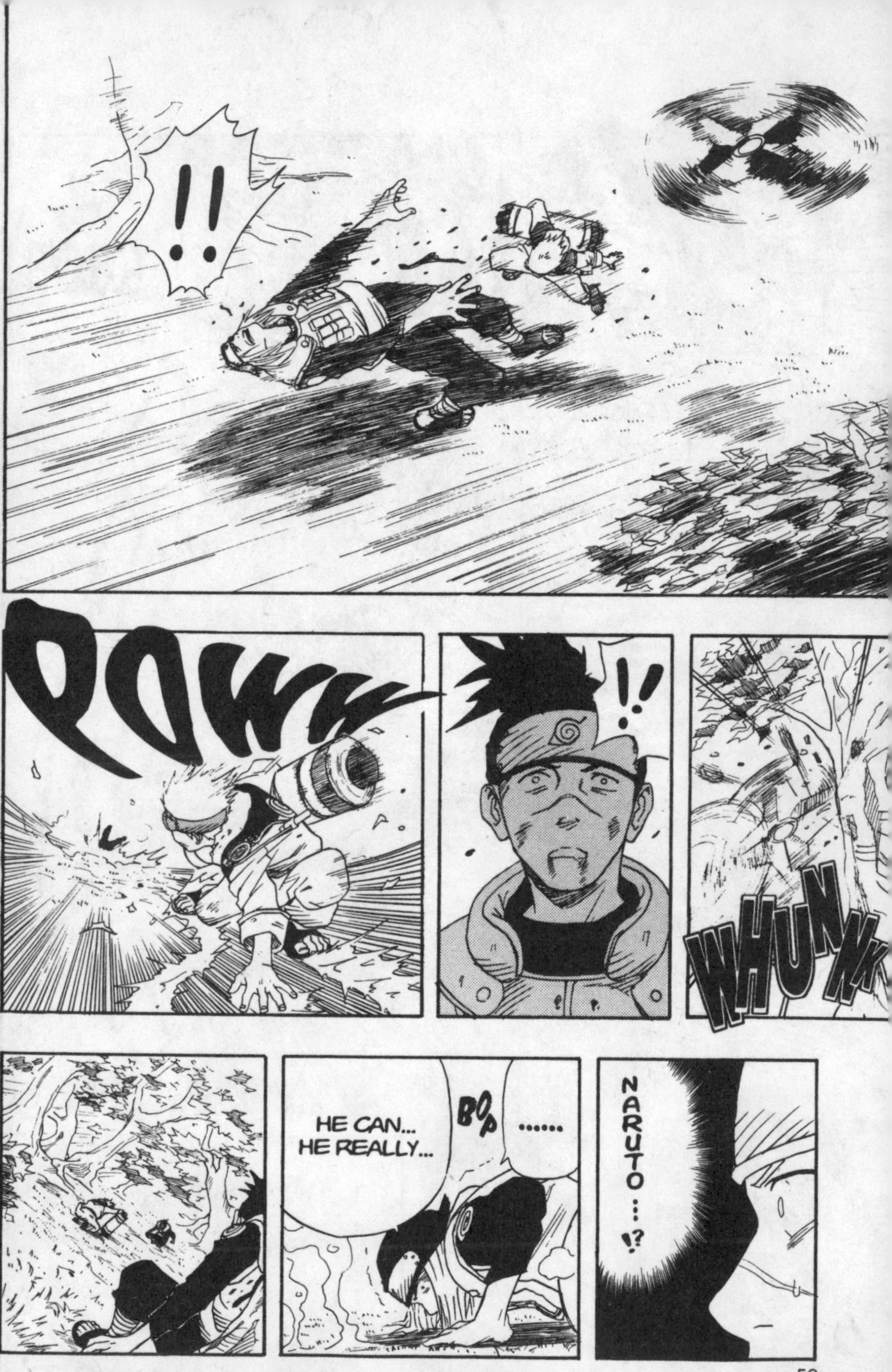
!!
WHUNK
!!
POWW
NARUTO...!?
......
BOP
HE CAN...
HE REALLY...

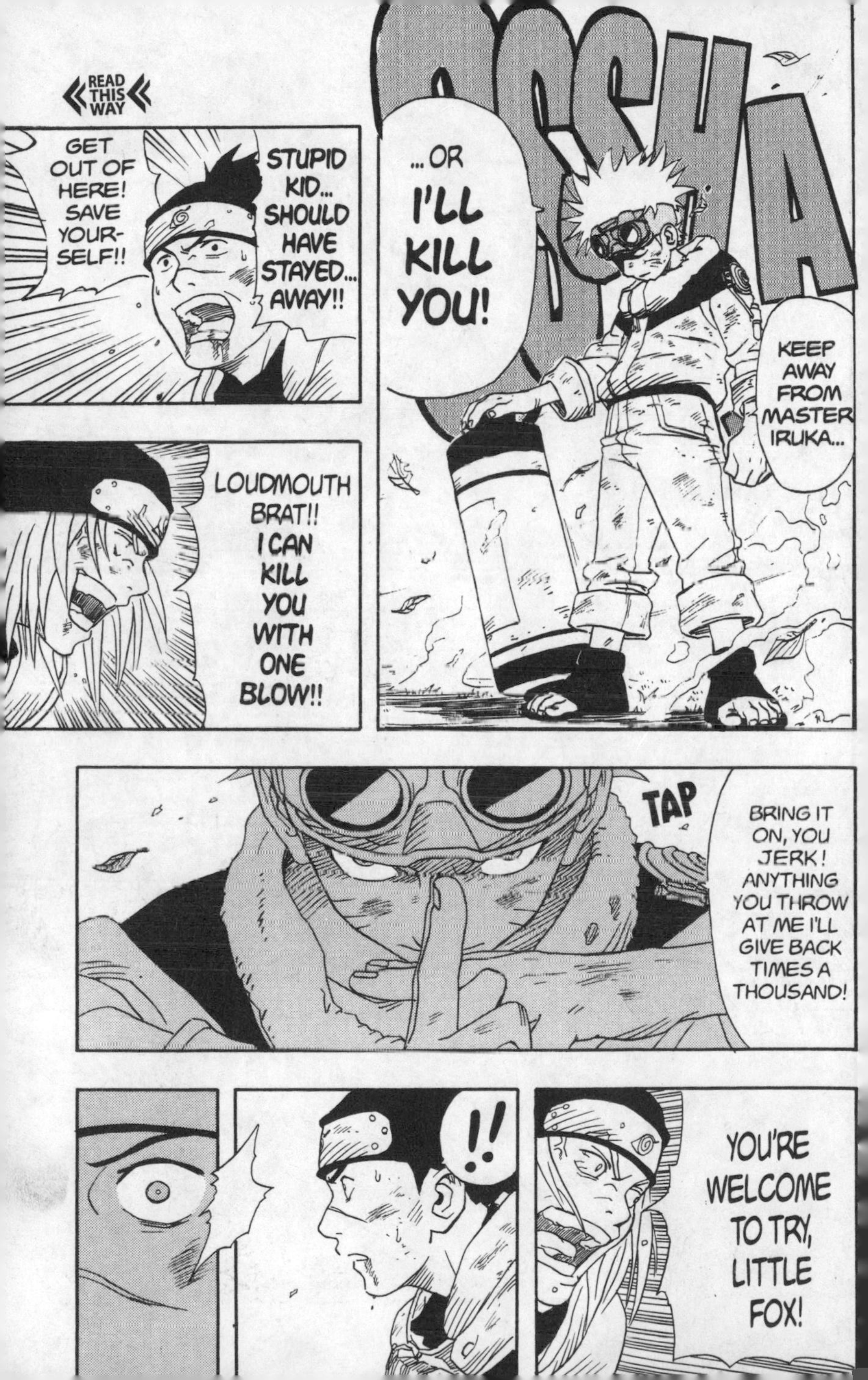
READ THIS WAY
KEEP AWAY FROM MASTER IRUKA...
...OR I'LL KILL YOU!
STUPID KID... SHOULD HAVE STAYED... AWAY!!
GET OUT OF HERE! SAVE YOURSELF!!
LOUDMOUTH BRAT!! I CAN KILL YOU WITH ONE BLOW!!
BRING IT ON, YOU JERK! ANYTHING YOU THROW AT ME I'LL GIVE BACK TIMES A THOUSAND!
TAP
YOU'RE WELCOME TO TRY, LITTLE FOX!
!!

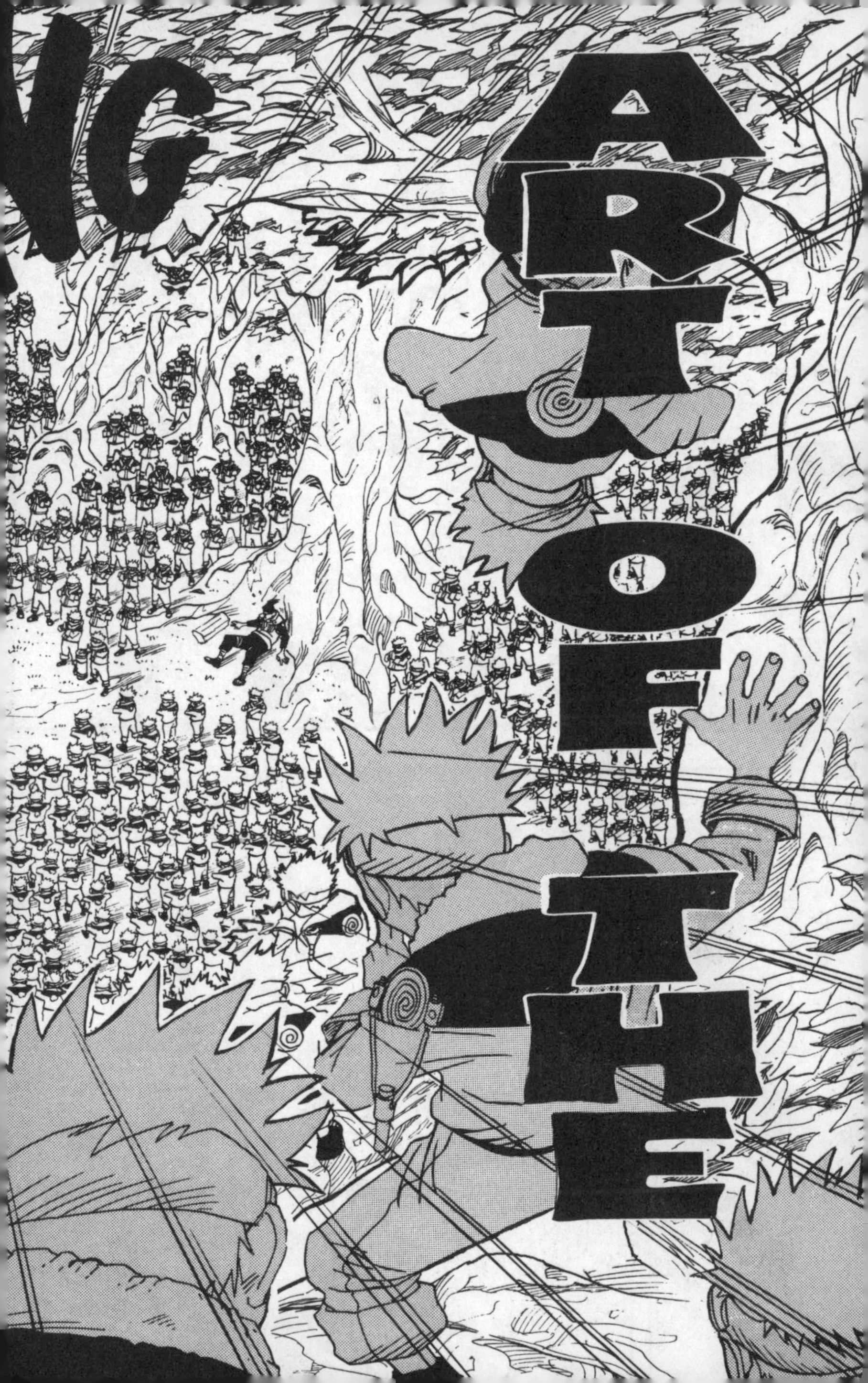
ART OF THE
NG

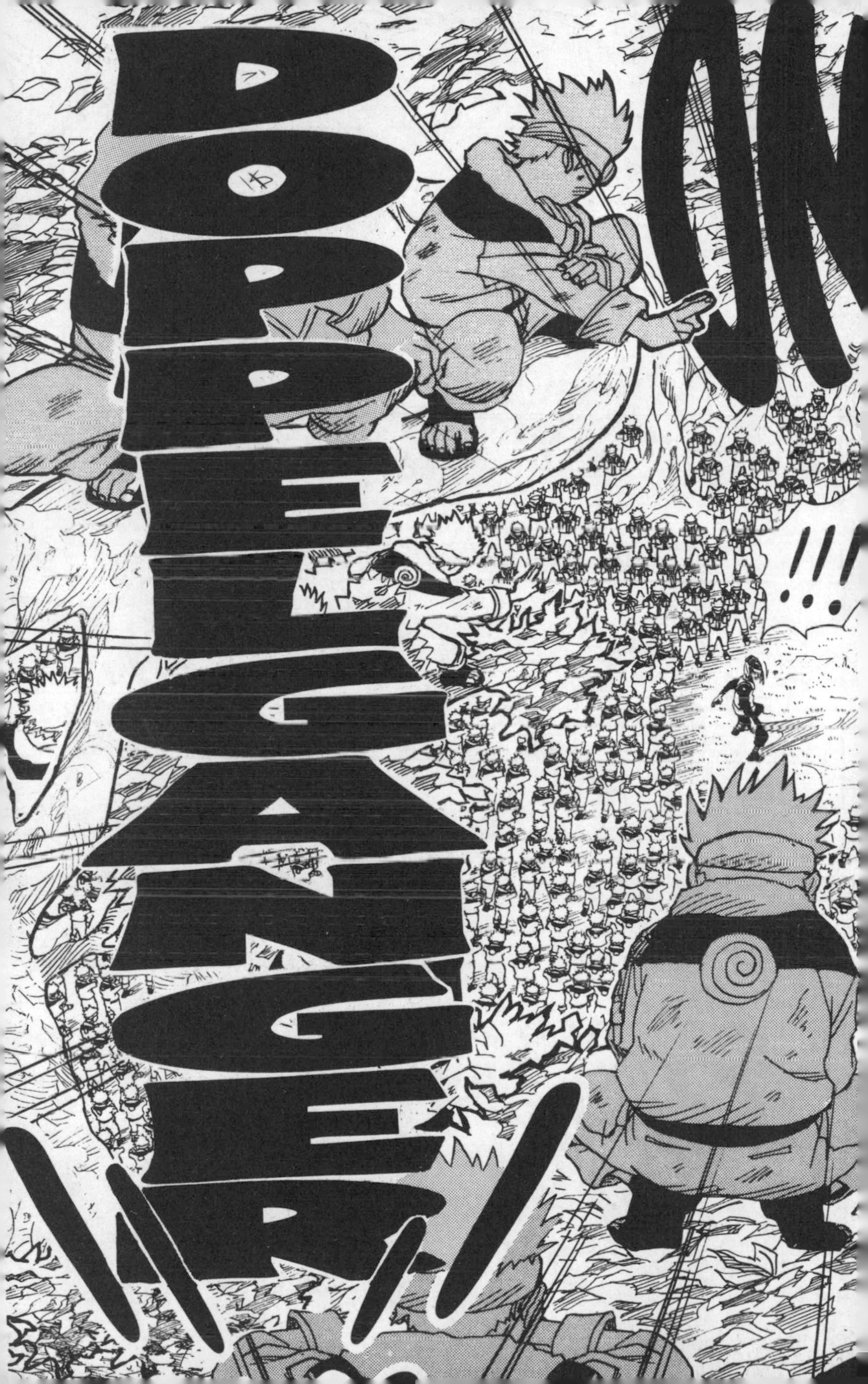
!!...
DOPPELGANGER!!

READ THIS WAY

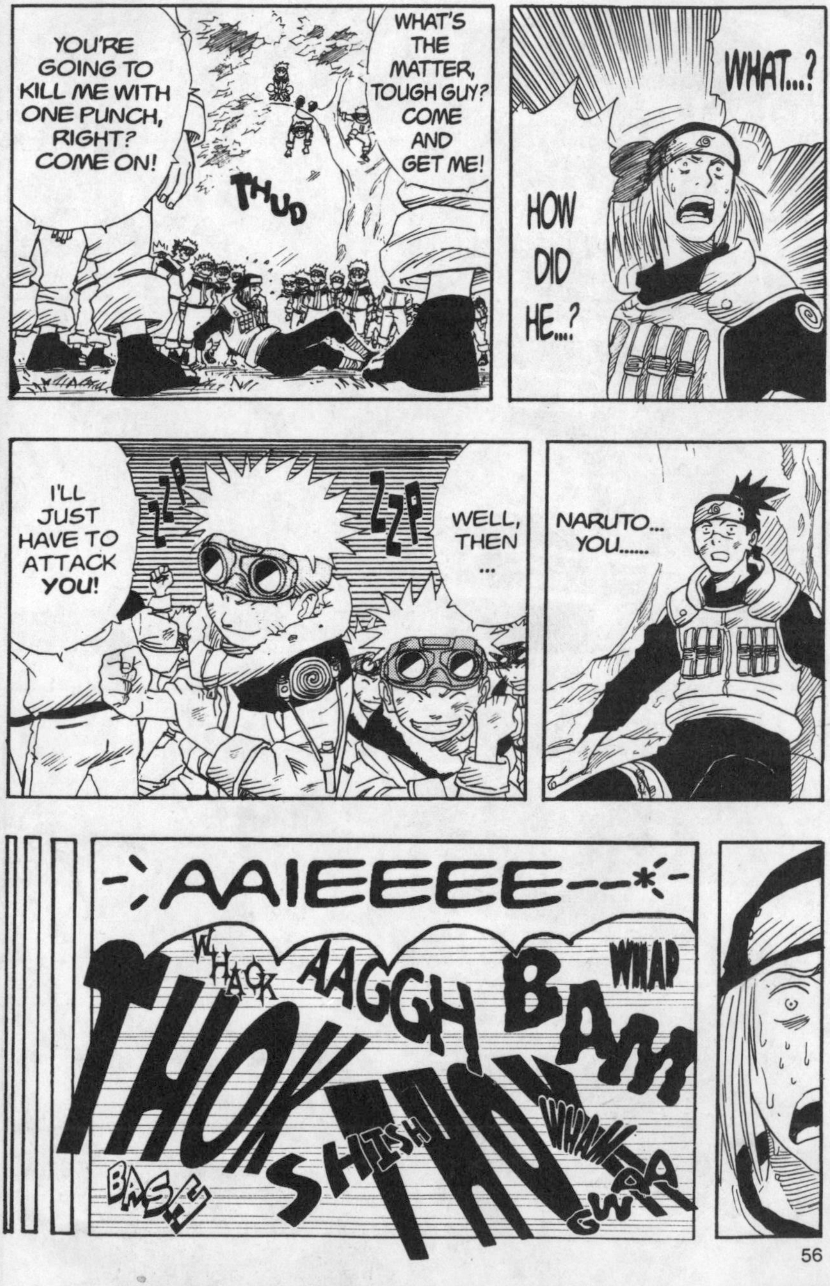
WHAT...?
HOW DID HE...?
WHAT'S THE MATTER, TOUGH GUY? COME AND GET ME!
YOU'RE GOING TO KILL ME WITH ONE PUNCH, RIGHT? COME ON!
THUD
NARUTO... YOU......
WELL, THEN ...
ZZP
ZZP
I'LL JUST HAVE TO ATTACK YOU!
AAIEEEE--*
WHACK
AAGGH
BAM
WHAP
THOK
SHISH
THOK
BASH

READ THIS WAY

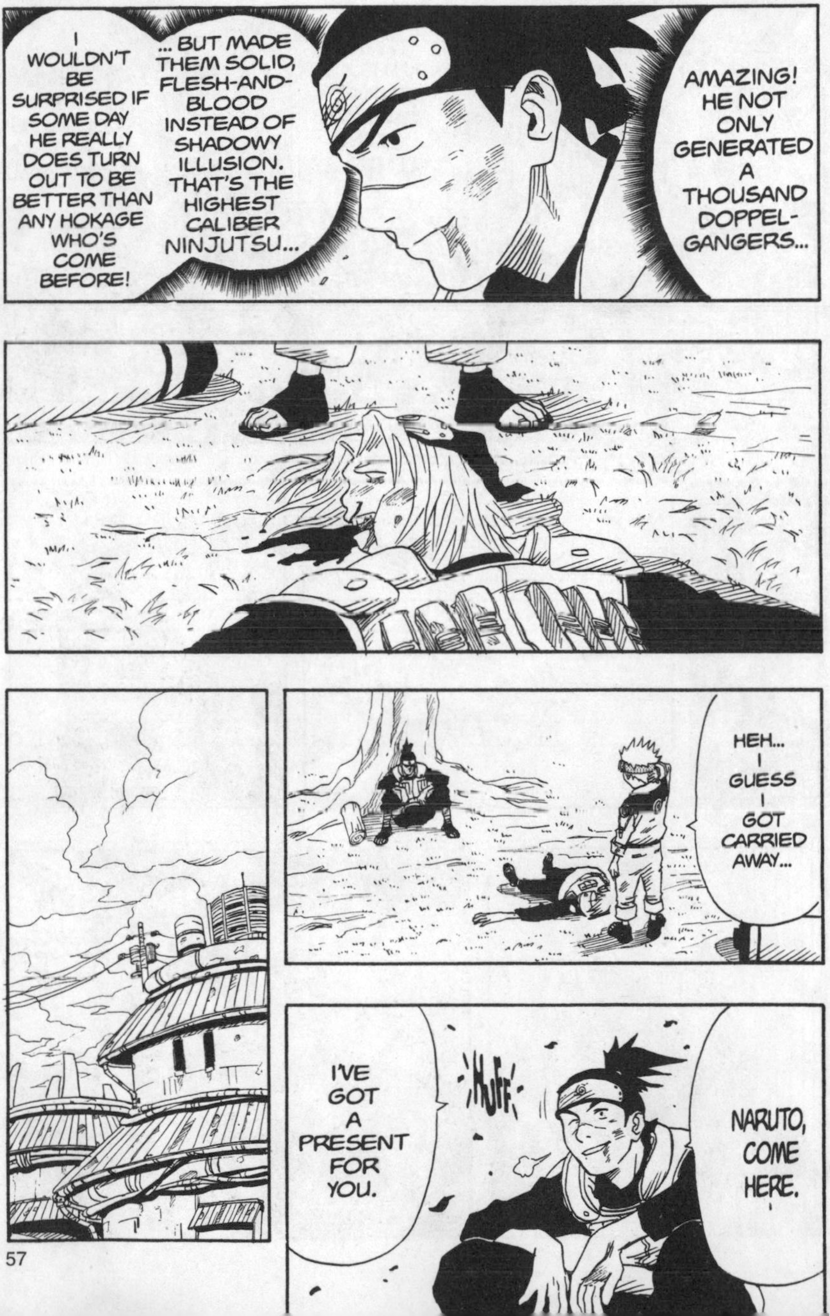

AMAZING! HE NOT ONLY GENERATED A THOUSAND DOPPEL-GANGERS...
... BUT MADE THEM SOLID, FLESH-AND-BLOOD INSTEAD OF SHADOWY ILLUSION. THAT'S THE HIGHEST CALIBER NINJUTSU...
I WOULDN'T BE SURPRISED IF SOME DAY HE REALLY DOES TURN OUT TO BE BETTER THAN ANY HOKAGE WHO'S COME BEFORE!
HEH... I GUESS I GOT CARRIED AWAY...
NARUTO, COME HERE.
HUFF
I'VE GOT A PRESENT FOR YOU.

READ THIS WAY

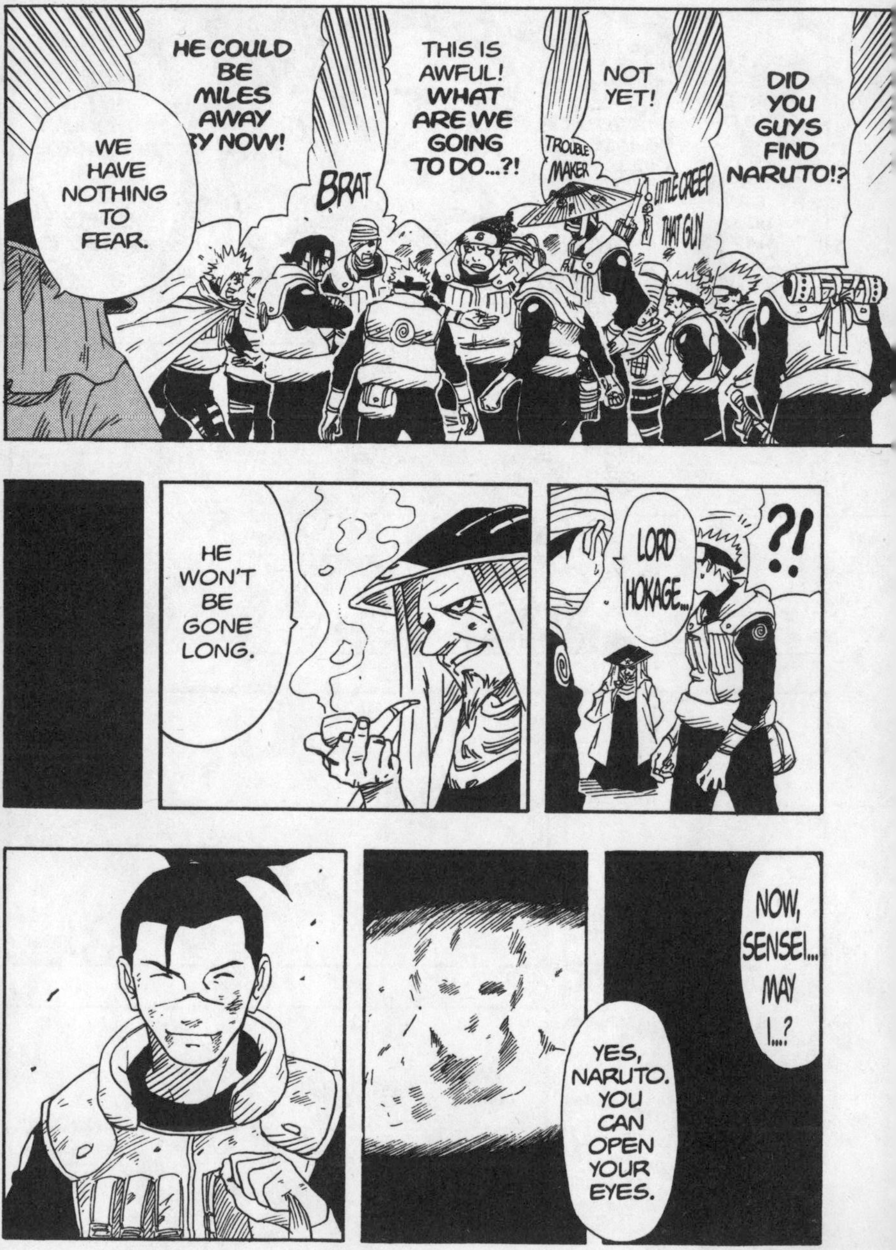
DID YOU GUYS FIND NARUTO!?
THAT GUY
LITTLE CREEP
NOT YET!
TROUBLE MAKER
THIS IS AWFUL! WHAT ARE WE GOING TO DO...?!
BRAT
HE COULD BE MILES AWAY BY NOW!
WE HAVE NOTHING TO FEAR.
?!
LORD HOKAGE...
HE WON'T BE GONE LONG.
NOW, SENSEI... MAY I...?
YES, NARUTO. YOU CAN OPEN YOUR EYES.

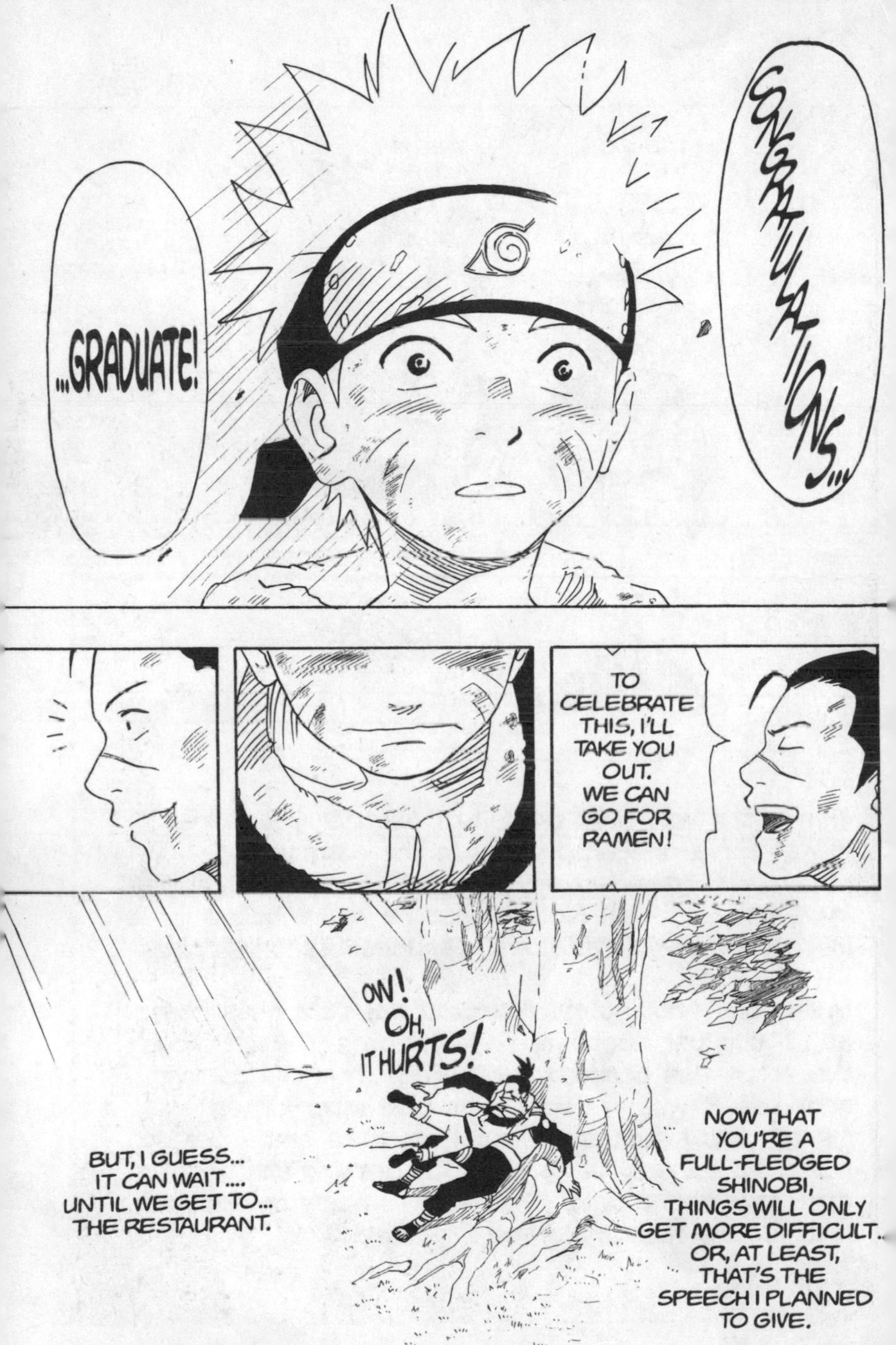
CONGRATULATIONS...
...GRADUATE!
TO CELEBRATE THIS, I'LL TAKE YOU OUT. WE CAN GO FOR RAMEN!
NOW THAT YOU'RE A FULL-FLEDGED SHINOBI, THINGS WILL ONLY GET MORE DIFFICULT... OR, AT LEAST, THAT'S THE SPEECH I PLANNED TO GIVE.
OW! OH, IT HURTS!
BUT, I GUESS... IT CAN WAIT.... UNTIL WE GET TO... THE RESTAURANT.

This is the very first sketch of Naruto that I drew.
It was for a one-shot story in the Japanese
Weekly Shonen Jump's special seasonal edition,
Akamaru Jump. Notice that he wears boots
instead of *zori* (traditional Japanese sandals).

In the one-shot story, *Naruto* wasn't a ninja comic
at all, but just about magic and sorcery. Even though
the setup was completely different from the current
storyline, it was the very first character-driven
manga that I ever drew, and I liked the character so
I decided to keep using him. But drawing the goggles
each time was a pain! That's why I came up with the
idea for the ninja *hitai-ate* (headband).

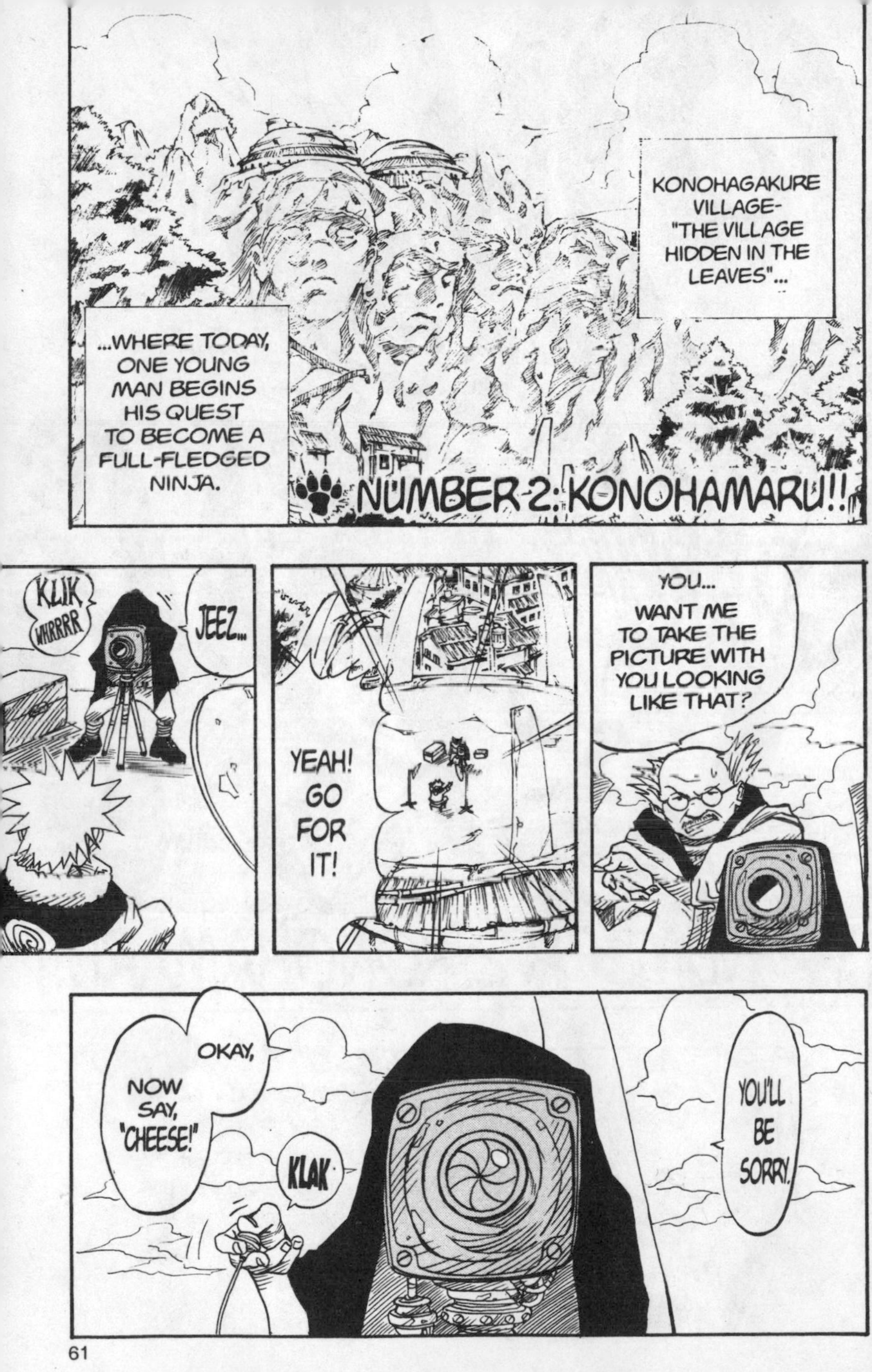
KONOHAGAKURE VILLAGE- "THE VILLAGE HIDDEN IN THE LEAVES"...
...WHERE TODAY, ONE YOUNG MAN BEGINS HIS QUEST TO BECOME A FULL-FLEDGED NINJA.
NUMBER 2: KONOHAMARU!!
YOU... WANT ME TO TAKE THE PICTURE WITH YOU LOOKING LIKE THAT?
YEAH! GO FOR IT!
KLIK
WHRRRR
JEEZ...
YOU'LL BE SORRY.
OKAY,
NOW SAY, "CHEESE!"
KLAK

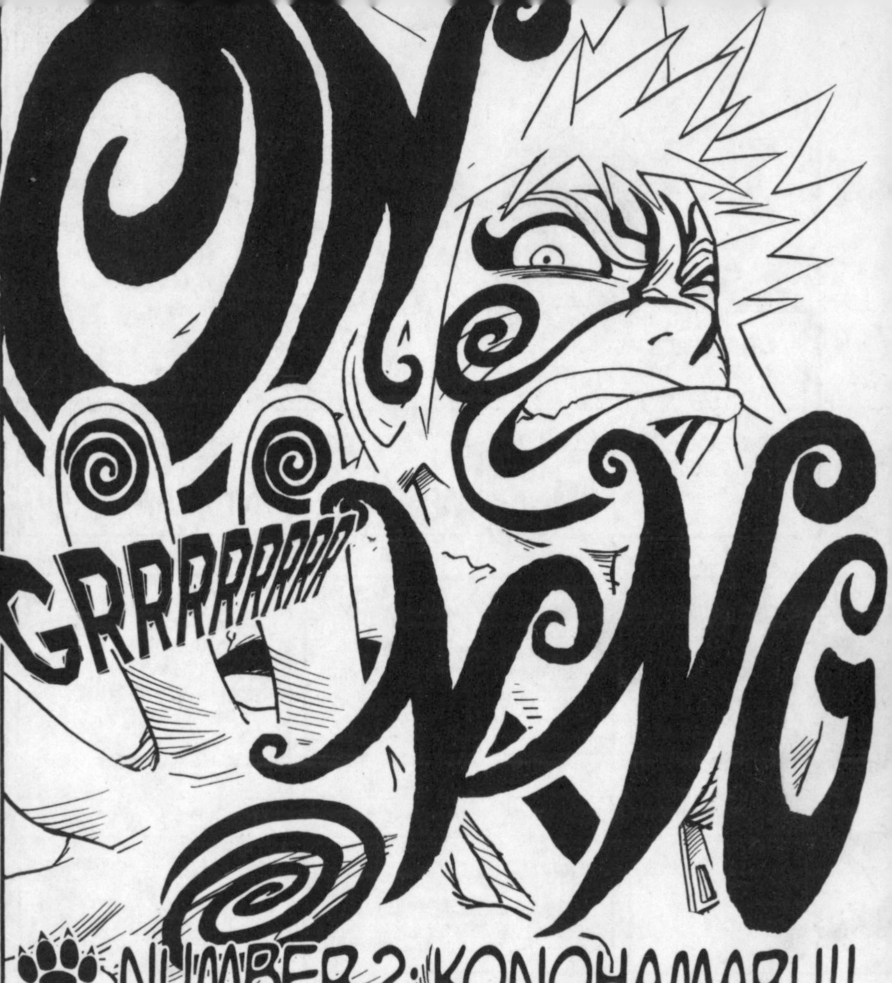
GRRRRRRRR
NUMBER 2: KONOHAMARU!!

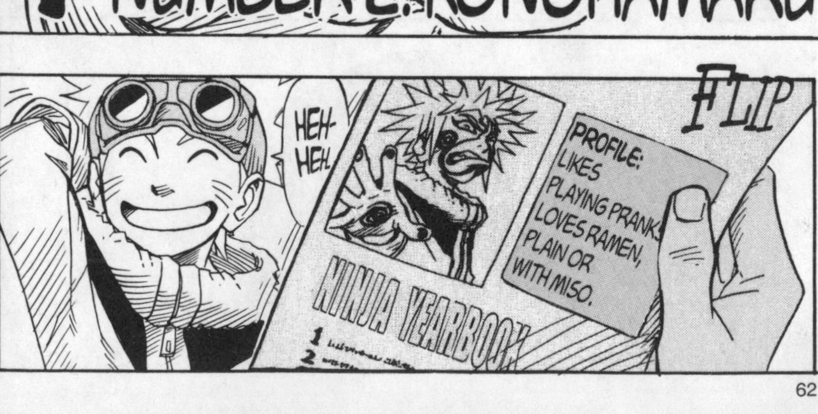
FLIP
HEH-HEH.
PROFILE:
LIKES
PLAYING PRANKS
LOVES RAMEN,
PLAIN OR
WITH MISO.
NINJA YEARBOOK

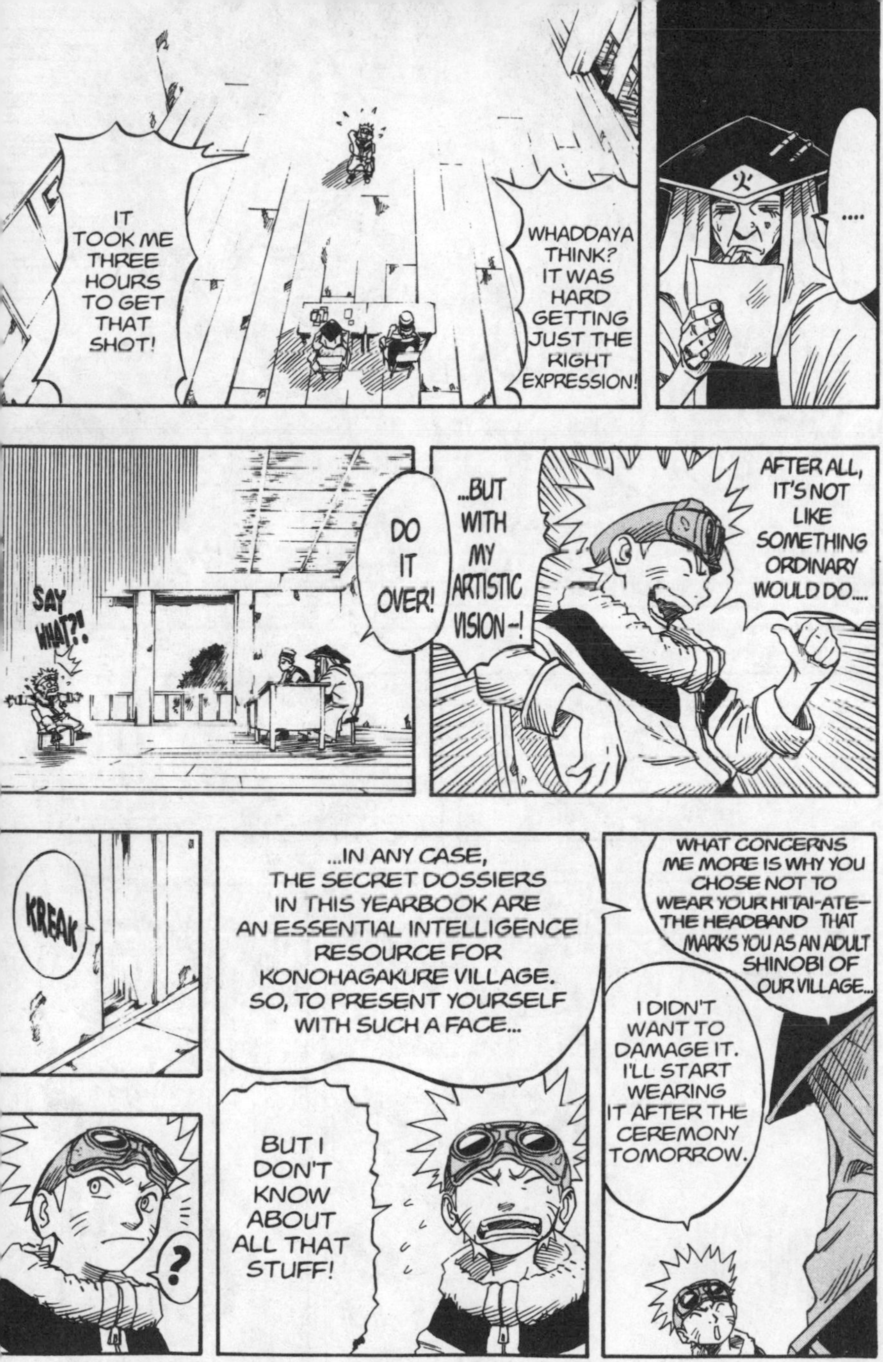
....
WHADDAYA THINK? IT WAS HARD GETTING JUST THE RIGHT EXPRESSION!
IT TOOK ME THREE HOURS TO GET THAT SHOT!
AFTER ALL, IT'S NOT LIKE SOMETHING ORDINARY WOULD DO....
...BUT WITH MY ARTISTIC VISION--!
DO IT OVER!
SAY WHAT?!
WHAT CONCERNS ME MORE IS WHY YOU CHOSE NOT TO WEAR YOUR HITAI-ATE-THE HEADBAND THAT MARKS YOU AS AN ADULT SHINOBI OF OUR VILLAGE...
I DIDN'T WANT TO DAMAGE IT. I'LL START WEARING IT AFTER THE CEREMONY TOMORROW.
...IN ANY CASE, THE SECRET DOSSIERS IN THIS YEARBOOK ARE AN ESSENTIAL INTELLIGENCE RESOURCE FOR KONOHAGAKURE VILLAGE. SO, TO PRESENT YOURSELF WITH SUCH A FACE...
KREAK
BUT I DON'T KNOW ABOUT ALL THAT STUFF!
?

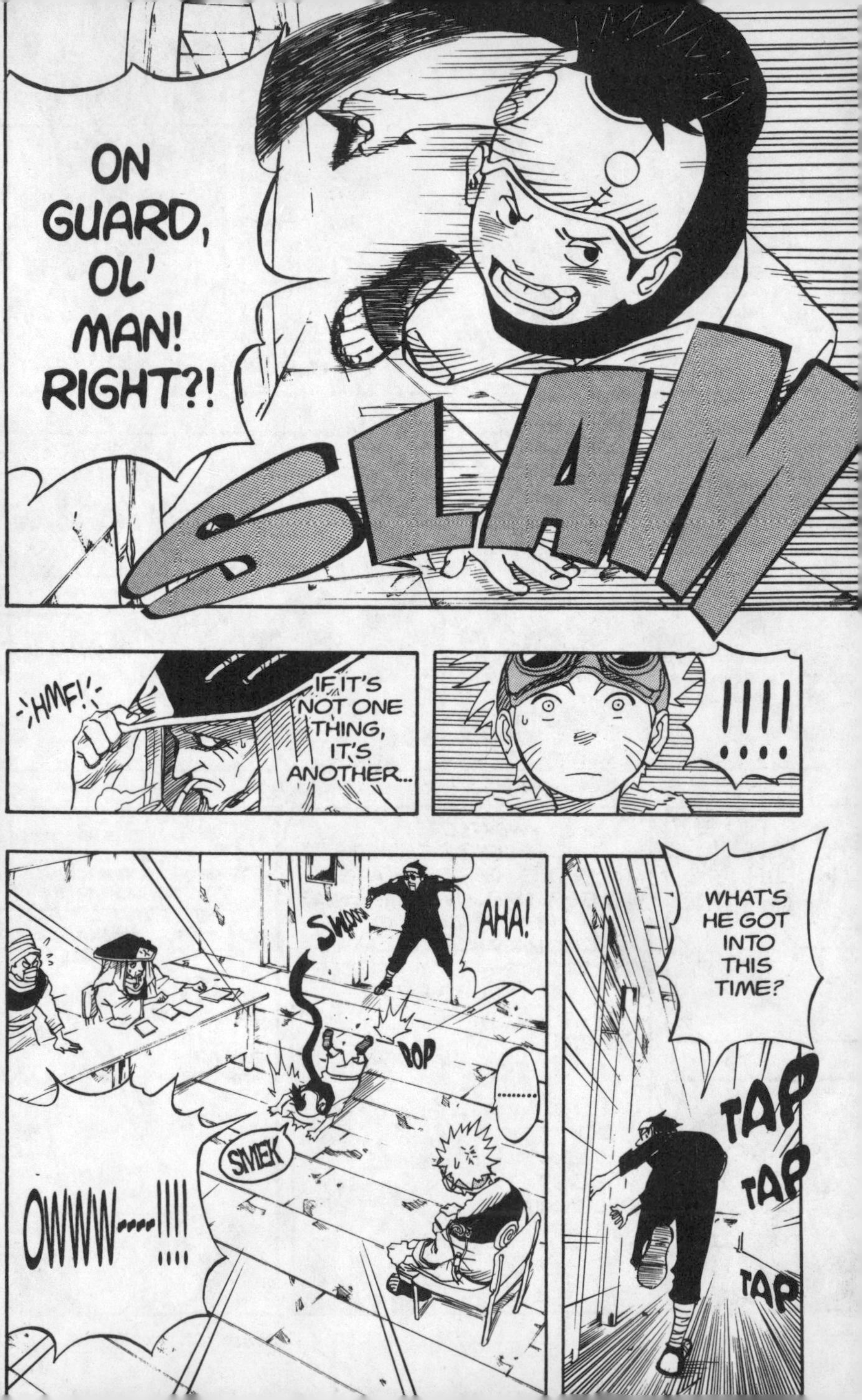

ON GUARD, OL' MAN! RIGHT?!
SLAM
!!!!
HMF!
IF IT'S NOT ONE THING, IT'S ANOTHER...
WHAT'S HE GOT INTO THIS TIME?
TAP
TAP
TAP
AHA!
BOP
......
SMEK
OWWW----!!!!

READ THIS WAY

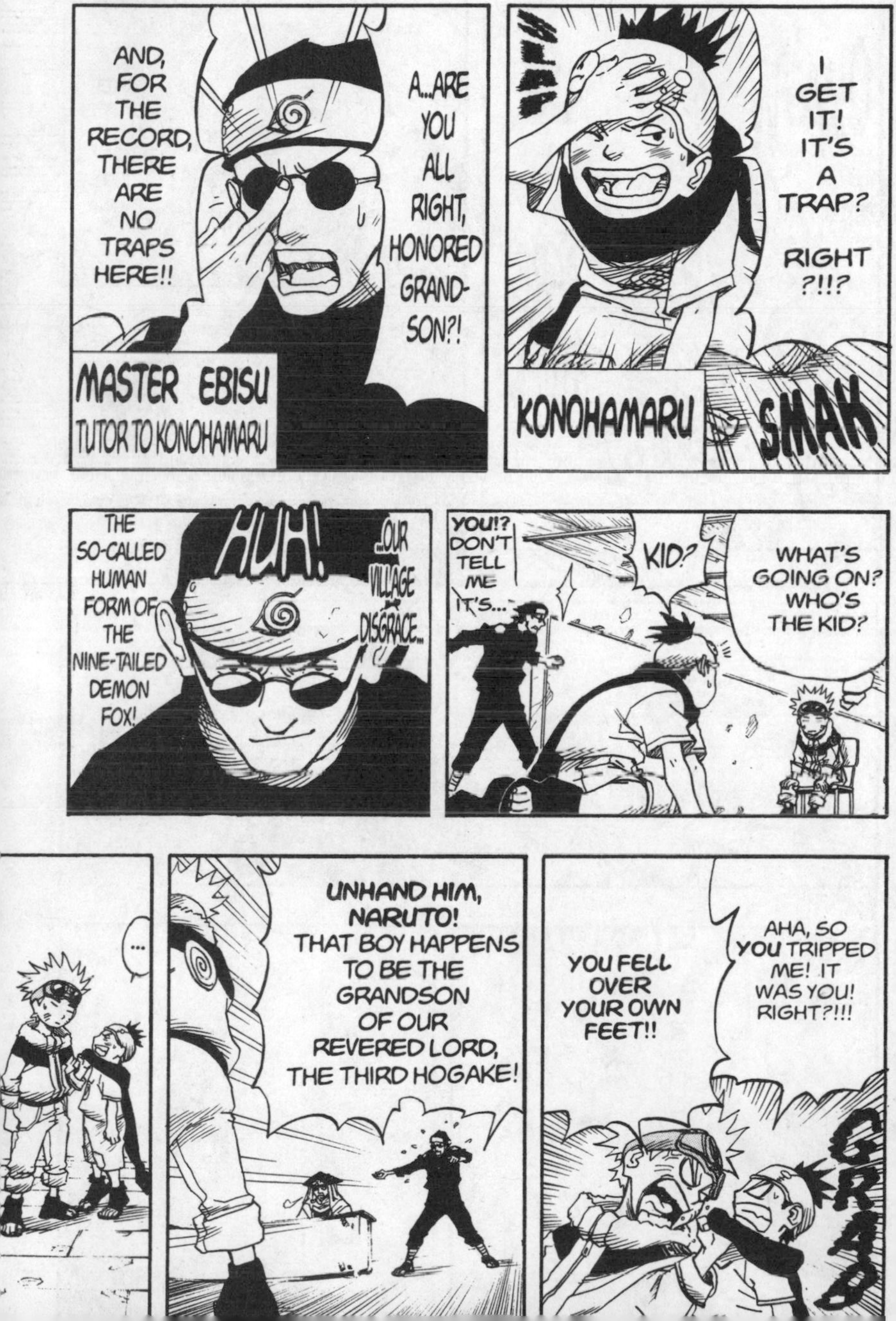
SLAP
I GET IT! IT'S A TRAP? RIGHT ?!!?
KONOHAMARU
SMAK
A...ARE YOU ALL RIGHT, HONORED GRANDSON?!
AND, FOR THE RECORD, THERE ARE NO TRAPS HERE!!
MASTER EBISU
TUTOR TO KONOHAMARU
WHAT'S GOING ON? WHO'S THE KID?
KID?
YOU!? DON'T TELL ME IT'S...
HUH!
...OUR VILLAGE DISGRACE...
THE SO-CALLED HUMAN FORM OF THE NINE-TAILED DEMON FOX!
GRAB
AHA, SO YOU TRIPPED ME! IT WAS YOU! RIGHT?!!!
YOU FELL OVER YOUR OWN FEET!!
UNHAND HIM, NARUTO! THAT BOY HAPPENS TO BE THE GRANDSON OF OUR REVERED LORD, THE THIRD HOGAKE!
...

READ THIS WAY

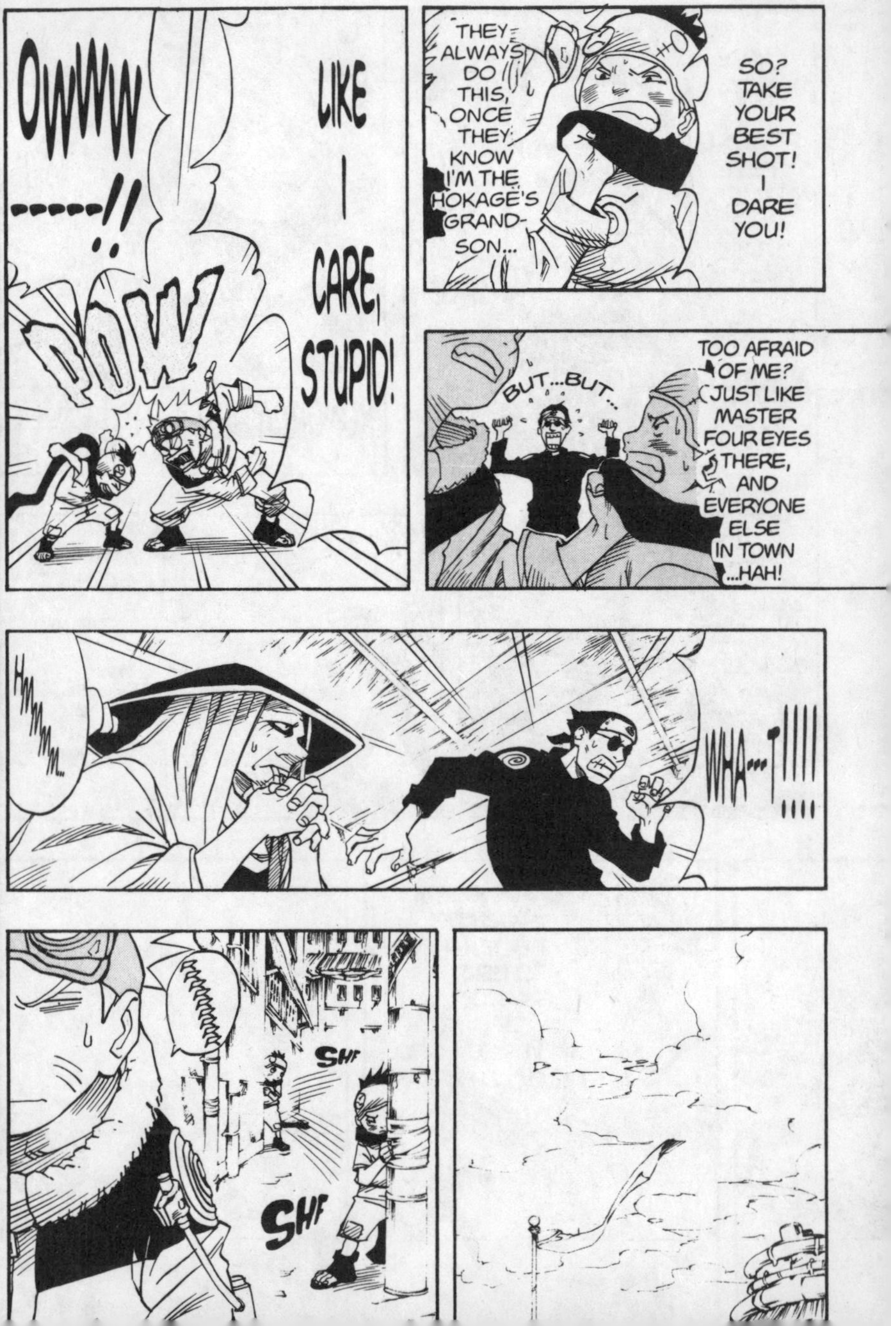
SO? TAKE YOUR BEST SHOT! I DARE YOU!
THEY ALWAYS DO THIS, ONCE THEY KNOW I'M THE HOKAGE'S GRANDSON...
TOO AFRAID OF ME? JUST LIKE MASTER FOUR EYES THERE, AND EVERYONE ELSE IN TOWN ...HAH!
BUT...BUT...
LIKE I CARE, STUPID!
OWWW------!!
POW
WHA---T!!!!!
HMMMM...
SHF
SHF

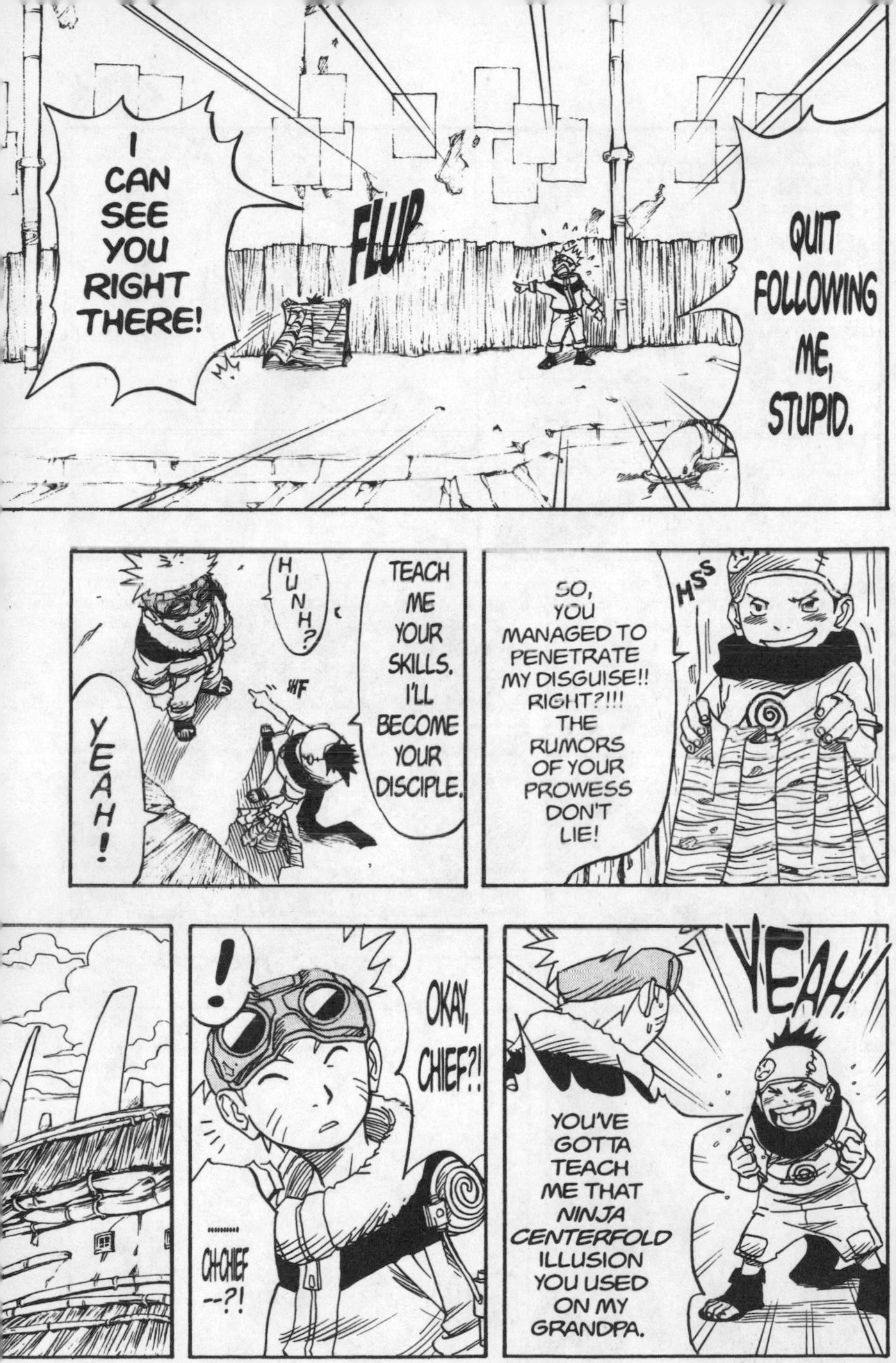
QUIT FOLLOWING ME, STUPID.
FLUP
I CAN SEE YOU RIGHT THERE!
HSS
SO, YOU MANAGED TO PENETRATE MY DISGUISE!! RIGHT?!!! THE RUMORS OF YOUR PROWESS DON'T LIE!
TEACH ME YOUR SKILLS. I'LL BECOME YOUR DISCIPLE.
HUNH?
HF
YEAH!
YEAH!!
YOU'VE GOTTA TEACH ME THAT NINJA CENTERFOLD ILLUSION YOU USED ON MY GRANDPA.
OKAY, CHIEF?!
!
....
CH-CHIEF--?!

READ THIS WAY

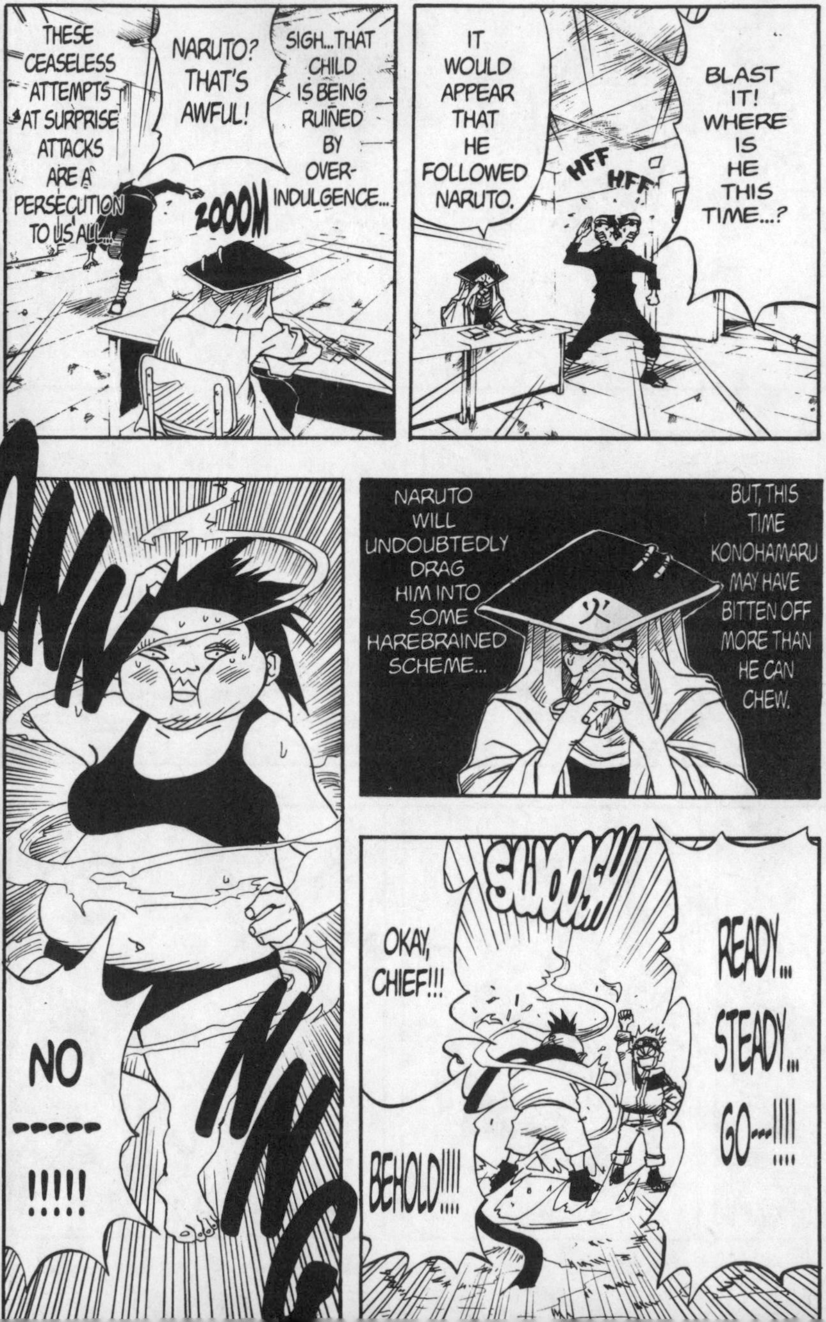
BLAST IT! WHERE IS HE THIS TIME...?
HFF HFF
IT WOULD APPEAR THAT HE FOLLOWED NARUTO.
SIGH...THAT CHILD IS BEING RUINED BY OVER-INDULGENCE...
NARUTO? THAT'S AWFUL!
THESE CEASELESS ATTEMPTS AT SURPRISE ATTACKS ARE A PERSECUTION TO US ALL...
ZOOOM
BUT, THIS TIME KONOHAMARU MAY HAVE BITTEN OFF MORE THAN HE CAN CHEW.
NARUTO WILL UNDOUBTEDLY DRAG HIM INTO SOME HAREBRAINED SCHEME...
READY... STEADY... GO---!!!!
OKAY, CHIEF!!!
BEHOLD!!!!
NO ------ !!!!!!

READ THIS WAY

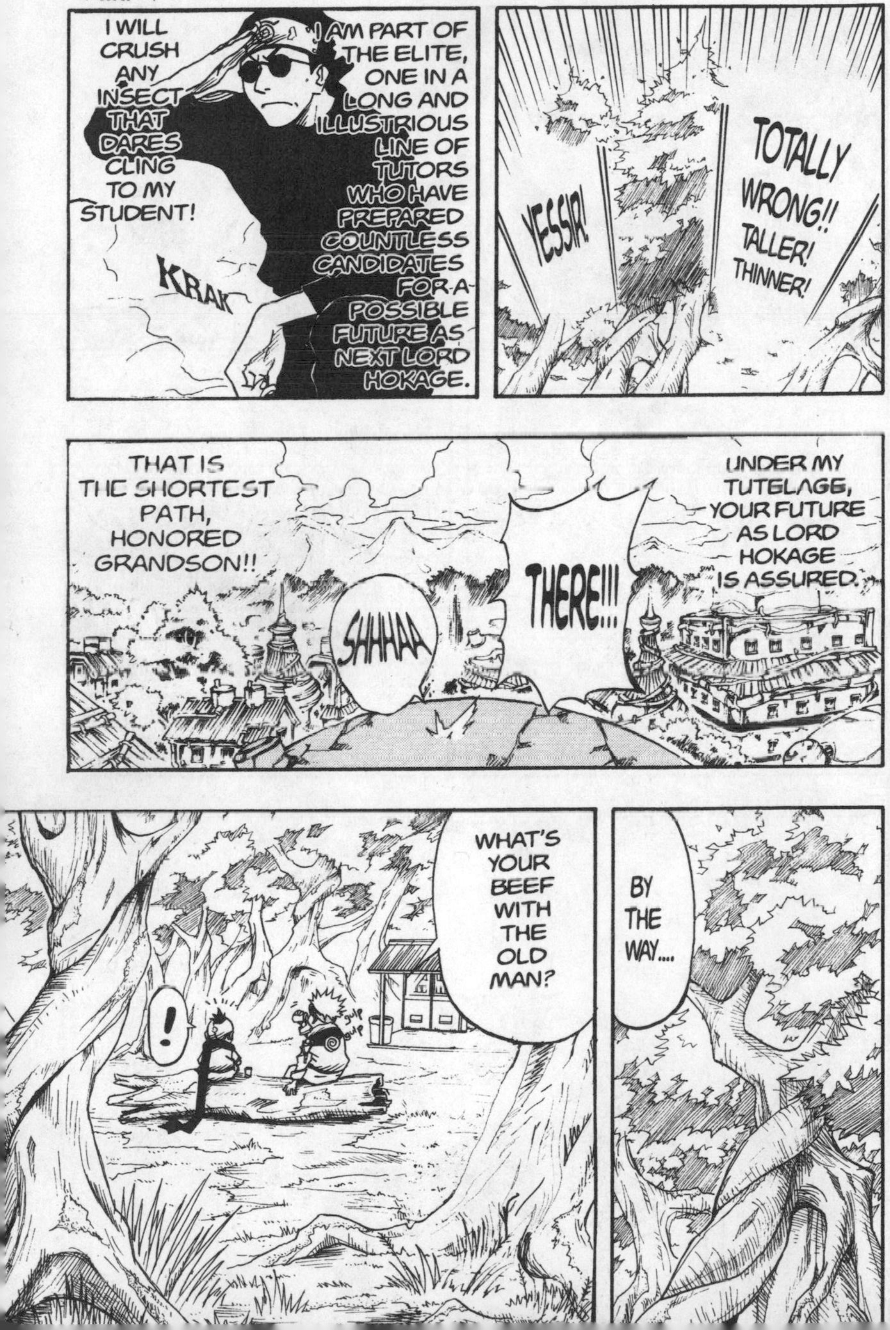
TOTALLY WRONG!!
TALLER! THINNER!
YESSIR!
I AM PART OF THE ELITE, ONE IN A LONG AND ILLUSTRIOUS LINE OF TUTORS WHO HAVE PREPARED COUNTLESS CANDIDATES FOR A POSSIBLE FUTURE AS NEXT LORD HOKAGE.
I WILL CRUSH ANY INSECT THAT DARES CLING TO MY STUDENT!
KRAK
UNDER MY TUTELAGE, YOUR FUTURE AS LORD HOKAGE IS ASSURED.
THERE!!!
SHHHAA
THAT IS THE SHORTEST PATH, HONORED GRANDSON!!
BY THE WAY....
WHAT'S YOUR BEEF WITH THE OLD MAN?
!
gulp gulp

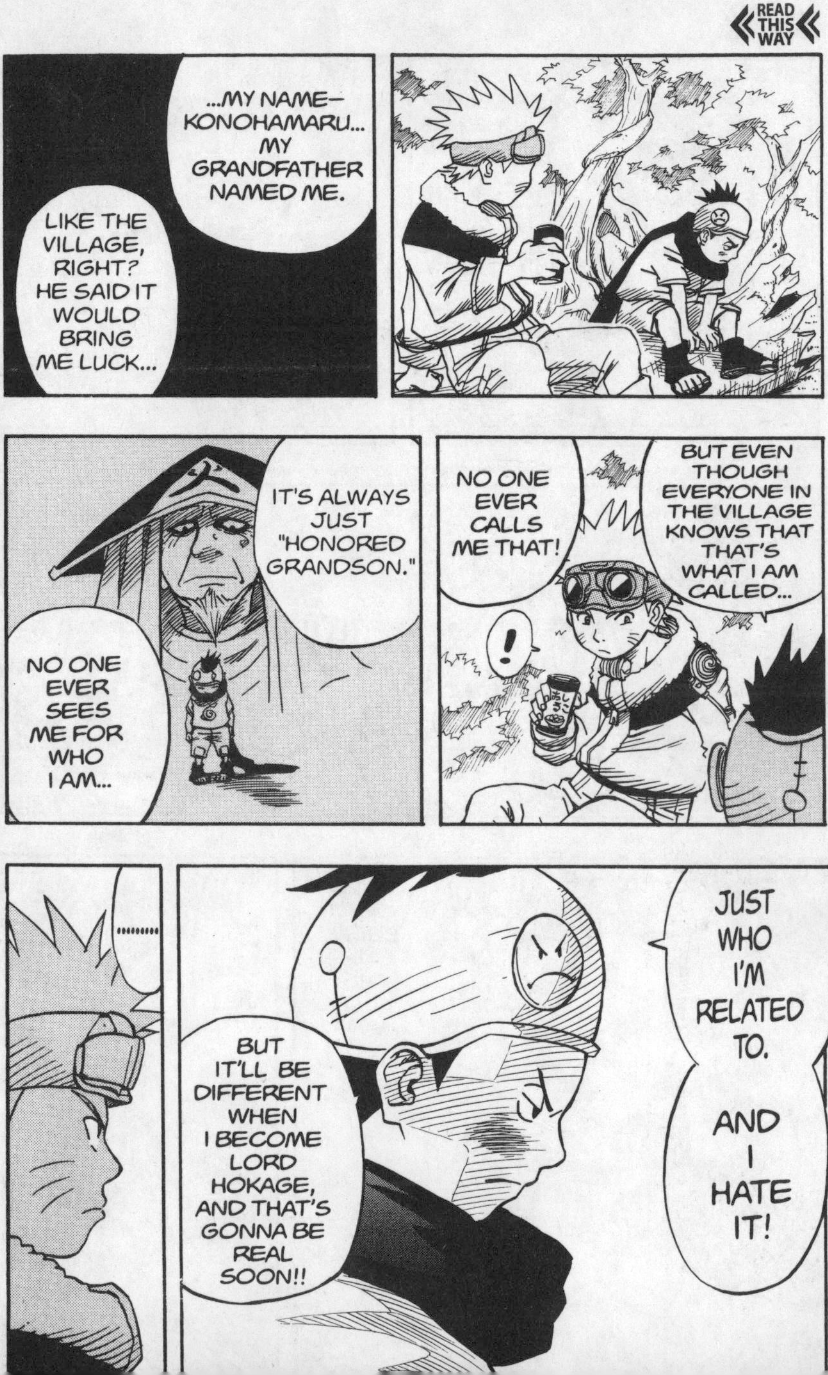
READ THIS WAY
...MY NAME— KONOHAMARU... MY GRANDFATHER NAMED ME.
LIKE THE VILLAGE, RIGHT? HE SAID IT WOULD BRING ME LUCK...
BUT EVEN THOUGH EVERYONE IN THE VILLAGE KNOWS THAT THAT'S WHAT I AM CALLED...
NO ONE EVER CALLS ME THAT!
!
IT'S ALWAYS JUST "HONORED GRANDSON."
NO ONE EVER SEES ME FOR WHO I AM...
JUST WHO I'M RELATED TO.
AND I HATE IT!
BUT IT'LL BE DIFFERENT WHEN I BECOME LORD HOKAGE, AND THAT'S GONNA BE REAL SOON!!
....

READ THIS WAY

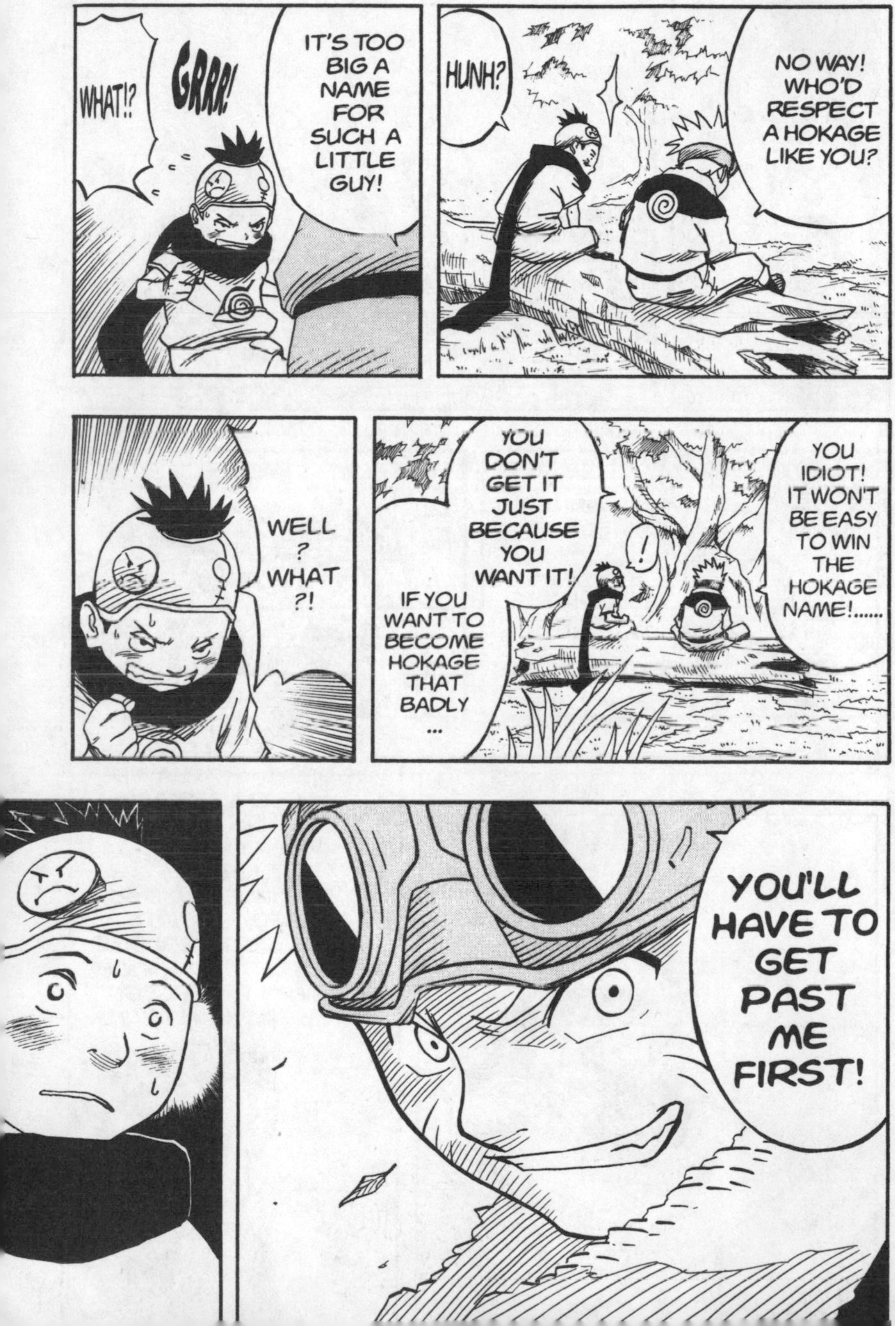

NO WAY! WHO'D RESPECT A HOKAGE LIKE YOU?
HUNH?
IT'S TOO BIG A NAME FOR SUCH A LITTLE GUY!
GRRR!
WHAT!?
YOU IDIOT! IT WON'T BE EASY TO WIN THE HOKAGE NAME!......
!
YOU DON'T GET IT JUST BECAUSE YOU WANT IT!
IF YOU WANT TO BECOME HOKAGE THAT BADLY ...
WELL? WHAT?!
YOU'LL HAVE TO GET PAST ME FIRST!

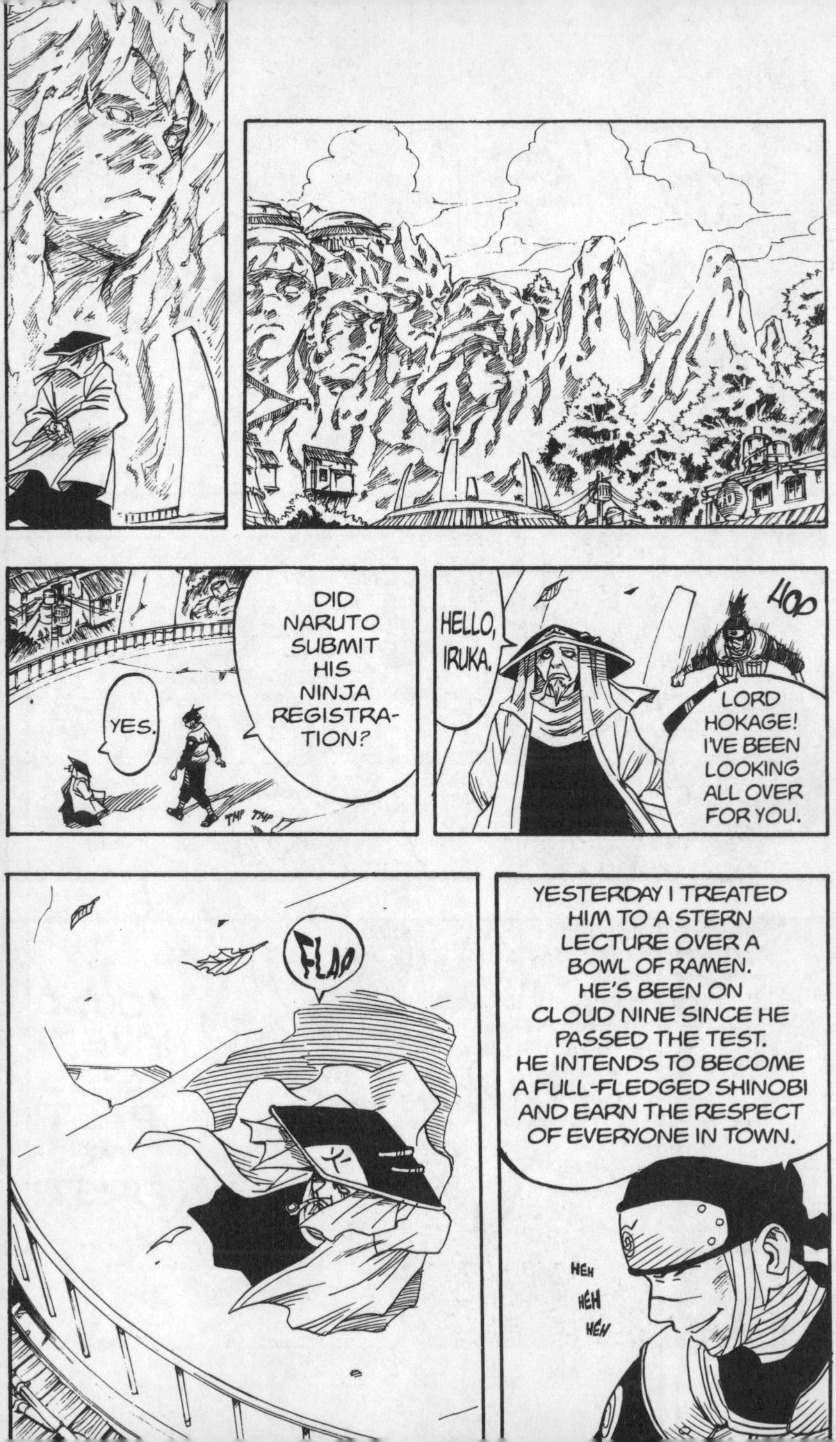
HOP
LORD HOKAGE! I'VE BEEN LOOKING ALL OVER FOR YOU.
HELLO, IRUKA.
DID NARUTO SUBMIT HIS NINJA REGISTRATION?
YES.
TMP TMP
YESTERDAY I TREATED HIM TO A STERN LECTURE OVER A BOWL OF RAMEN. HE'S BEEN ON CLOUD NINE SINCE HE PASSED THE TEST. HE INTENDS TO BECOME A FULL-FLEDGED SHINOBI AND EARN THE RESPECT OF EVERYONE IN TOWN.
HEH HEH HEH
FLAP

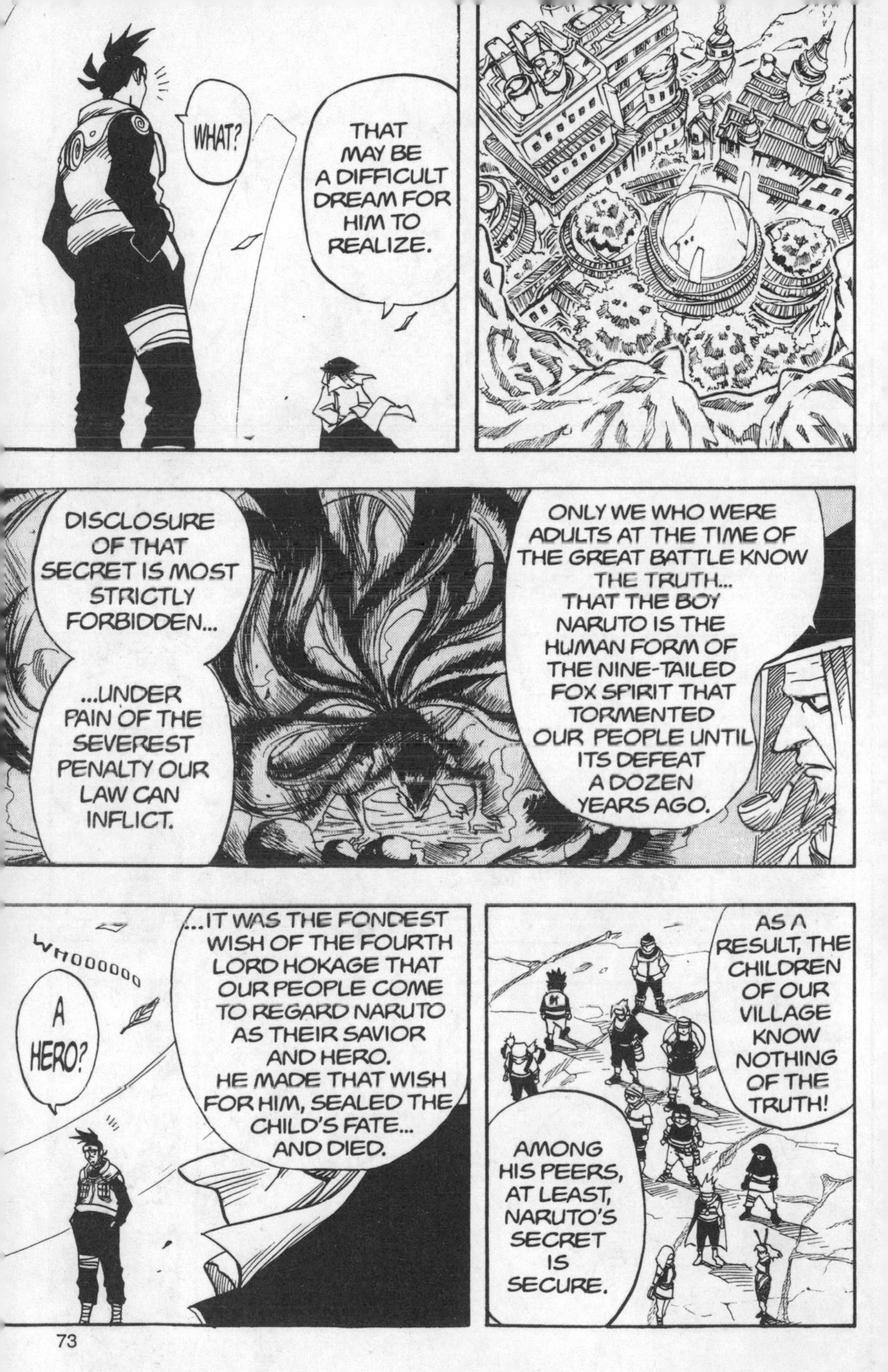
THAT MAY BE A DIFFICULT DREAM FOR HIM TO REALIZE.
WHAT?
ONLY WE WHO WERE ADULTS AT THE TIME OF THE GREAT BATTLE KNOW THE TRUTH... THAT THE BOY NARUTO IS THE HUMAN FORM OF THE NINE-TAILED FOX SPIRIT THAT TORMENTED OUR PEOPLE UNTIL ITS DEFEAT A DOZEN YEARS AGO.
DISCLOSURE OF THAT SECRET IS MOST STRICTLY FORBIDDEN...
...UNDER PAIN OF THE SEVEREST PENALTY OUR LAW CAN INFLICT.
AS A RESULT, THE CHILDREN OF OUR VILLAGE KNOW NOTHING OF THE TRUTH!
AMONG HIS PEERS, AT LEAST, NARUTO'S SECRET IS SECURE.
...IT WAS THE FONDEST WISH OF THE FOURTH LORD HOKAGE THAT OUR PEOPLE COME TO REGARD NARUTO AS THEIR SAVIOR AND HERO. HE MADE THAT WISH FOR HIM, SEALED THE CHILD'S FATE... AND DIED.
WHOOOOOOO
A HERO?

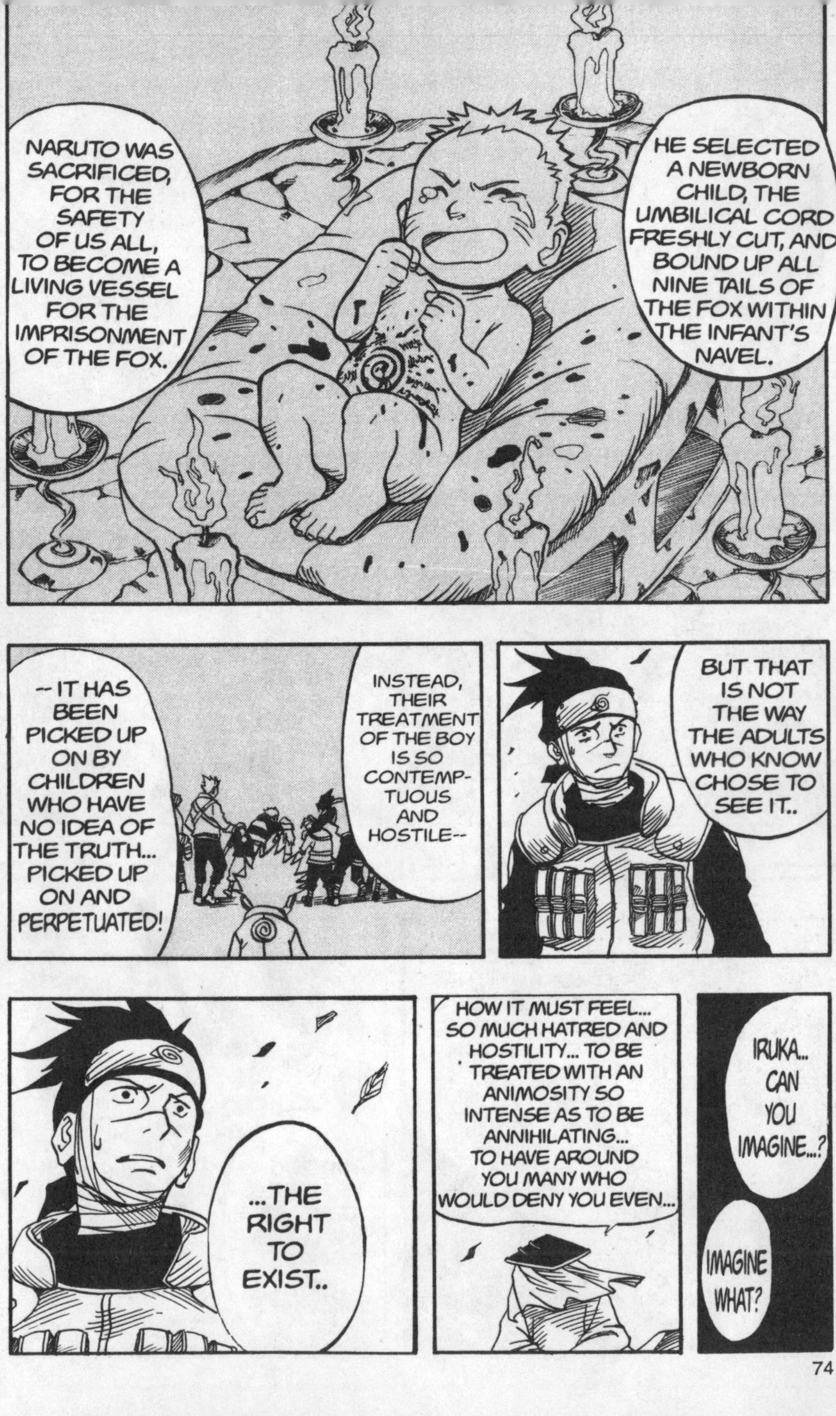
HE SELECTED A NEWBORN CHILD, THE UMBILICAL CORD FRESHLY CUT, AND BOUND UP ALL NINE TAILS OF THE FOX WITHIN THE INFANT'S NAVEL.
NARUTO WAS SACRIFICED, FOR THE SAFETY OF US ALL, TO BECOME A LIVING VESSEL FOR THE IMPRISONMENT OF THE FOX.
BUT THAT IS NOT THE WAY THE ADULTS WHO KNOW CHOSE TO SEE IT..
INSTEAD, THEIR TREATMENT OF THE BOY IS SO CONTEMP-TUOUS AND HOSTILE--
--IT HAS BEEN PICKED UP ON BY CHILDREN WHO HAVE NO IDEA OF THE TRUTH... PICKED UP ON AND PERPETUATED!
IRUKA... CAN YOU IMAGINE...?
IMAGINE WHAT?
HOW IT MUST FEEL... SO MUCH HATRED AND HOSTILITY... TO BE TREATED WITH AN ANIMOSITY SO INTENSE AS TO BE ANNIHILATING... TO HAVE AROUND YOU MANY WHO WOULD DENY YOU EVEN...
...THE RIGHT TO EXIST..

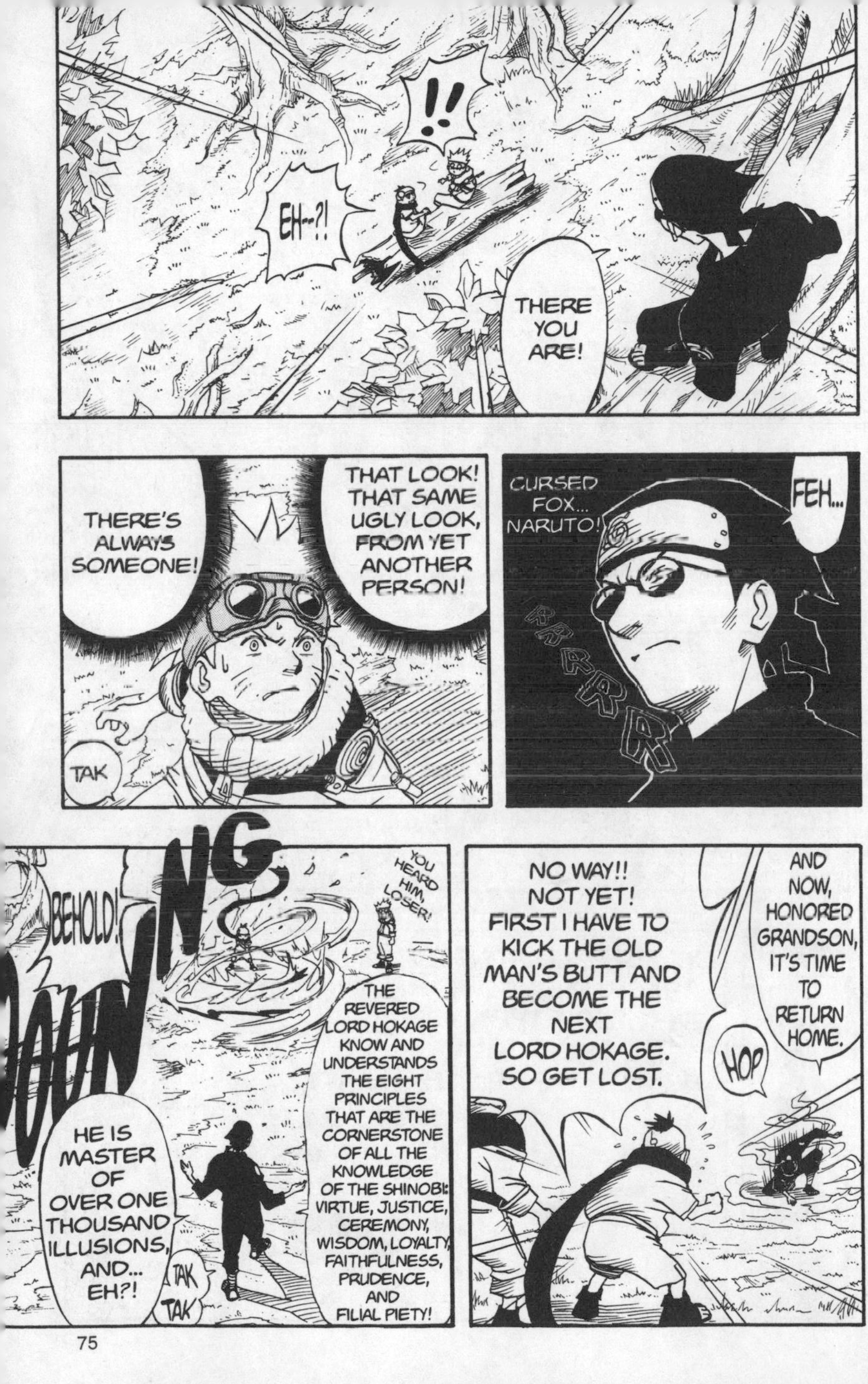
!!
EH--?!
THERE YOU ARE!
FEH...
CURSED FOX... NARUTO!
RRRRR
THAT LOOK! THAT SAME UGLY LOOK, FROM YET ANOTHER PERSON!
THERE'S ALWAYS SOMEONE!
TAK
AND NOW, HONORED GRANDSON, IT'S TIME TO RETURN HOME.
HOP
NO WAY!! NOT YET! FIRST I HAVE TO KICK THE OLD MAN'S BUTT AND BECOME THE NEXT LORD HOKAGE. SO GET LOST.
YOU HEARD HIM, LOSER!
BEHOLD!
THE REVERED LORD HOKAGE KNOW AND UNDERSTANDS THE EIGHT PRINCIPLES THAT ARE THE CORNERSTONE OF ALL THE KNOWLEDGE OF THE SHINOBI: VIRTUE, JUSTICE, CEREMONY, WISDOM, LOYALTY, FAITHFULNESS, PRUDENCE, AND FILIAL PIETY!
HE IS MASTER OF OVER ONE THOUSAND ILLUSIONS, AND... EH?!
TAK TAK

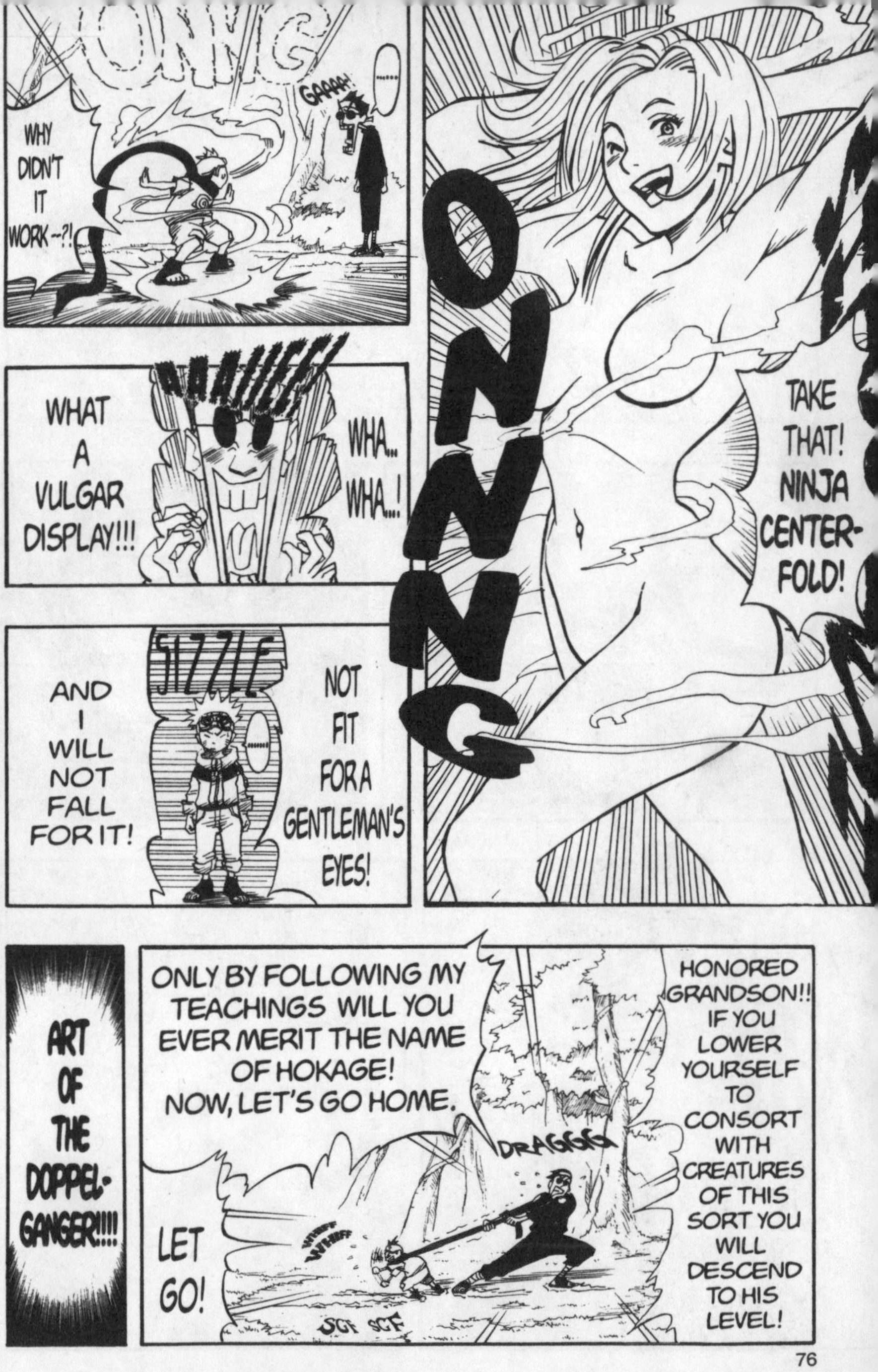
ONNNG
TAKE THAT! NINJA CENTER-FOLD!
GAAAA!
......
WHY DIDN'T IT WORK--?!
WHA... WHA..!
WHAT A VULGAR DISPLAY!!!
SIZZLE
......
NOT FIT FOR A GENTLEMAN'S EYES!
AND I WILL NOT FALL FOR IT!
HONORED GRANDSON!! IF YOU LOWER YOURSELF TO CONSORT WITH CREATURES OF THIS SORT YOU WILL DESCEND TO HIS LEVEL!
ONLY BY FOLLOWING MY TEACHINGS WILL YOU EVER MERIT THE NAME OF HOKAGE! NOW, LET'S GO HOME.
DRAGGG
WHIFF WHIFF
LET GO!
SCF SCF
ART OF THE DOPPEL-GANGER!!!!

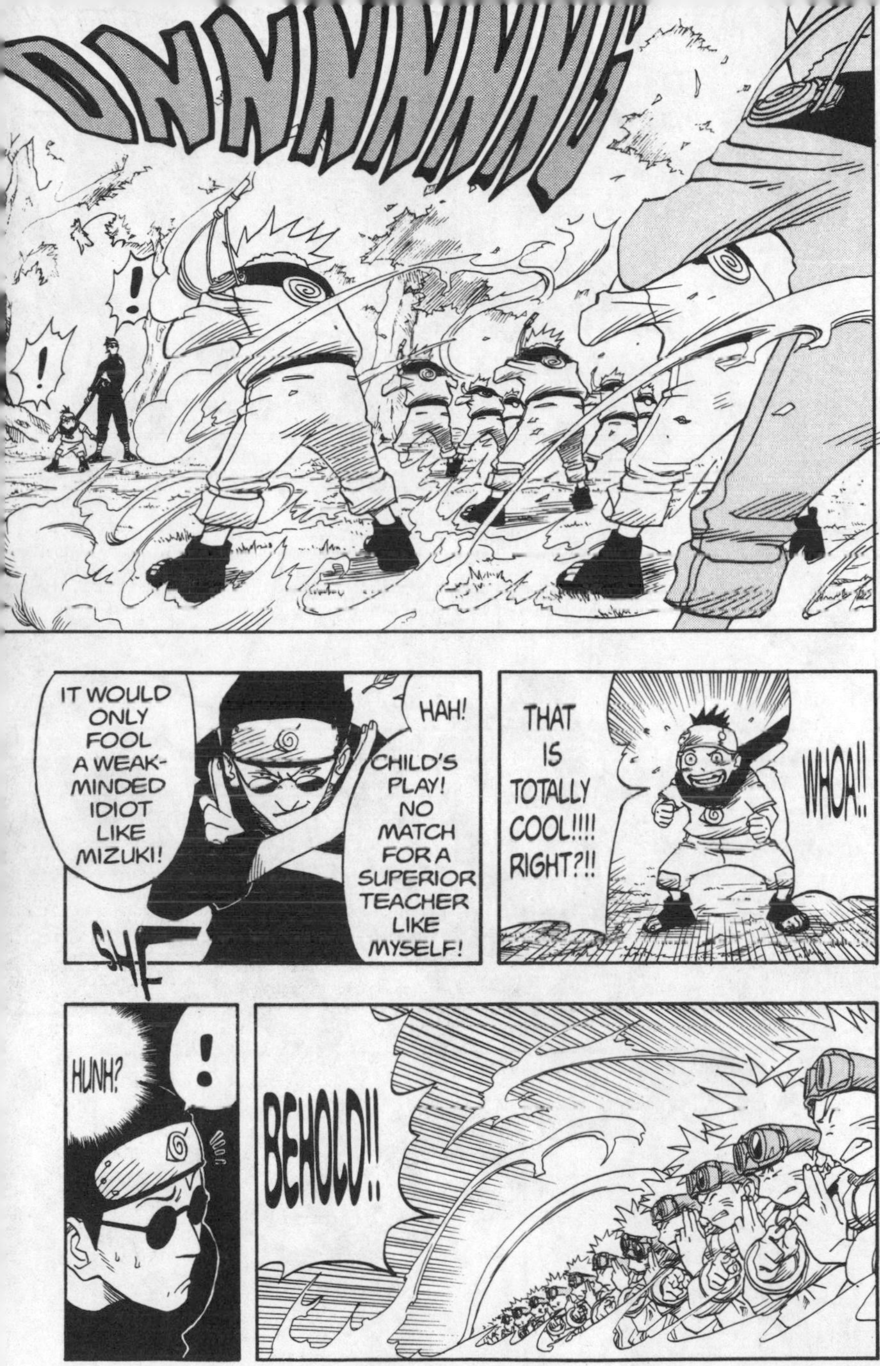
!
!
WHOA!!
THAT IS TOTALLY COOL!!!! RIGHT?!!
HAH!
CHILD'S PLAY! NO MATCH FOR A SUPERIOR TEACHER LIKE MYSELF!
IT WOULD ONLY FOOL A WEAK-MINDED IDIOT LIKE MIZUKI!
SHF
BEHOLD!!
!
HUNH?

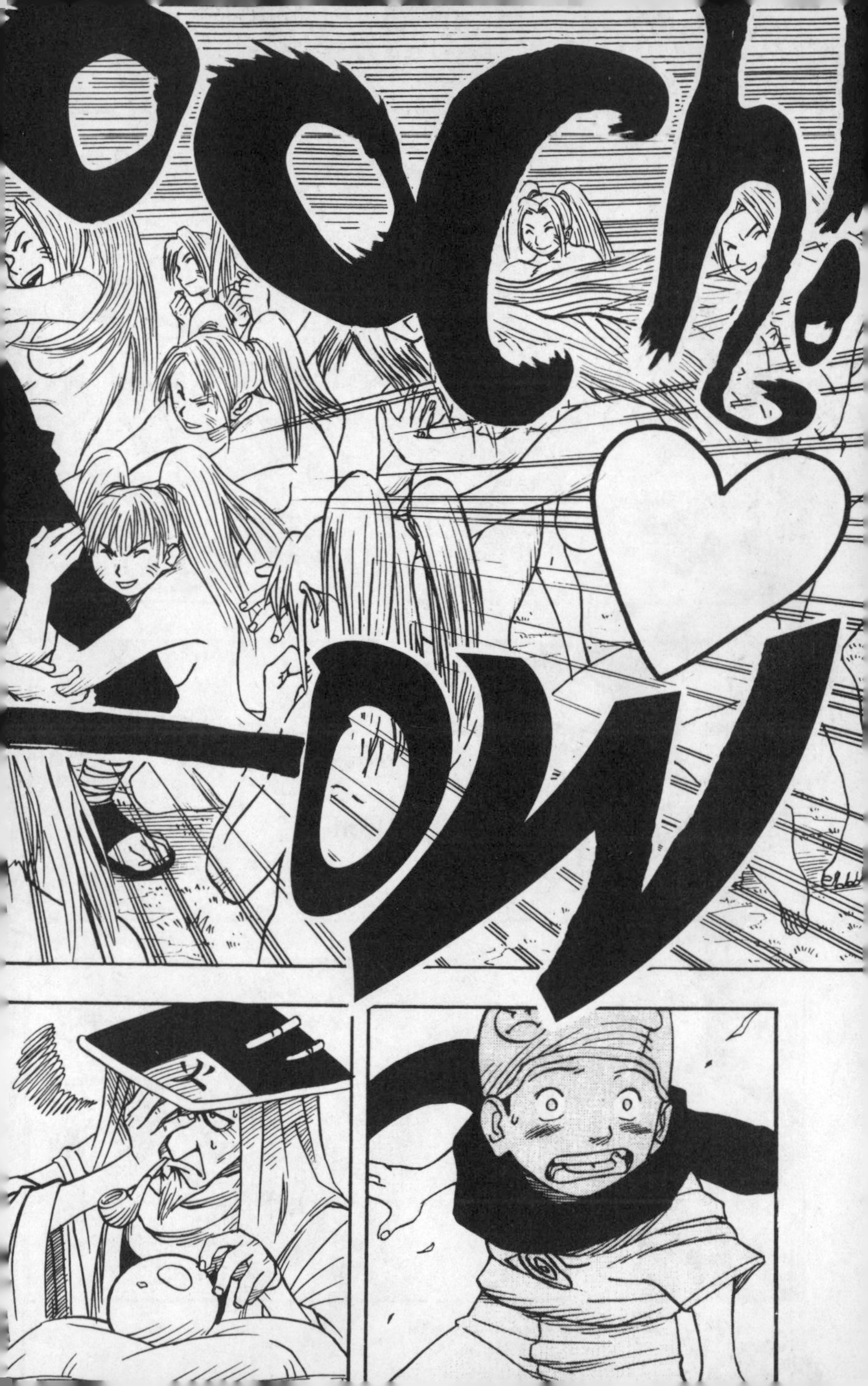
Ooch!
♥
OW

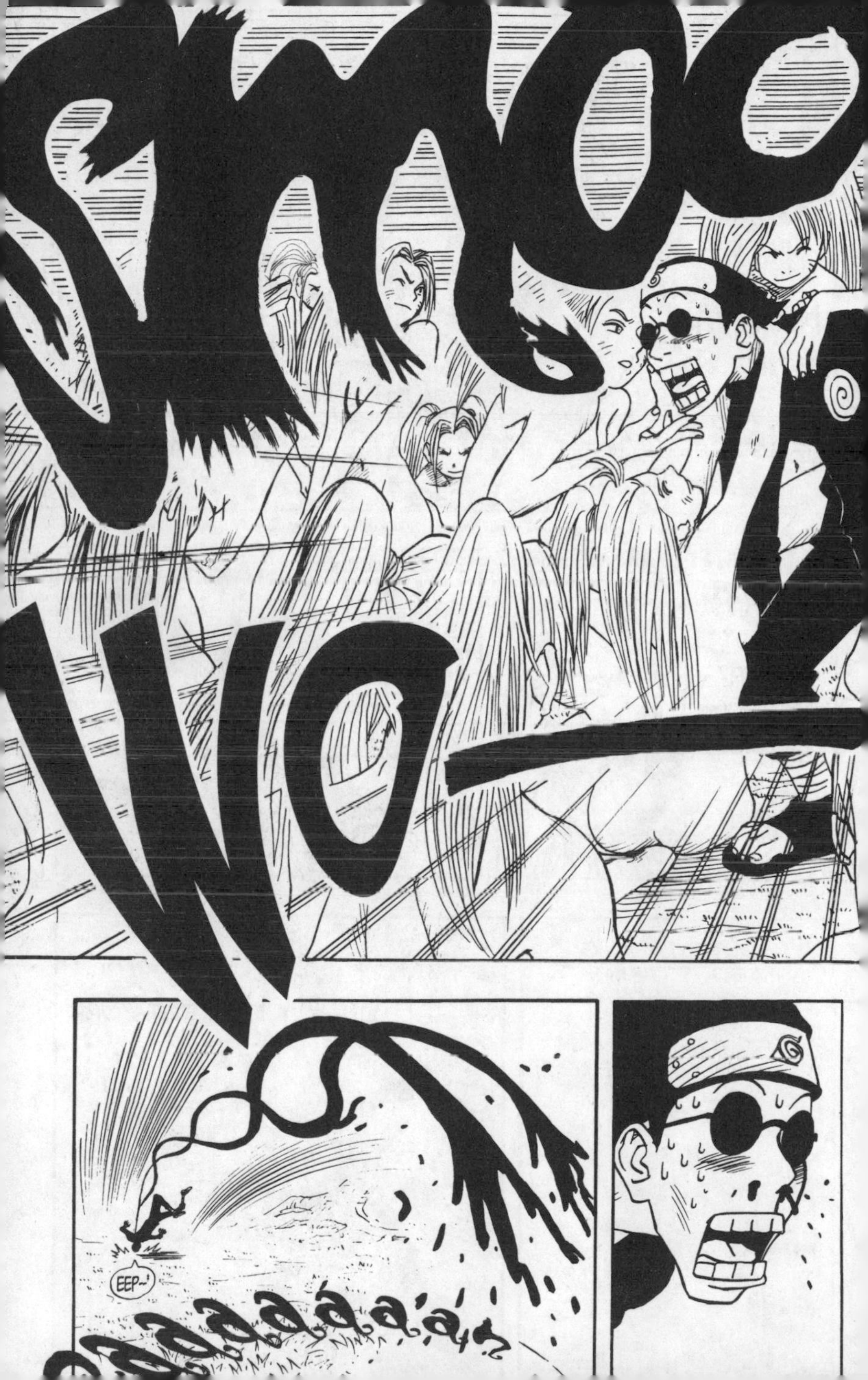
EEP~!

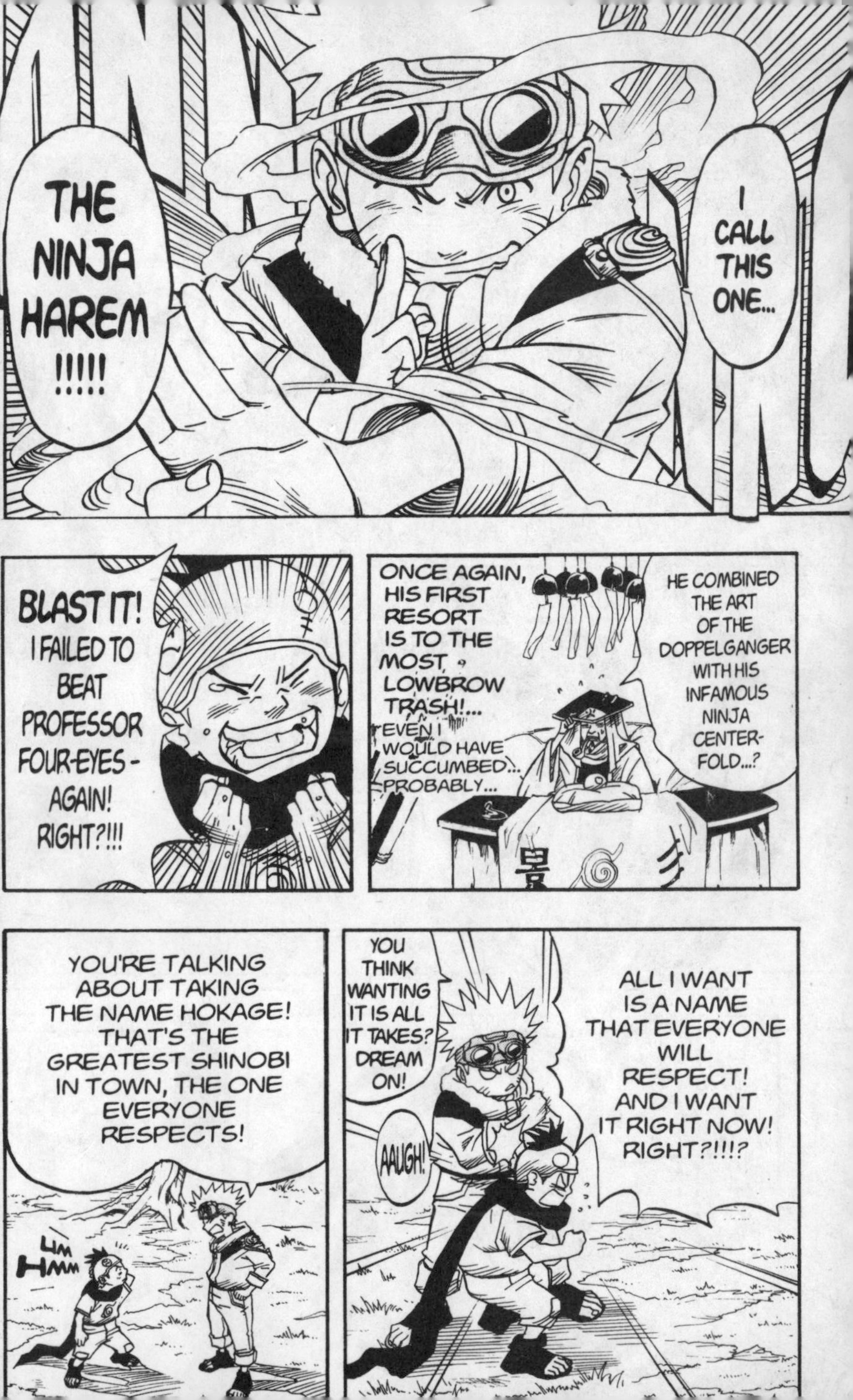
I CALL THIS ONE...
THE NINJA HAREM !!!!!
HE COMBINED THE ART OF THE DOPPELGANGER WITH HIS INFAMOUS NINJA CENTER-FOLD...?
ONCE AGAIN, HIS FIRST RESORT IS TO THE MOST LOWBROW TRASH!...
EVEN I WOULD HAVE SUCCUMBED... PROBABLY...
BLAST IT! I FAILED TO BEAT PROFESSOR FOUR-EYES - AGAIN! RIGHT?!!!
ALL I WANT IS A NAME THAT EVERYONE WILL RESPECT! AND I WANT IT RIGHT NOW! RIGHT?!!!?
YOU THINK WANTING IT IS ALL IT TAKES? DREAM ON!
AAUGH!
YOU'RE TALKING ABOUT TAKING THE NAME HOKAGE! THAT'S THE GREATEST SHINOBI IN TOWN, THE ONE EVERYONE RESPECTS!
UH HMM

READ THIS WAY

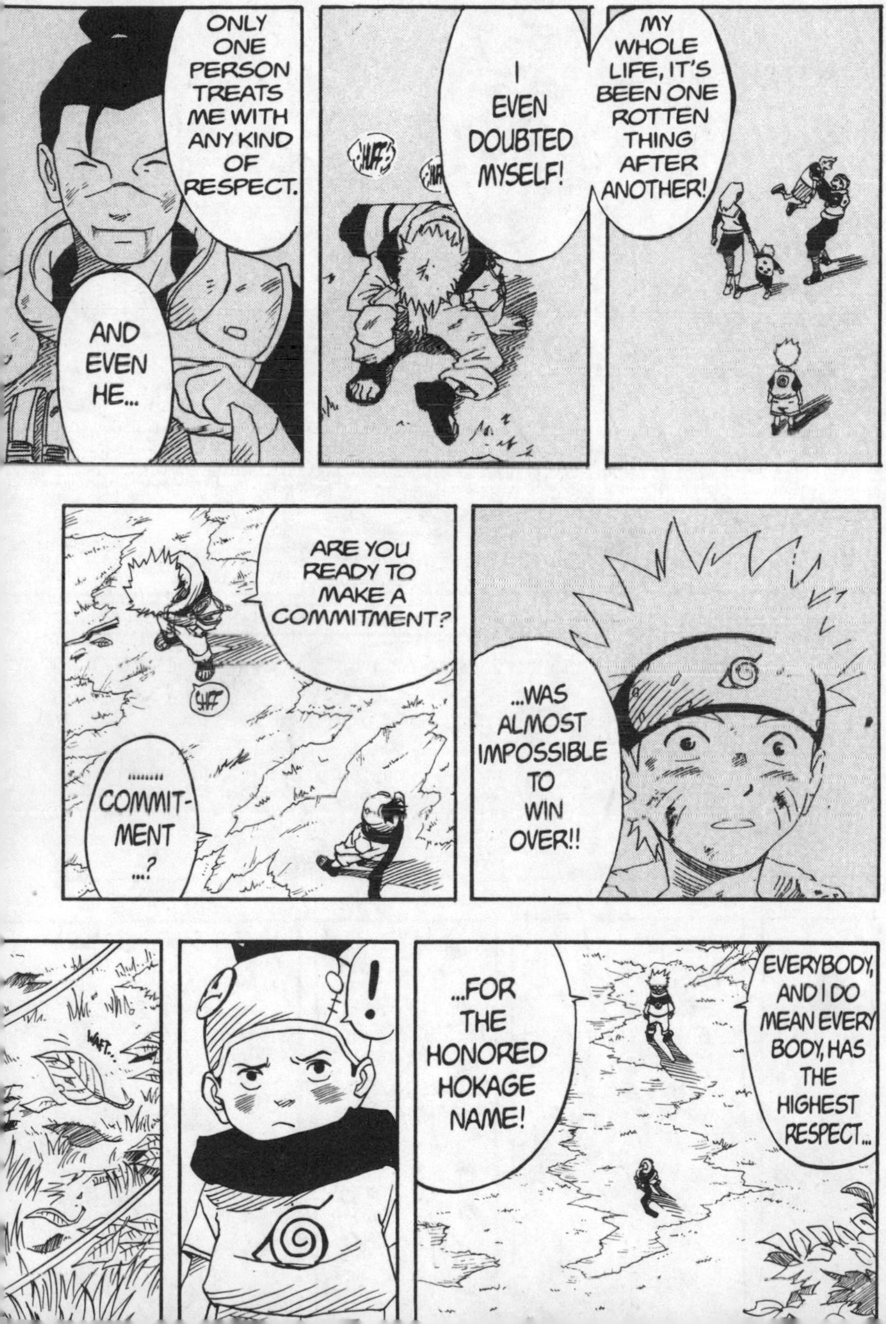
MY WHOLE LIFE, IT'S BEEN ONE ROTTEN THING AFTER ANOTHER!
I EVEN DOUBTED MYSELF!
HUFF
ONLY ONE PERSON TREATS ME WITH ANY KIND OF RESPECT.
AND EVEN HE...
...WAS ALMOST IMPOSSIBLE TO WIN OVER!!
ARE YOU READY TO MAKE A COMMITMENT?
SHFF
.... COMMIT-MENT ...?
EVERYBODY, AND I DO MEAN EVERY BODY, HAS THE HIGHEST RESPECT...
...FOR THE HONORED HOKAGE NAME!
!
WAFT...

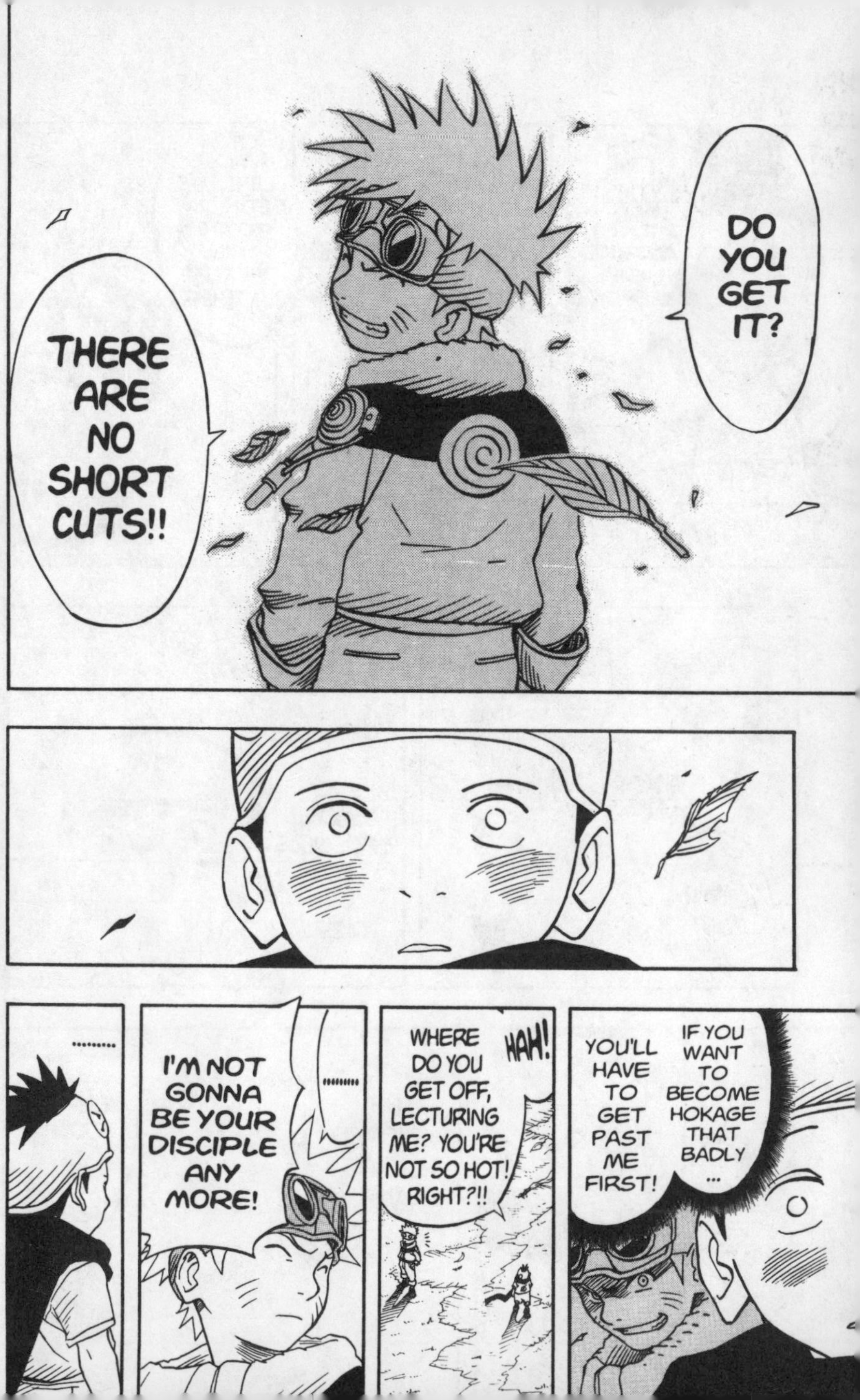
DO YOU GET IT?
THERE ARE NO SHORT CUTS!!
IF YOU WANT TO BECOME HOKAGE THAT BADLY ...
YOU'LL HAVE TO GET PAST ME FIRST!
HAH!
WHERE DO YOU GET OFF, LECTURING ME? YOU'RE NOT SO HOT! RIGHT?!!
....
I'M NOT GONNA BE YOUR DISCIPLE ANY MORE!
....

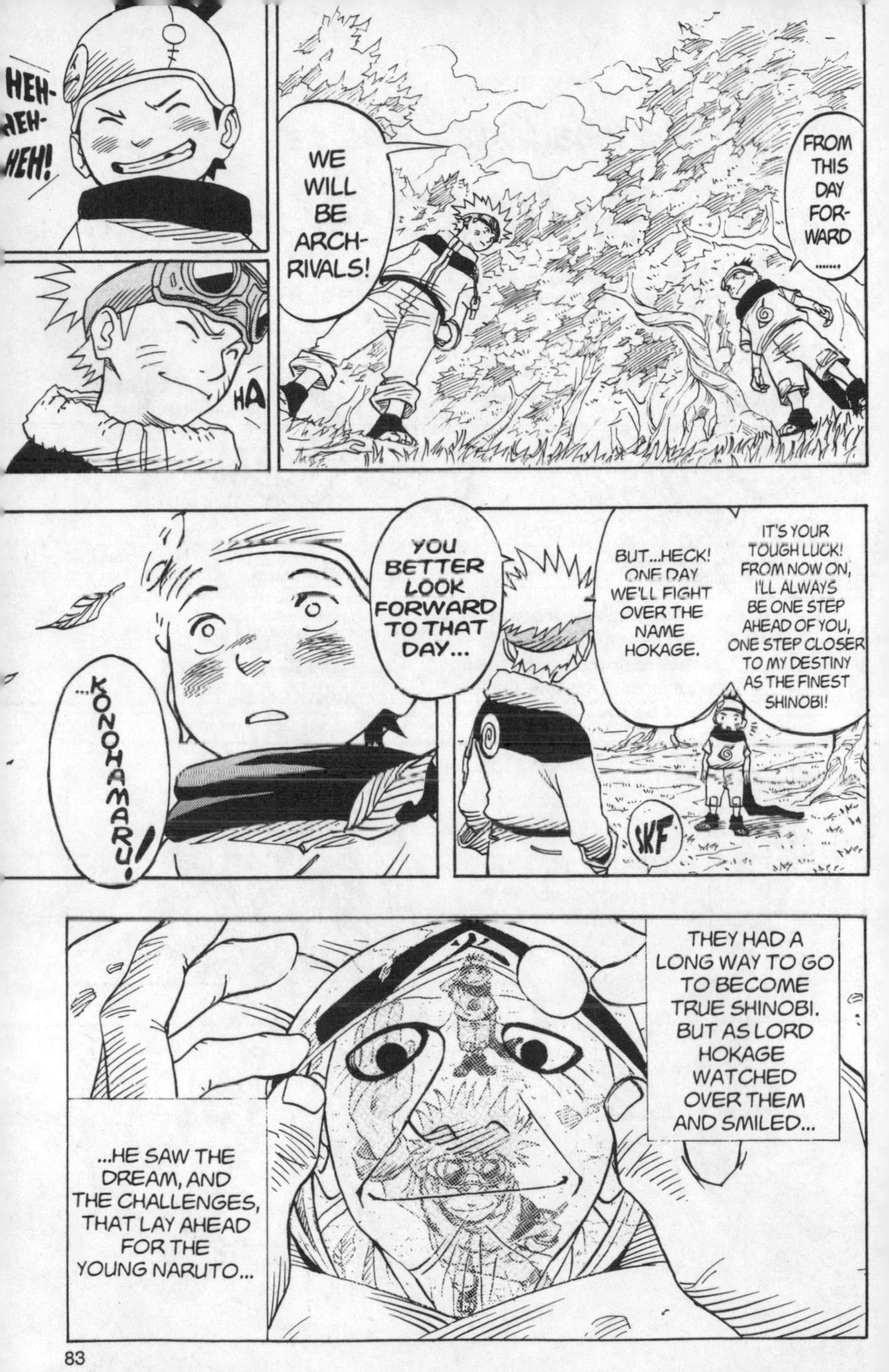

FROM THIS DAY FORWARD......
WE WILL BE ARCH-RIVALS!
HEH-HEH-HEH!
HA
IT'S YOUR TOUGH LUCK! FROM NOW ON, I'LL ALWAYS BE ONE STEP AHEAD OF YOU, ONE STEP CLOSER TO MY DESTINY AS THE FINEST SHINOBI!
BUT...HECK! ONE DAY WE'LL FIGHT OVER THE NAME HOKAGE.
SKF
YOU BETTER LOOK FORWARD TO THAT DAY...
...KONOHAMARU!
THEY HAD A LONG WAY TO GO TO BECOME TRUE SHINOBI. BUT AS LORD HOKAGE WATCHED OVER THEM AND SMILED...
...HE SAW THE DREAM, AND THE CHALLENGES, THAT LAY AHEAD FOR THE YOUNG NARUTO...

Konohagakure Basics:

SHINOBI STYLE

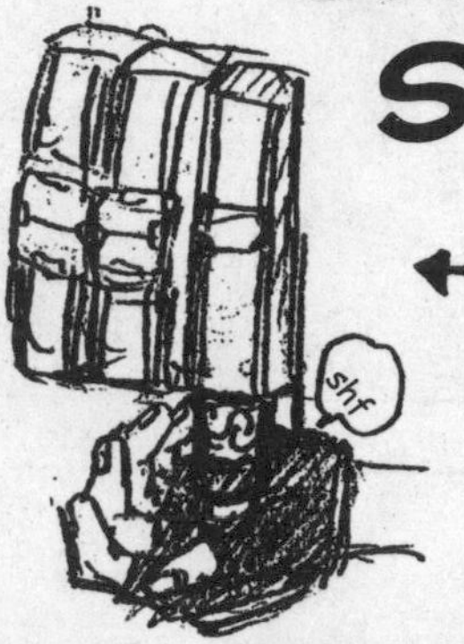
shf

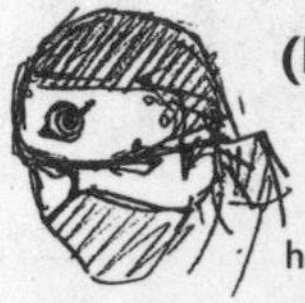

***Hitai-ate* (Forehead Band)**
Can be worn either as a headband, or a cover for the entire head.

***Makimono* Pouch (Scroll Pouch)**
The classic Konohagakure pouch, worn on both the right and left sides of the vest. Scrolls, medicine and ninja tools are extracted from the bottom of the pouches.

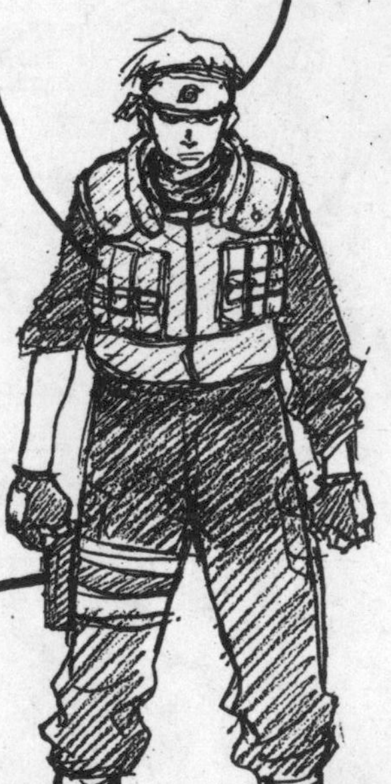

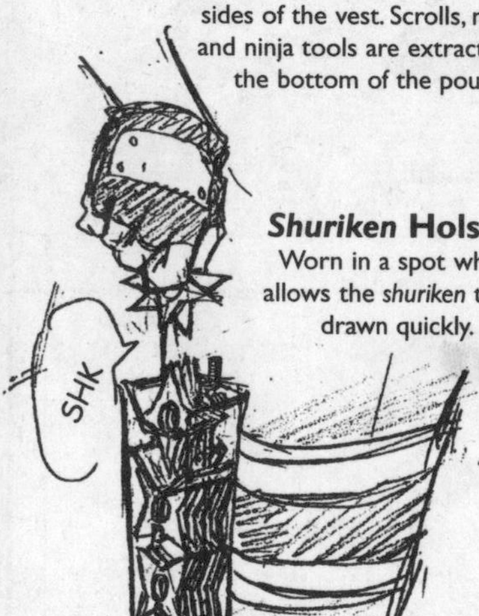
SHK

***Shuriken* Holster**
Worn in a spot which allows the *shuriken* to be drawn quickly.

number 3: Enter Sasuke!

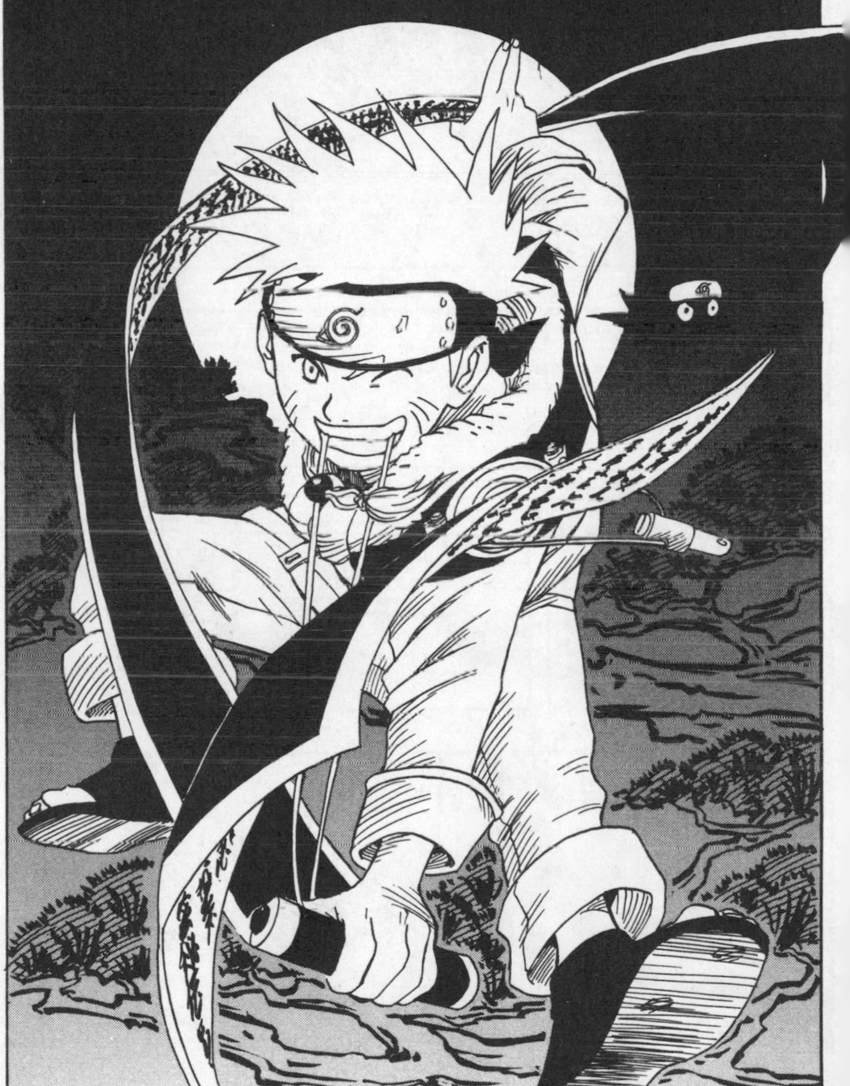

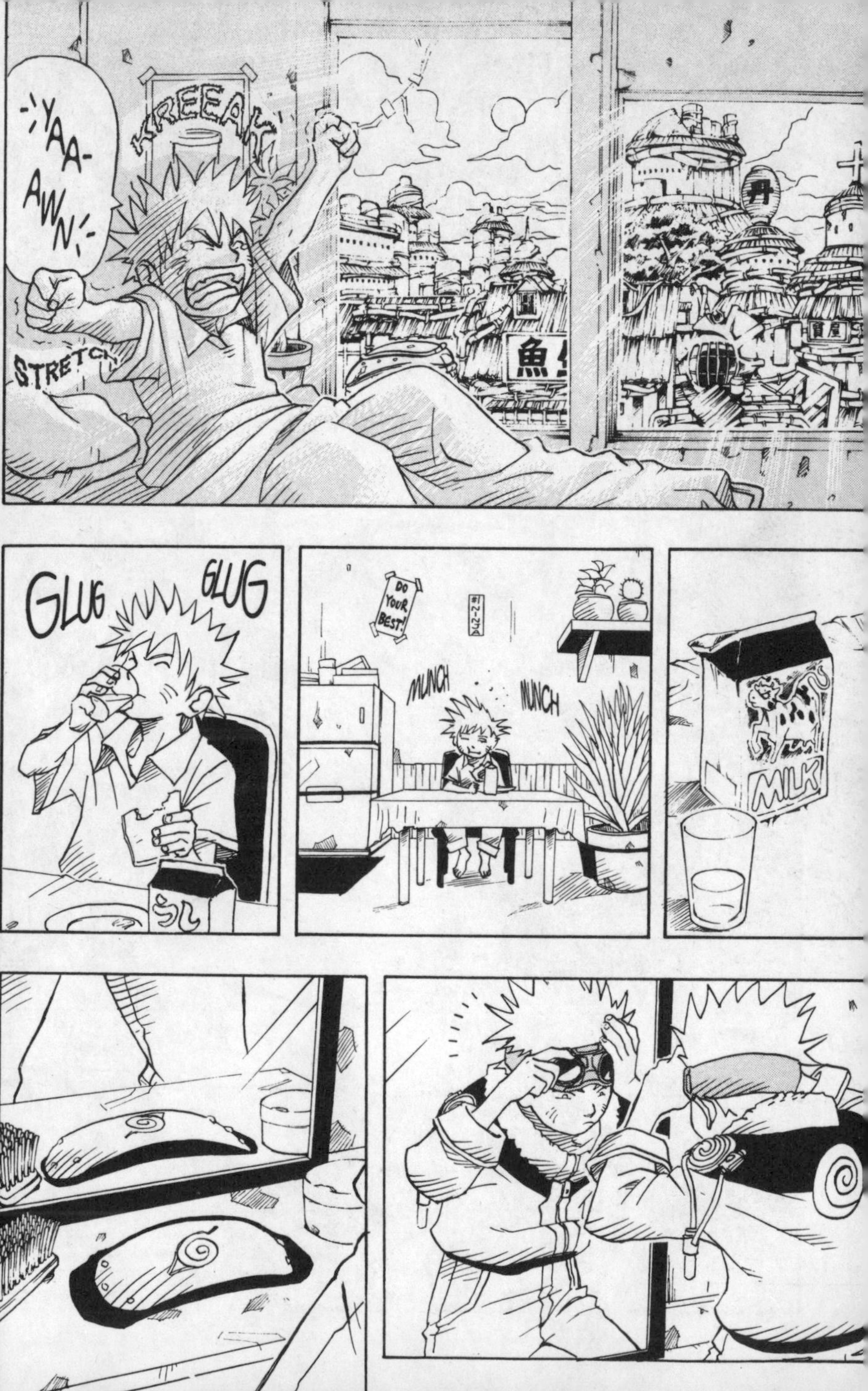
KREEAK
YAAA-AWWN
STRETCH
魚
MILK
DO YOUR BEST!
#1 NINJA
MUNCH
MUNCH
GLUG
GLUG
うし

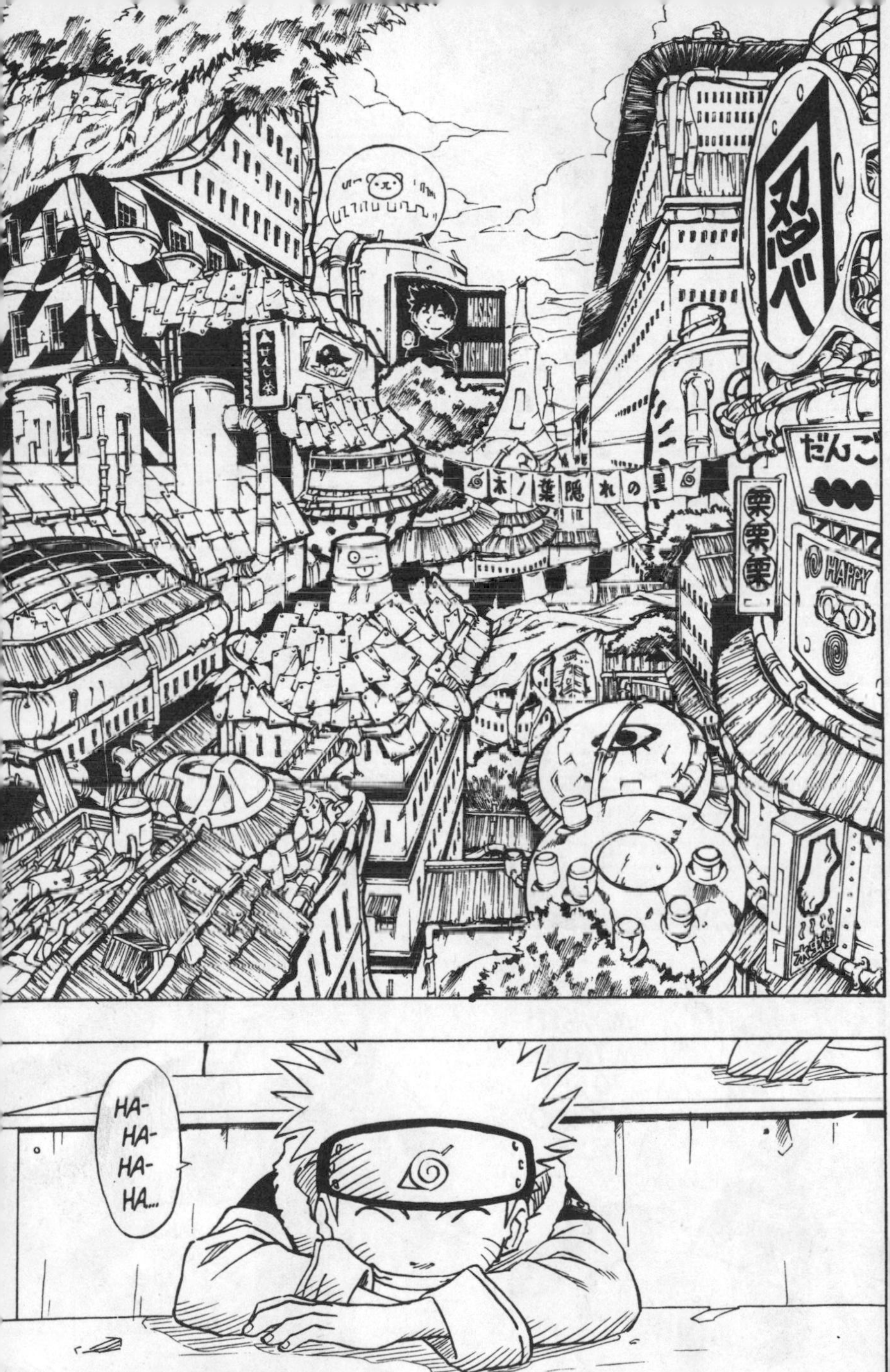
MASASHI KISHIMOTO
木ノ葉隠れの里
だんご
HAPPY
HA-HA-HA-HA...

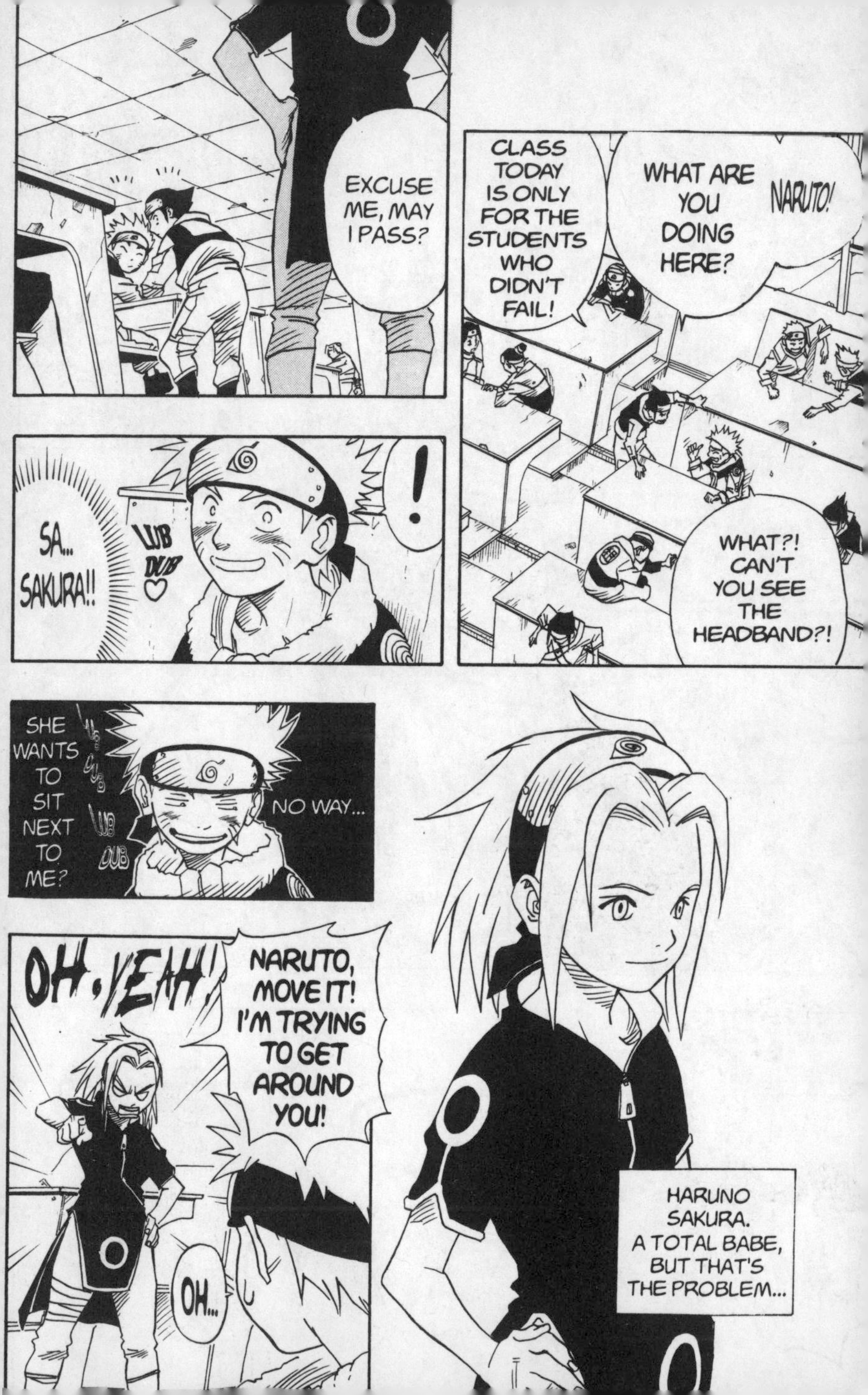
NARUTO!
WHAT ARE YOU DOING HERE?
CLASS TODAY IS ONLY FOR THE STUDENTS WHO DIDN'T FAIL!
WHAT?! CAN'T YOU SEE THE HEADBAND?!
EXCUSE ME, MAY I PASS?
!
LUB DUB
SA... SAKURA!!
HARUNO SAKURA. A TOTAL BABE, BUT THAT'S THE PROBLEM...
NO WAY...
LUB DUB LUB DUB
SHE WANTS TO SIT NEXT TO ME?
NARUTO, MOVE IT! I'M TRYING TO GET AROUND YOU!
OH, YEAH!
OH...

READ THIS WAY

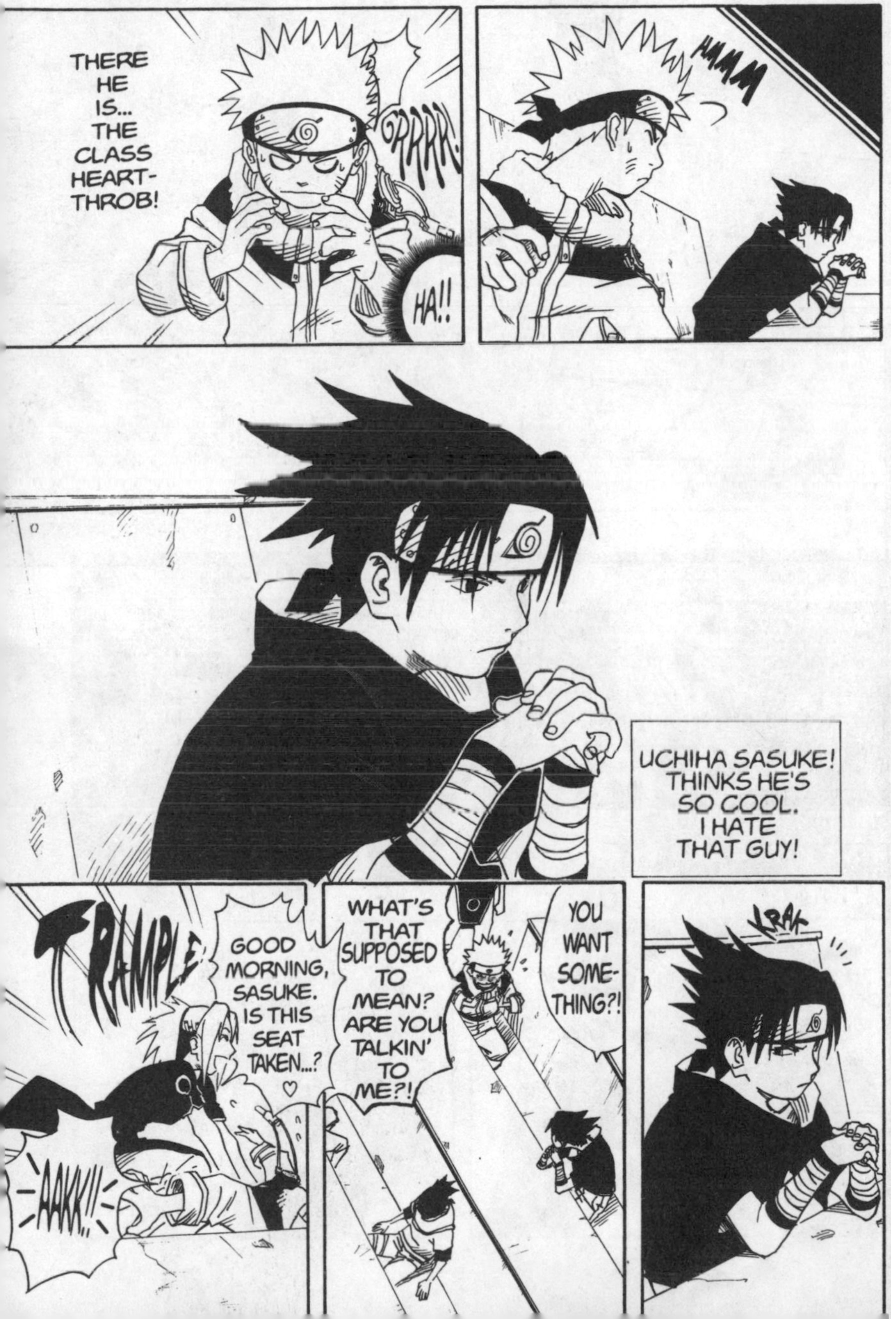
HMMM
THERE HE IS... THE CLASS HEART-THROB!
GRRRR!
HA!!
UCHIHA SASUKE! THINKS HE'S SO COOL. I HATE THAT GUY!
KRAK
YOU WANT SOME-THING?!
WHAT'S THAT SUPPOSED TO MEAN? ARE YOU TALKIN' TO ME?!
GOOD MORNING, SASUKE. IS THIS SEAT TAKEN...? ♡
TRAMPLE
AAKK!!

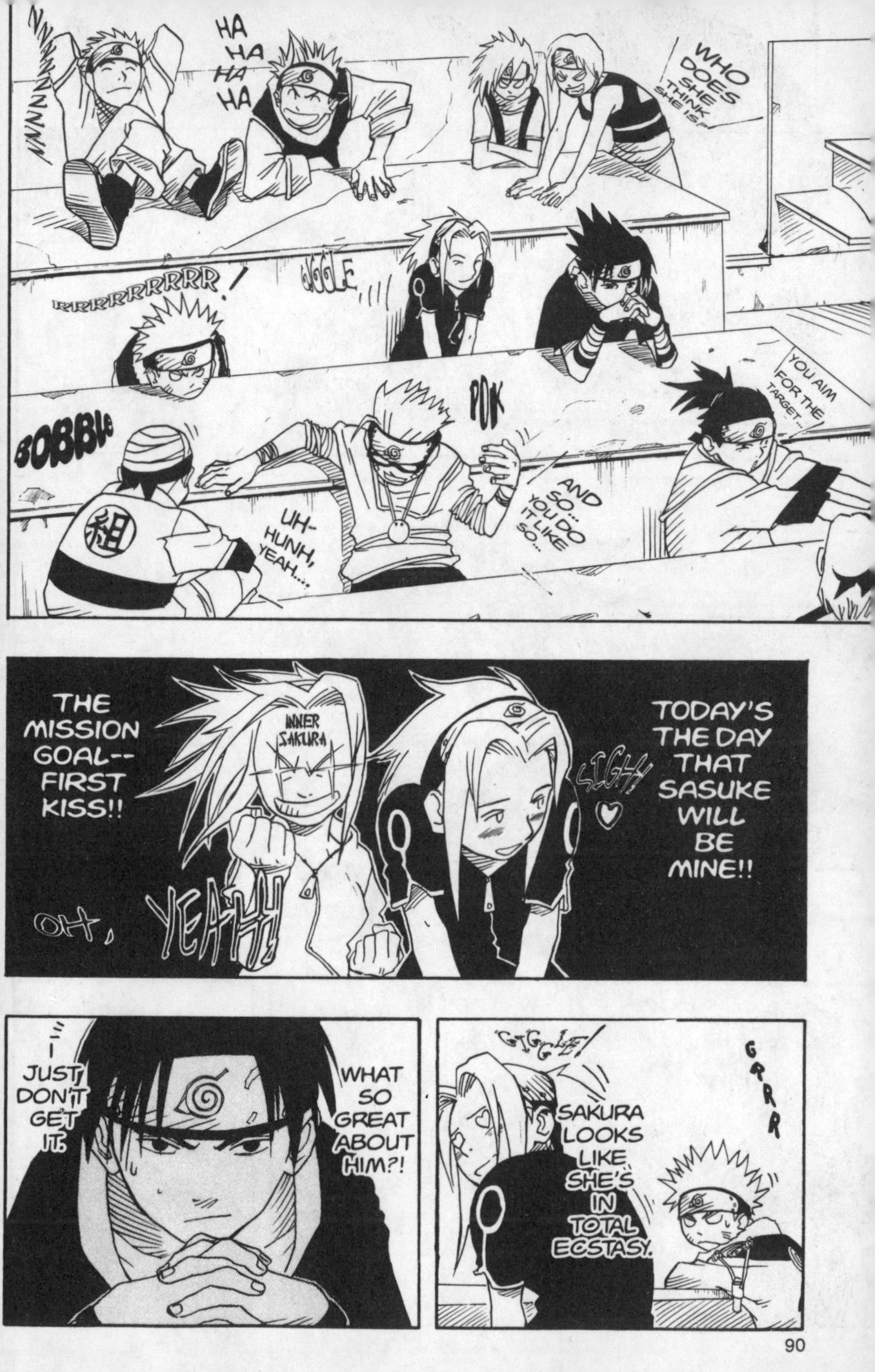
WHO DOES SHE THINK SHE IS?
HA HA HA HA
YOU AIM FOR THE TARGET...
POK
GIGGLE
AND SO... YOU DO IT LIKE SO...
UH-HUNH, YEAH....
BOBBLE
TODAY'S THE DAY THAT SASUKE WILL BE MINE!!
SIGH ♥
INNER SAKURA
THE MISSION GOAL-- FIRST KISS!!
OH, YEAHH
GRRR
GIGGLE!
SAKURA LOOKS LIKE SHE'S IN TOTAL ECSTASY.
WHAT SO GREAT ABOUT HIM?!
I JUST DON'T GET IT.

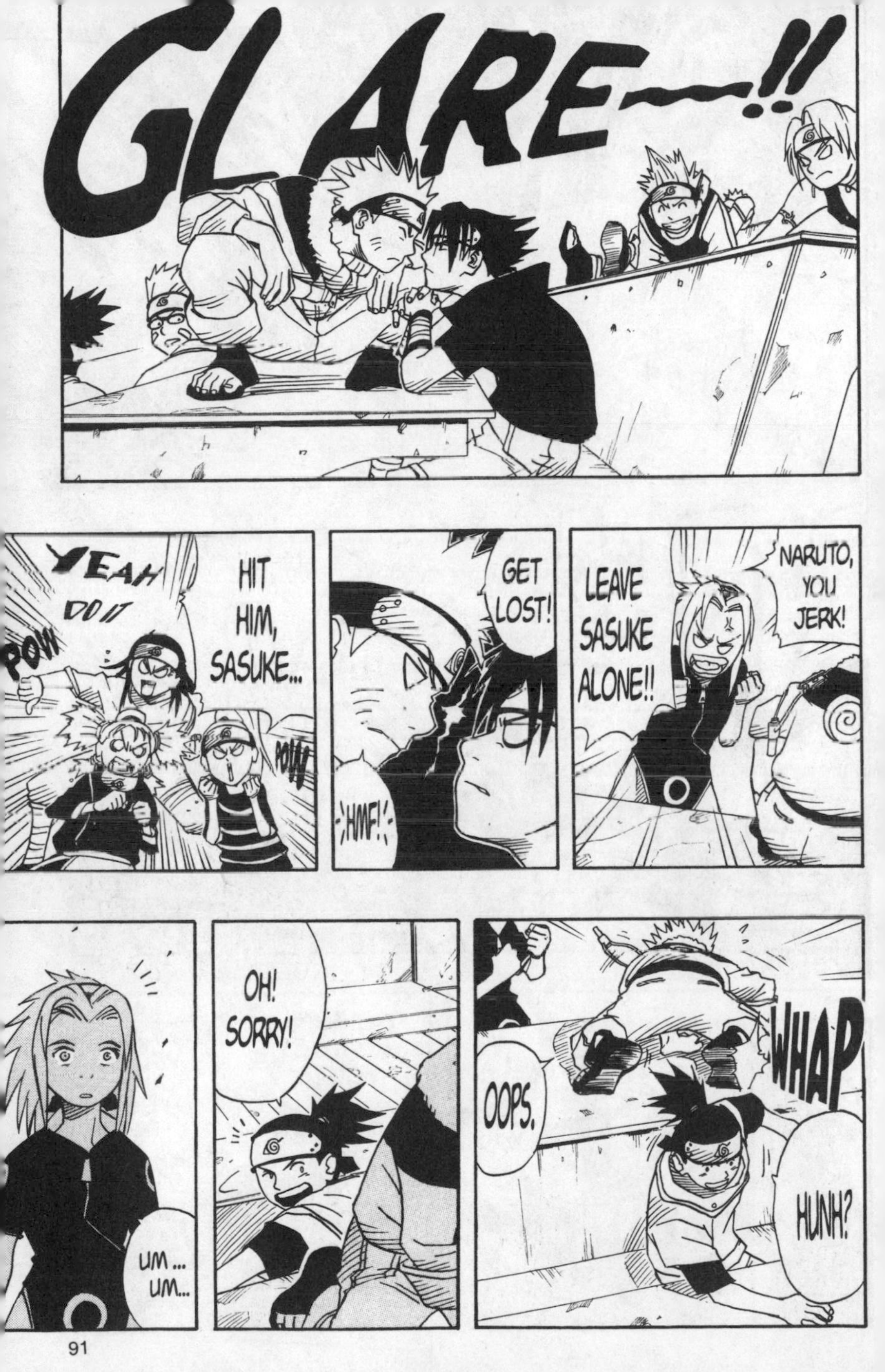

GLARE--!!
NARUTO, YOU JERK!
LEAVE SASUKE ALONE!!
GET LOST!
HMF!
HIT HIM, SASUKE...
YEAH
DO IT
POW
POW
WHAP
OOPS.
HUNH?
OH! SORRY!
UM... UM...

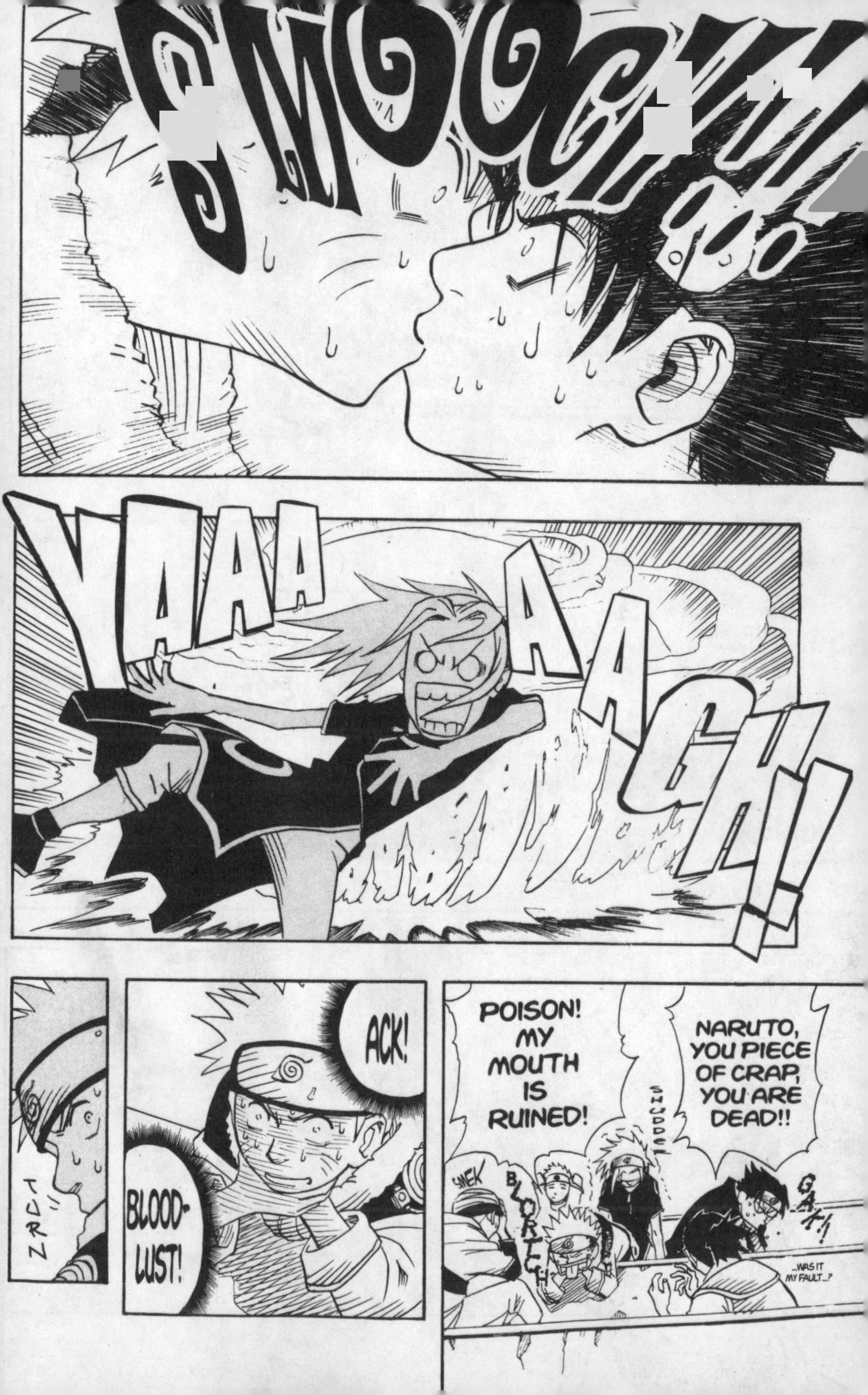
SMOOCH!!
YAAAAACH!!
NARUTO, YOU PIECE OF CRAP, YOU ARE DEAD!!
POISON! MY MOUTH IS RUINED!
SHUDDER
GAK!!
BLORTCH
SMEK
...WAS IT MY FAULT...?
ACK!
BLOOD-LUST!
TURN

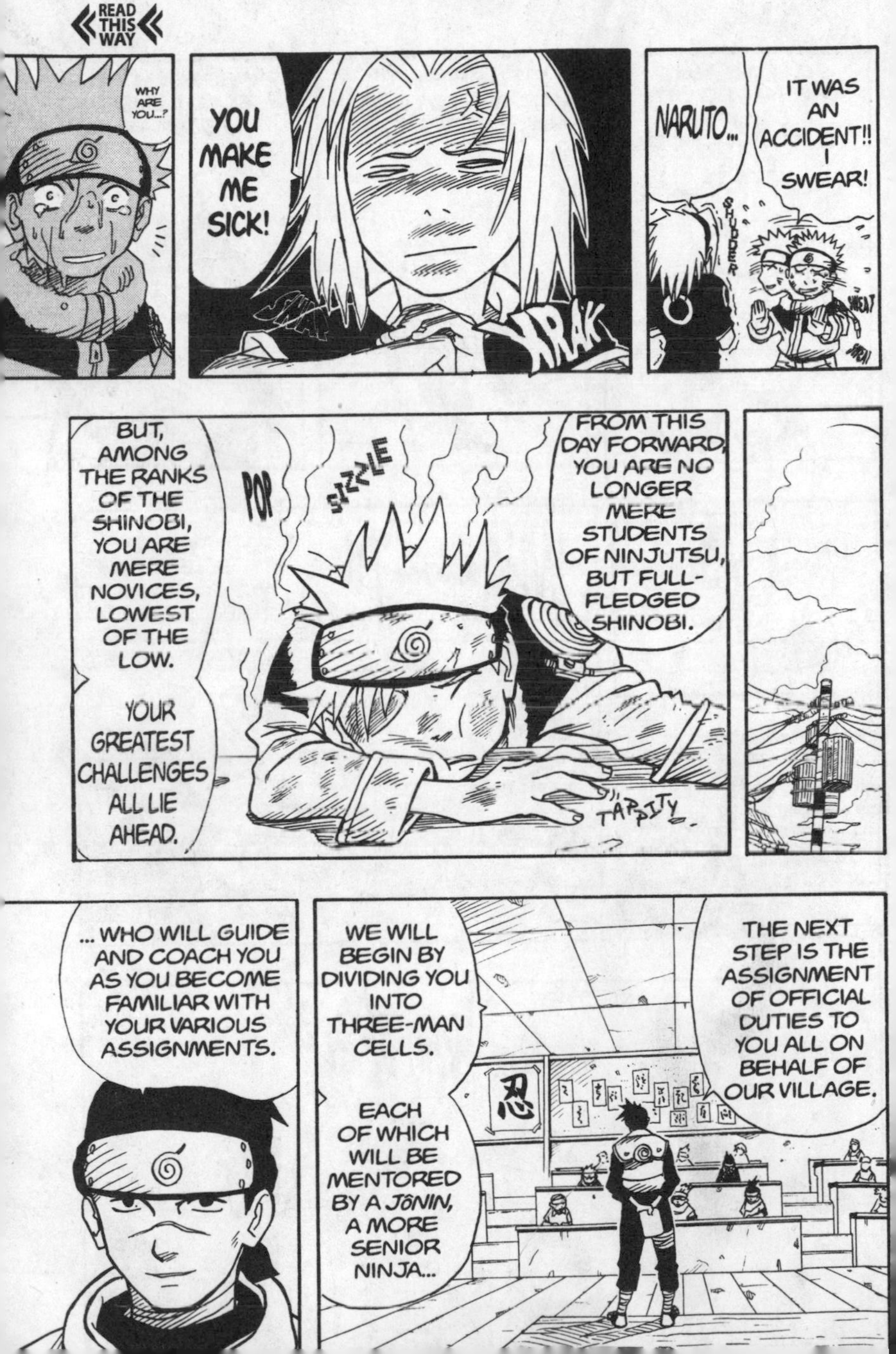
READ THIS WAY
IT WAS AN ACCIDENT!! I SWEAR!
NARUTO...
SHUDDER
SWEAT
YOU MAKE ME SICK!
KRAK
WHY ARE YOU...?
FROM THIS DAY FORWARD, YOU ARE NO LONGER MERE STUDENTS OF NINJUTSU, BUT FULL-FLEDGED SHINOBI.
SIZZLE
POP
BUT, AMONG THE RANKS OF THE SHINOBI, YOU ARE MERE NOVICES, LOWEST OF THE LOW.
YOUR GREATEST CHALLENGES ALL LIE AHEAD.
TAPPITY
THE NEXT STEP IS THE ASSIGNMENT OF OFFICIAL DUTIES TO YOU ALL ON BEHALF OF OUR VILLAGE.
WE WILL BEGIN BY DIVIDING YOU INTO THREE-MAN CELLS.
EACH OF WHICH WILL BE MENTORED BY A JÔNIN, A MORE SENIOR NINJA...
... WHO WILL GUIDE AND COACH YOU AS YOU BECOME FAMILIAR WITH YOUR VARIOUS ASSIGNMENTS.

READ THIS WAY

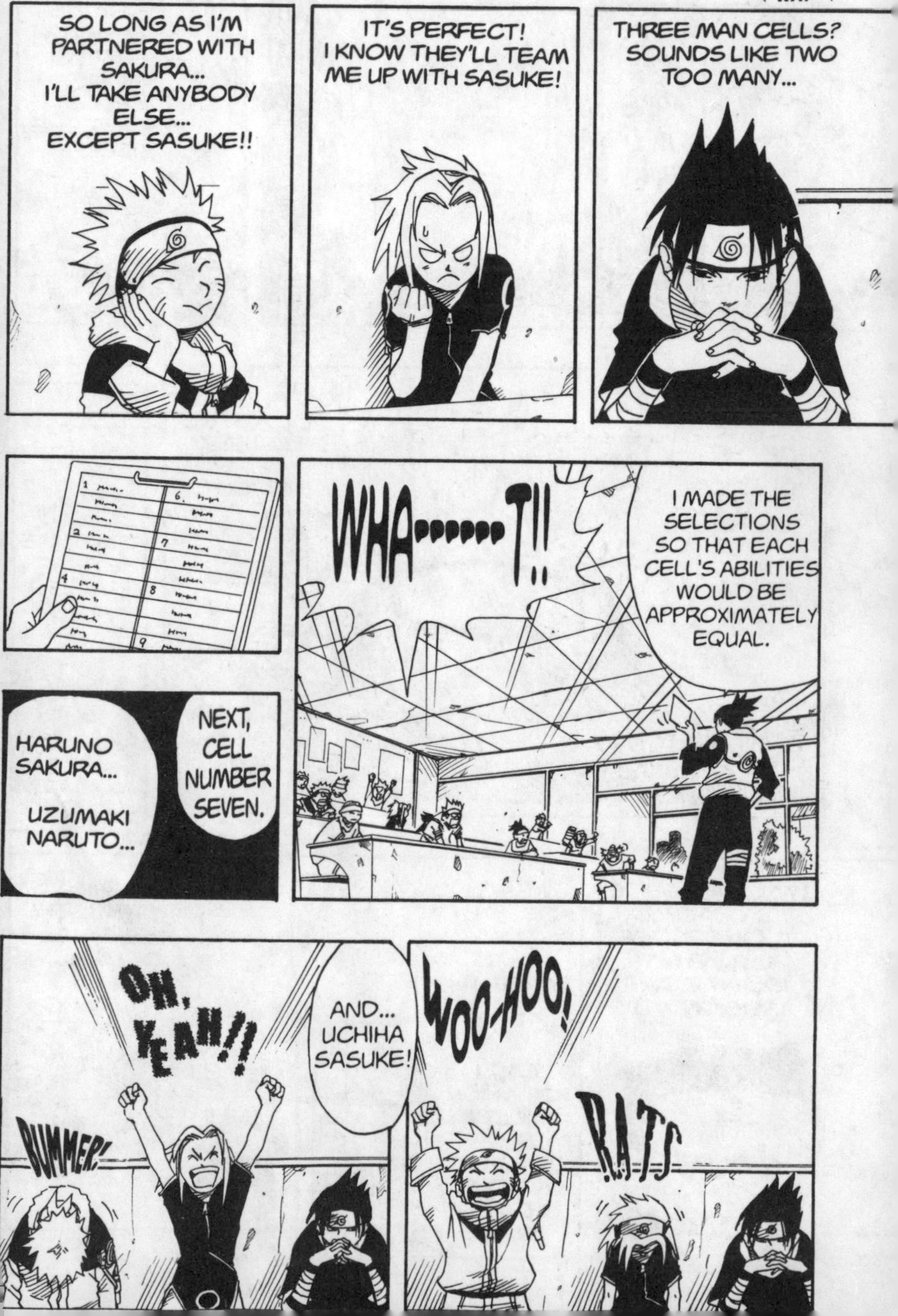
THREE MAN CELLS? SOUNDS LIKE TWO TOO MANY...
IT'S PERFECT! I KNOW THEY'LL TEAM ME UP WITH SASUKE!
SO LONG AS I'M PARTNERED WITH SAKURA... I'LL TAKE ANYBODY ELSE... EXCEPT SASUKE!!
I MADE THE SELECTIONS SO THAT EACH CELL'S ABILITIES WOULD BE APPROXIMATELY EQUAL.
WHA......T!!
NEXT, CELL NUMBER SEVEN.
HARUNO SAKURA...
UZUMAKI NARUTO...
WOO-HOO!
RATS
AND... UCHIHA SASUKE!
OH, YEAH!!
BUMMER!

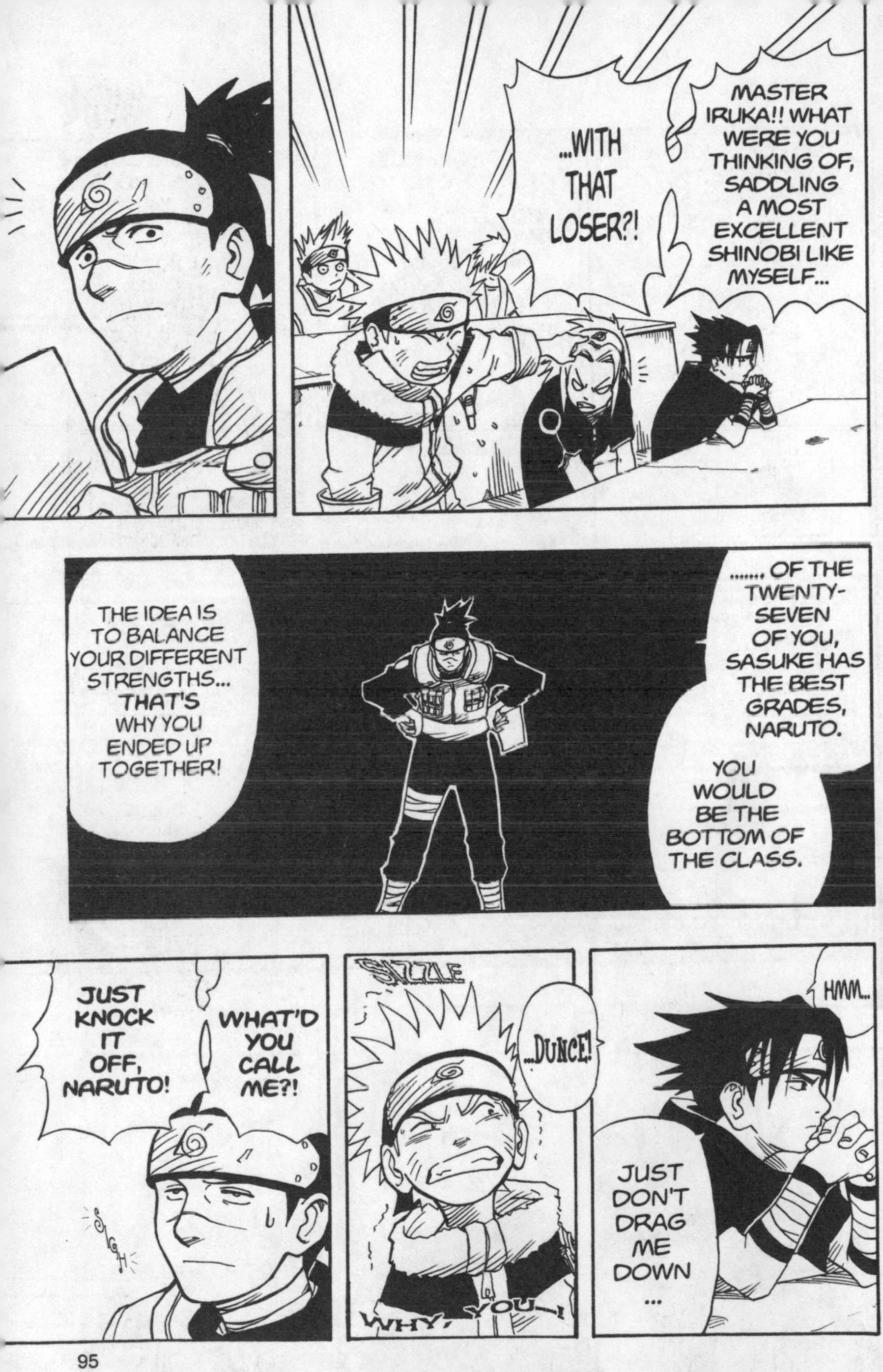
MASTER IRUKA!! WHAT WERE YOU THINKING OF, SADDLING A MOST EXCELLENT SHINOBI LIKE MYSELF...
...WITH THAT LOSER?!
.... OF THE TWENTY-SEVEN OF YOU, SASUKE HAS THE BEST GRADES, NARUTO.
YOU WOULD BE THE BOTTOM OF THE CLASS.
THE IDEA IS TO BALANCE YOUR DIFFERENT STRENGTHS... THAT'S WHY YOU ENDED UP TOGETHER!
HMM...
JUST DON'T DRAG ME DOWN ...
...DUNCE!
SIZZLE
WHY, YOU--!
WHAT'D YOU CALL ME?!
JUST KNOCK IT OFF, NARUTO!
SIGH

READ THIS WAY

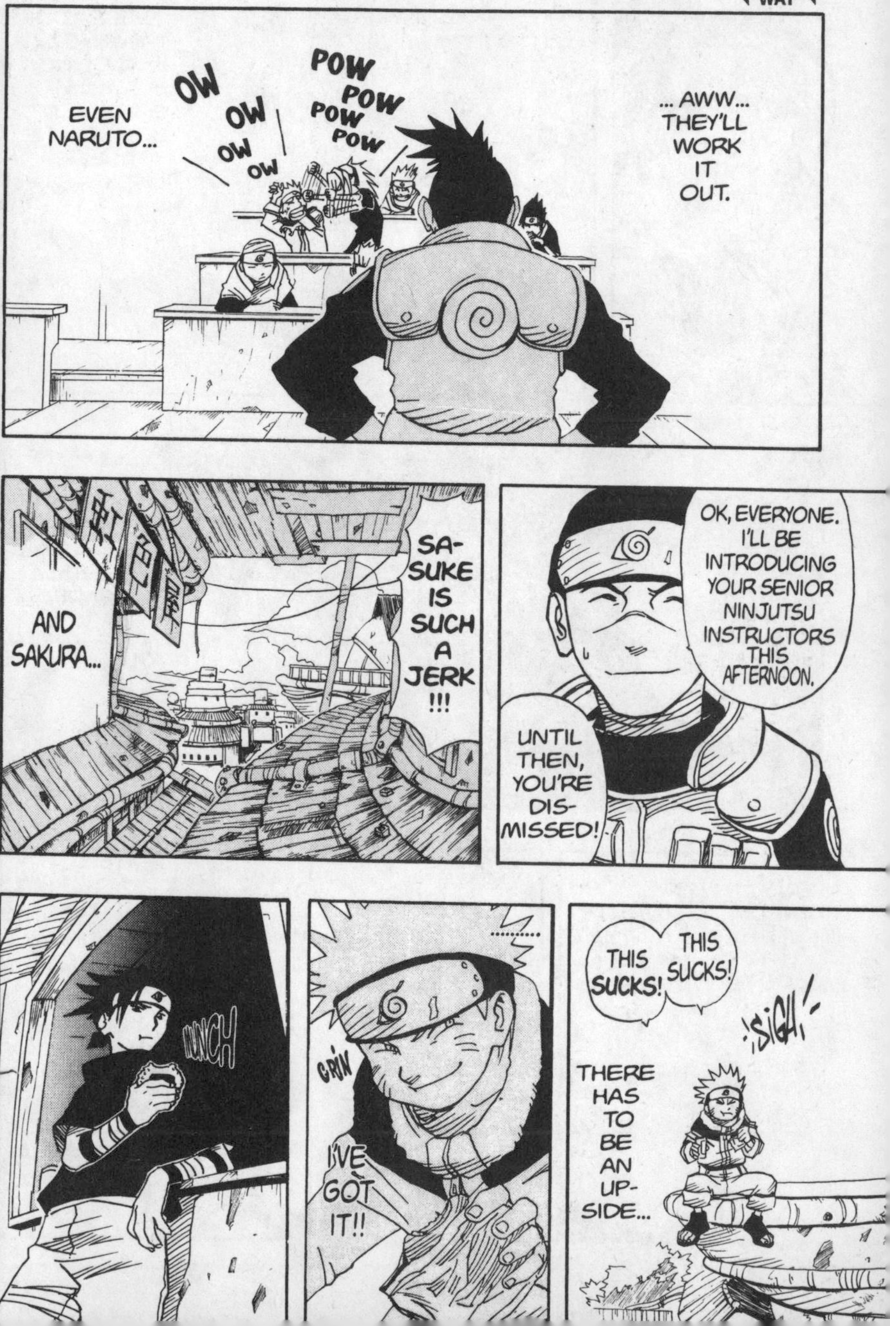
... AWW... THEY'LL WORK IT OUT.
POW
POW
POW
POW
OW
OW
OW
OW
EVEN NARUTO...
OK, EVERYONE. I'LL BE INTRODUCING YOUR SENIOR NINJUTSU INSTRUCTORS THIS AFTERNOON.
UNTIL THEN, YOU'RE DIS-MISSED!
SA-SUKE IS SUCH A JERK!!!
AND SAKURA...
THIS SUCKS!
THIS SUCKS!
SIGH
THERE HAS TO BE AN UP-SIDE...
....
GRIN
I'VE GOT IT!!
MUNCH

READ THIS WAY

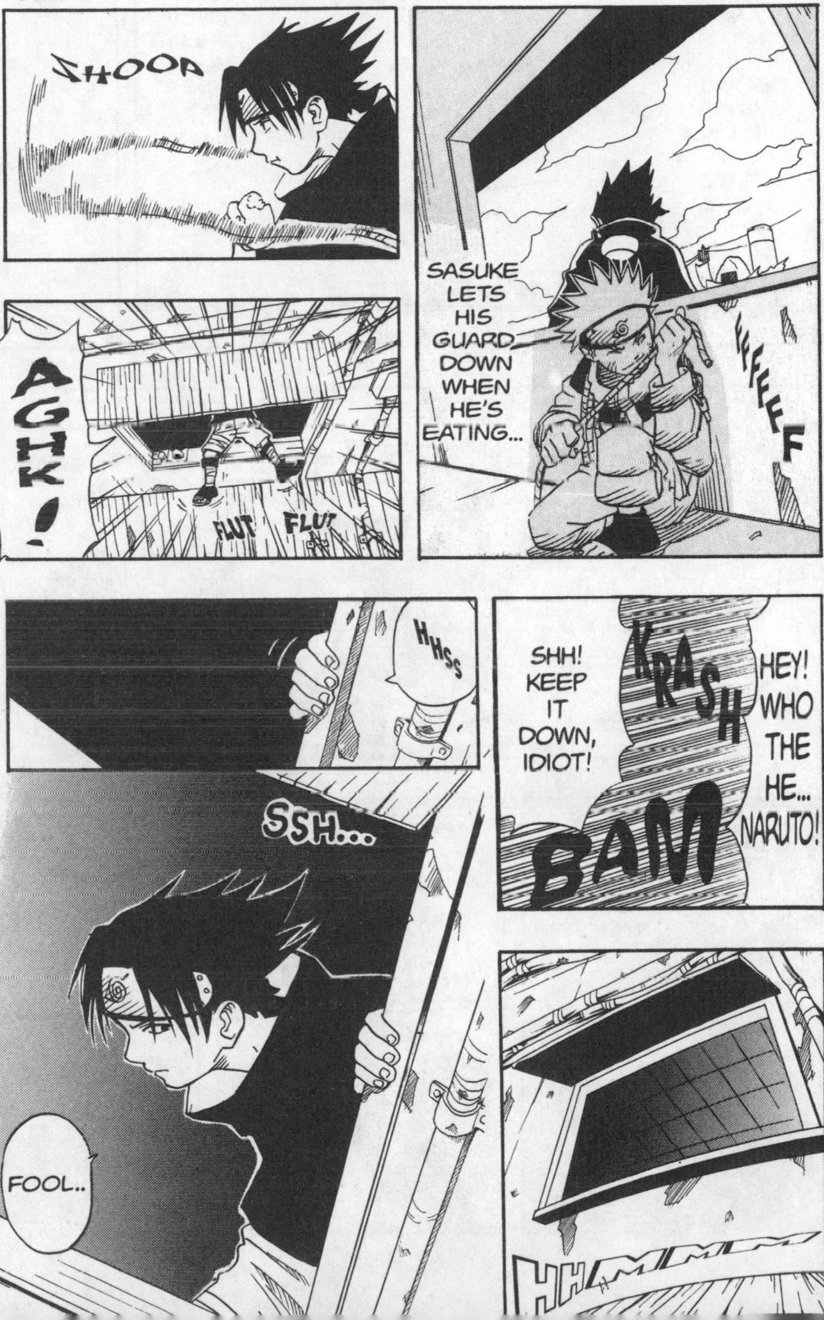
SASUKE LETS HIS GUARD DOWN WHEN HE'S EATING...
FFFFF
SHOOP
AGHK!
FLUT FLUT
HEY! WHO THE HE... NARUTO!
KRASH
SHH! KEEP IT DOWN, IDIOT!
BAM
HHMMMM
HHSS
SSH...
FOOL..

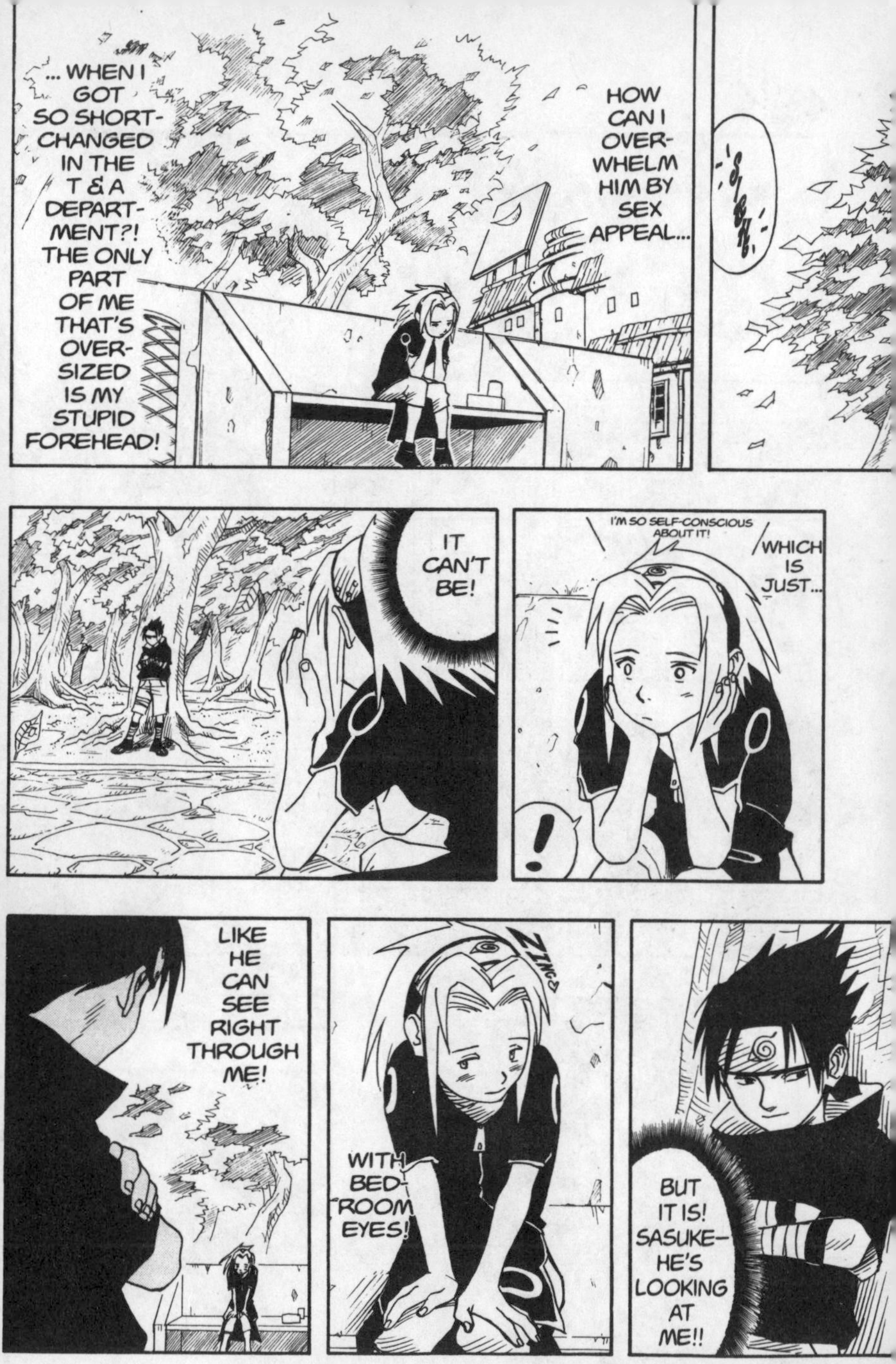
SIGH
HOW CAN I OVER-WHELM HIM BY SEX APPEAL...
... WHEN I GOT SO SHORT-CHANGED IN THE T & A DEPART-MENT?! THE ONLY PART OF ME THAT'S OVER-SIZED IS MY STUPID FOREHEAD!
I'M SO SELF-CONSCIOUS ABOUT IT!
WHICH IS JUST...
IT CAN'T BE!
BUT IT IS! SASUKE-HE'S LOOKING AT ME!!
ZING
WITH BED-ROOM EYES!
LIKE HE CAN SEE RIGHT THROUGH ME!

READ THIS WAY

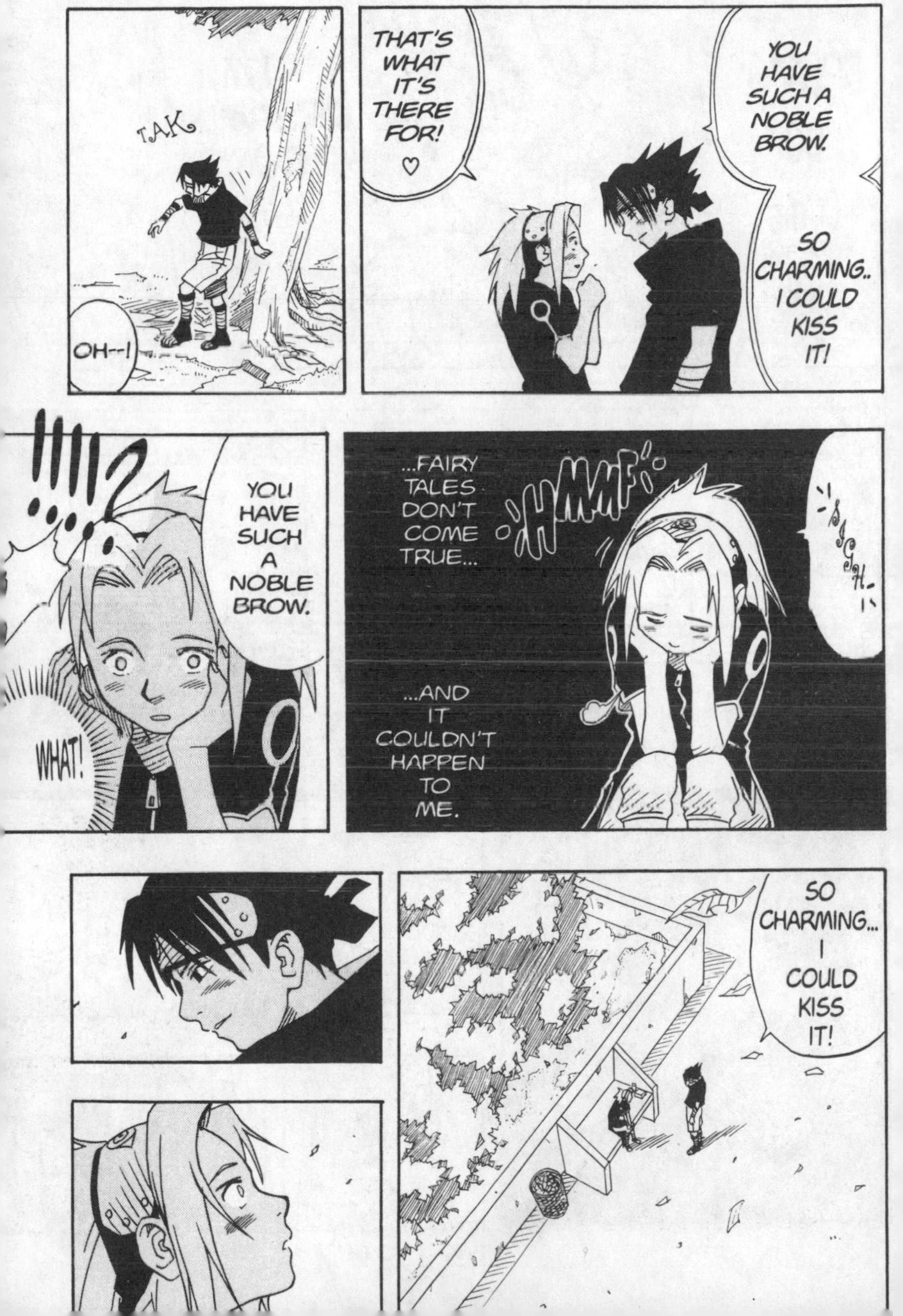
YOU HAVE SUCH A NOBLE BROW.
SO CHARMING.. I COULD KISS IT!
THAT'S WHAT IT'S THERE FOR! ♥
TAK
OH--!
HMMF
SIGH
...FAIRY TALES DON'T COME TRUE...
...AND IT COULDN'T HAPPEN TO ME.
!!!!?
YOU HAVE SUCH A NOBLE BROW.
WHAT!
SO CHARMING... I COULD KISS IT!

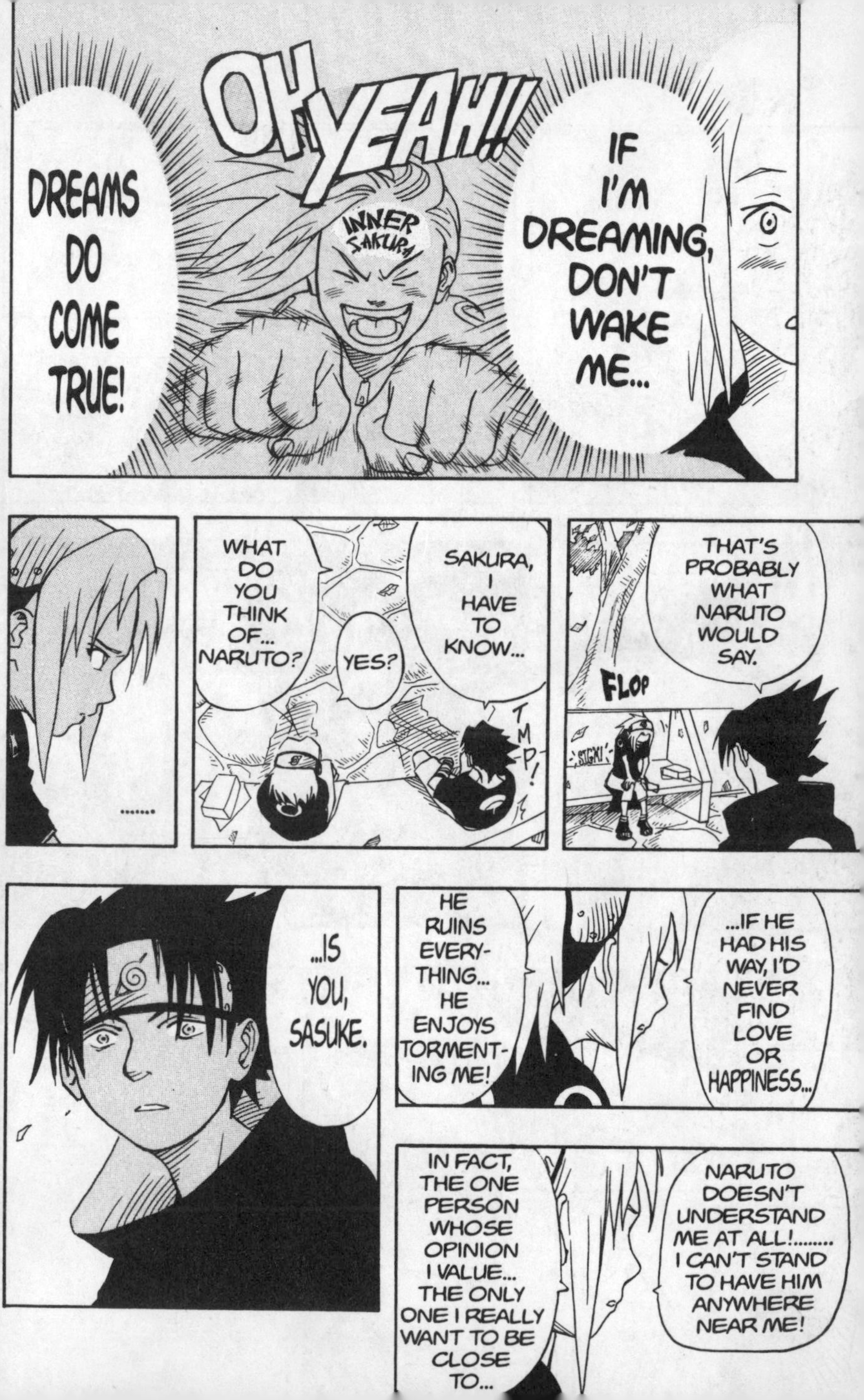
IF I'M DREAMING, DON'T WAKE ME...
OH YEAH!!
INNER SAKURA
DREAMS DO COME TRUE!
THAT'S PROBABLY WHAT NARUTO WOULD SAY.
FLOP
SAKURA, I HAVE TO KNOW...
YES?
WHAT DO YOU THINK OF... NARUTO?
TMP!
....
...IF HE HAD HIS WAY, I'D NEVER FIND LOVE OR HAPPINESS...
HE RUINS EVERYTHING... HE ENJOYS TORMENTING ME!
NARUTO DOESN'T UNDERSTAND ME AT ALL!........ I CAN'T STAND TO HAVE HIM ANYWHERE NEAR ME!
IN FACT, THE ONE PERSON WHOSE OPINION I VALUE... THE ONLY ONE I REALLY WANT TO BE CLOSE TO...
...IS YOU, SASUKE.

READ THIS WAY

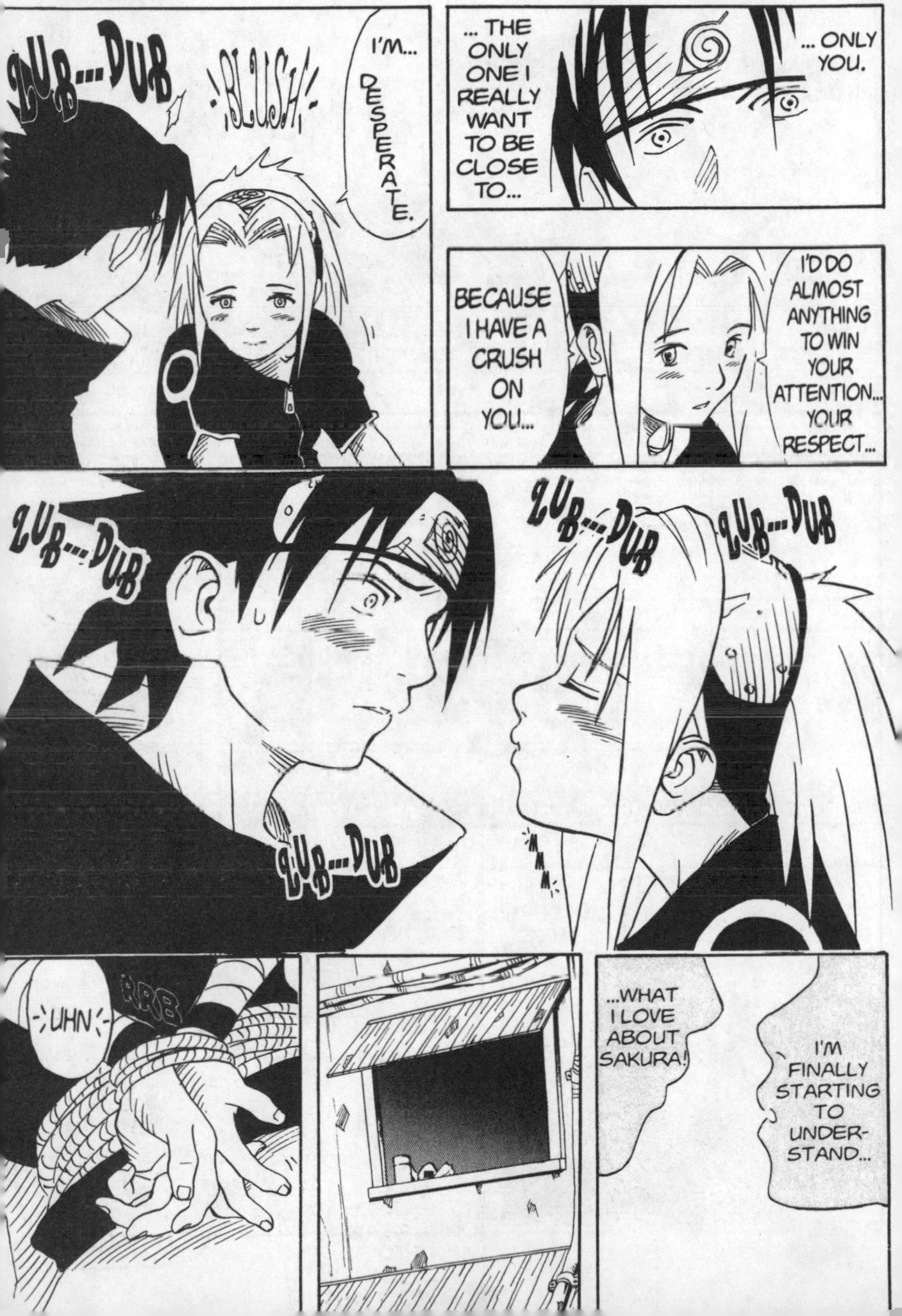

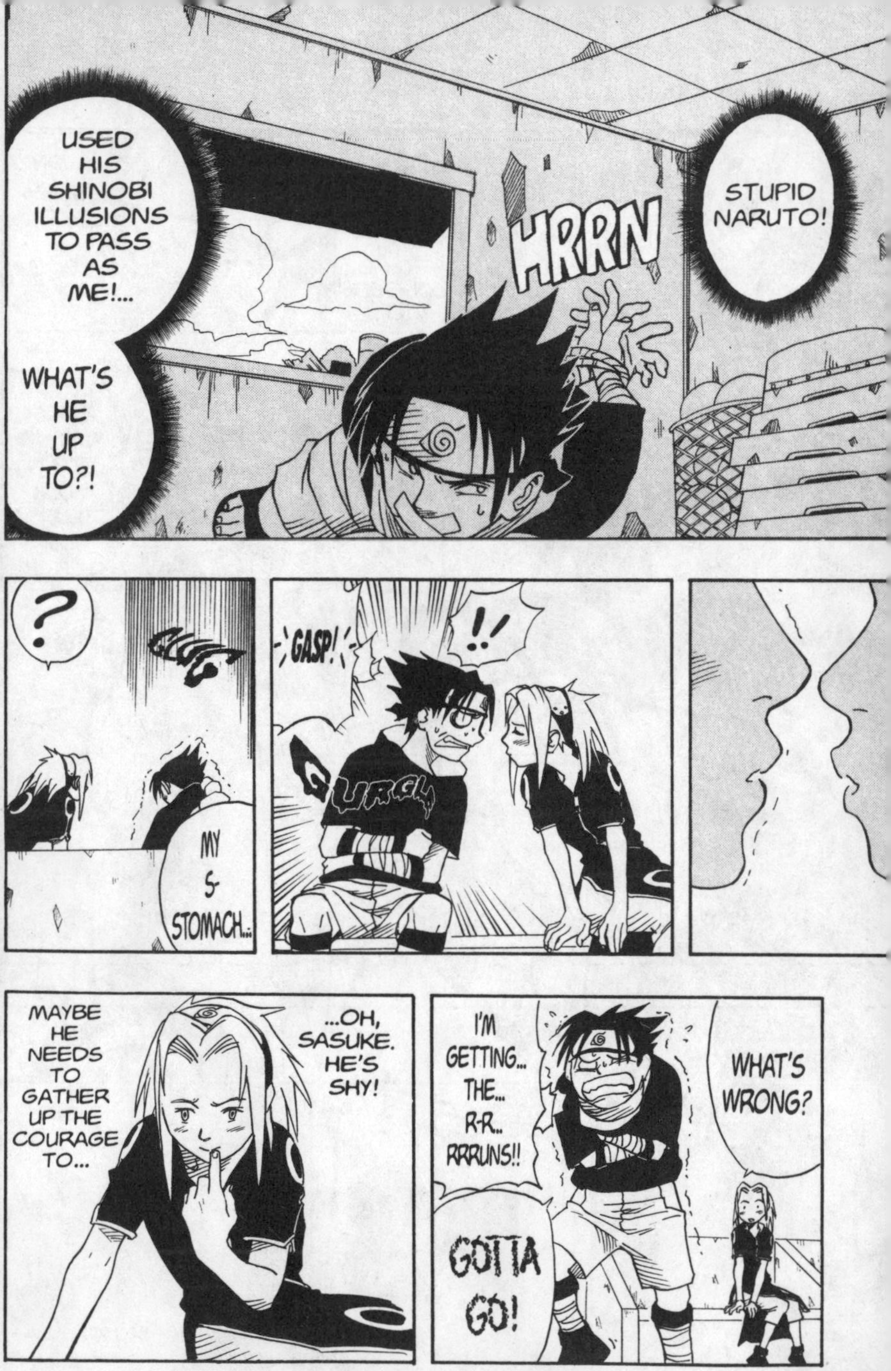
STUPID NARUTO!
HRRN
USED HIS SHINOBI ILLUSIONS TO PASS AS ME!...
WHAT'S HE UP TO?!
!!
GASP!
GURGL
?
MY S-STOMACH...
WHAT'S WRONG?
I'M GETTING... THE... R-R... RRRUNS!!
GOTTA GO!
...OH, SASUKE. HE'S SHY!
MAYBE HE NEEDS TO GATHER UP THE COURAGE TO...

READ THIS WAY

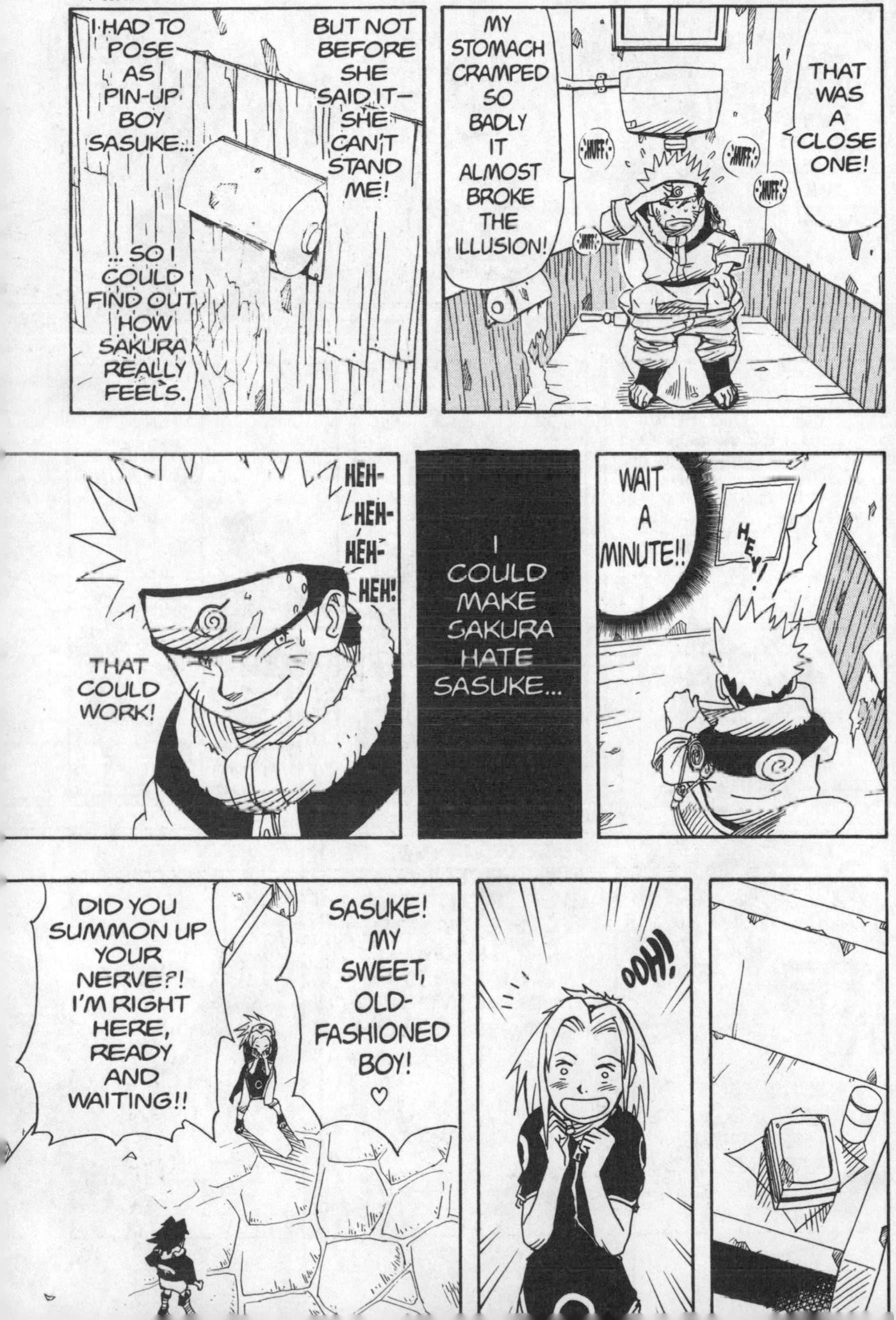

THAT WAS A CLOSE ONE!
HUFF
HUFF
HUFF
HUFF
MY STOMACH CRAMPED SO BADLY IT ALMOST BROKE THE ILLUSION!
I HAD TO POSE AS PIN-UP BOY SASUKE...
... SO I COULD FIND OUT HOW SAKURA REALLY FEELS.
BUT NOT BEFORE SHE SAID IT— SHE CAN'T STAND ME!
WAIT A MINUTE!!
HEY!
I COULD MAKE SAKURA HATE SASUKE...
HEH-HEH-HEH-HEH!
THAT COULD WORK!
OOH!
SASUKE! MY SWEET, OLD-FASHIONED BOY! ♡
DID YOU SUMMON UP YOUR NERVE?! I'M RIGHT HERE, READY AND WAITING!!

READ THIS WAY

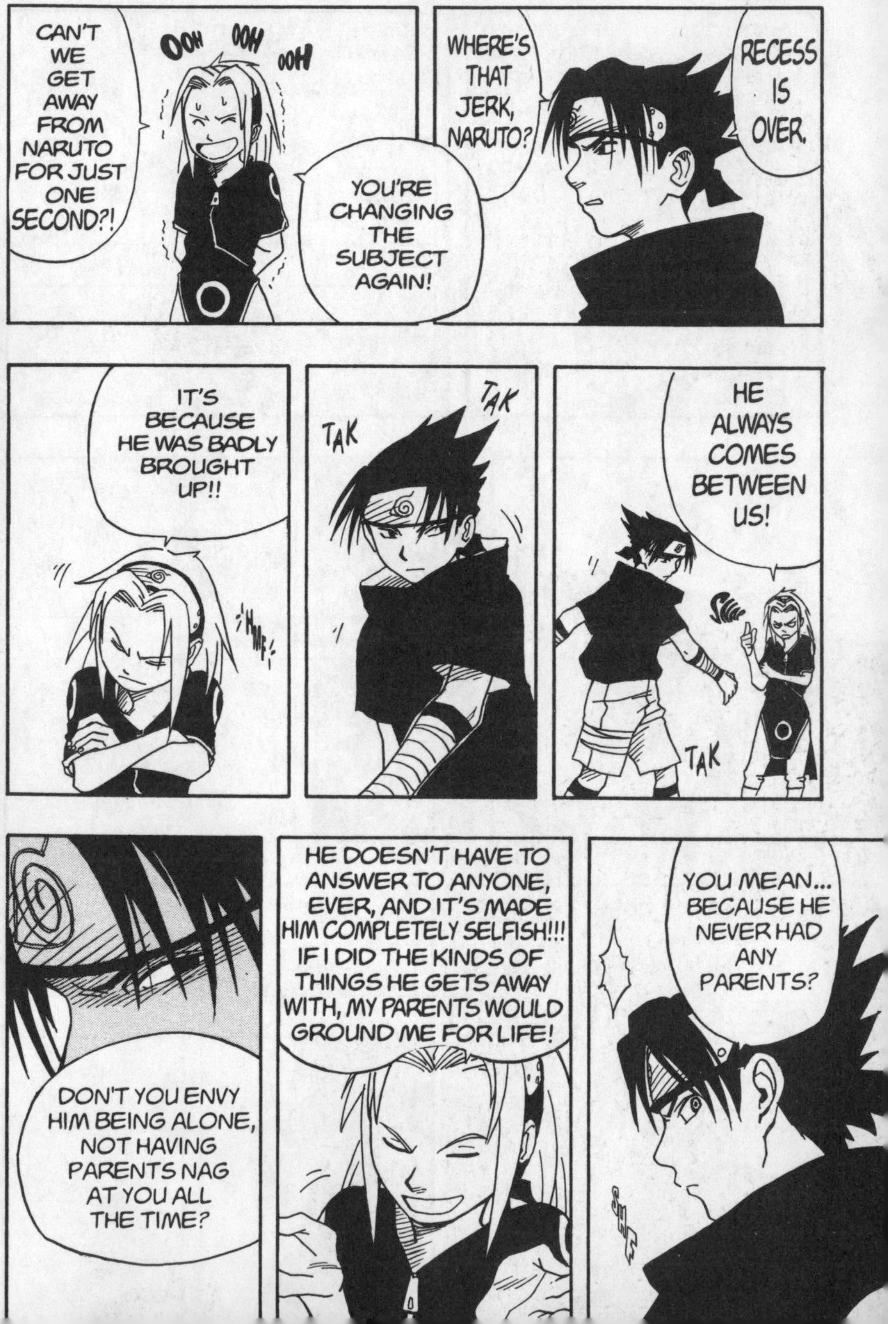
RECESS IS OVER.
WHERE'S THAT JERK, NARUTO?
YOU'RE CHANGING THE SUBJECT AGAIN!
OOH OOH OOH
CAN'T WE GET AWAY FROM NARUTO FOR JUST ONE SECOND?!
HE ALWAYS COMES BETWEEN US!
TAK
TAK
TAK
IT'S BECAUSE HE WAS BADLY BROUGHT UP!!
HMF
YOU MEAN... BECAUSE HE NEVER HAD ANY PARENTS?
HE DOESN'T HAVE TO ANSWER TO ANYONE, EVER, AND IT'S MADE HIM COMPLETELY SELFISH!!! IF I DID THE KINDS OF THINGS HE GETS AWAY WITH, MY PARENTS WOULD GROUND ME FOR LIFE!
DON'T YOU ENVY HIM BEING ALONE, NOT HAVING PARENTS NAG AT YOU ALL THE TIME?

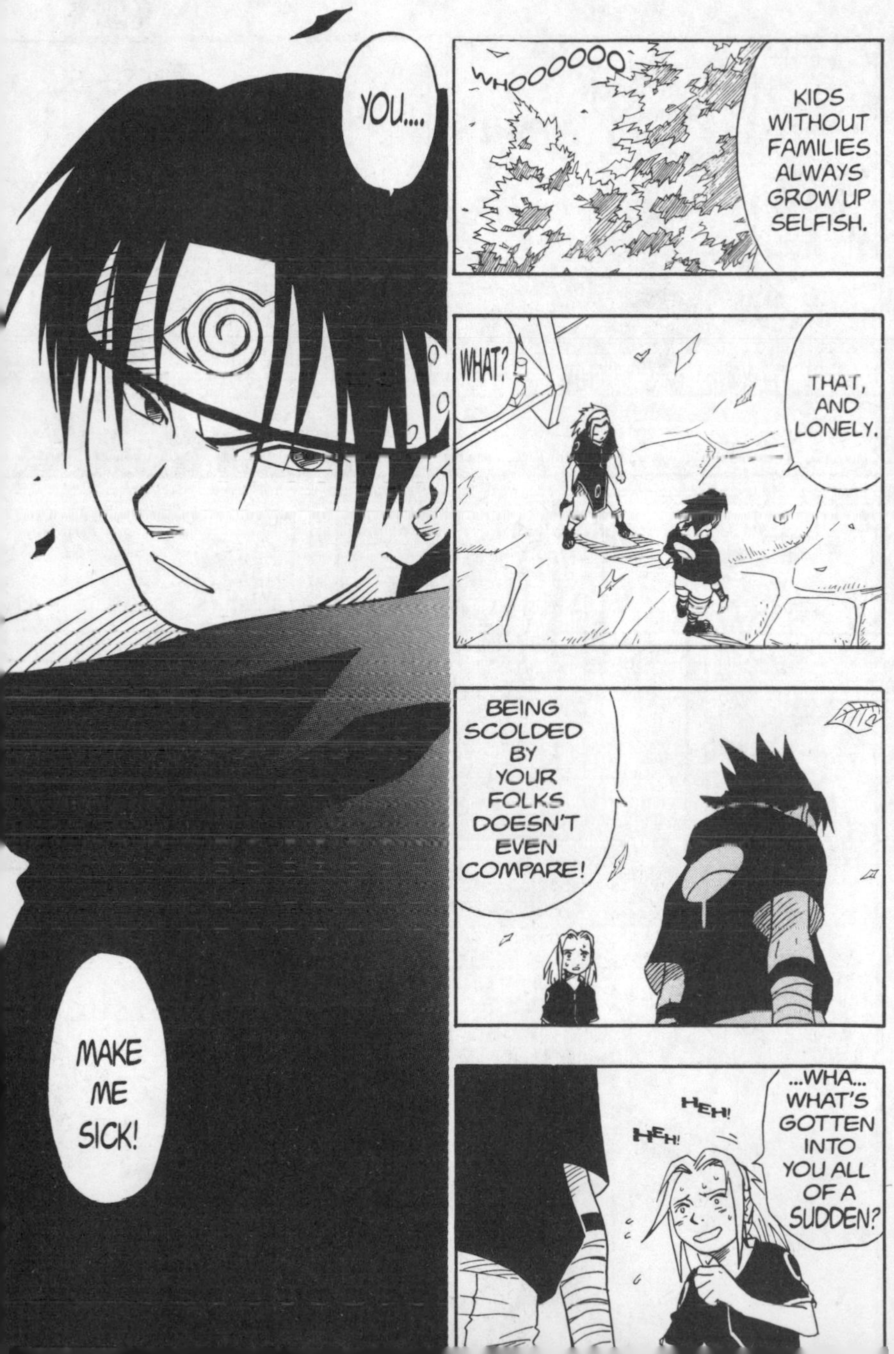
KIDS WITHOUT FAMILIES ALWAYS GROW UP SELFISH.
WHOOOOOO
THAT, AND LONELY.
WHAT?
BEING SCOLDED BY YOUR FOLKS DOESN'T EVEN COMPARE!
...WHA... WHAT'S GOTTEN INTO YOU ALL OF A SUDDEN?
HEH!
HEH!
YOU....
MAKE ME SICK!

READ THIS WAY

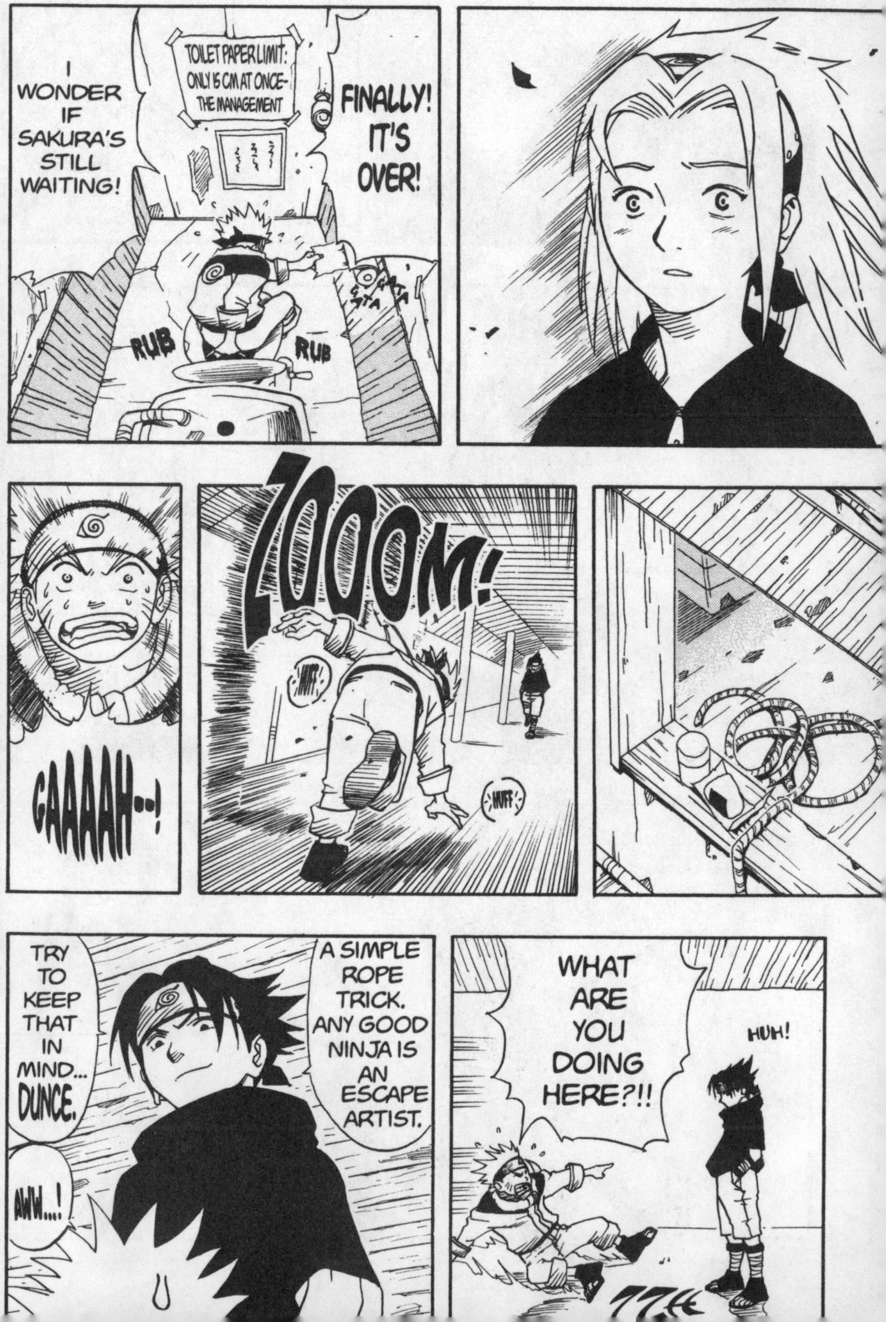
FINALLY! IT'S OVER!
I WONDER IF SAKURA'S STILL WAITING!
TOILET PAPER LIMIT: ONLY 15 CM AT ONCE- THE MANAGEMENT
GATA GATA
RUB
RUB
ZOOOM!
HUFF
HUFF
GAAAAH--!
WHAT ARE YOU DOING HERE?!!
HUH!
A SIMPLE ROPE TRICK. ANY GOOD NINJA IS AN ESCAPE ARTIST.
TRY TO KEEP THAT IN MIND... DUNCE.
AWW...!

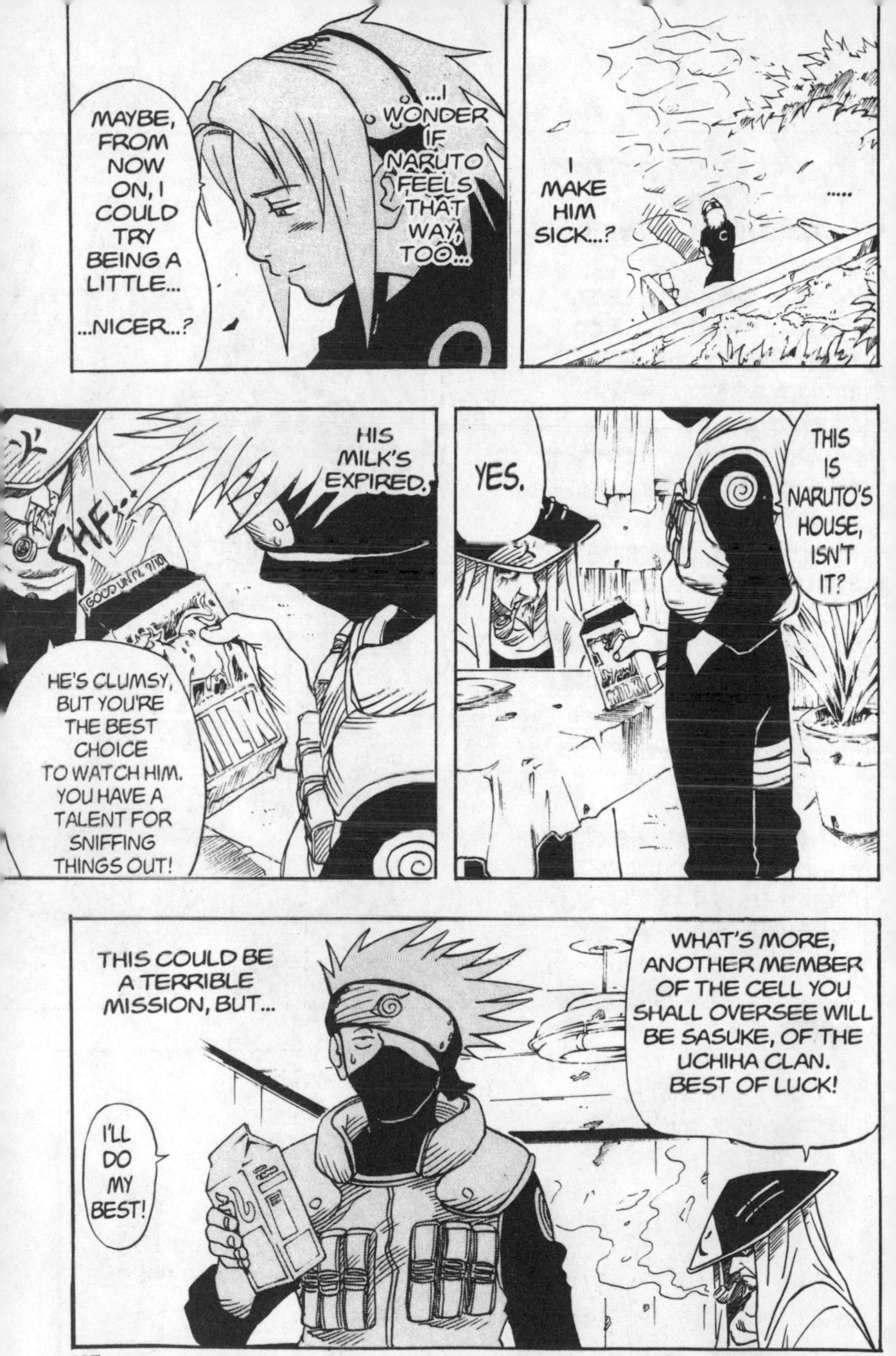
.....
I MAKE HIM SICK...?
...I WONDER IF NARUTO FEELS THAT WAY, TOO...
MAYBE, FROM NOW ON, I COULD TRY BEING A LITTLE...
...NICER...?
THIS IS NARUTO'S HOUSE, ISN'T IT?
YES.
HIS MILK'S EXPIRED.
SHF...
HE'S CLUMSY, BUT YOU'RE THE BEST CHOICE TO WATCH HIM. YOU HAVE A TALENT FOR SNIFFING THINGS OUT!
WHAT'S MORE, ANOTHER MEMBER OF THE CELL YOU SHALL OVERSEE WILL BE SASUKE, OF THE UCHIHA CLAN. BEST OF LUCK!
THIS COULD BE A TERRIBLE MISSION, BUT...
I'LL DO MY BEST!

The picture on the right is from Karakuri ("mechanism"), the first story I submitted to Weekly Shonen Jump. Karakuri won the Hop Step Award for new manga artists, which allowed me to get picked up by my current editor and helped me begin my journey down the road of a manga artist. It's a manga that brings back a lot of memories for me. But, man, the hero sure does have intensely terrifying eyes.

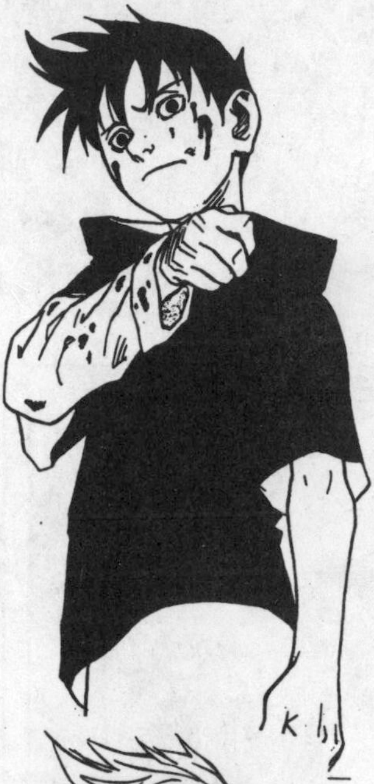

The picture on the right is another one from the first manga I published in Weekly Shonen Jump...that's right, Karakuri! But when the reader polls came in, its popularity was rock bottom! Still, this manga also brings back a lot of memories for me.

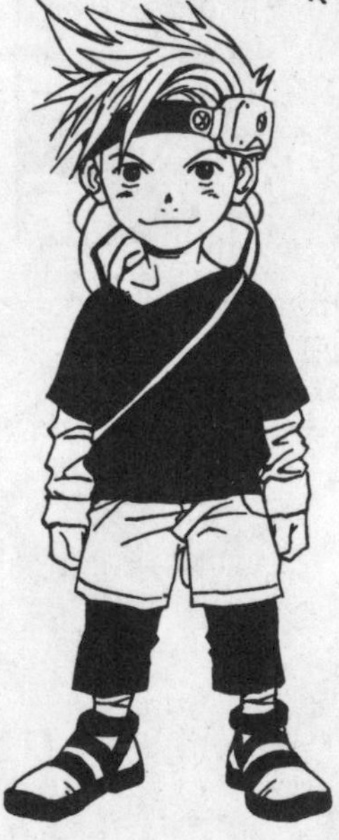

number 4: Hatake Kakashi!!

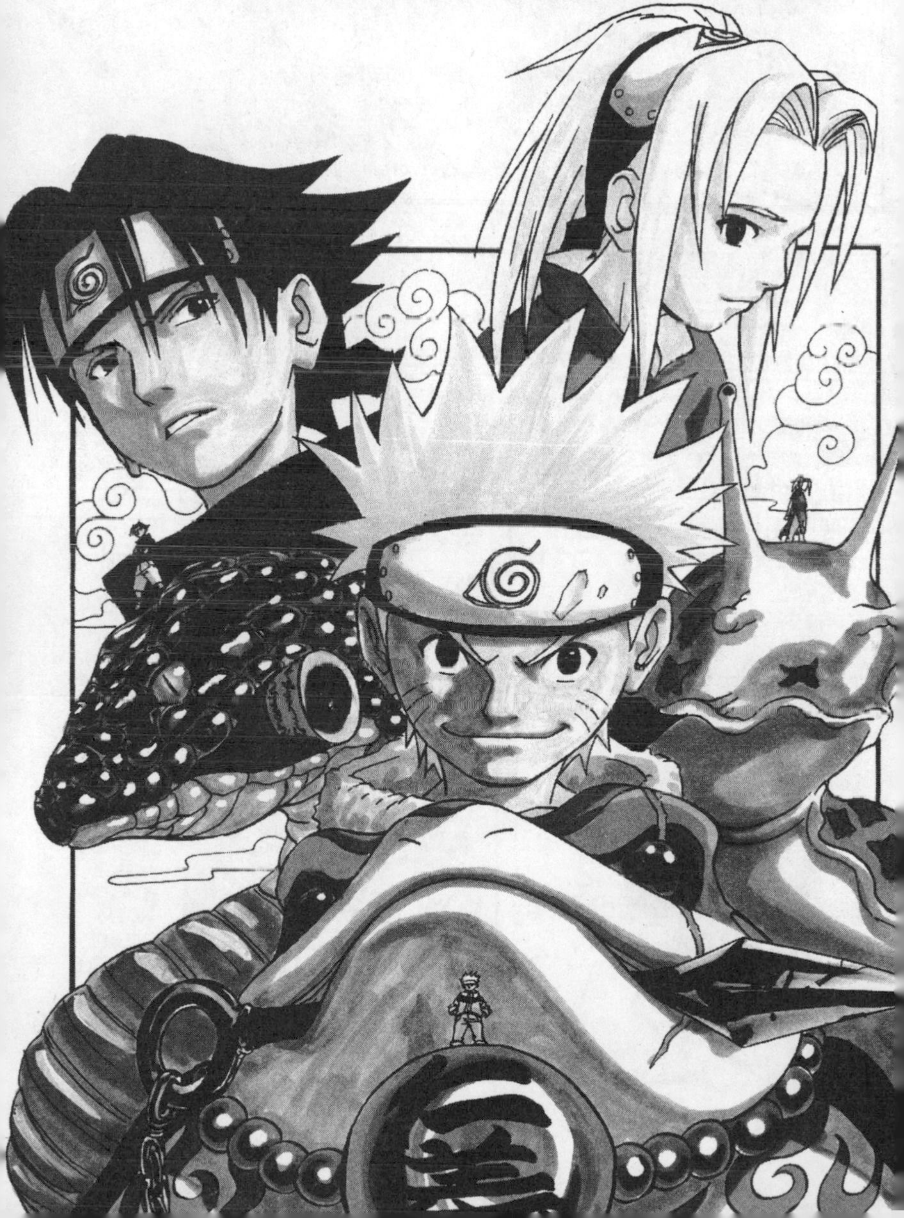

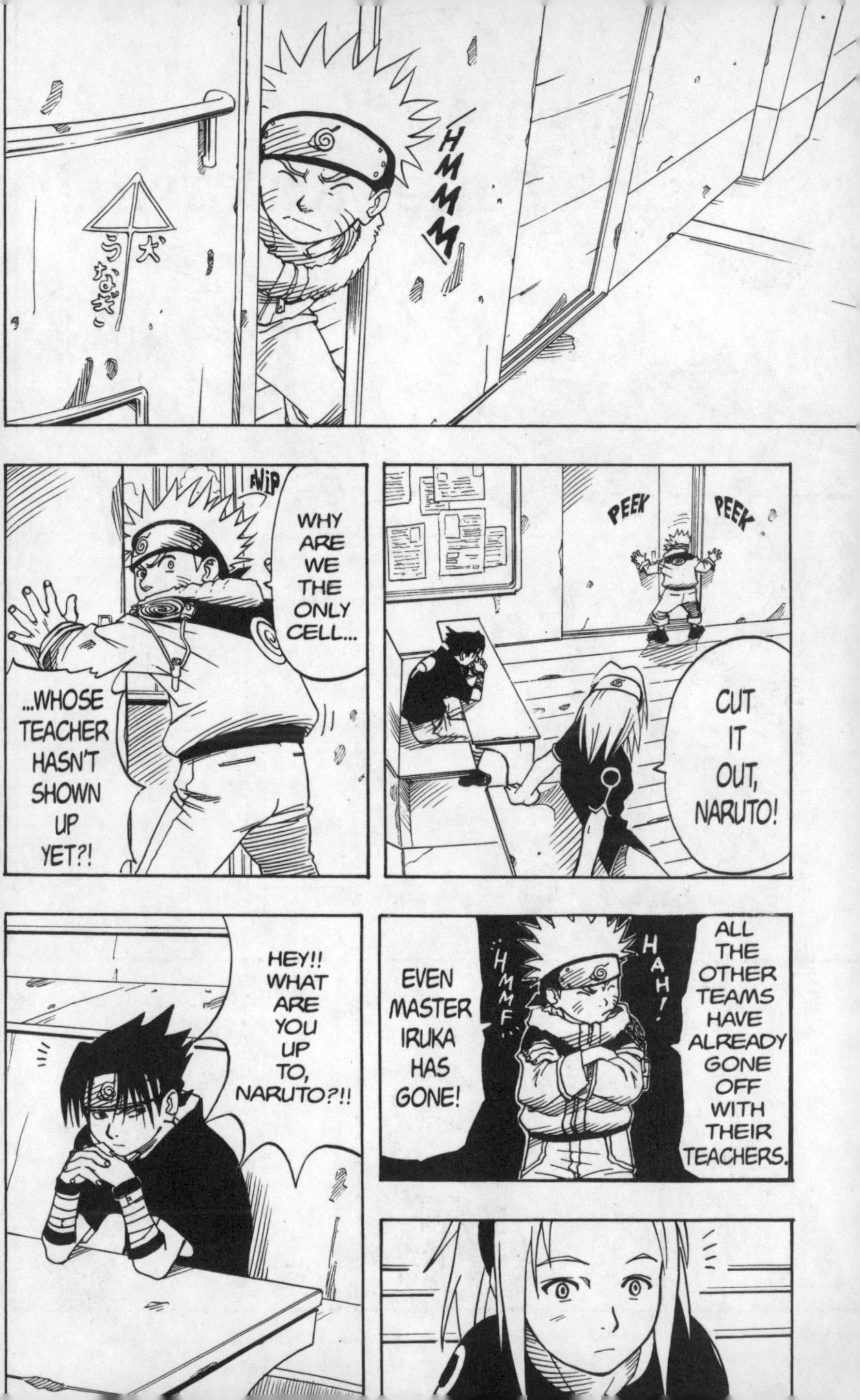
HMMM
犬
うなぎ
PEEK
PEEK
CUT IT OUT, NARUTO!
FWIP
WHY ARE WE THE ONLY CELL...
...WHOSE TEACHER HASN'T SHOWN UP YET?!
ALL THE OTHER TEAMS HAVE ALREADY GONE OFF WITH THEIR TEACHERS.
HAH!
HMMF
EVEN MASTER IRUKA HAS GONE!
HEY!! WHAT ARE YOU UP TO, NARUTO?!!

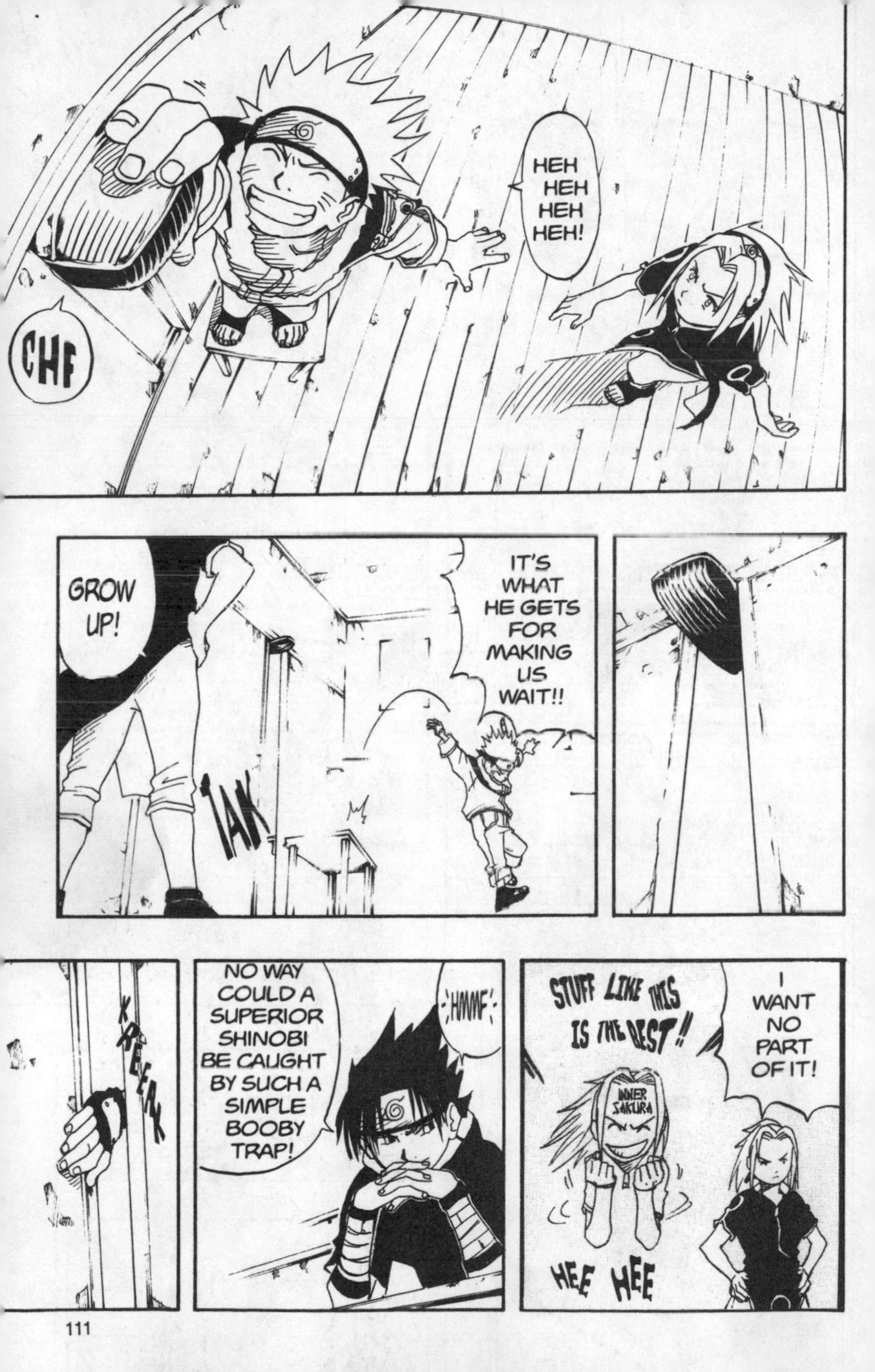
HEH HEH HEH HEH!
CHF
IT'S WHAT HE GETS FOR MAKING US WAIT!!
GROW UP!
TAK
I WANT NO PART OF IT!
STUFF LIKE THIS IS THE BEST!!
INNER SAKURA
HEE HEE
HMMF
NO WAY COULD A SUPERIOR SHINOBI BE CAUGHT BY SUCH A SIMPLE BOOBY TRAP!
KREEAK

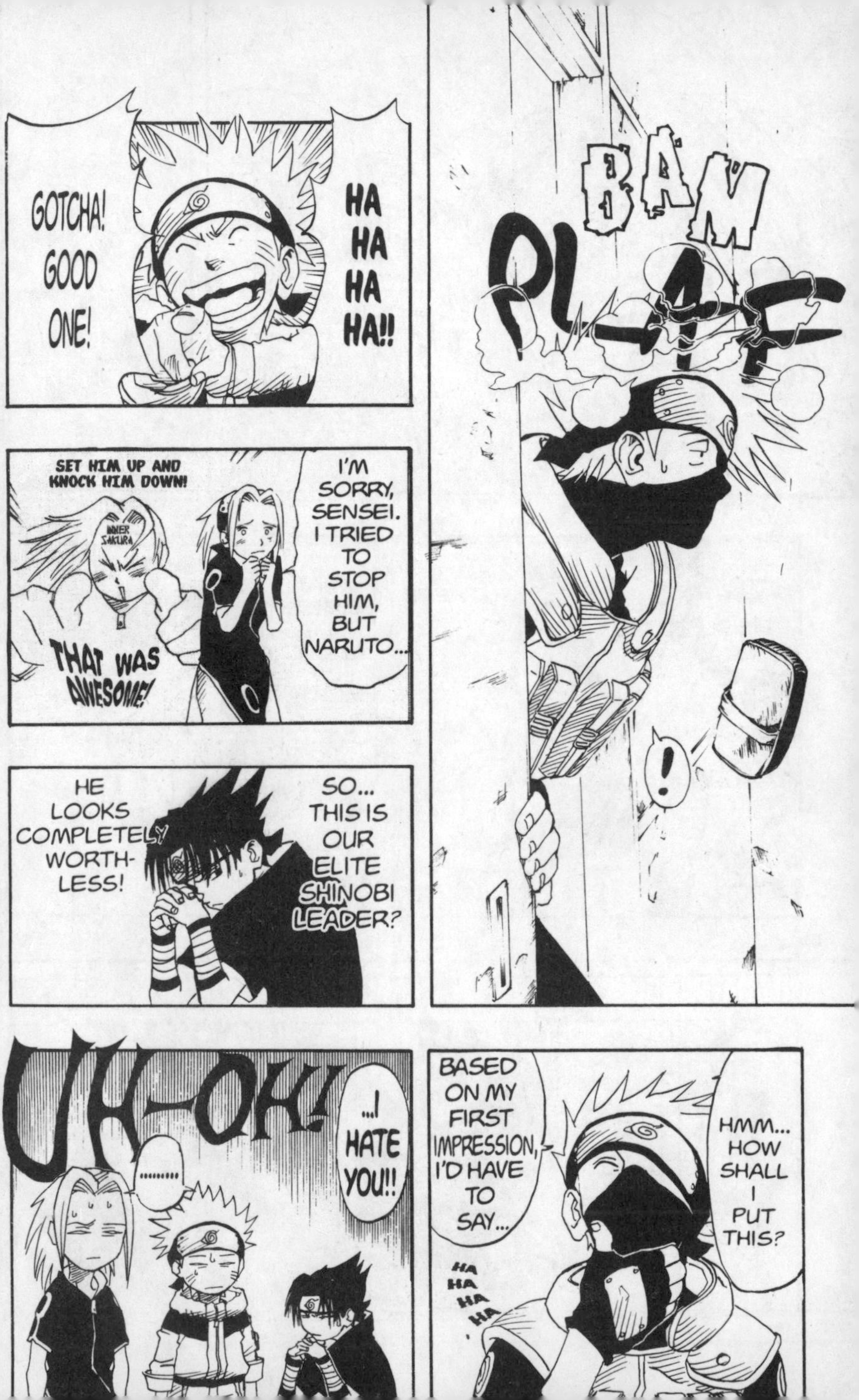
BAM
PLAF
!
HA HA HA HA!!
GOTCHA! GOOD ONE!
I'M SORRY, SENSEI. I TRIED TO STOP HIM, BUT NARUTO...
SET HIM UP AND KNOCK HIM DOWN!
INNER SAKURA
THAT WAS AWESOME!
SO... THIS IS OUR ELITE SHINOBI LEADER?
HE LOOKS COMPLETELY WORTHLESS!
HMM... HOW SHALL I PUT THIS?
BASED ON MY FIRST IMPRESSION, I'D HAVE TO SAY...
HA HA HA HA
...I HATE YOU!!
UH-OH!
....

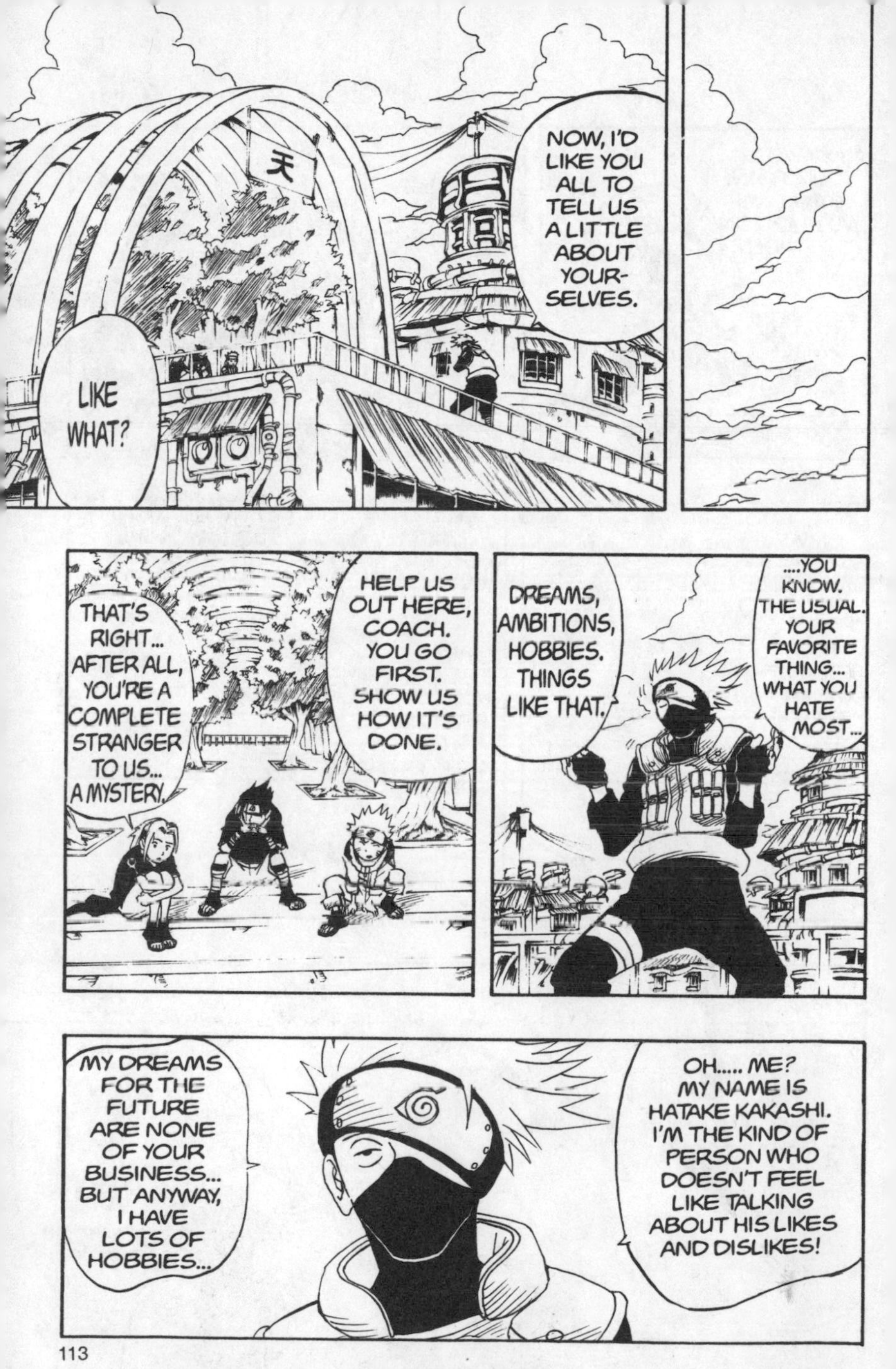

NOW, I'D LIKE YOU ALL TO TELL US A LITTLE ABOUT YOUR-SELVES.
LIKE WHAT?
....YOU KNOW. THE USUAL. YOUR FAVORITE THING... WHAT YOU HATE MOST...
DREAMS, AMBITIONS, HOBBIES. THINGS LIKE THAT.
HELP US OUT HERE, COACH. YOU GO FIRST. SHOW US HOW IT'S DONE.
THAT'S RIGHT... AFTER ALL, YOU'RE A COMPLETE STRANGER TO US... A MYSTERY.
OH..... ME? MY NAME IS HATAKE KAKASHI. I'M THE KIND OF PERSON WHO DOESN'T FEEL LIKE TALKING ABOUT HIS LIKES AND DISLIKES!
MY DREAMS FOR THE FUTURE ARE NONE OF YOUR BUSINESS... BUT ANYWAY, I HAVE LOTS OF HOBBIES...

READ THIS WAY

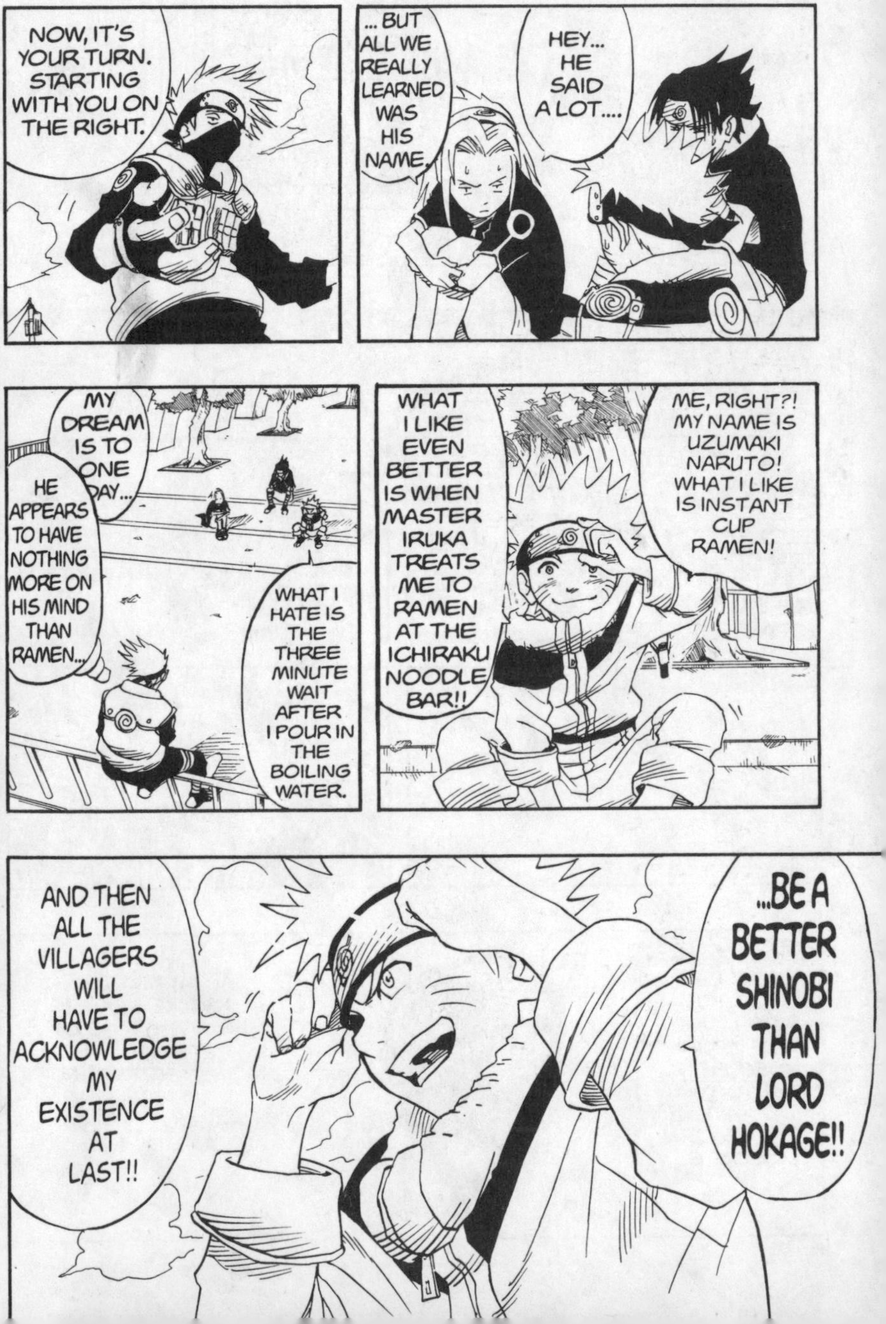
HEY... HE SAID A LOT....
... BUT ALL WE REALLY LEARNED WAS HIS NAME.
NOW, IT'S YOUR TURN. STARTING WITH YOU ON THE RIGHT.
ME, RIGHT?! MY NAME IS UZUMAKI NARUTO! WHAT I LIKE IS INSTANT CUP RAMEN!
WHAT I LIKE EVEN BETTER IS WHEN MASTER IRUKA TREATS ME TO RAMEN AT THE ICHIRAKU NOODLE BAR!!
WHAT I HATE IS THE THREE MINUTE WAIT AFTER I POUR IN THE BOILING WATER.
MY DREAM IS TO ONE DAY...
HE APPEARS TO HAVE NOTHING MORE ON HIS MIND THAN RAMEN...
...BE A BETTER SHINOBI THAN LORD HOKAGE!!
AND THEN ALL THE VILLAGERS WILL HAVE TO ACKNOWLEDGE MY EXISTENCE AT LAST!!

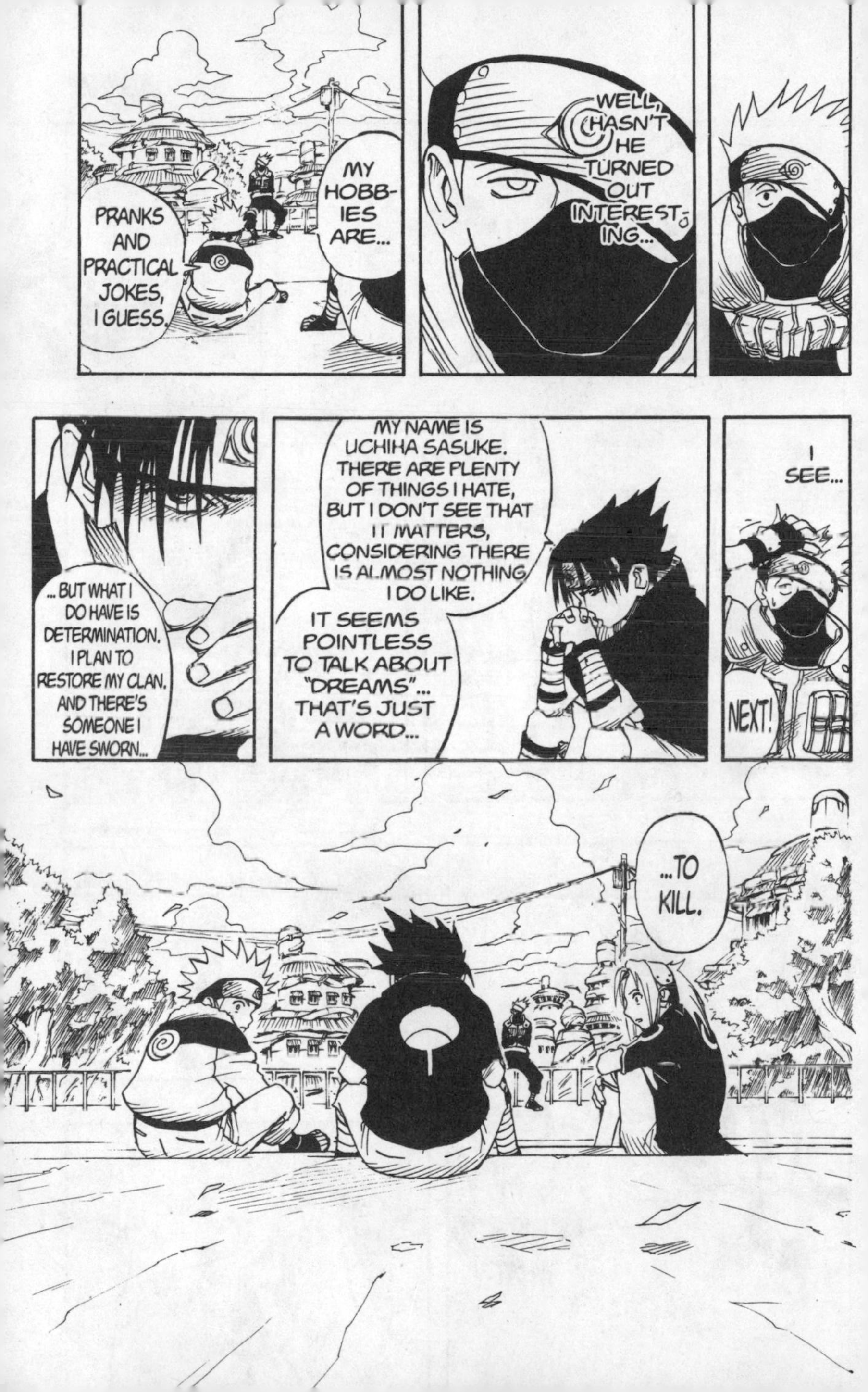
WELL, HASN'T HE TURNED OUT INTERESTING...
MY HOBBIES ARE...
PRANKS AND PRACTICAL JOKES, I GUESS.
I SEE...
NEXT!
MY NAME IS UCHIHA SASUKE. THERE ARE PLENTY OF THINGS I HATE, BUT I DON'T SEE THAT IT MATTERS, CONSIDERING THERE IS ALMOST NOTHING I DO LIKE.
IT SEEMS POINTLESS TO TALK ABOUT "DREAMS"... THAT'S JUST A WORD...
...BUT WHAT I DO HAVE IS DETERMINATION. I PLAN TO RESTORE MY CLAN. AND THERE'S SOMEONE I HAVE SWORN...
...TO KILL.

READ THIS WAY

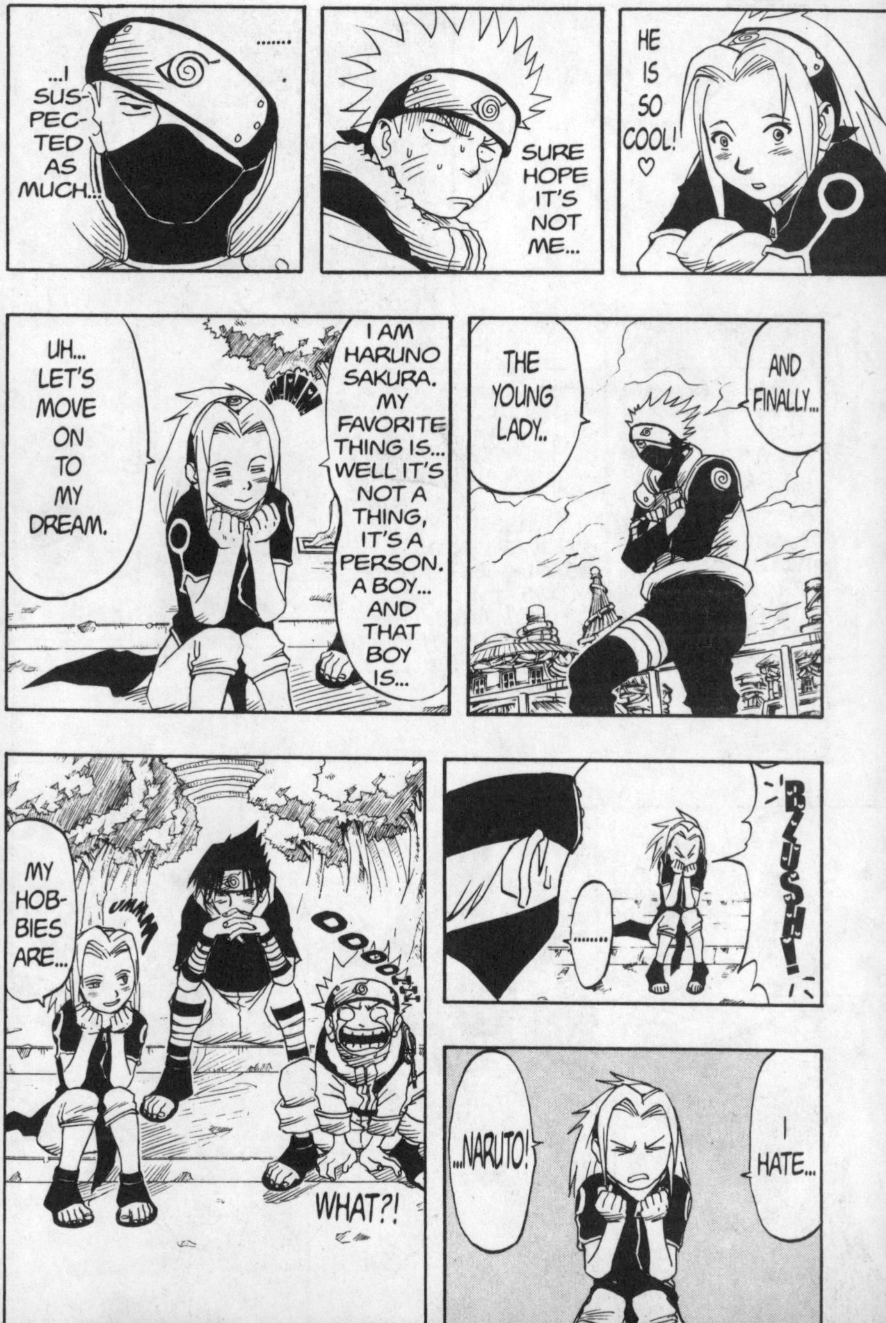

HE IS SO COOL! ♡
SURE HOPE IT'S NOT ME...
....
...I SUS-PEC-TED AS MUCH...
AND FINALLY...
THE YOUNG LADY..
I AM HARUNO SAKURA. MY FAVORITE THING IS... WELL IT'S NOT A THING, IT'S A PERSON. A BOY... AND THAT BOY IS...
UH... LET'S MOVE ON TO MY DREAM.
BLUSH!
....
I HATE...
...NARUTO!
MY HOB-BIES ARE...
UMMM
DOOOO?!!
WHAT?!

READ THIS WAY

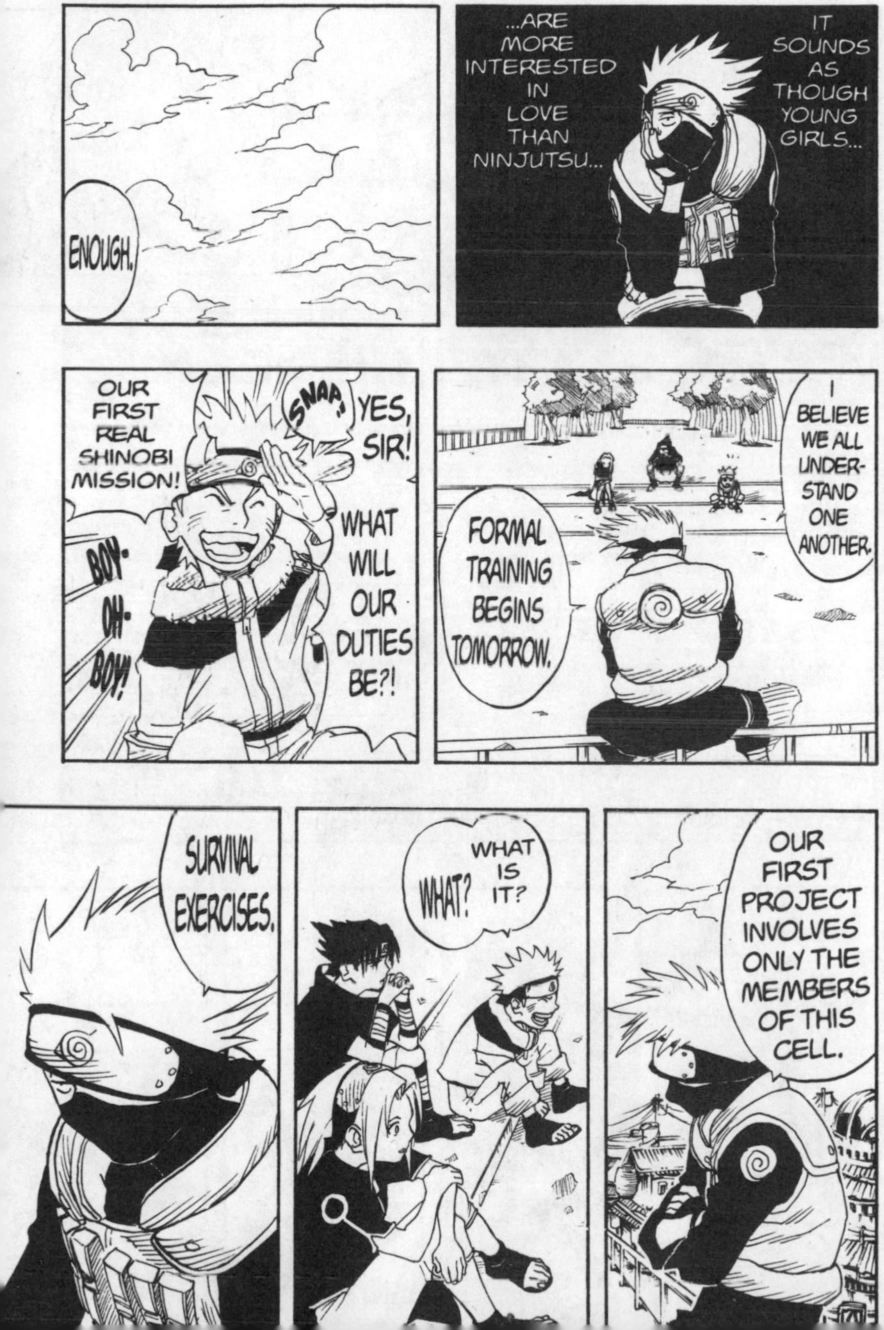

IT SOUNDS AS THOUGH YOUNG GIRLS...
...ARE MORE INTERESTED IN LOVE THAN NINJUTSU...
ENOUGH.
I BELIEVE WE ALL UNDERSTAND ONE ANOTHER.
FORMAL TRAINING BEGINS TOMORROW.
SNAP!
YES, SIR!
OUR FIRST REAL SHINOBI MISSION!
WHAT WILL OUR DUTIES BE?!
BOY-OH-BOY!
OUR FIRST PROJECT INVOLVES ONLY THE MEMBERS OF THIS CELL.
WHAT IS IT?
WHAT?
SURVIVAL EXERCISES.

READ THIS WAY

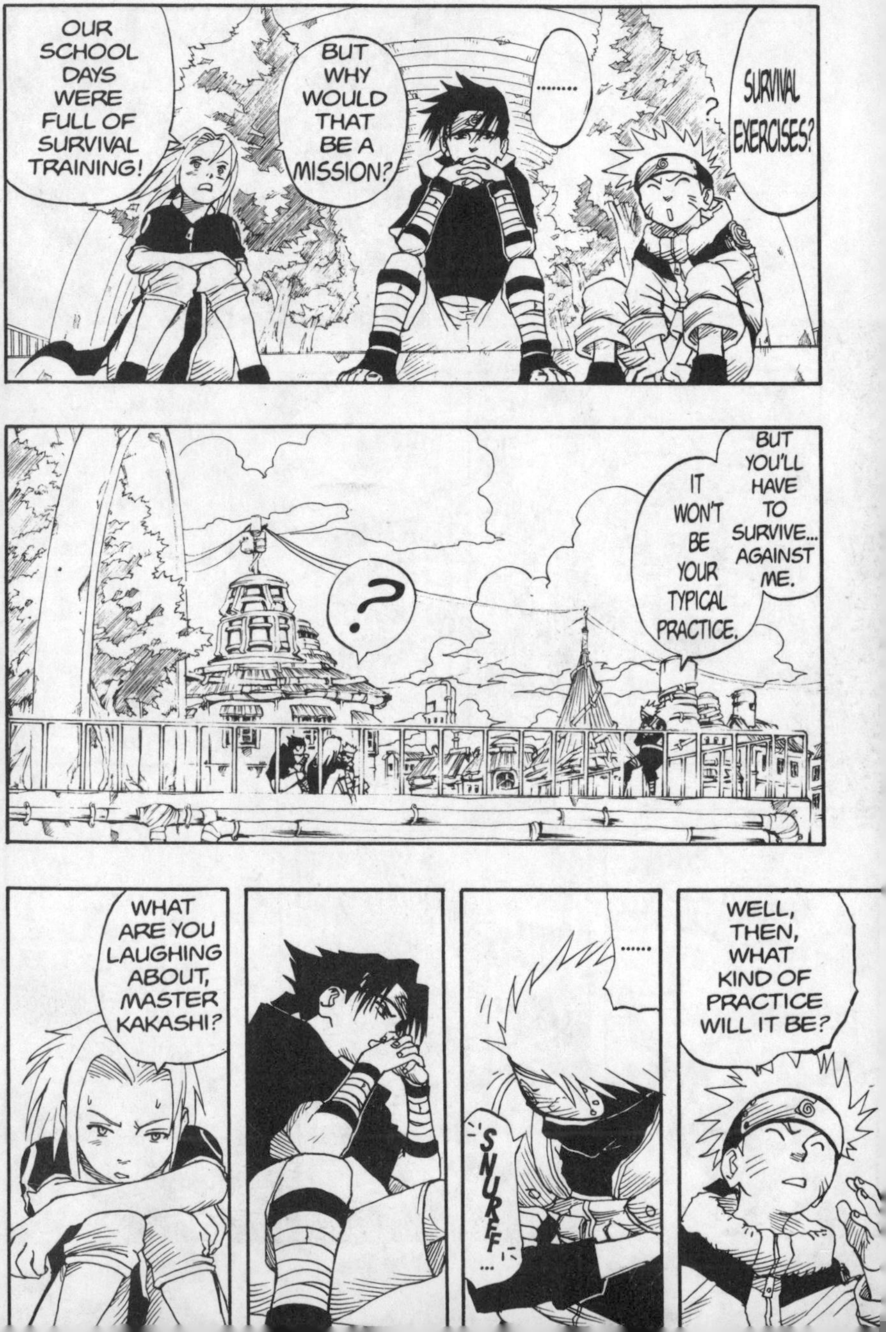
SURVIVAL EXERCISES?
?
....
BUT WHY WOULD THAT BE A MISSION?
OUR SCHOOL DAYS WERE FULL OF SURVIVAL TRAINING!
BUT YOU'LL HAVE TO SURVIVE... AGAINST ME.
IT WON'T BE YOUR TYPICAL PRACTICE.
?
WELL, THEN, WHAT KIND OF PRACTICE WILL IT BE?
......
SNURFF...
WHAT ARE YOU LAUGHING ABOUT, MASTER KAKASHI?

READ THIS WAY

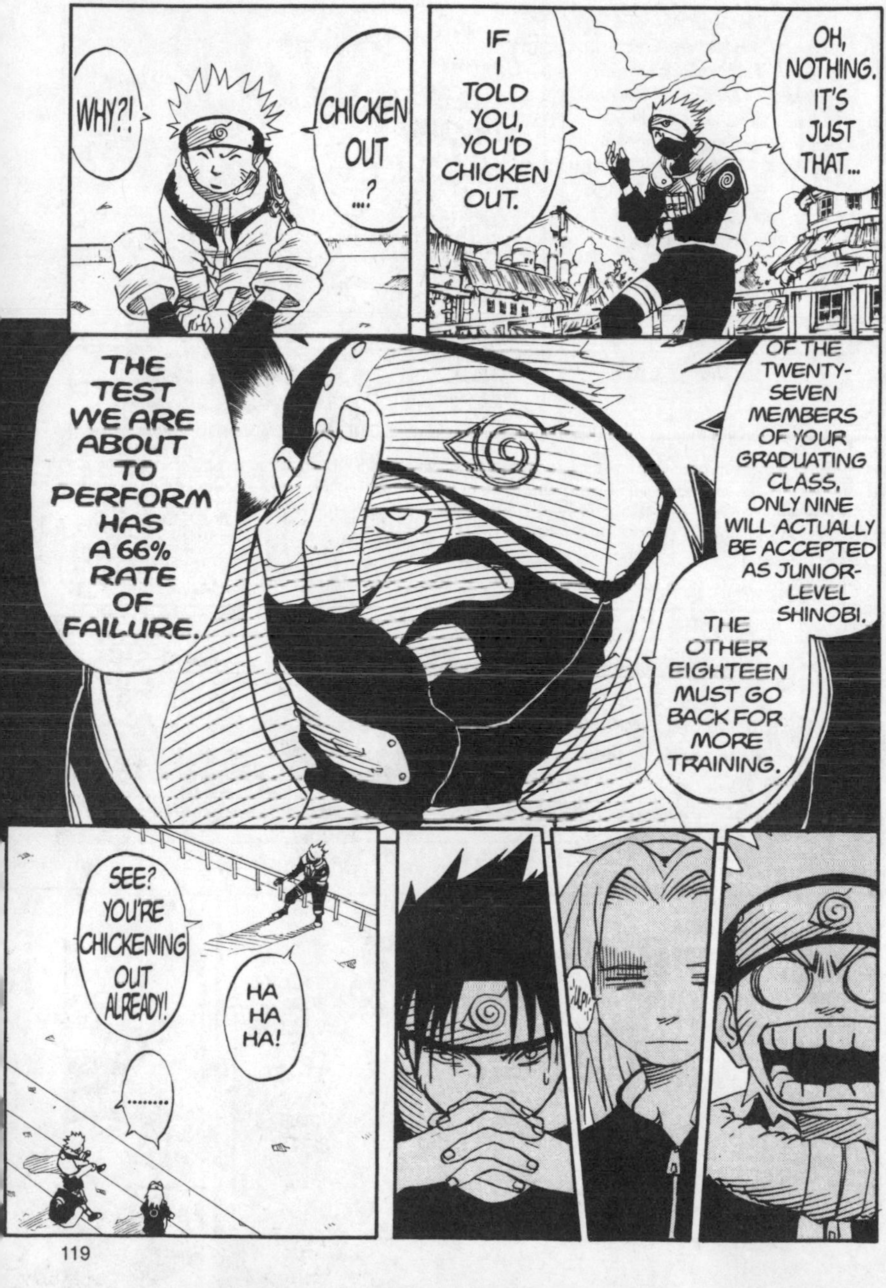
OH, NOTHING. IT'S JUST THAT...
IF I TOLD YOU, YOU'D CHICKEN OUT.
CHICKEN OUT ...?
WHY?!
OF THE TWENTY-SEVEN MEMBERS OF YOUR GRADUATING CLASS, ONLY NINE WILL ACTUALLY BE ACCEPTED AS JUNIOR-LEVEL SHINOBI.
THE OTHER EIGHTEEN MUST GO BACK FOR MORE TRAINING.
THE TEST WE ARE ABOUT TO PERFORM HAS A 66% RATE OF FAILURE.
GULP!
SEE? YOU'RE CHICKENING OUT ALREADY!
HA HA HA!
....

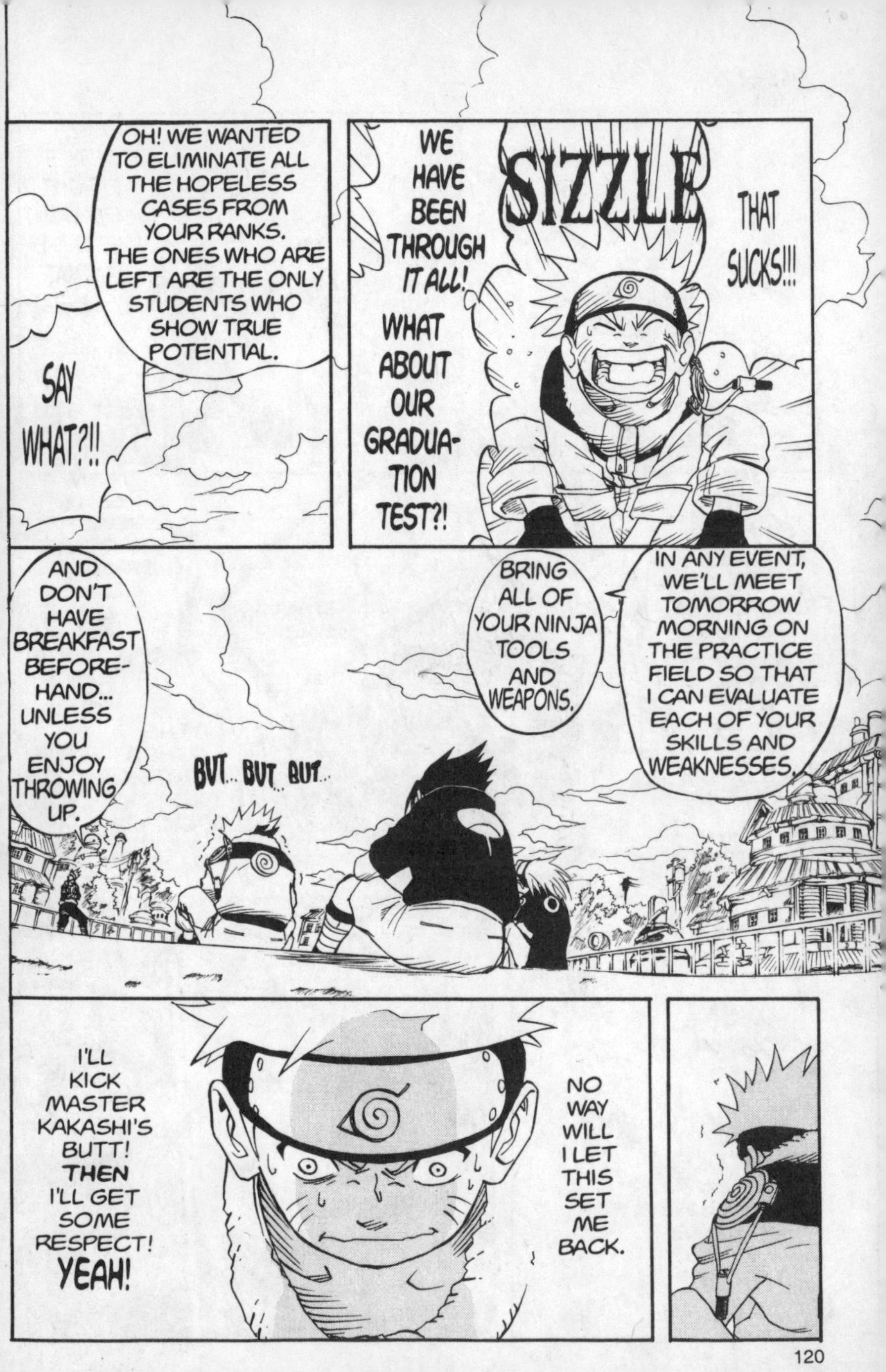
SIZZLE
THAT SUCKS!!!
WE HAVE BEEN THROUGH IT ALL! WHAT ABOUT OUR GRADUATION TEST?!
OH! WE WANTED TO ELIMINATE ALL THE HOPELESS CASES FROM YOUR RANKS. THE ONES WHO ARE LEFT ARE THE ONLY STUDENTS WHO SHOW TRUE POTENTIAL.
SAY WHAT?!!
IN ANY EVENT, WE'LL MEET TOMORROW MORNING ON THE PRACTICE FIELD SO THAT I CAN EVALUATE EACH OF YOUR SKILLS AND WEAKNESSES.
BRING ALL OF YOUR NINJA TOOLS AND WEAPONS.
AND DON'T HAVE BREAKFAST BEFOREHAND... UNLESS YOU ENJOY THROWING UP.
BUT... BUT BUT...
NO WAY WILL I LET THIS SET ME BACK.
I'LL KICK MASTER KAKASHI'S BUTT! THEN I'LL GET SOME RESPECT! YEAH!

READ THIS WAY

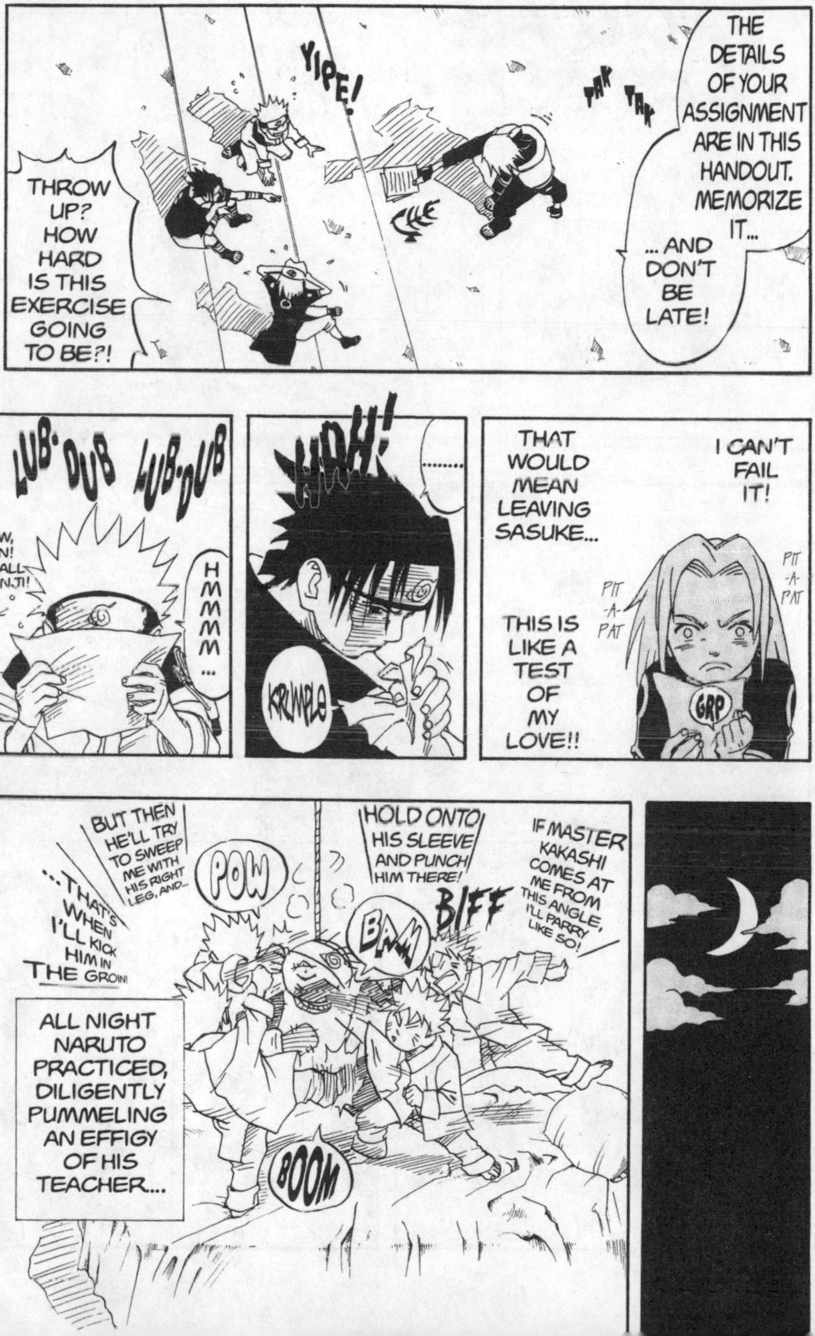
THE DETAILS OF YOUR ASSIGNMENT ARE IN THIS HANDOUT. MEMORIZE IT...
...AND DON'T BE LATE!
TAK TAK
YIPE!
THROW UP? HOW HARD IS THIS EXERCISE GOING TO BE?!
I CAN'T FAIL IT!
PIT -A- PAT
PIT -A- PAT
THAT WOULD MEAN LEAVING SASUKE...
THIS IS LIKE A TEST OF MY LOVE!!
GRP
....
KRUMPLE
LUB-DUB LUB-DUB
HMMMM...
AWW, MAN! IT'S ALL IN KANJI!
IF MASTER KAKASHI COMES AT ME FROM THIS ANGLE, I'LL PARRY LIKE SO!
HOLD ONTO HIS SLEEVE AND PUNCH HIM THERE!
BUT THEN HE'LL TRY TO SWEEP ME WITH HIS RIGHT LEG, AND...
...THAT'S WHEN I'LL KICK HIM IN THE GROIN!
BIFF
BAM
POW
ALL NIGHT NARUTO PRACTICED, DILIGENTLY PUMMELING AN EFFIGY OF HIS TEACHER...
BOOM

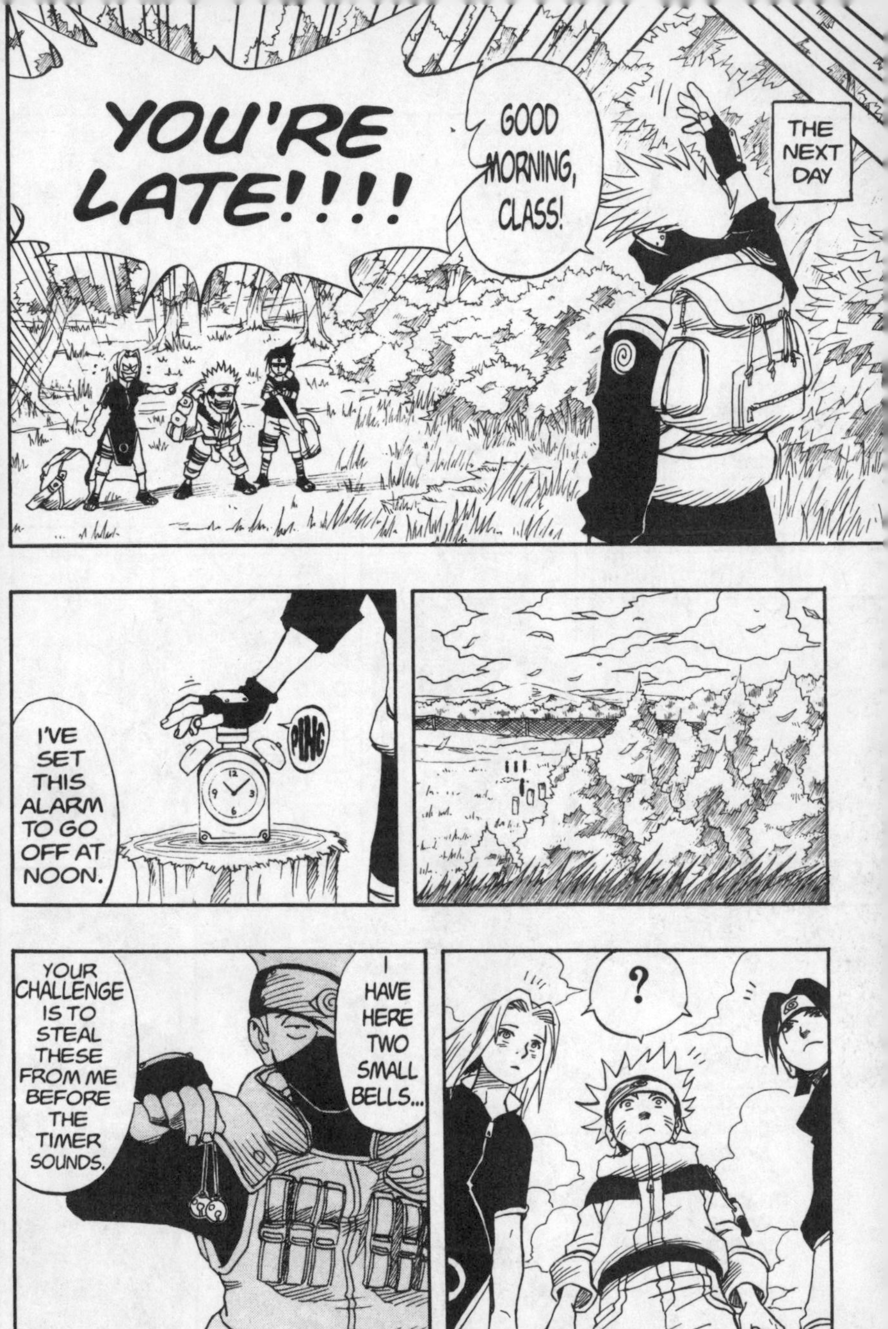
THE NEXT DAY
GOOD MORNING, CLASS!
YOU'RE LATE!!!!
I'VE SET THIS ALARM TO GO OFF AT NOON.
?
I HAVE HERE TWO SMALL BELLS...
YOUR CHALLENGE IS TO STEAL THESE FROM ME BEFORE THE TIMER SOUNDS.

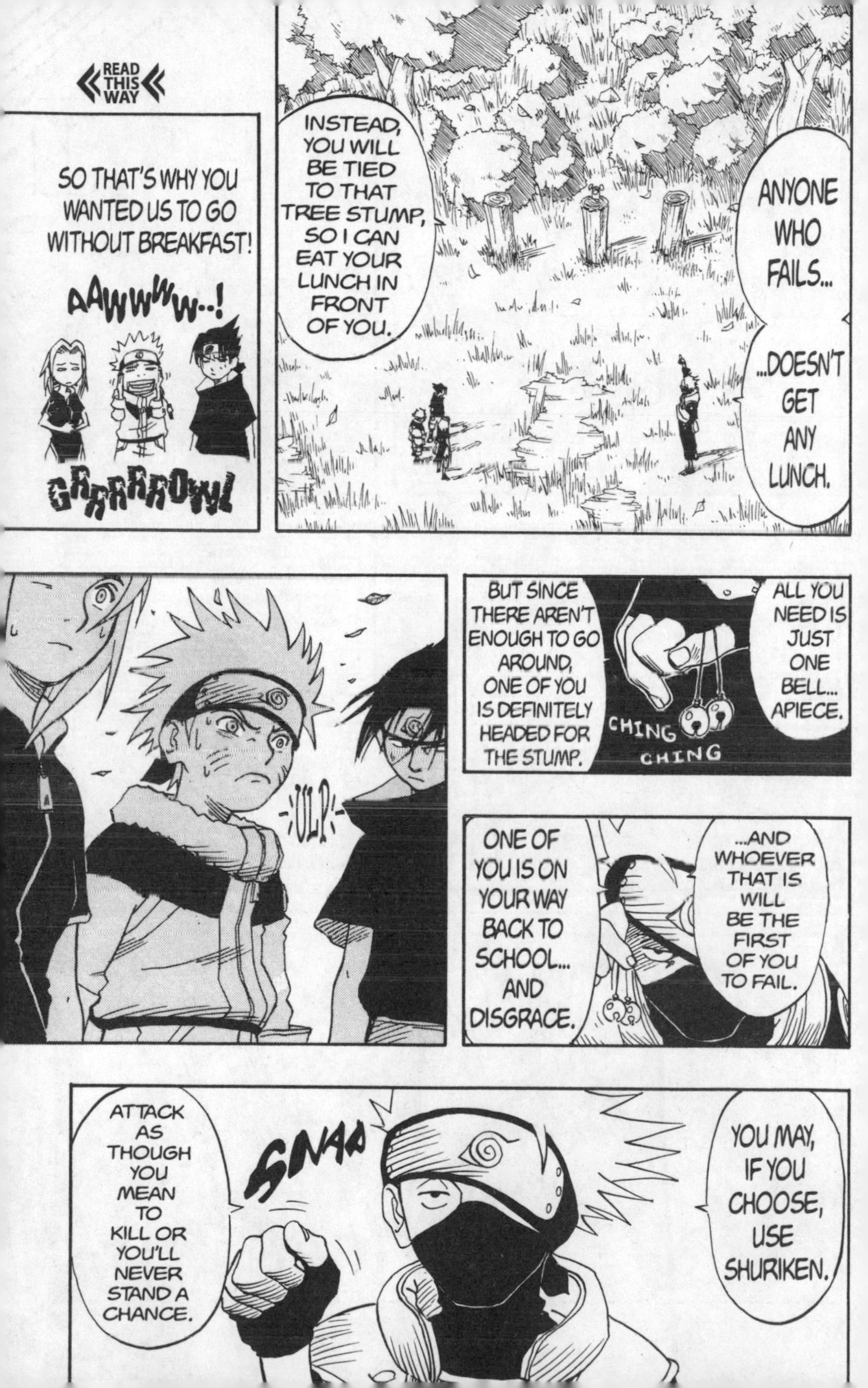
READ THIS WAY
ANYONE WHO FAILS...
...DOESN'T GET ANY LUNCH.
INSTEAD, YOU WILL BE TIED TO THAT TREE STUMP, SO I CAN EAT YOUR LUNCH IN FRONT OF YOU.
SO THAT'S WHY YOU WANTED US TO GO WITHOUT BREAKFAST!
AAWWWW..!
GRRRRROWL!
ALL YOU NEED IS JUST ONE BELL... APIECE.
CHING
CHING
BUT SINCE THERE AREN'T ENOUGH TO GO AROUND, ONE OF YOU IS DEFINITELY HEADED FOR THE STUMP.
...AND WHOEVER THAT IS WILL BE THE FIRST OF YOU TO FAIL.
ONE OF YOU IS ON YOUR WAY BACK TO SCHOOL... AND DISGRACE.
ULP
YOU MAY, IF YOU CHOOSE, USE SHURIKEN.
ATTACK AS THOUGH YOU MEAN TO KILL OR YOU'LL NEVER STAND A CHANCE.

READ THIS WAY

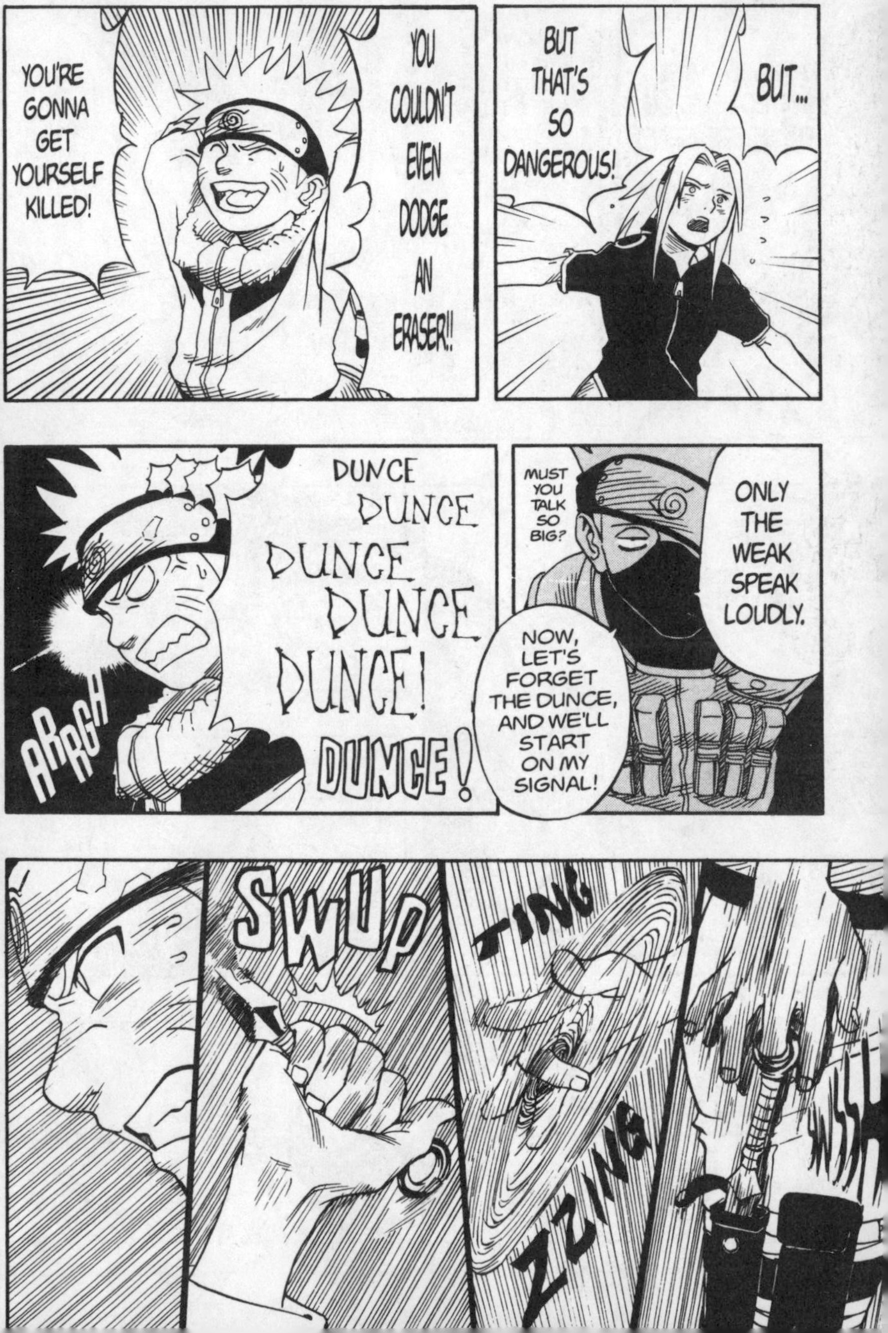
BUT...
BUT THAT'S SO DANGEROUS!
YOU COULDN'T EVEN DODGE AN ERASER!!
YOU'RE GONNA GET YOURSELF KILLED!
ONLY THE WEAK SPEAK LOUDLY.
MUST YOU TALK SO BIG?
NOW, LET'S FORGET THE DUNCE, AND WE'LL START ON MY SIGNAL!
DUNCE
DUNCE
DUNCE
DUNCE
DUNCE!
DUNCE!
ARRGH
WSSH
ZZING
TING
SWUP

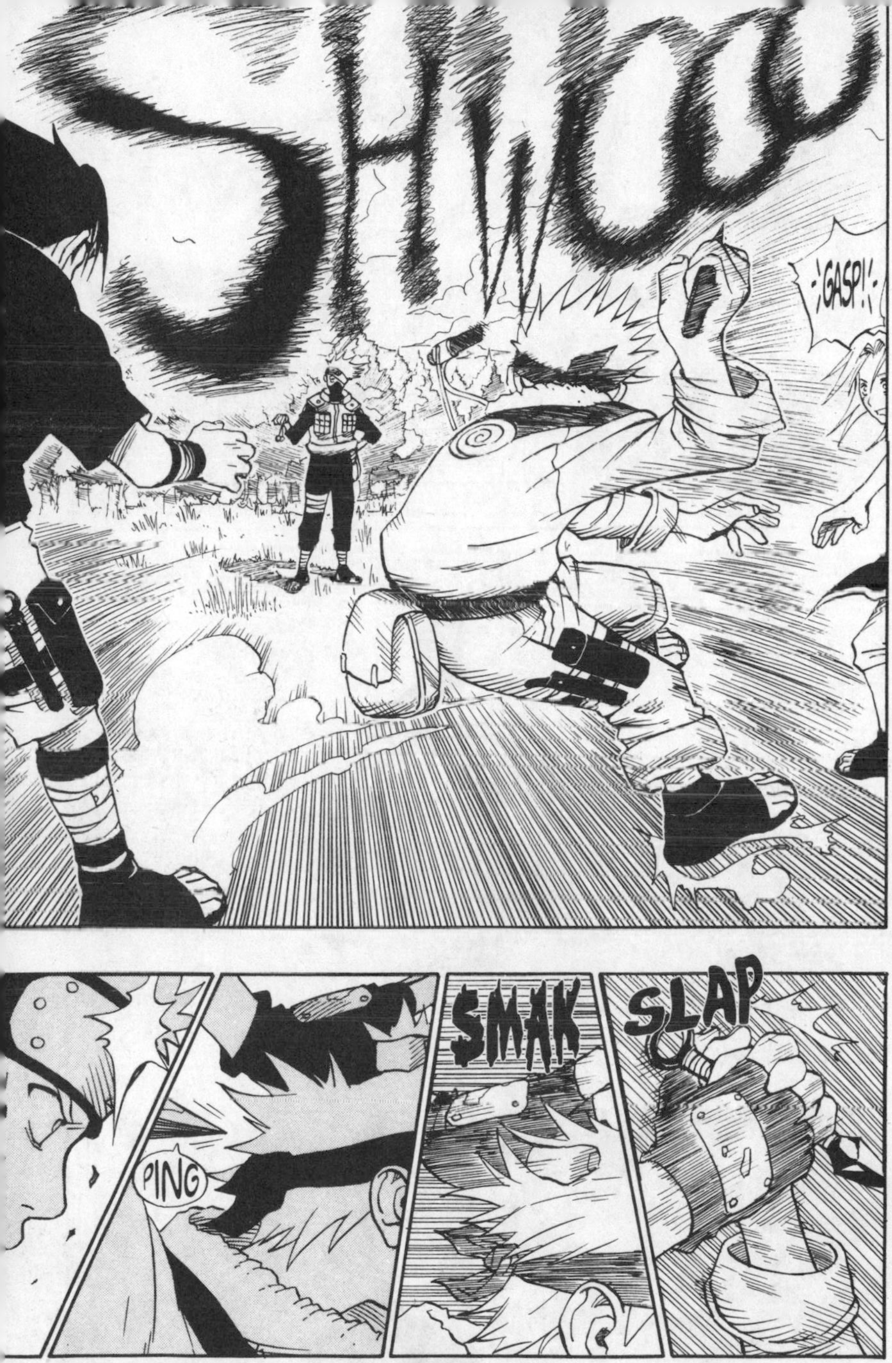
SHWOOSH
¡GASP!
SLAP
SMAK
PING

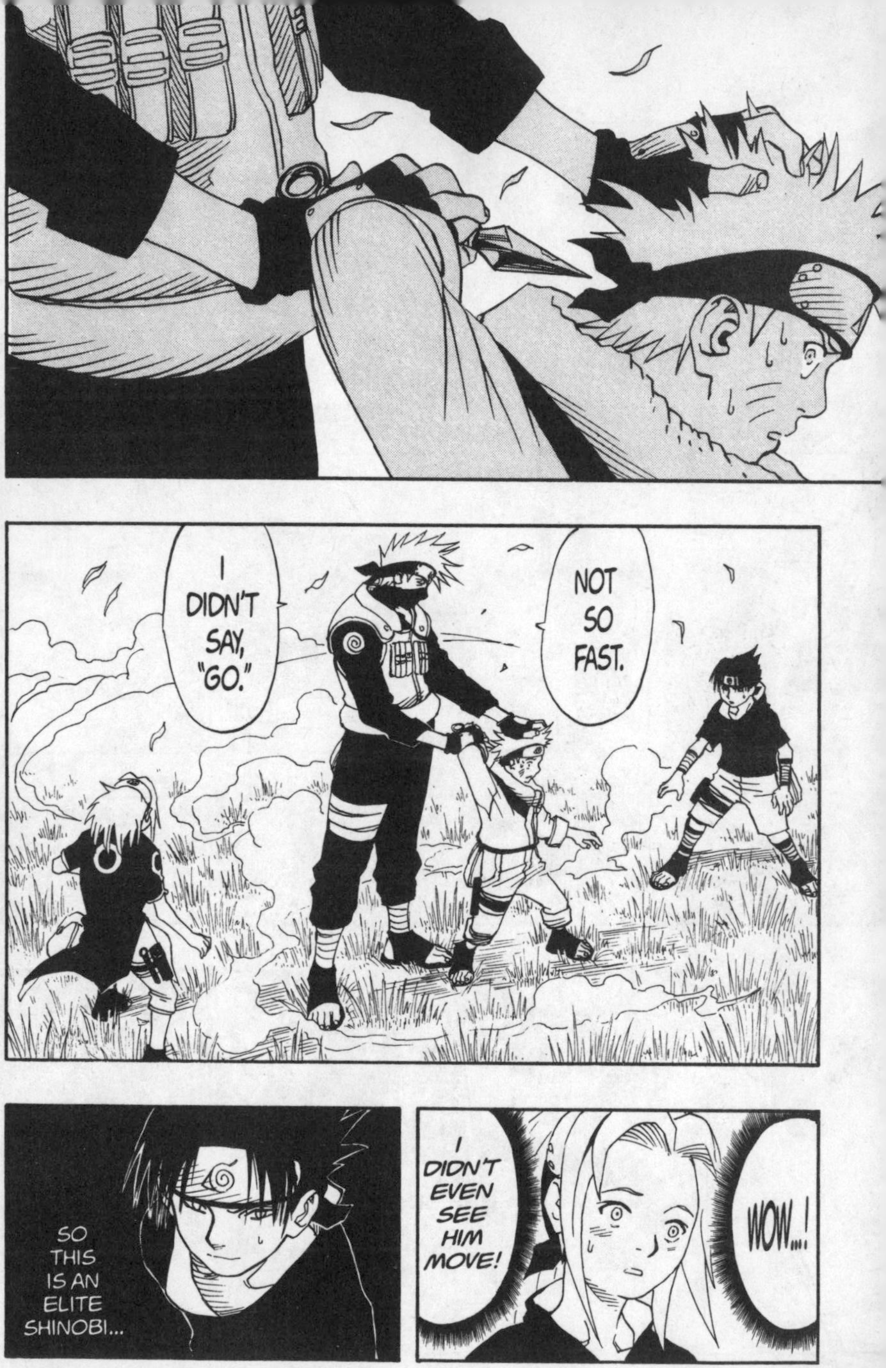
NOT SO FAST.
I DIDN'T SAY, "GO."
WOW...!
I DIDN'T EVEN SEE HIM MOVE!
SO THIS IS AN ELITE SHINOBI...

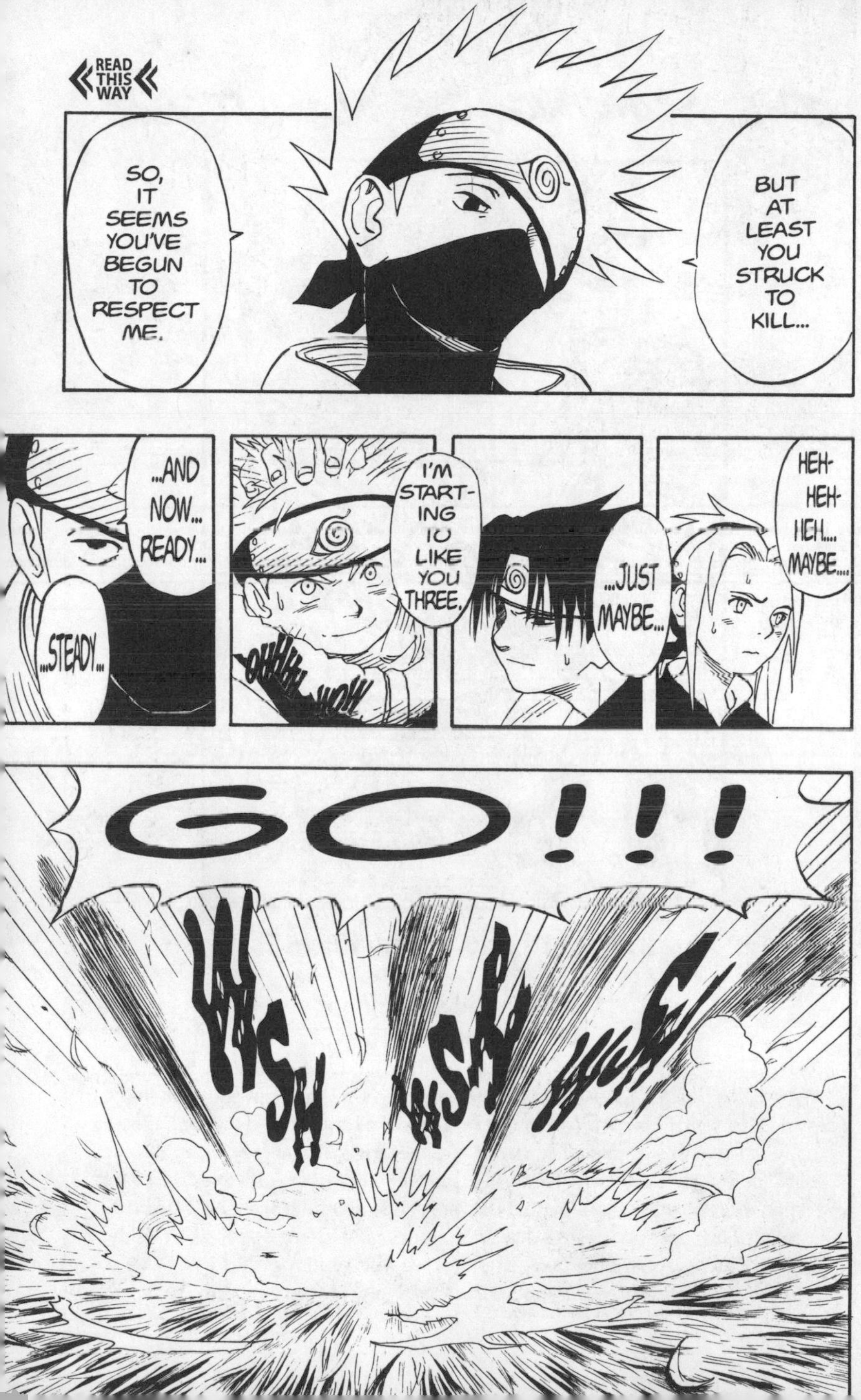
READ THIS WAY
BUT AT LEAST YOU STRUCK TO KILL...
SO, IT SEEMS YOU'VE BEGUN TO RESPECT ME.
HEH-HEH-HEH... MAYBE...
...JUST MAYBE...
I'M STARTING TO LIKE YOU THREE.
...AND NOW... READY...
...STEADY...
GO!!!

THE MAKING OF NARUTO!!!

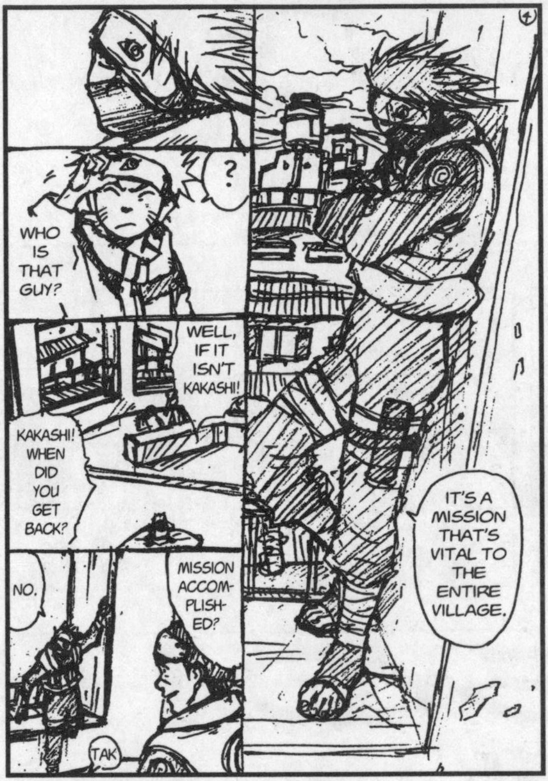
IT'S A MISSION THAT'S VITAL TO THE ENTIRE VILLAGE.
?
WHO IS THAT GUY?
WELL, IF IT ISN'T KAKASHI!
KAKASHI! WHEN DID YOU GET BACK?
MISSION ACCOMPLISHED?
NO.
TAK

The Kakashi That Might Have Been

The Rejected Outline for the Second Chapter

My original plan for Kakashi's first appearance was to have him show up in the second chapter of **Naruto** (see **page #61**). He was meant to be a cool, affected, upper-level ninja who ended sentences (in the original Japanese) with the very polite "*de gozaru*" verb form. This was going to be before Sakura and Sasuke had been introduced. Kakashi would suddenly appear on the scene as Naruto's teacher. This idea was discarded after a discussion with my editor at **Weekly Shonen Jump**. As an outgrowth of things we discussed together, I was able to flesh out Kakashi, Sasuke, and Sakura into the characters they are today.

number 5:

Pride Goeth Before a Fall

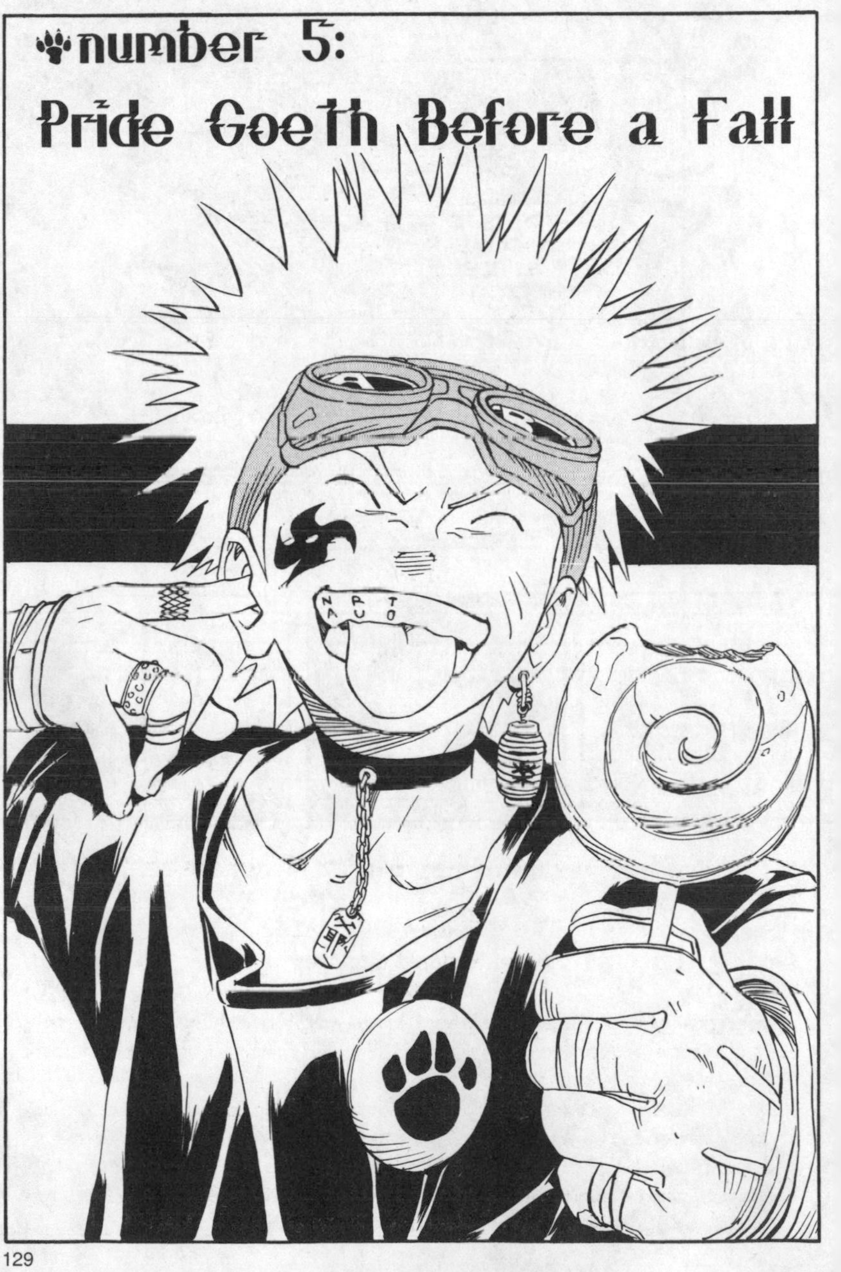

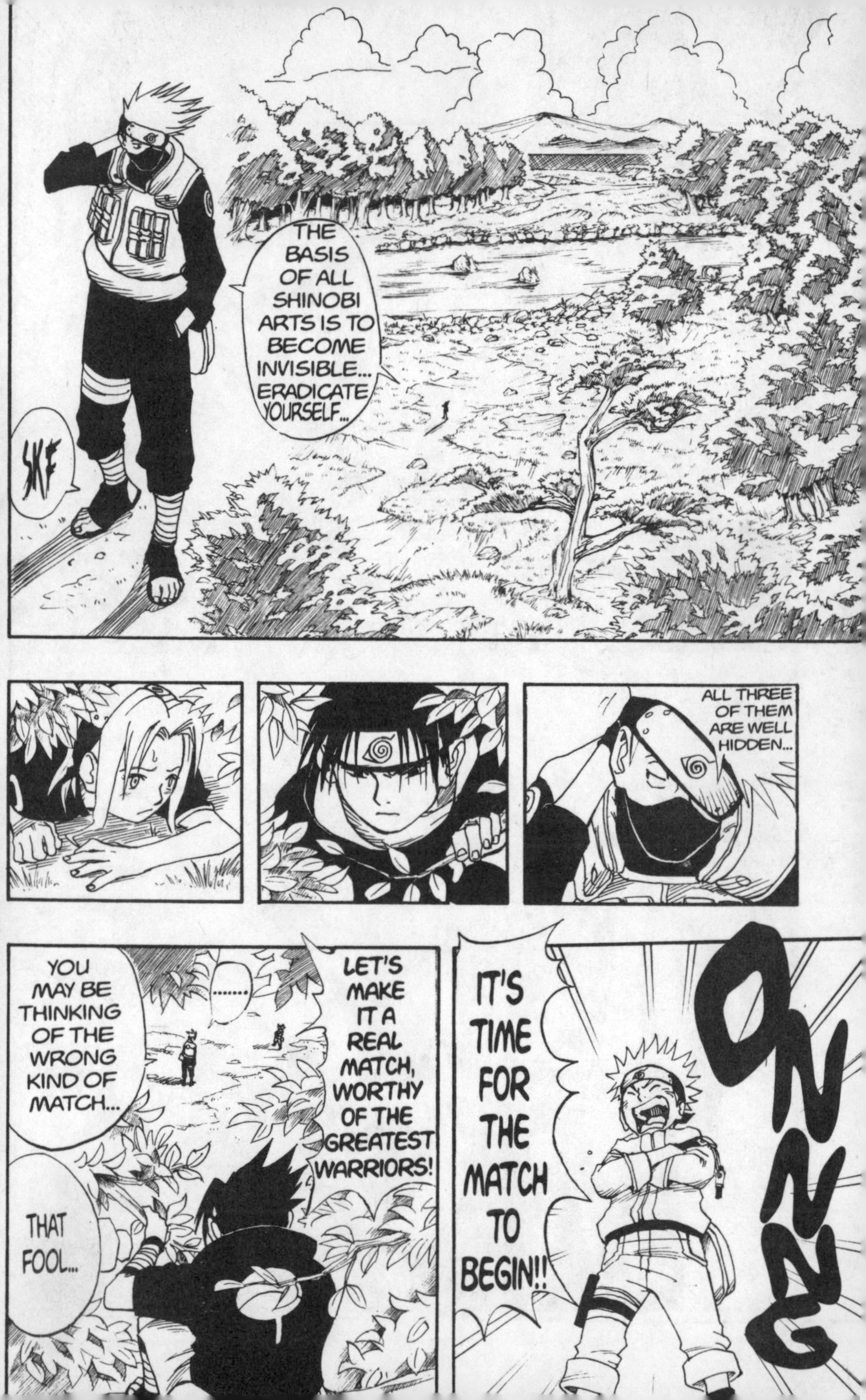
THE BASIS OF ALL SHINOBI ARTS IS TO BECOME INVISIBLE... ERADICATE YOURSELF...
SKF
ALL THREE OF THEM ARE WELL HIDDEN...
ONNNG
IT'S TIME FOR THE MATCH TO BEGIN!!
LET'S MAKE IT A REAL MATCH, WORTHY OF THE GREATEST WARRIORS!
....
YOU MAY BE THINKING OF THE WRONG KIND OF MATCH...
THAT FOOL...

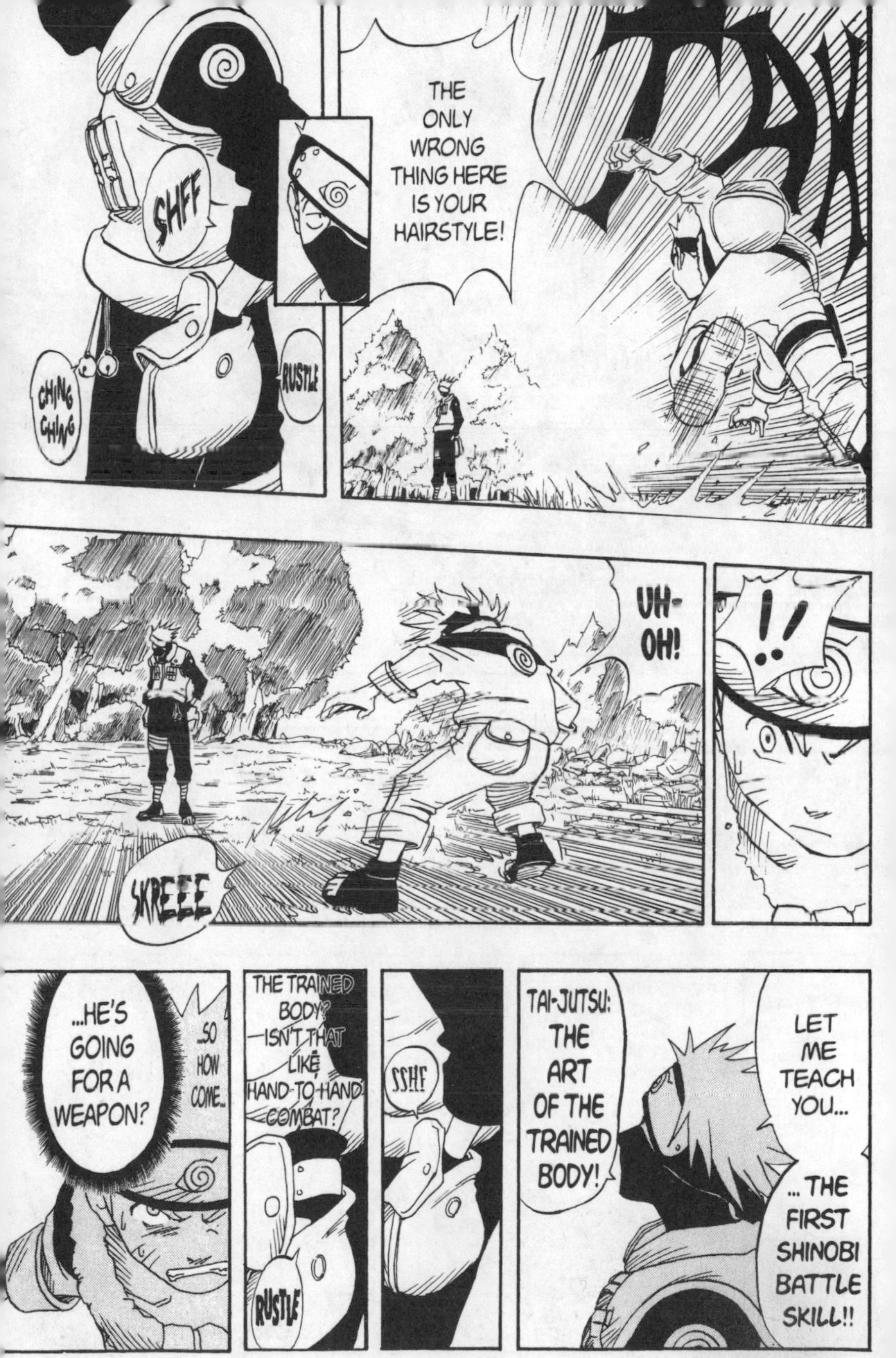

TAH
THE ONLY WRONG THING HERE IS YOUR HAIRSTYLE!
SHFF
RUSTLE
CHING CHING
!!
UH-OH!
SKREEE
LET ME TEACH YOU...
... THE FIRST SHINOBI BATTLE SKILL!!
TAI-JUTSU: THE ART OF THE TRAINED BODY!
SSHF
THE TRAINED BODY? ISN'T THAT LIKE, HAND-TO-HAND COMBAT?
RUSTLE
...SO HOW COME...
...HE'S GOING FOR A WEAPON?

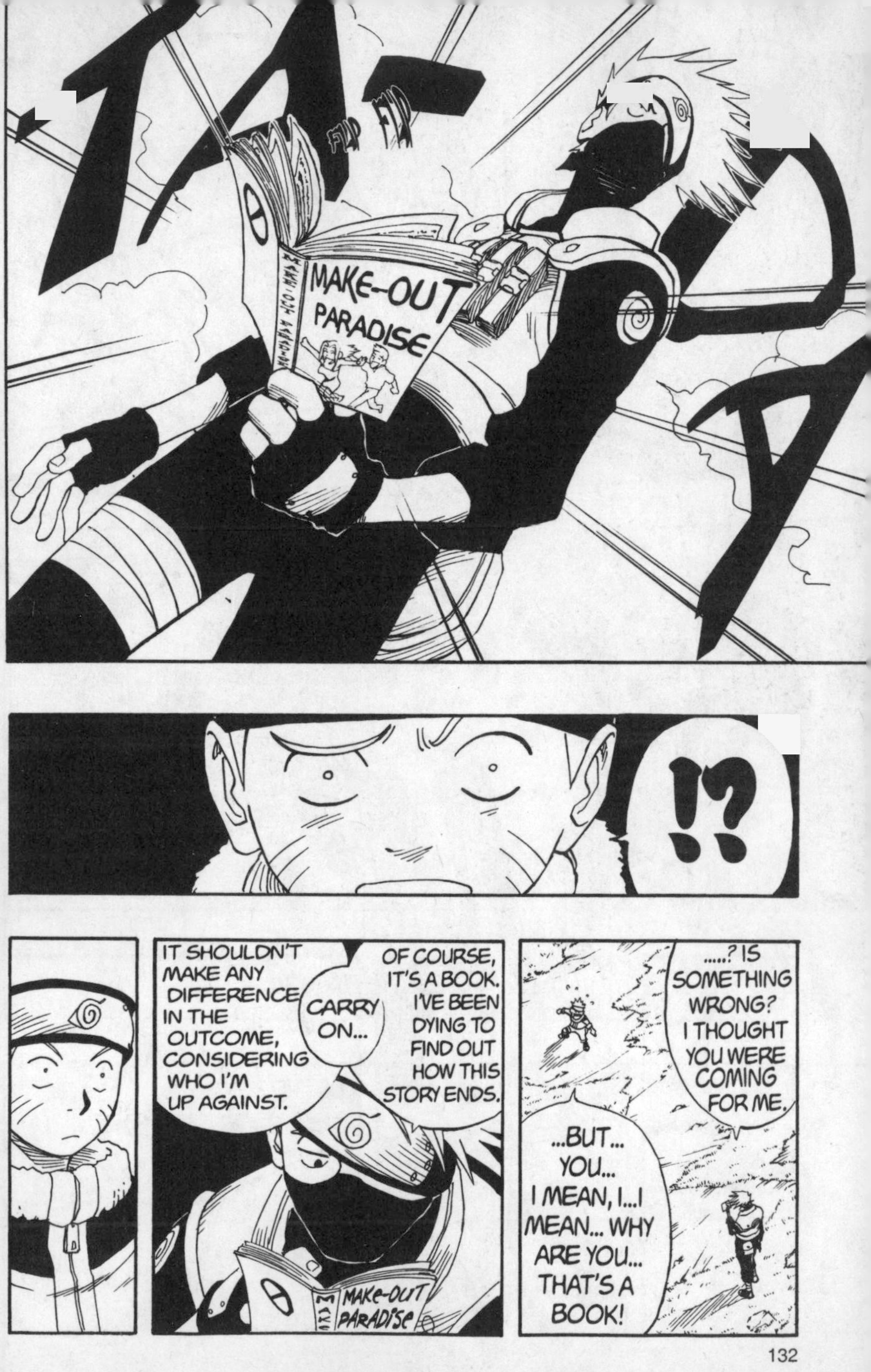
FLIP FLIP
MAKE-OUT PARADISE
!?
.....? IS SOMETHING WRONG? I THOUGHT YOU WERE COMING FOR ME.
...BUT... YOU... I MEAN, I...I MEAN... WHY ARE YOU... THAT'S A BOOK!
OF COURSE, IT'S A BOOK. I'VE BEEN DYING TO FIND OUT HOW THIS STORY ENDS.
CARRY ON...
IT SHOULDN'T MAKE ANY DIFFERENCE IN THE OUTCOME, CONSIDERING WHO I'M UP AGAINST.
MAKE-OUT PARADISE

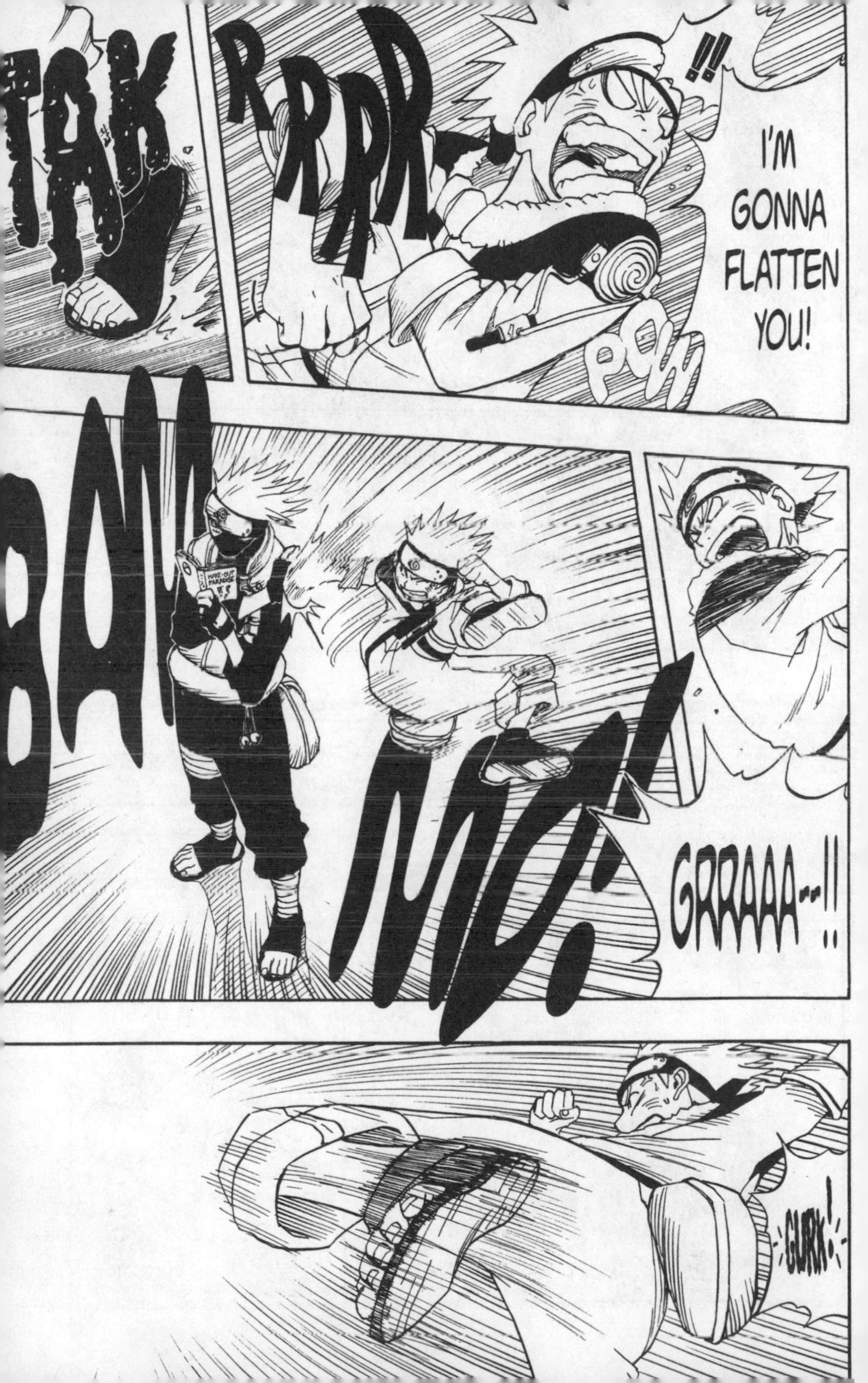
!!
I'M GONNA FLATTEN YOU!
POW
RRRRR
TAK
GRRAAA--!!
MAKE-OUT PARADISE
BAMM!
GURK!

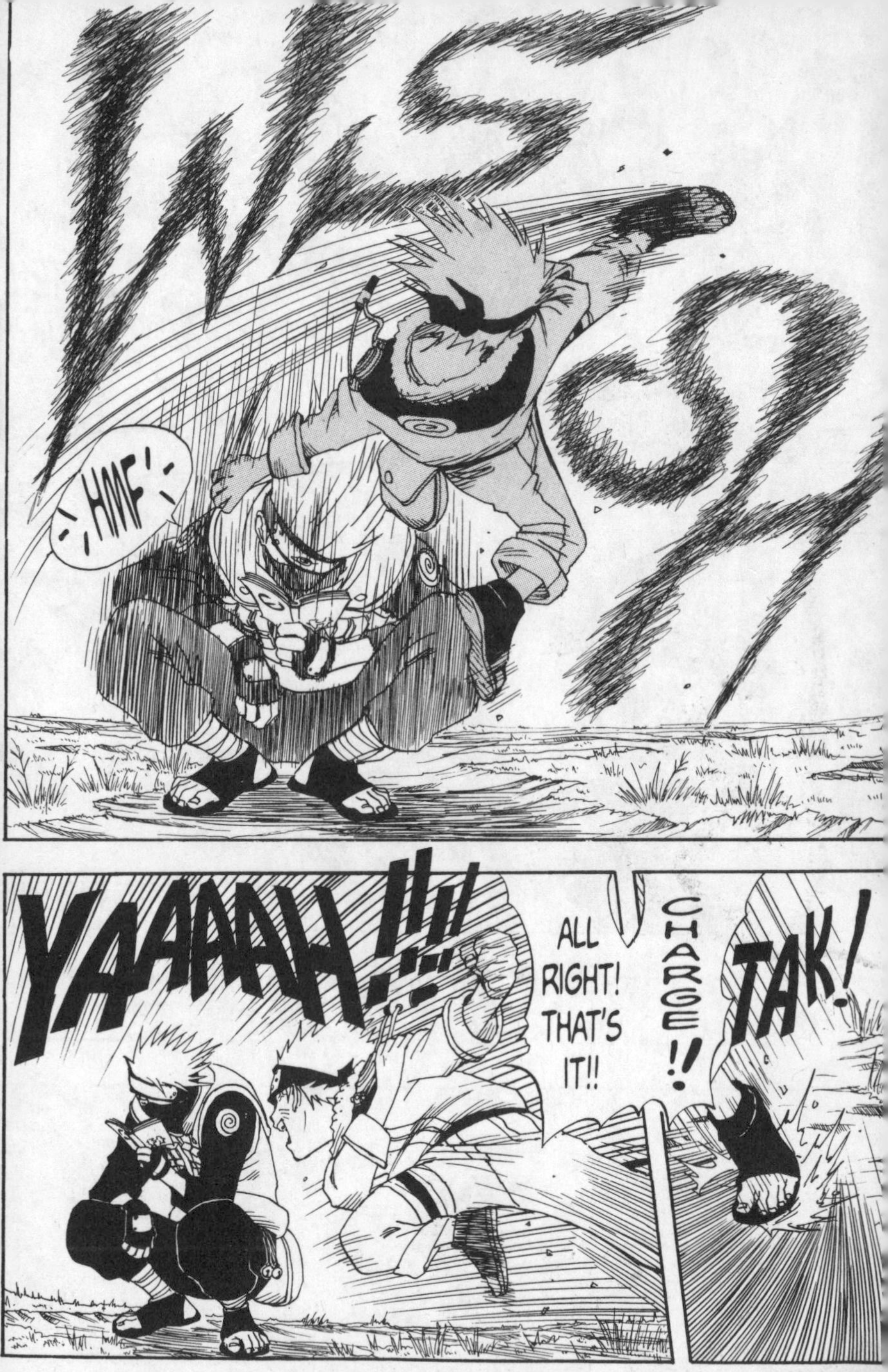
HMF
TAK!
CHARGE!!
ALL RIGHT! THAT'S IT!!
YAAAAH!!!

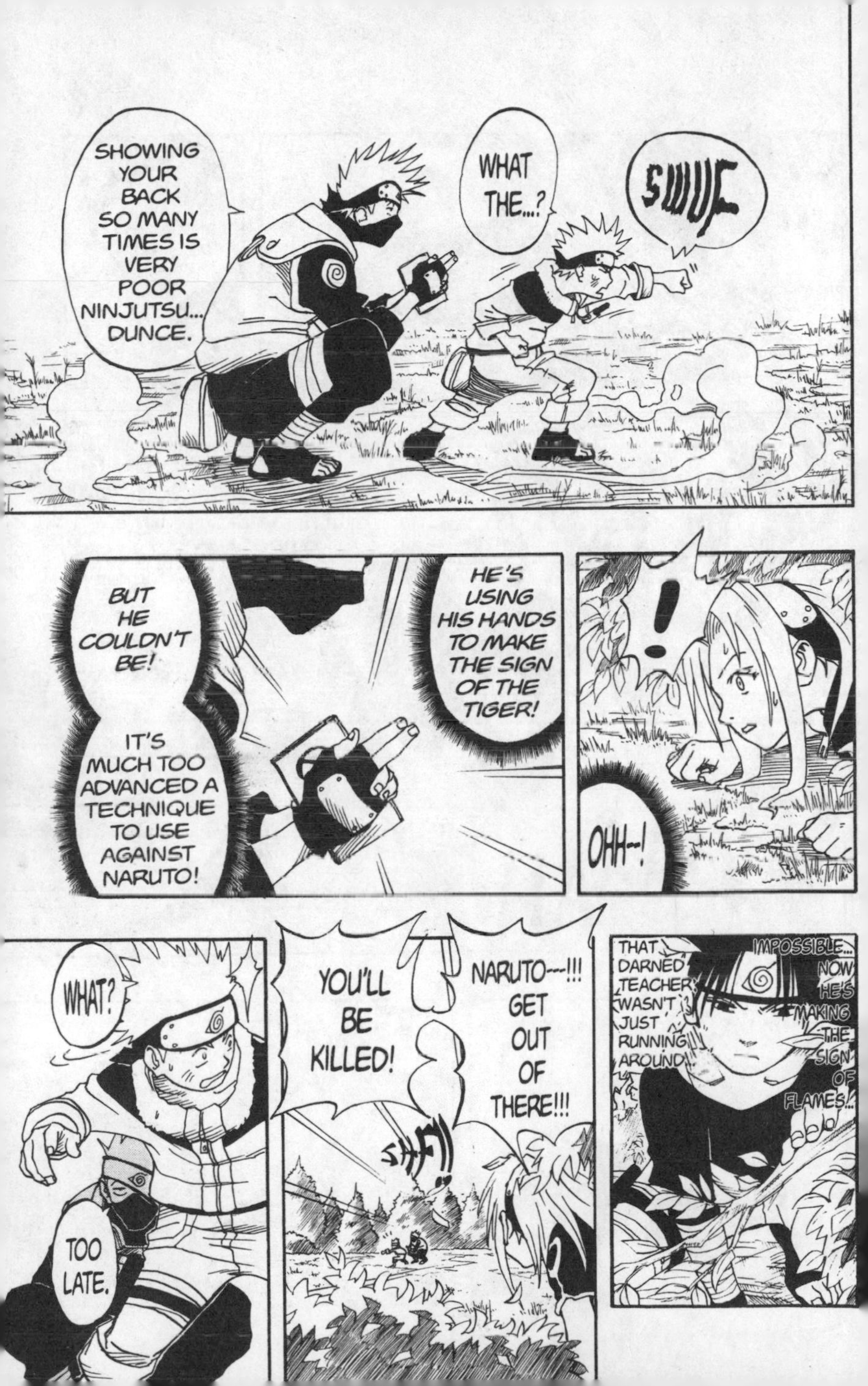
SWUF
WHAT THE...?
SHOWING YOUR BACK SO MANY TIMES IS VERY POOR NINJUTSU... DUNCE.
!
OHH--!
HE'S USING HIS HANDS TO MAKE THE SIGN OF THE TIGER!
BUT HE COULDN'T BE!
IT'S MUCH TOO ADVANCED A TECHNIQUE TO USE AGAINST NARUTO!
IMPOSSIBLE... NOW HE'S MAKING THE SIGN OF FLAMES...
THAT DARNED TEACHER WASN'T JUST RUNNING AROUND!
NARUTO---!!! GET OUT OF THERE!!!
YOU'LL BE KILLED!
WHAT?
TOO LATE.

READ THIS WAY

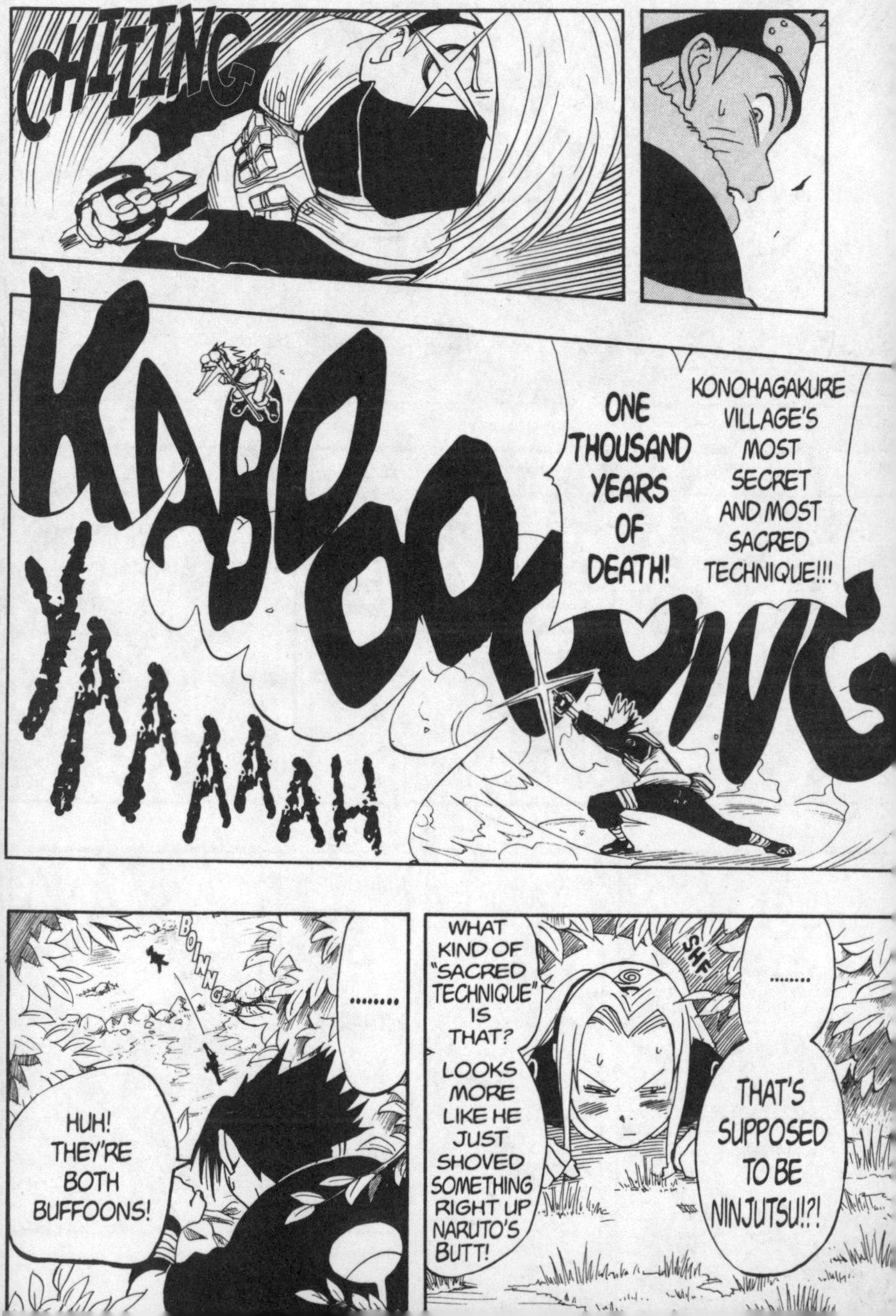
CHIIING
KONOHAGAKURE VILLAGE'S MOST SECRET AND MOST SACRED TECHNIQUE!!!
ONE THOUSAND YEARS OF DEATH!
KABOOOING
YAAAAAH
SHF
....
THAT'S SUPPOSED TO BE NINJUTSU!?!
WHAT KIND OF "SACRED TECHNIQUE" IS THAT?
LOOKS MORE LIKE HE JUST SHOVED SOMETHING RIGHT UP NARUTO'S BUTT!
BOINNG
....
HUH! THEY'RE BOTH BUFFOONS!

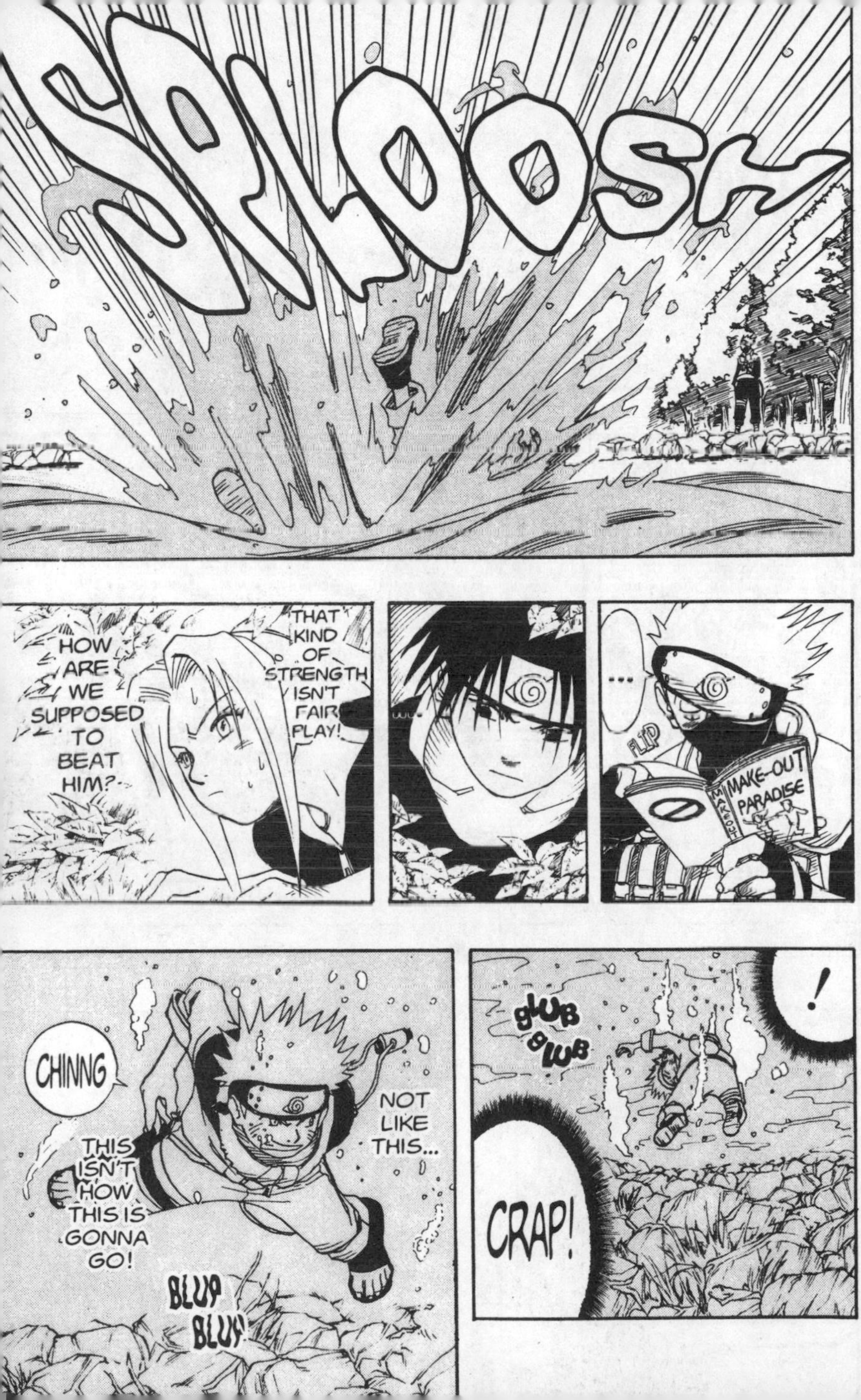
SPLOOSH
...
FLIP
MAKE-OUT PARADISE
...
THAT KIND OF STRENGTH ISN'T FAIR PLAY!
HOW ARE WE SUPPOSED TO BEAT HIM?
!
GLUB GLUB
CRAP!
CHINNG
NOT LIKE THIS...
THIS ISN'T HOW THIS IS GONNA GO!
BLUP BLUP

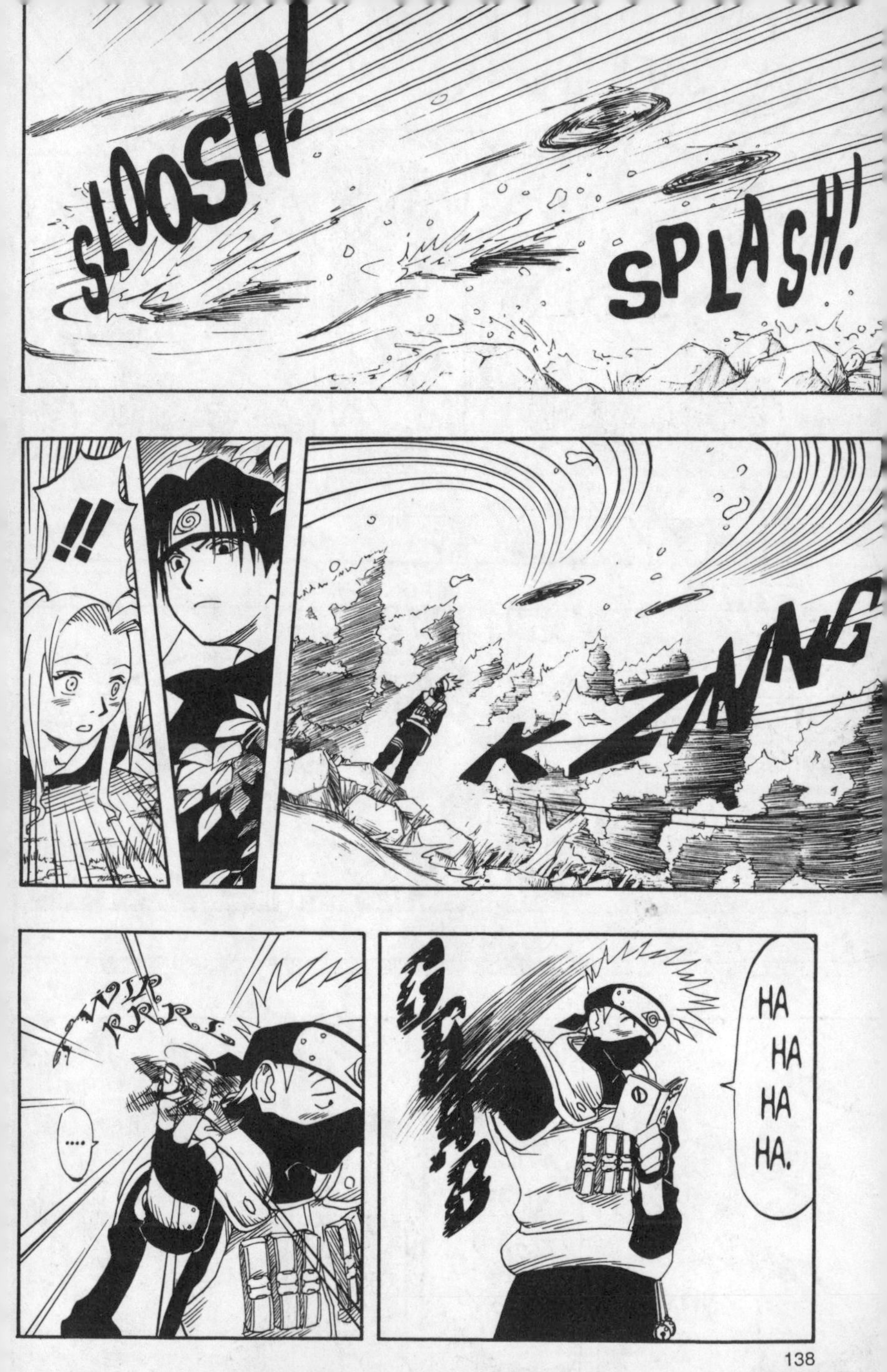
SPLASH!
SLOOSH!
KZANG
!!
HA HA HA HA.
SWIP
RRRR...
....

«READ THIS WAY«

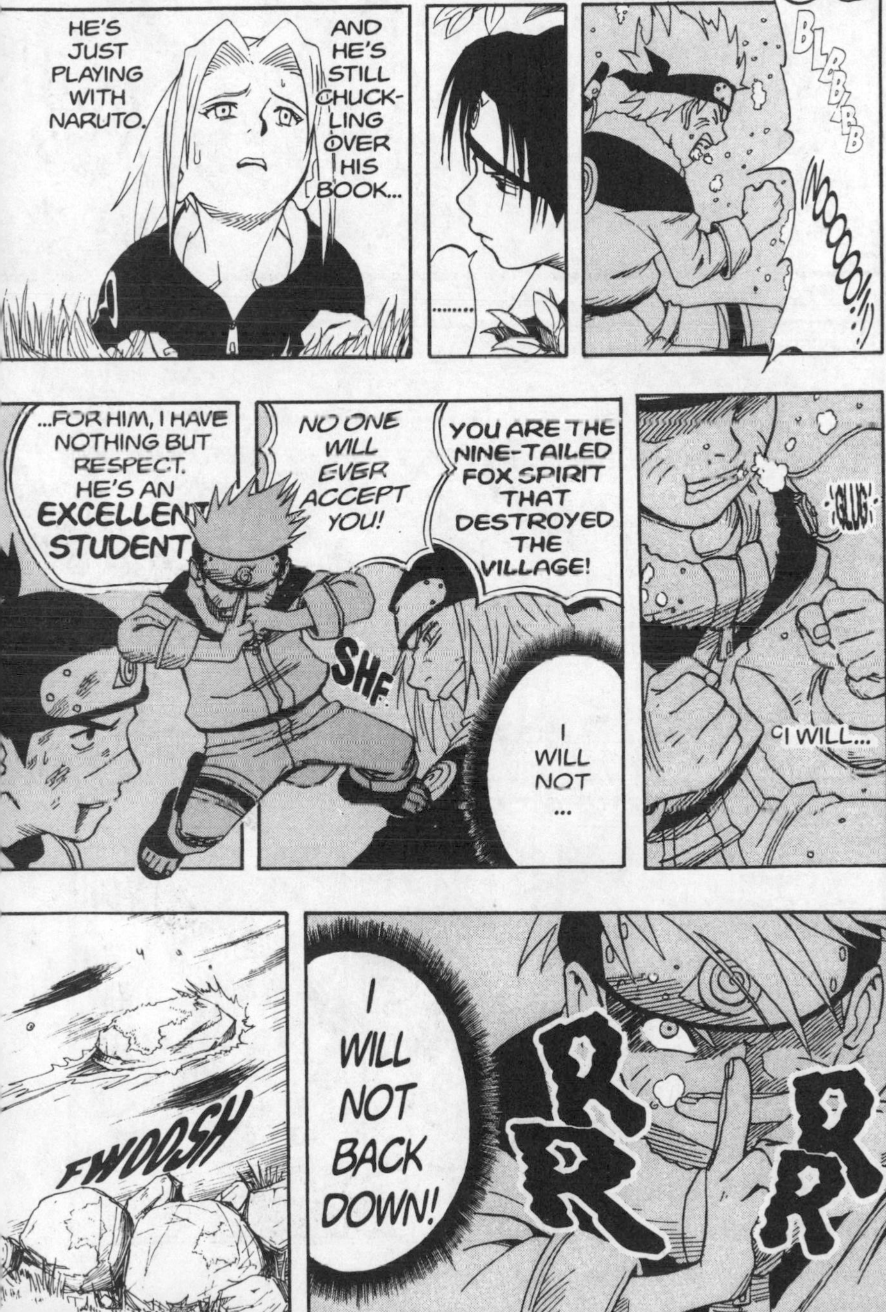
BLBBBB
NOOOOO!!
....
HE'S JUST PLAYING WITH NARUTO.
AND HE'S STILL CHUCKLING OVER HIS BOOK...
GLUG
I WILL...
YOU ARE THE NINE-TAILED FOX SPIRIT THAT DESTROYED THE VILLAGE!
NO ONE WILL EVER ACCEPT YOU!
SHF
I WILL NOT ...
...FOR HIM, I HAVE NOTHING BUT RESPECT. HE'S AN EXCELLENT STUDENT
I WILL NOT BACK DOWN!
RRRR
FWOOSH

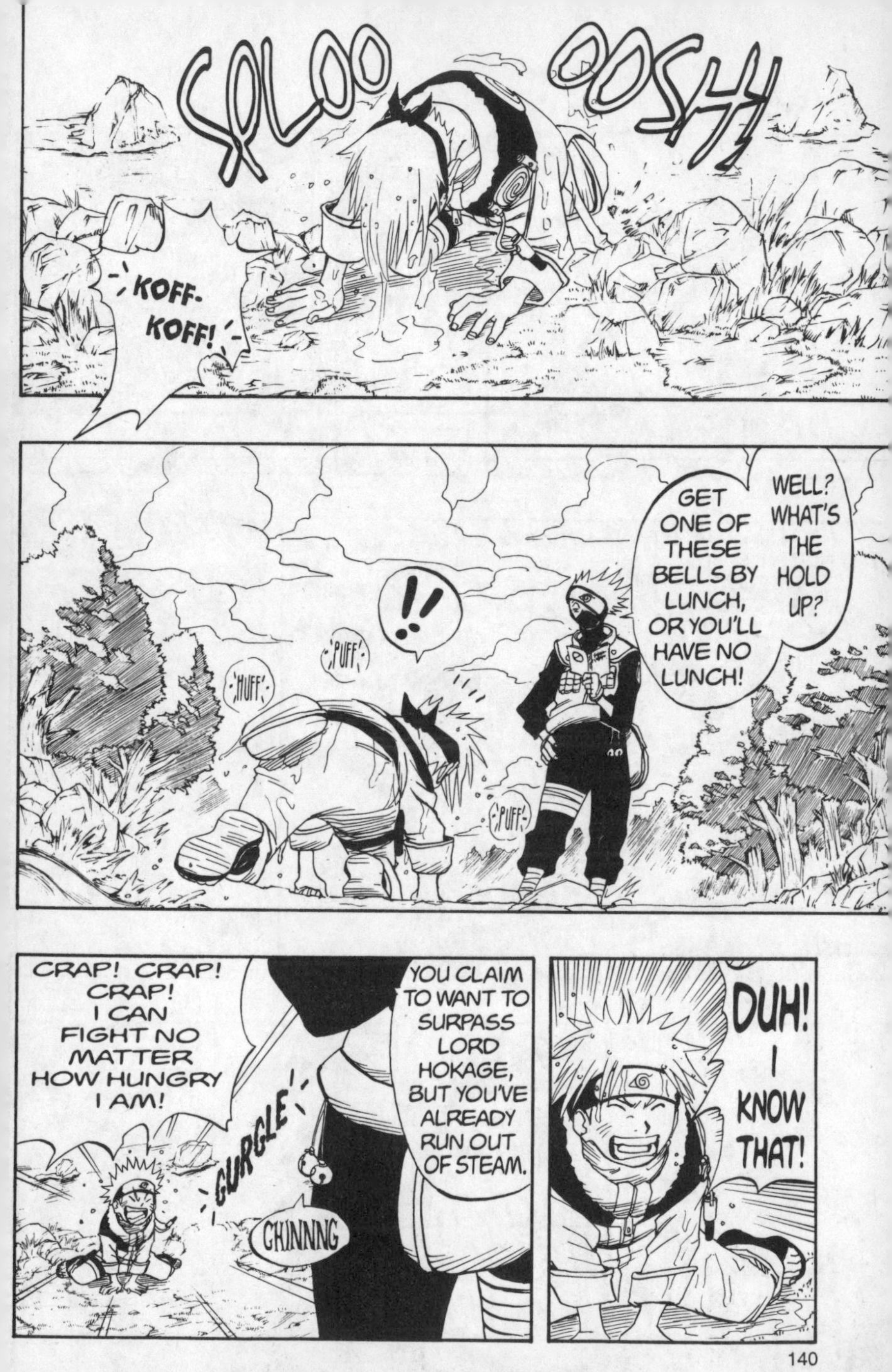
SPLOOOOSH
KOFF-KOFF!
WELL? WHAT'S THE HOLD UP?
GET ONE OF THESE BELLS BY LUNCH, OR YOU'LL HAVE NO LUNCH!
!!
PUFF
HUFF
PUFF
DUH! I KNOW THAT!
YOU CLAIM TO WANT TO SURPASS LORD HOKAGE, BUT YOU'VE ALREADY RUN OUT OF STEAM.
CHINNNG
CRAP! CRAP! CRAP! I CAN FIGHT NO MATTER HOW HUNGRY I AM!
GURGLE

READ THIS WAY

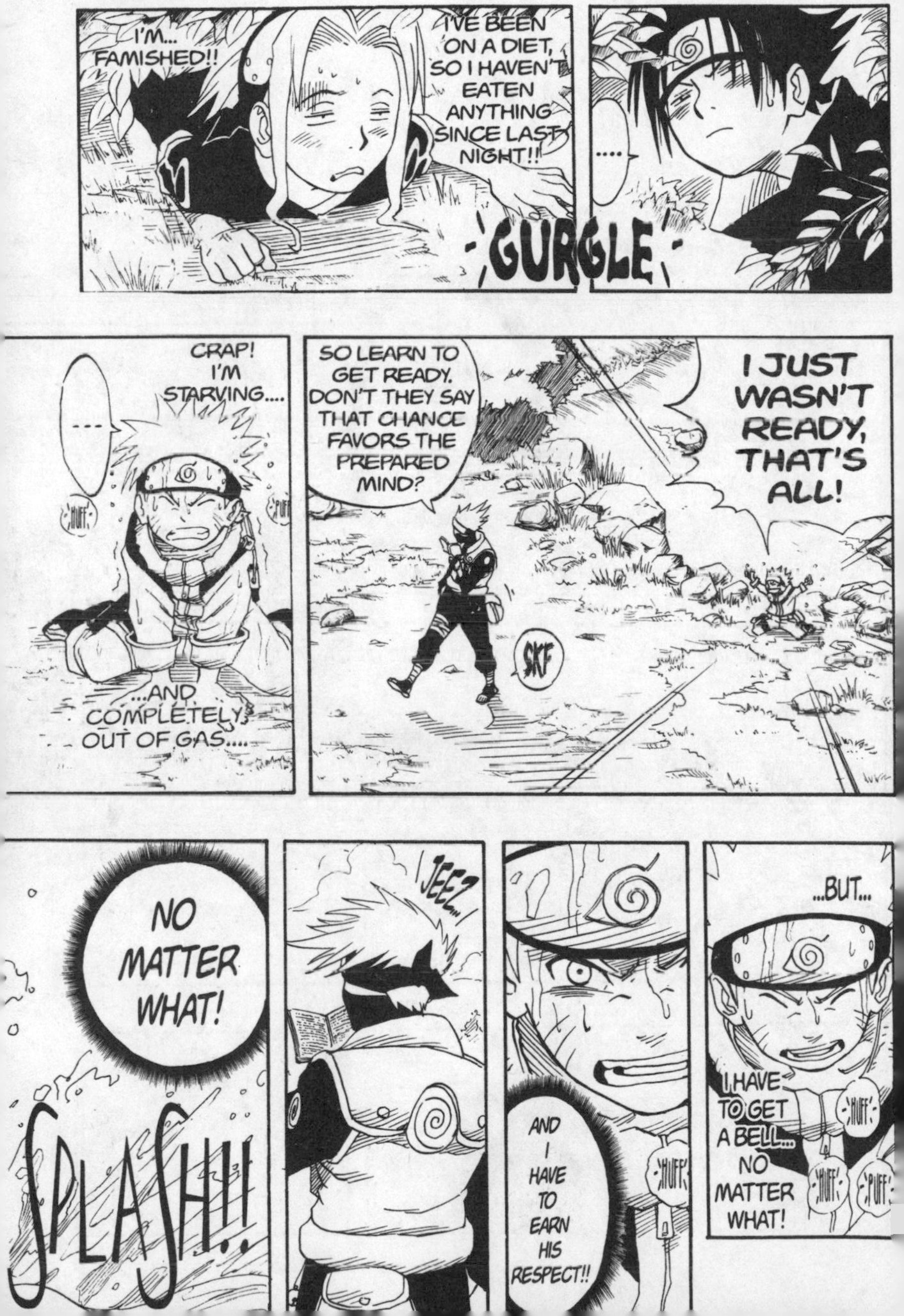
....
GURGLE
I'VE BEEN ON A DIET, SO I HAVEN'T EATEN ANYTHING SINCE LAST NIGHT!!
I'M... FAMISHED!!
I JUST WASN'T READY, THAT'S ALL!
SO LEARN TO GET READY. DON'T THEY SAY THAT CHANCE FAVORS THE PREPARED MIND?
SKF
CRAP! I'M STARVING....
...
HUFF
PUFF
...AND COMPLETELY OUT OF GAS....
...BUT...
I HAVE TO GET A BELL... NO MATTER WHAT!
HUFF
HUFF
PUFF
AND I HAVE TO EARN HIS RESPECT!!
HUFF
JEEZ...
NO MATTER WHAT!
SPLASH!!

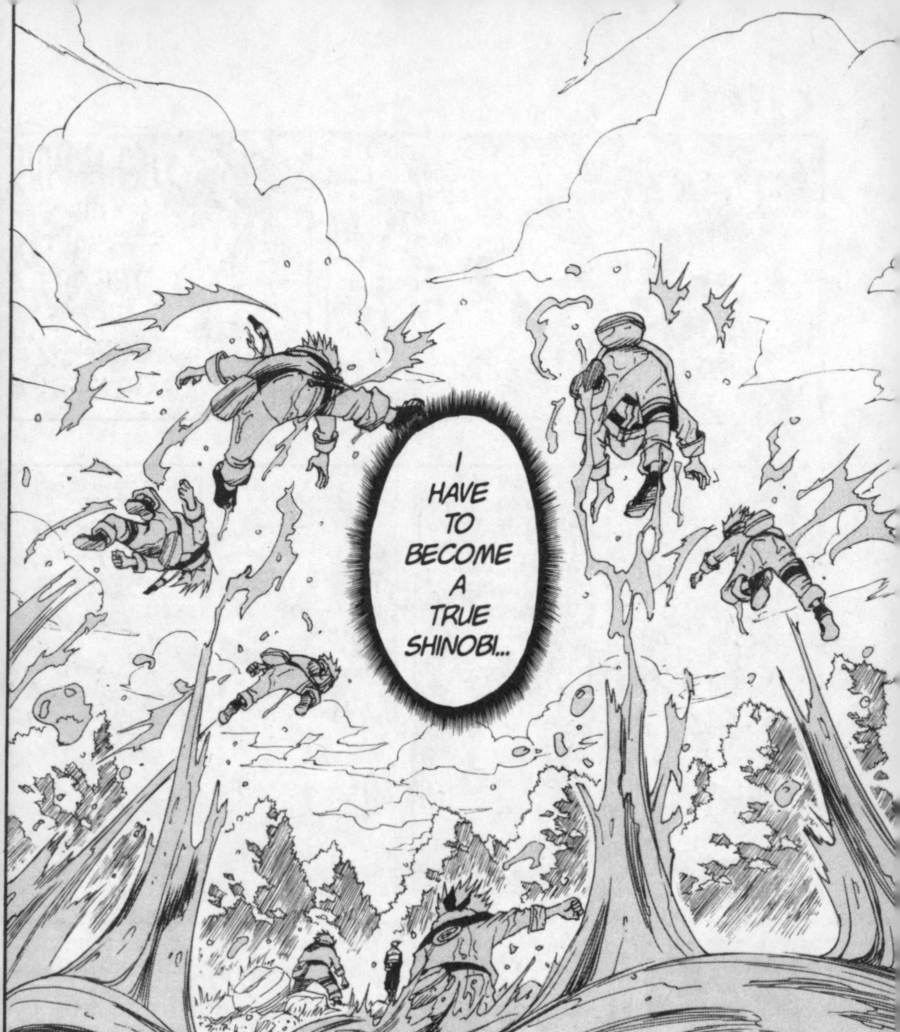
I HAVE TO BECOME A TRUE SHINOBI...
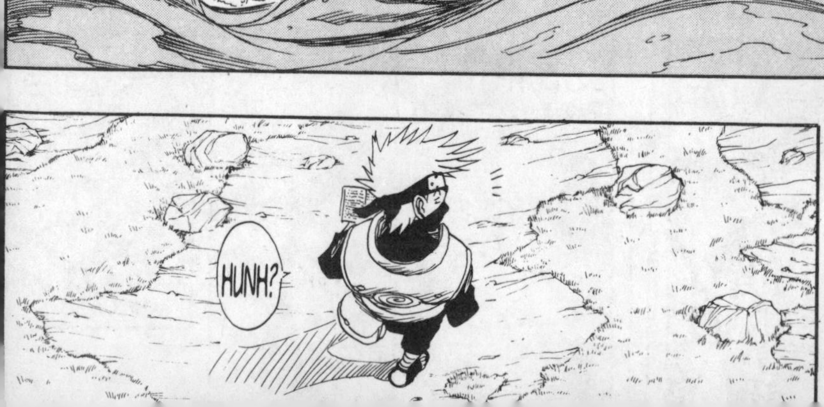
HUNH?

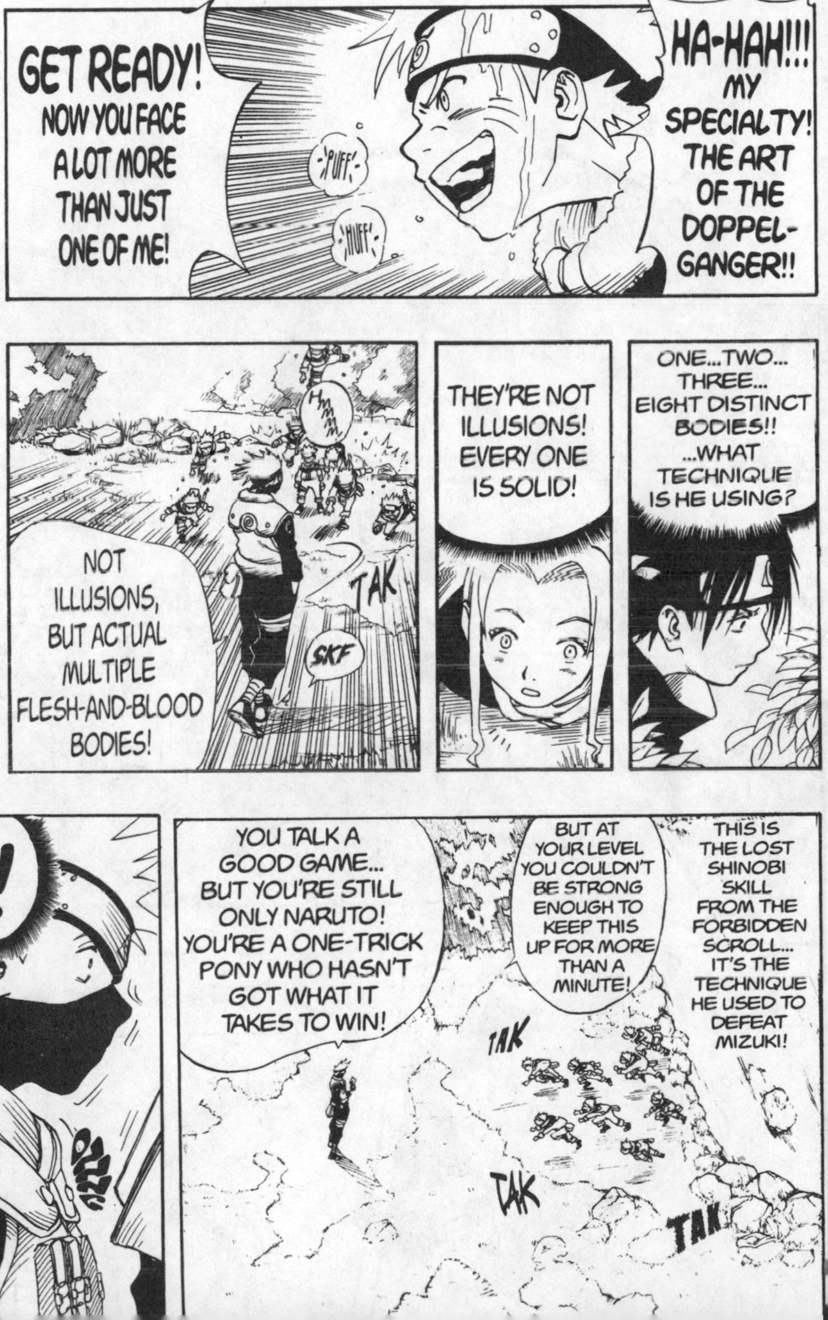
HA-HAH!!!! MY SPECIALTY! THE ART OF THE DOPPEL-GANGER!!
GET READY! NOW YOU FACE A LOT MORE THAN JUST ONE OF ME!
PUFF
HUFF
ONE...TWO... THREE... EIGHT DISTINCT BODIES!! ...WHAT TECHNIQUE IS HE USING?
THEY'RE NOT ILLUSIONS! EVERY ONE IS SOLID!
HMMM
NOT ILLUSIONS, BUT ACTUAL MULTIPLE FLESH-AND-BLOOD BODIES!
TAK
SKF
THIS IS THE LOST SHINOBI SKILL FROM THE FORBIDDEN SCROLL... IT'S THE TECHNIQUE HE USED TO DEFEAT MIZUKI!
BUT AT YOUR LEVEL YOU COULDN'T BE STRONG ENOUGH TO KEEP THIS UP FOR MORE THAN A MINUTE!
YOU TALK A GOOD GAME... BUT YOU'RE STILL ONLY NARUTO! YOU'RE A ONE-TRICK PONY WHO HASN'T GOT WHAT IT TAKES TO WIN!
TAK
TAK
TAK
!

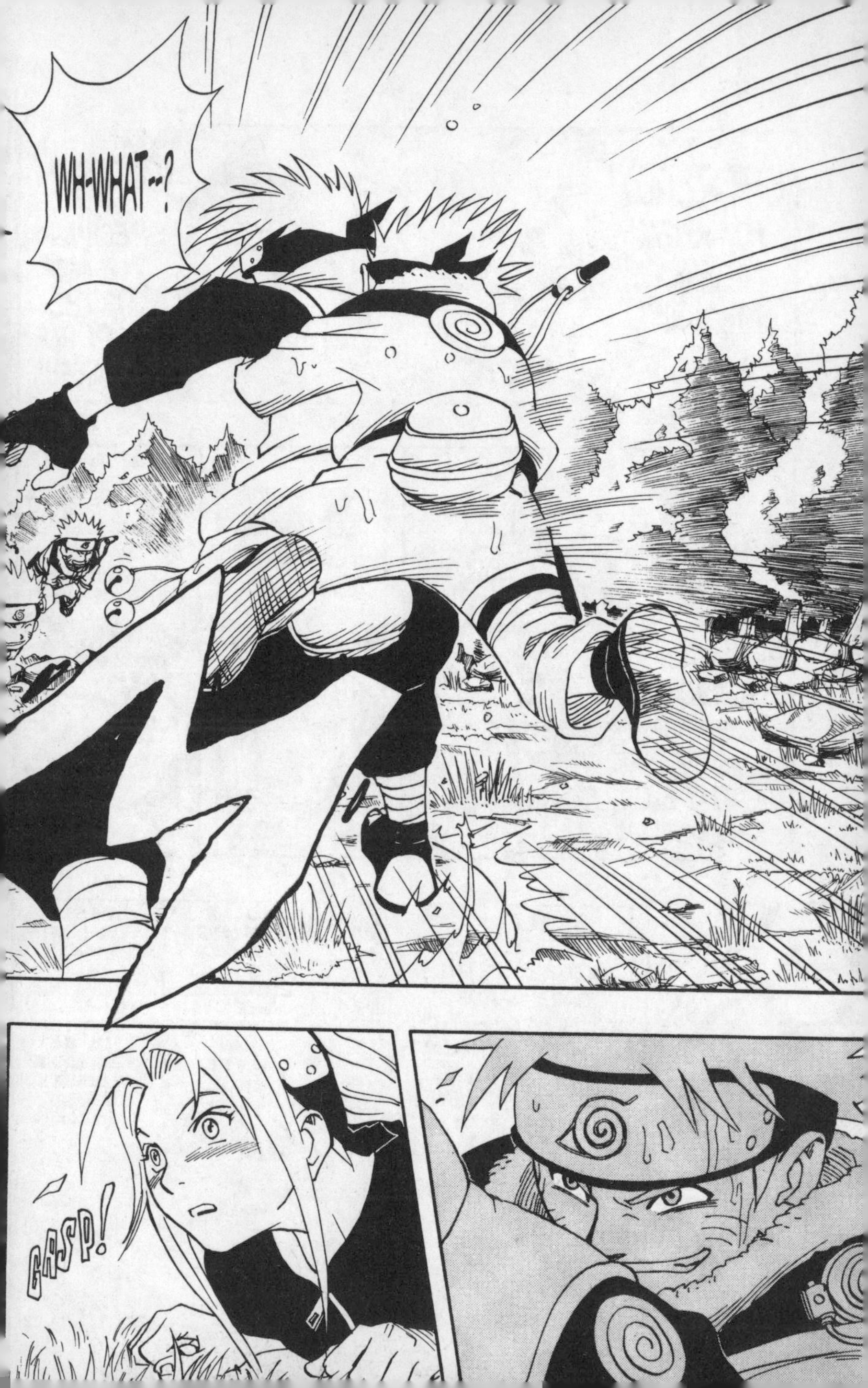
WH-WHAT--?
GASP!

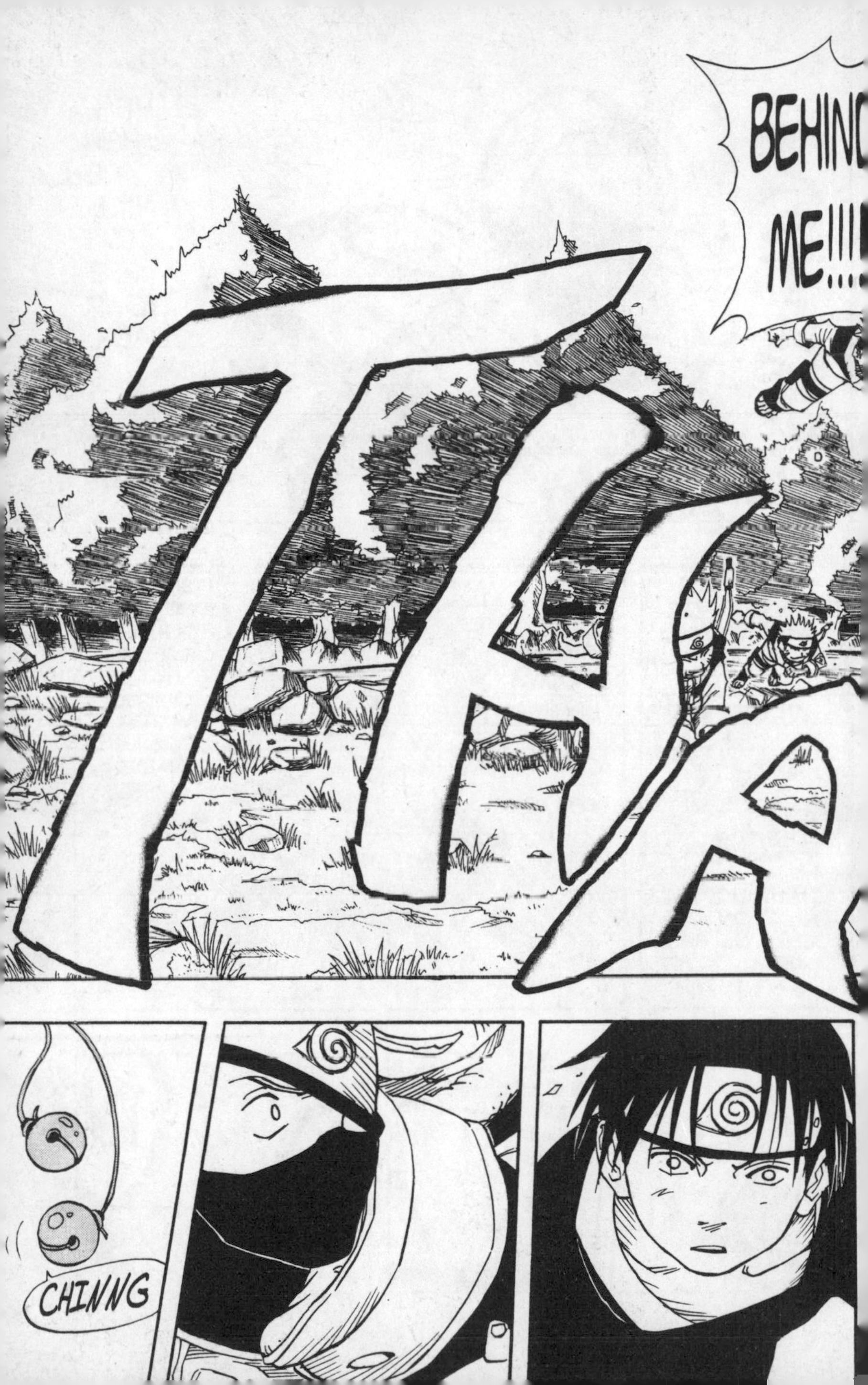
BEHIND ME!!!!
CHINNG

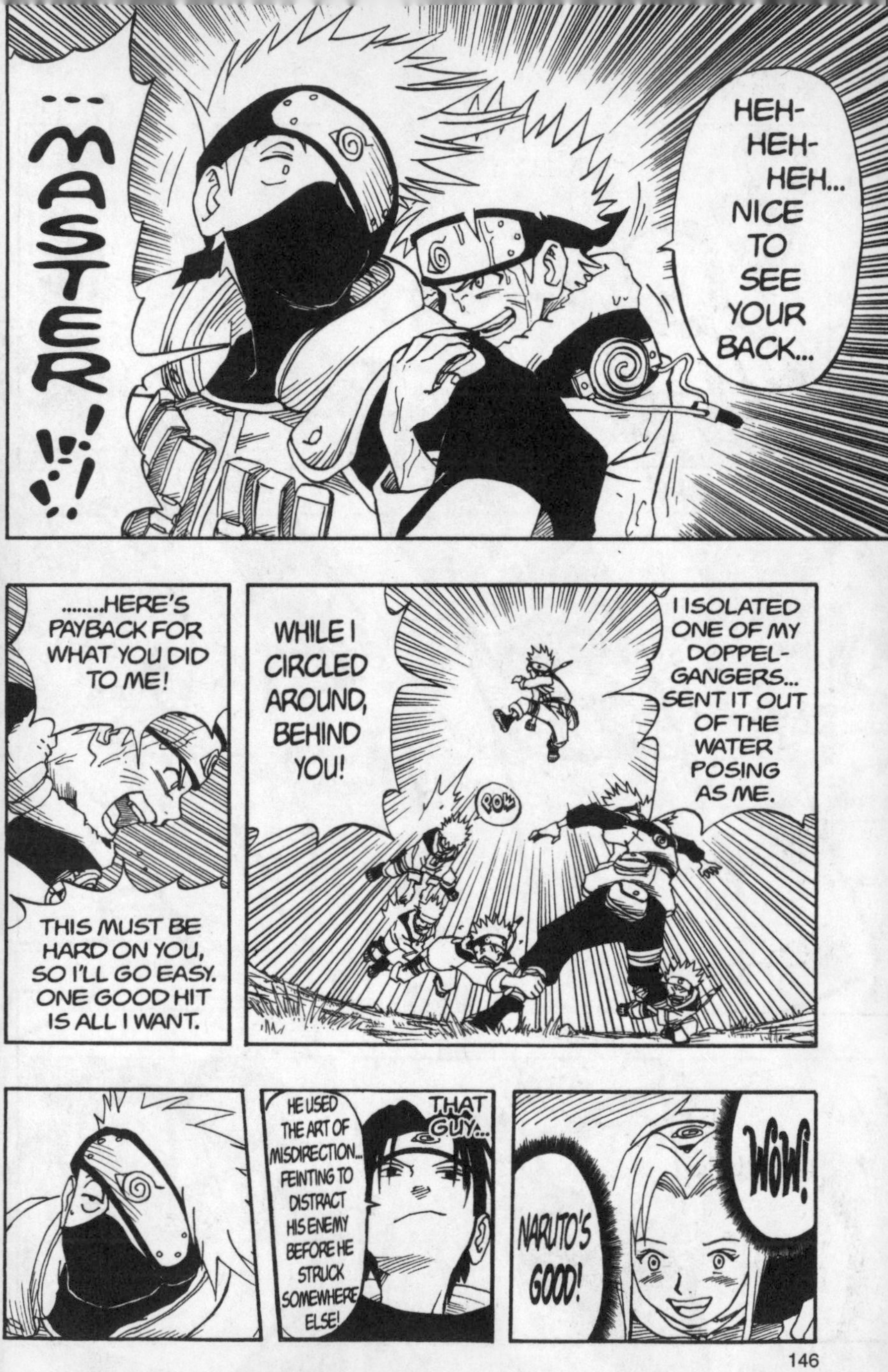
HEH-HEH-HEH... NICE TO SEE YOUR BACK...
...MASTER!!
I ISOLATED ONE OF MY DOPPEL-GANGERS... SENT IT OUT OF THE WATER POSING AS ME.
WHILE I CIRCLED AROUND, BEHIND YOU!
POW
........HERE'S PAYBACK FOR WHAT YOU DID TO ME!
THIS MUST BE HARD ON YOU, SO I'LL GO EASY. ONE GOOD HIT IS ALL I WANT.
WOW!
NARUTO'S GOOD!
THAT GUY...
HE USED THE ART OF MISDIRECTION... FEINTING TO DISTRACT HIS ENEMY BEFORE HE STRUCK SOMEWHERE ELSE!

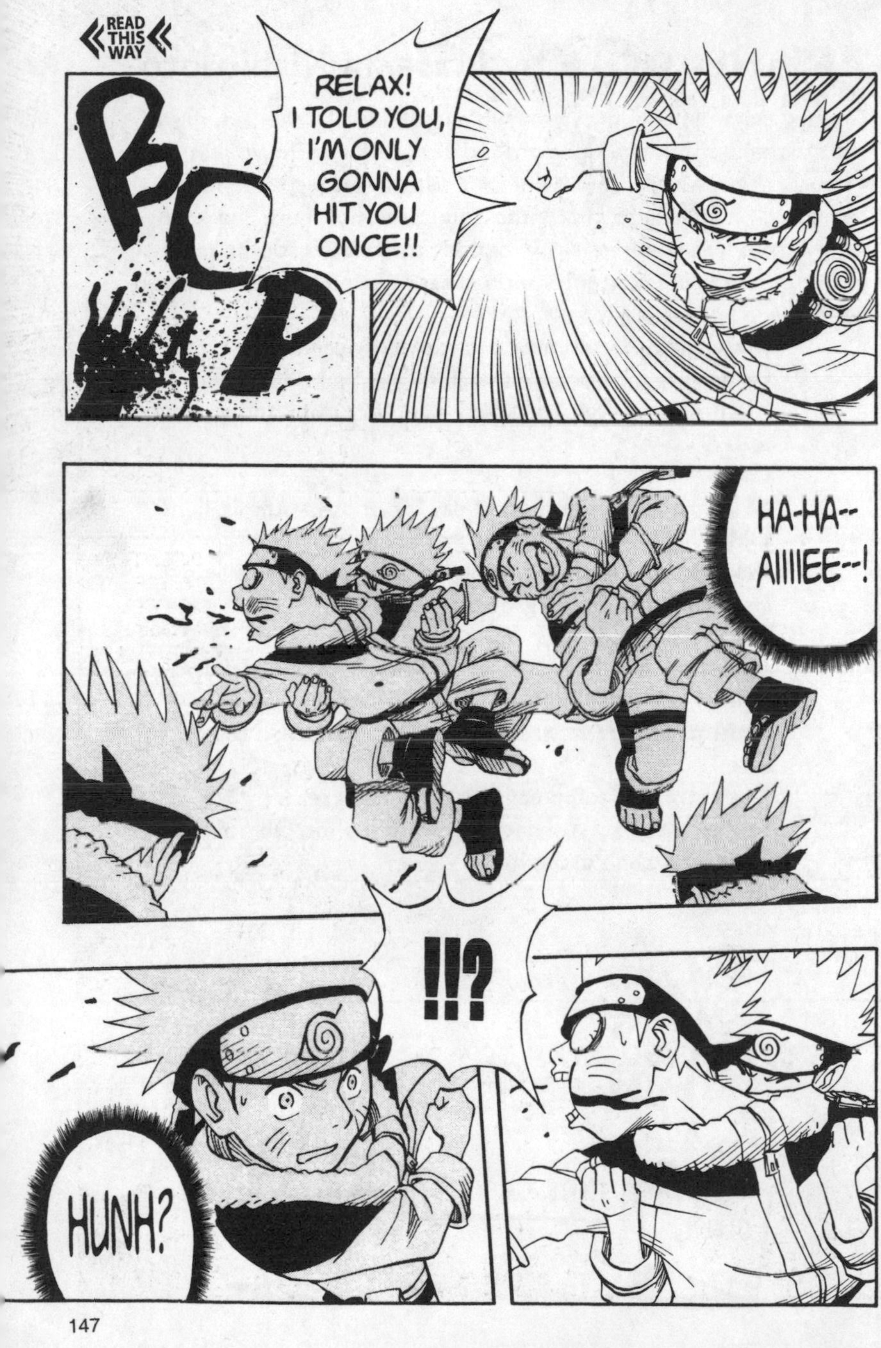
READ THIS WAY
RELAX! I TOLD YOU, I'M ONLY GONNA HIT YOU ONCE!!
BOP
HA-HA-- AIIIIEE--!
!!?
HUNH?

AN ANECDOTE by Masashi Kishimoto

Coming from the country, I grew up surrounded by the beauties of nature, trees, plants, and open ground. So moving to Tokyo was quite a shock. There was hardly a plant or a natural setting to be found. I had to do something to create the country atmosphere and keep myself from feeling homesick. Something that would soothe me enough that I could concentrate on creating good manga. So I decided to buy a houseplant for my desk.

Kishimoto: "From now on, you're my partner!"

I even gave my plant a name: *Ukki-kun*, as in "Mr. Ukki."

Kishimoto: "Well, Ukki, you look very shiny and green today!"

Ukki: "………"

Kishimoto: "It was a good day for photosynthesis, huh?"

Ukki: "………"

Kishimoto: "Today I'm going to give you an excellent fertilizer for vigorous growth!"

We were a super-team.

Assistant A: "What is this, Mr. Kishimoto? How did your plant get all dried out?"

Kishimoto: "What are you saying?! I gave Ukki the best care!"

Assistant A: "You mean this? This fertilizer is concentrated, so you need to dilute it a lot. Oh no! You mean you didn't dilute it?!"

Sigh…

Ukki-kun   (Three months later)   Ukki-kun

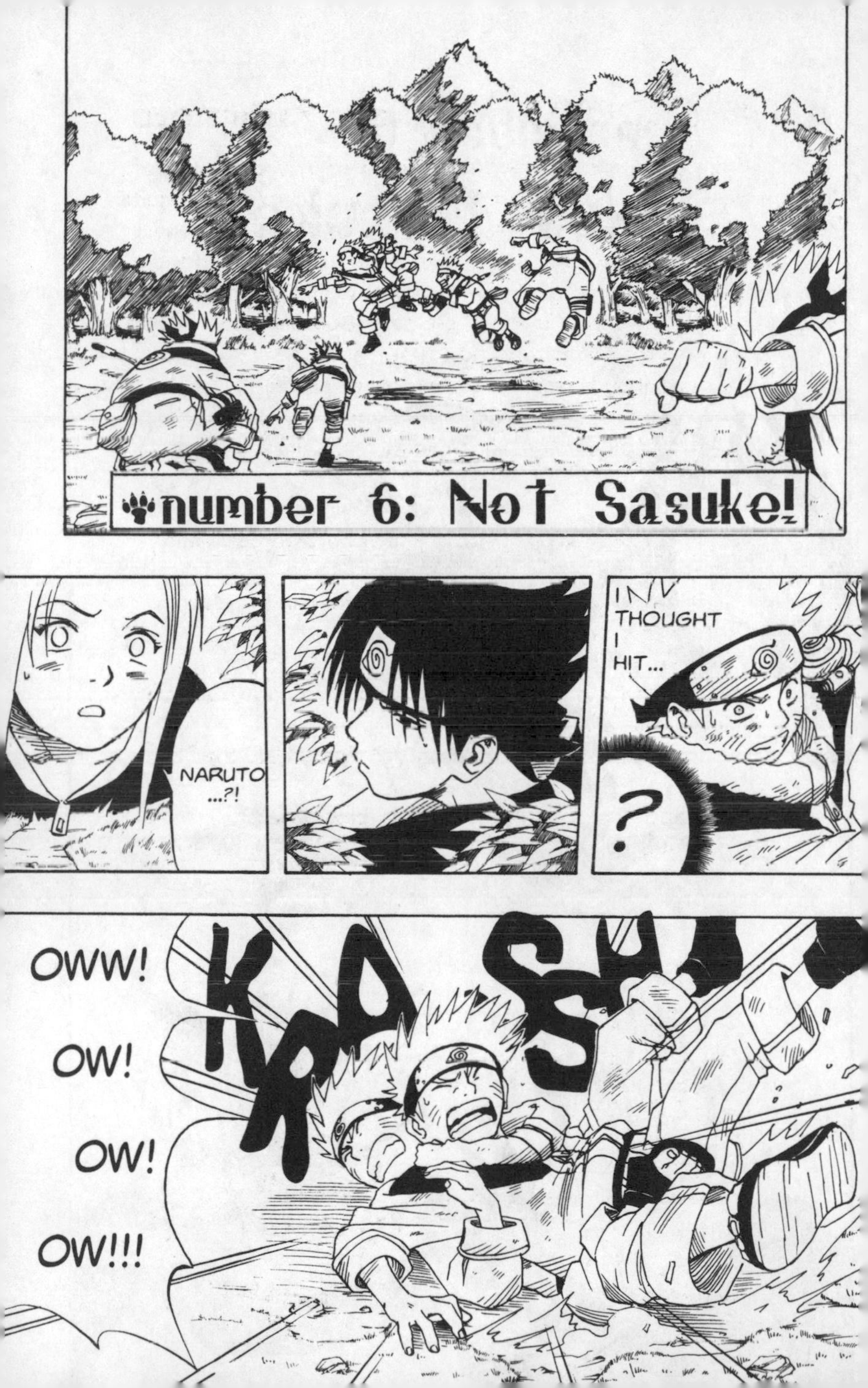
number 6: Not Sasuke!
I THOUGHT I HIT...
?
NARUTO ...?!
KASH
OWW!
OW!
OW!
OW!!!

number 6:

Not Sasuke!

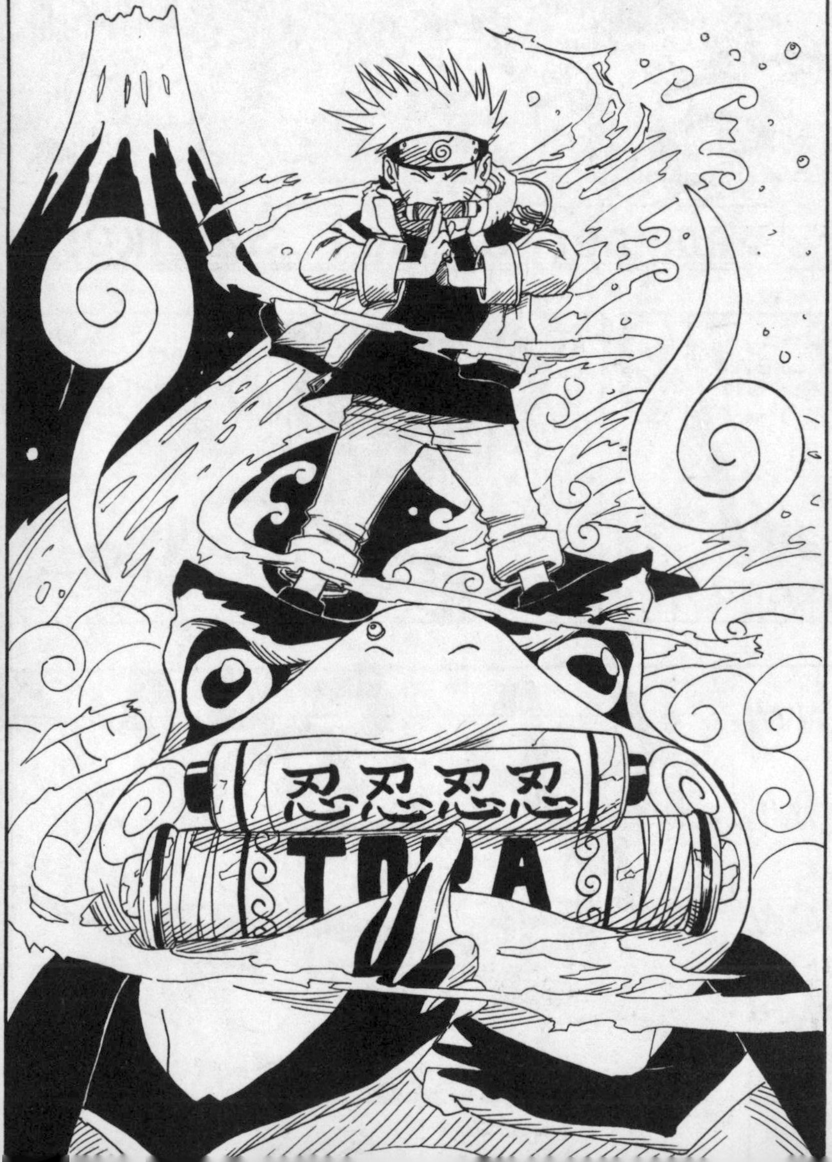
忍忍忍忍

READ THIS WAY

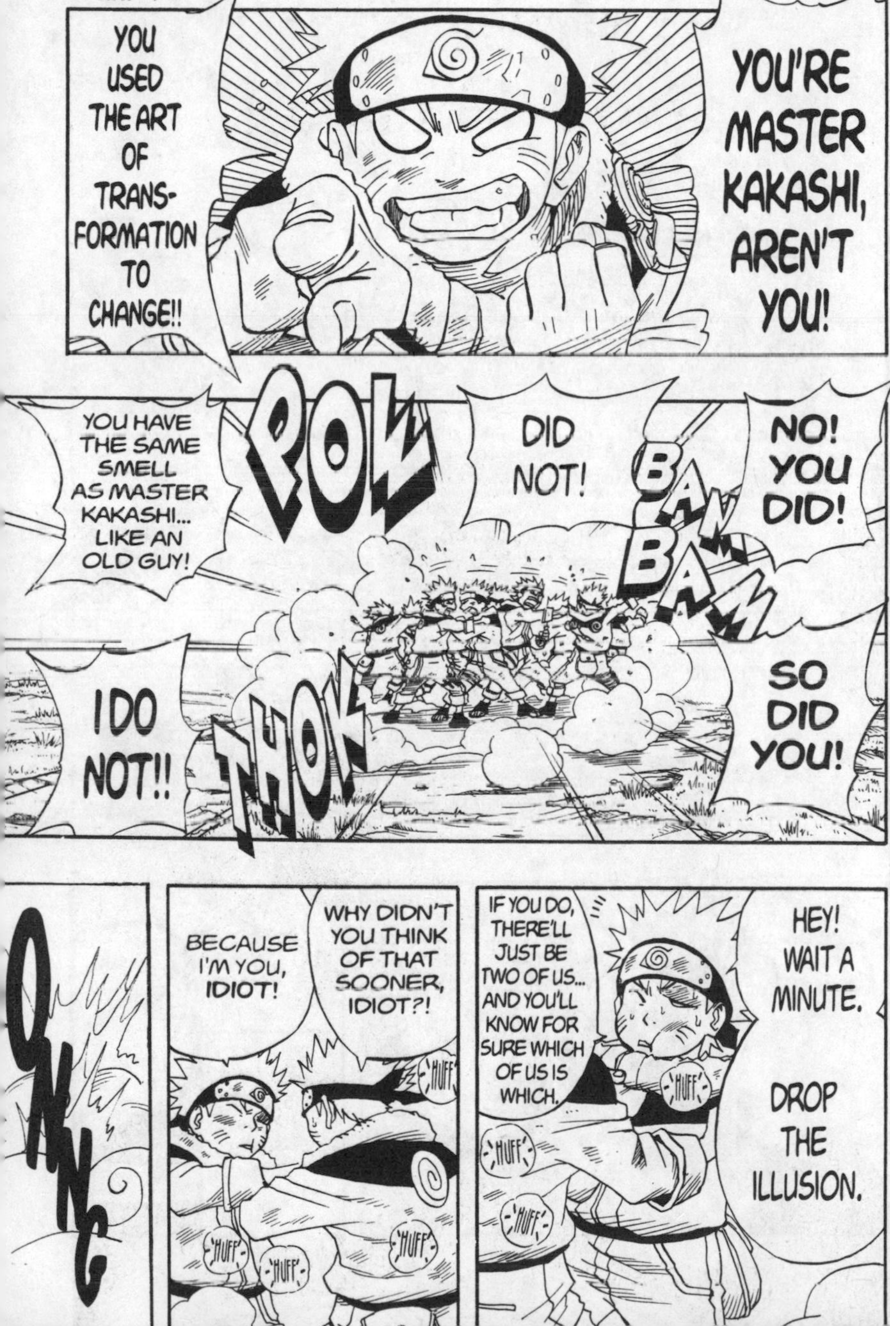

YOU'RE MASTER KAKASHI, AREN'T YOU!
YOU USED THE ART OF TRANS-FORMATION TO CHANGE!!
NO! YOU DID!
BAM BAM
DID NOT!
POW
YOU HAVE THE SAME SMELL AS MASTER KAKASHI... LIKE AN OLD GUY!
SO DID YOU!
THOK
I DO NOT!!
HEY! WAIT A MINUTE.
DROP THE ILLUSION.
IF YOU DO, THERE'LL JUST BE TWO OF US... AND YOU'LL KNOW FOR SURE WHICH OF US IS WHICH.
HUFF
HUFF
HUFF
WHY DIDN'T YOU THINK OF THAT SOONER, IDIOT?!
BECAUSE I'M YOU, IDIOT!
HUFF
HUFF
HUFF

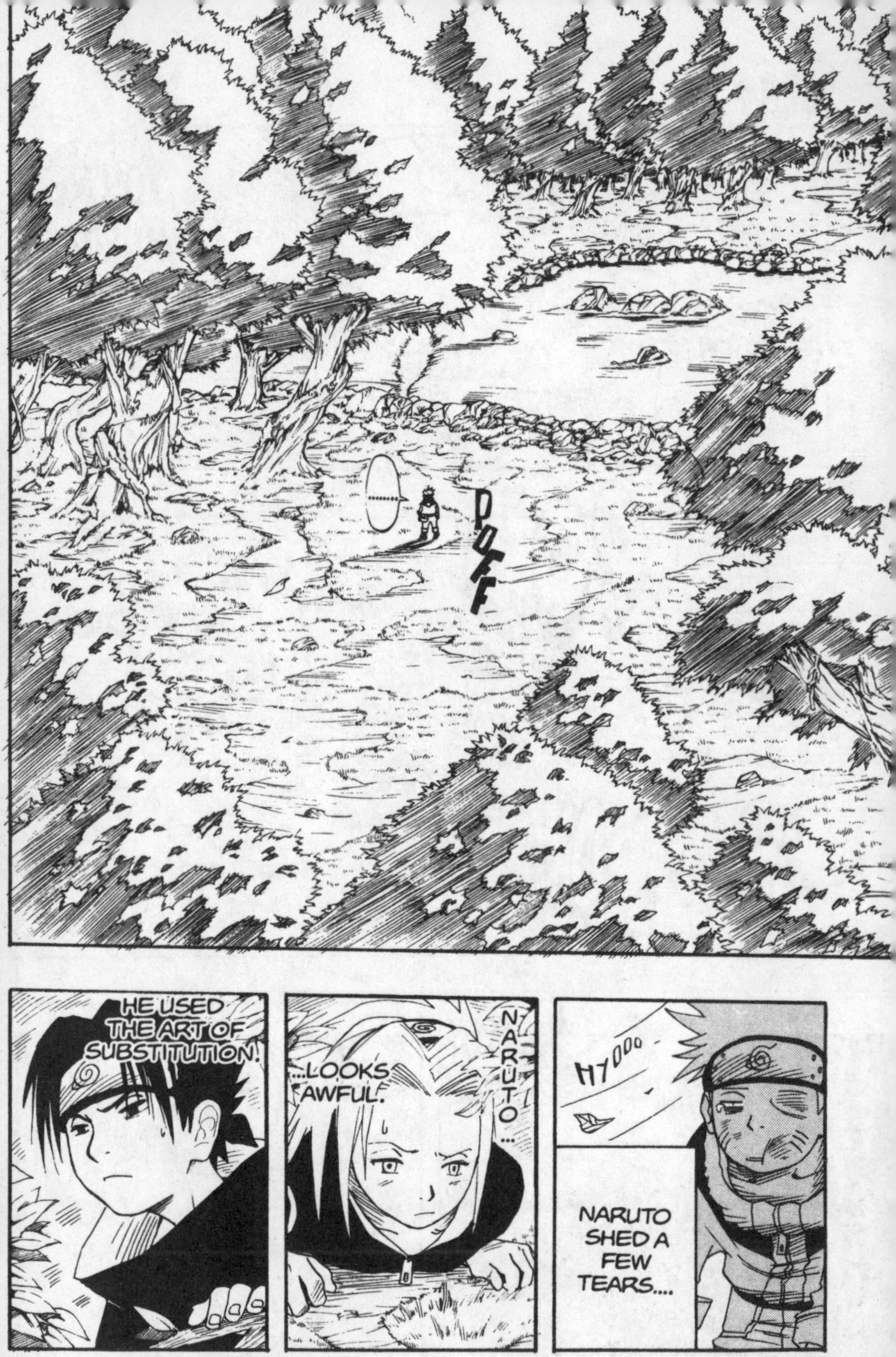
......
POFF
HYOOO
NARUTO SHED A FEW TEARS....
NARUTO...
...LOOKS AWFUL.
HE USED THE ART OF SUBSTITUTION!

READ THIS WAY

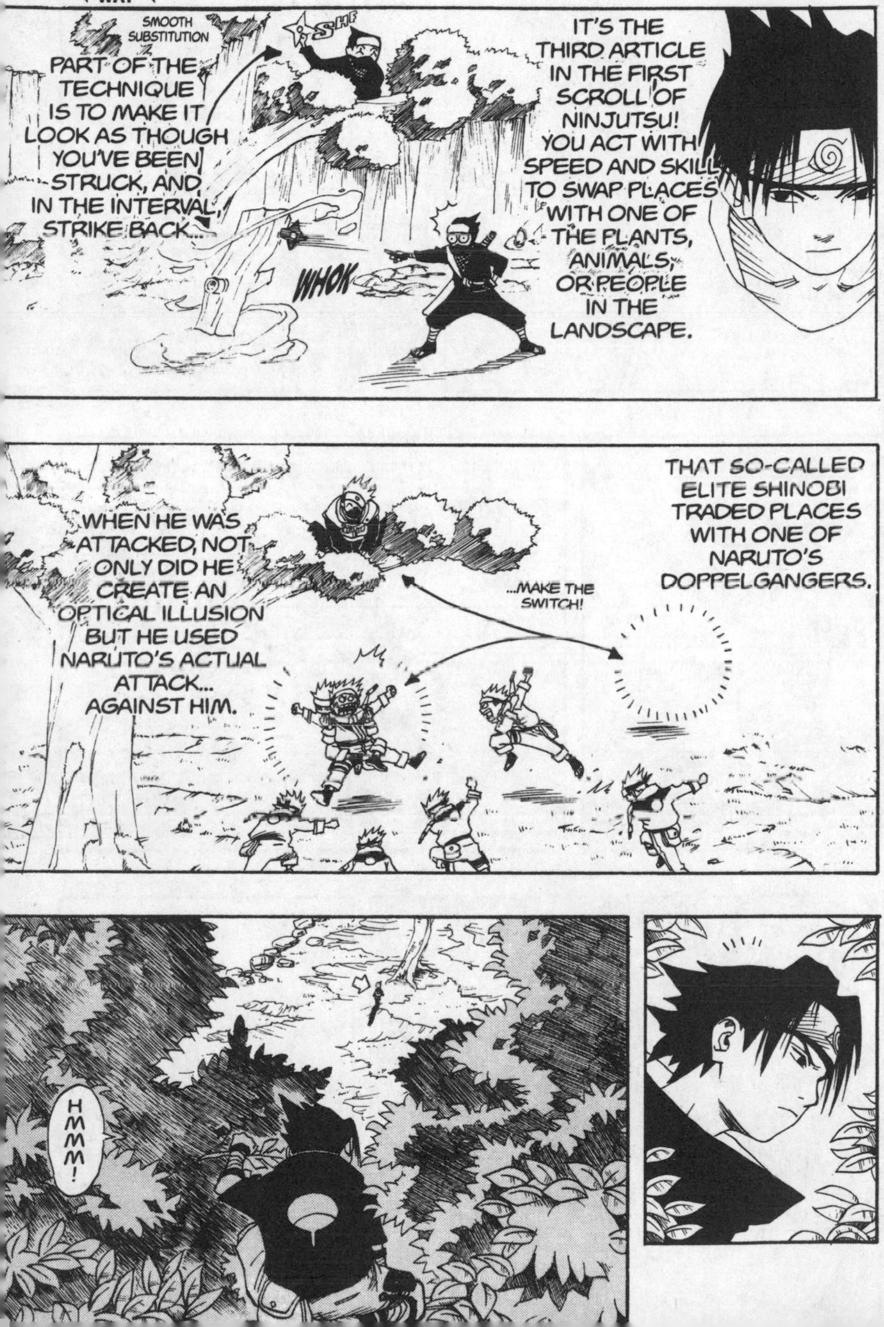
IT'S THE THIRD ARTICLE IN THE FIRST SCROLL OF NINJUTSU! YOU ACT WITH SPEED AND SKILL TO SWAP PLACES WITH ONE OF THE PLANTS, ANIMALS, OR PEOPLE IN THE LANDSCAPE.
SMOOTH SUBSTITUTION
SHF
PART OF THE TECHNIQUE IS TO MAKE IT LOOK AS THOUGH YOU'VE BEEN STRUCK, AND, IN THE INTERVAL, STRIKE BACK...
WHOK
THAT SO-CALLED ELITE SHINOBI TRADED PLACES WITH ONE OF NARUTO'S DOPPELGANGERS.
...MAKE THE SWITCH!
WHEN HE WAS ATTACKED, NOT ONLY DID HE CREATE AN OPTICAL ILLUSION BUT HE USED NARUTO'S ACTUAL ATTACK... AGAINST HIM.
HMMM!

READ THIS WAY

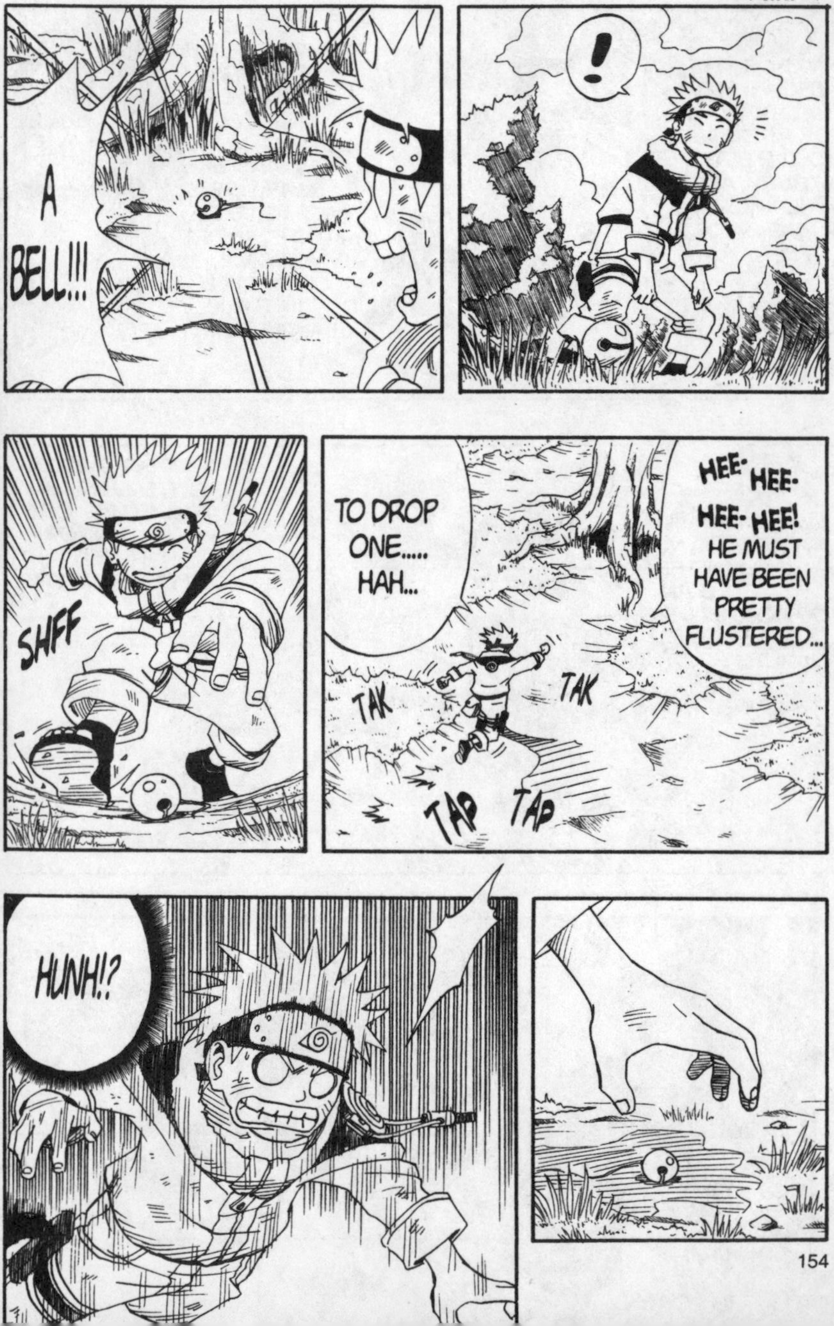
!
A BELL!!!
HEE-HEE-HEE-HEE! HE MUST HAVE BEEN PRETTY FLUSTERED...
TO DROP ONE..... HAH...
TAK
TAK
TAP
TAP
SHFF
HUNH!?

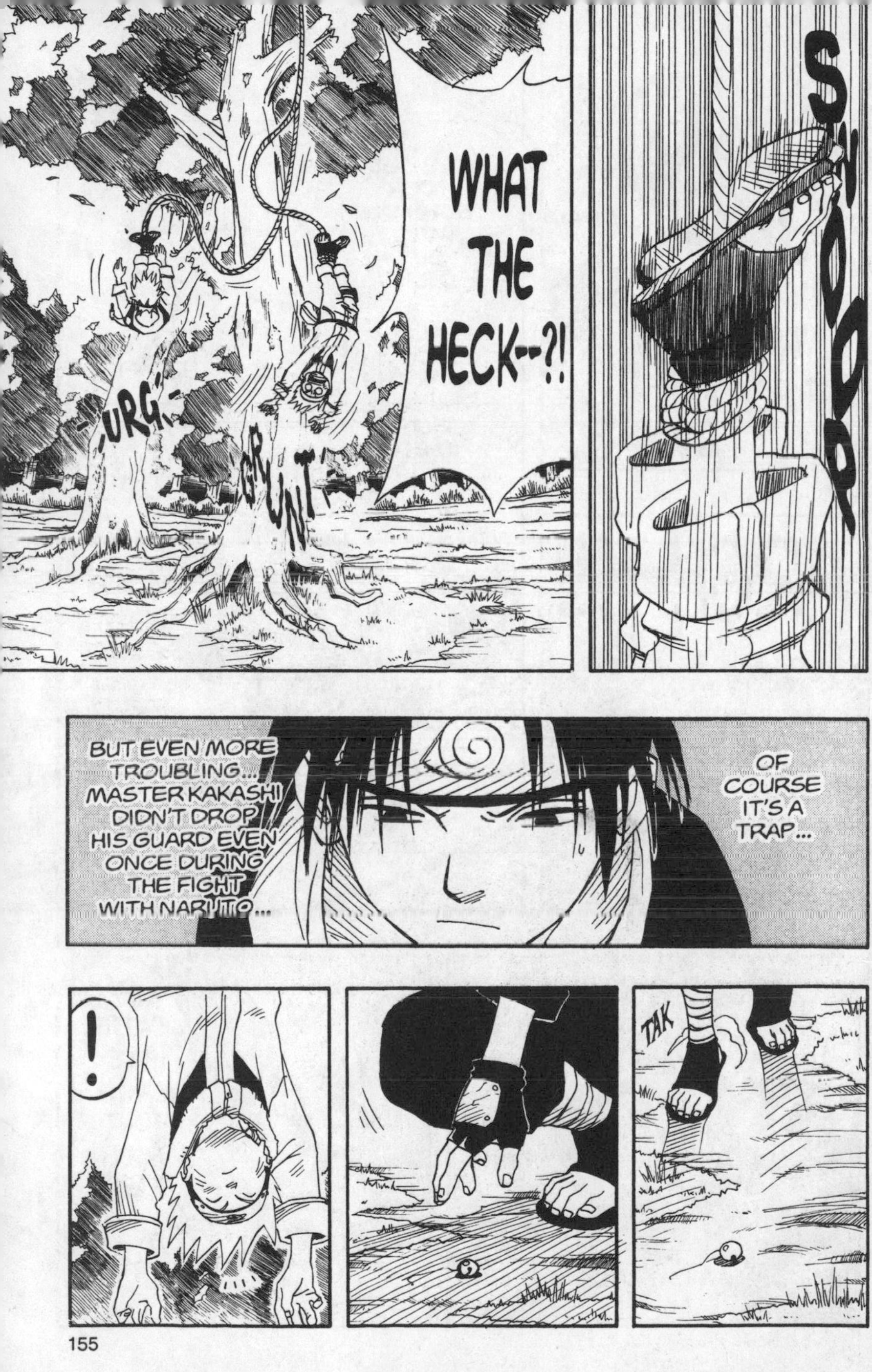
SNOOP
WHAT THE HECK--?!
URG
GRUNT
OF COURSE IT'S A TRAP...
BUT EVEN MORE TROUBLING... MASTER KAKASHI DIDN'T DROP HIS GUARD EVEN ONCE DURING THE FIGHT WITH NARUTO...
TAK
!

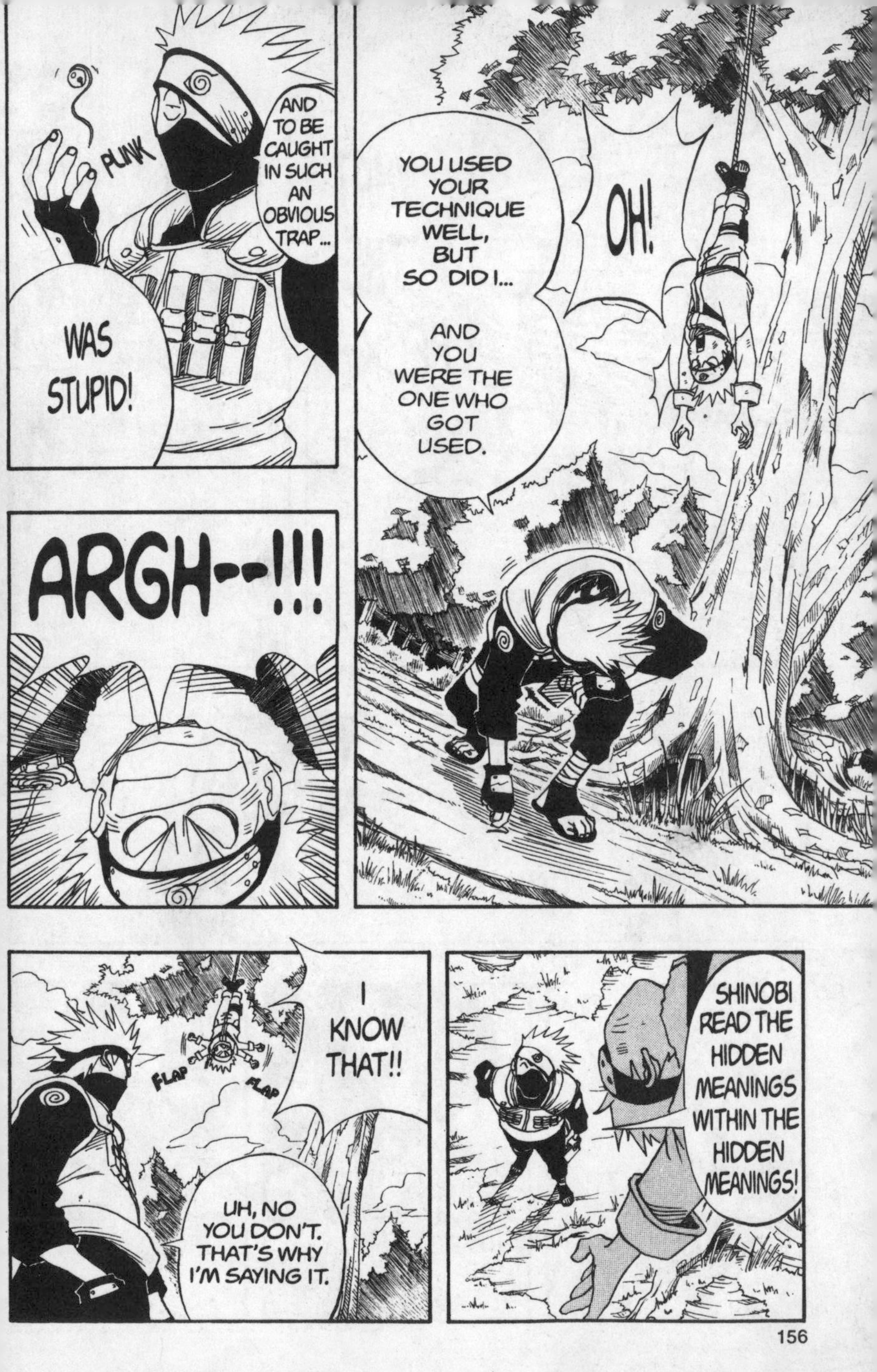
OH!
YOU USED YOUR TECHNIQUE WELL, BUT SO DID I... AND YOU WERE THE ONE WHO GOT USED.
PUNK
AND TO BE CAUGHT IN SUCH AN OBVIOUS TRAP...
WAS STUPID!
ARGH--!!!
SHINOBI READ THE HIDDEN MEANINGS WITHIN THE HIDDEN MEANINGS!
I KNOW THAT!!
FLAP
FLAP
UH, NO YOU DON'T. THAT'S WHY I'M SAYING IT.

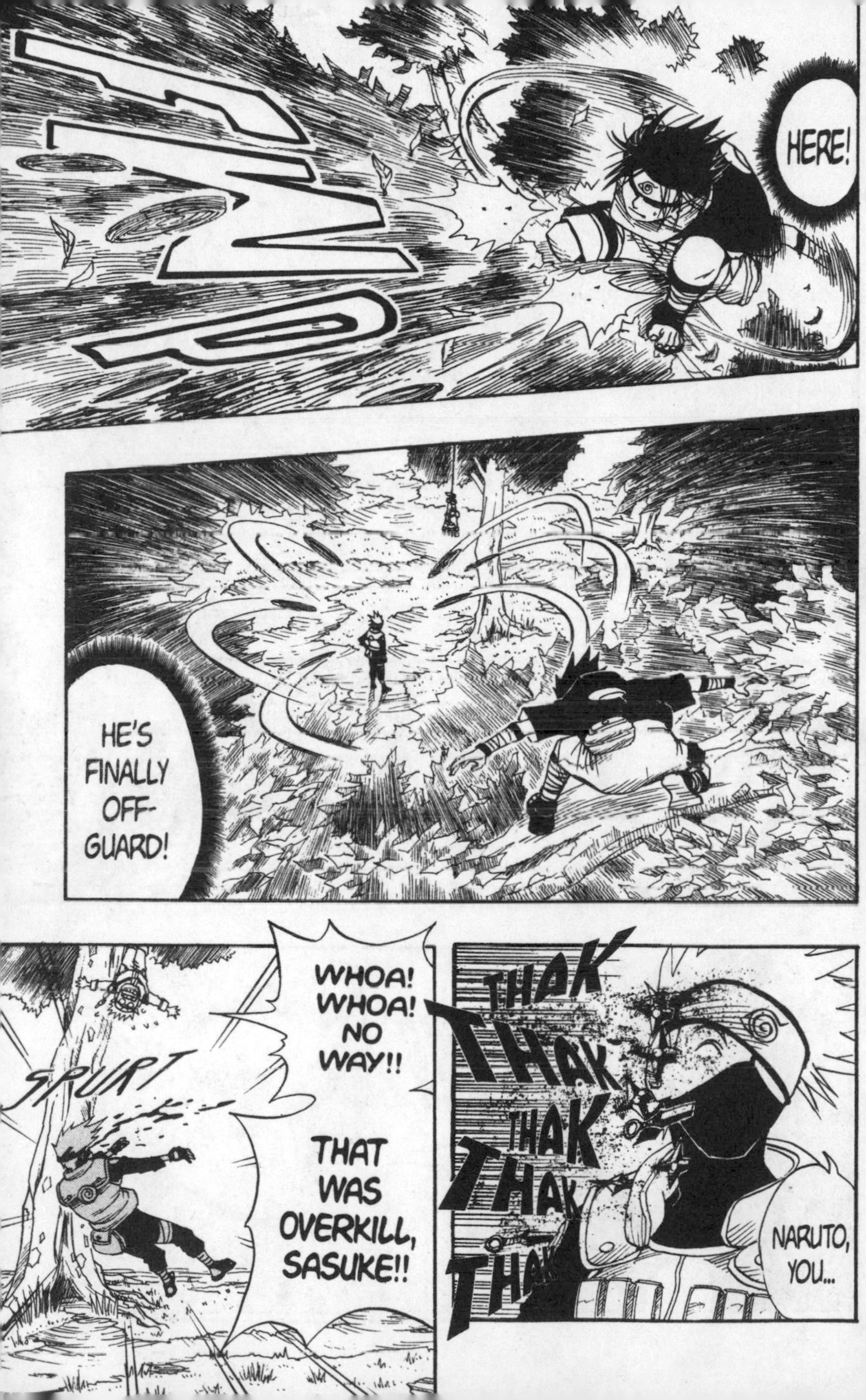
HERE!
HE'S FINALLY OFF-GUARD!
THAK THAK THAK THAK THAK
NARUTO, YOU...
WHOA! WHOA! NO WAY!!
THAT WAS OVERKILL, SASUKE!!
SPURT

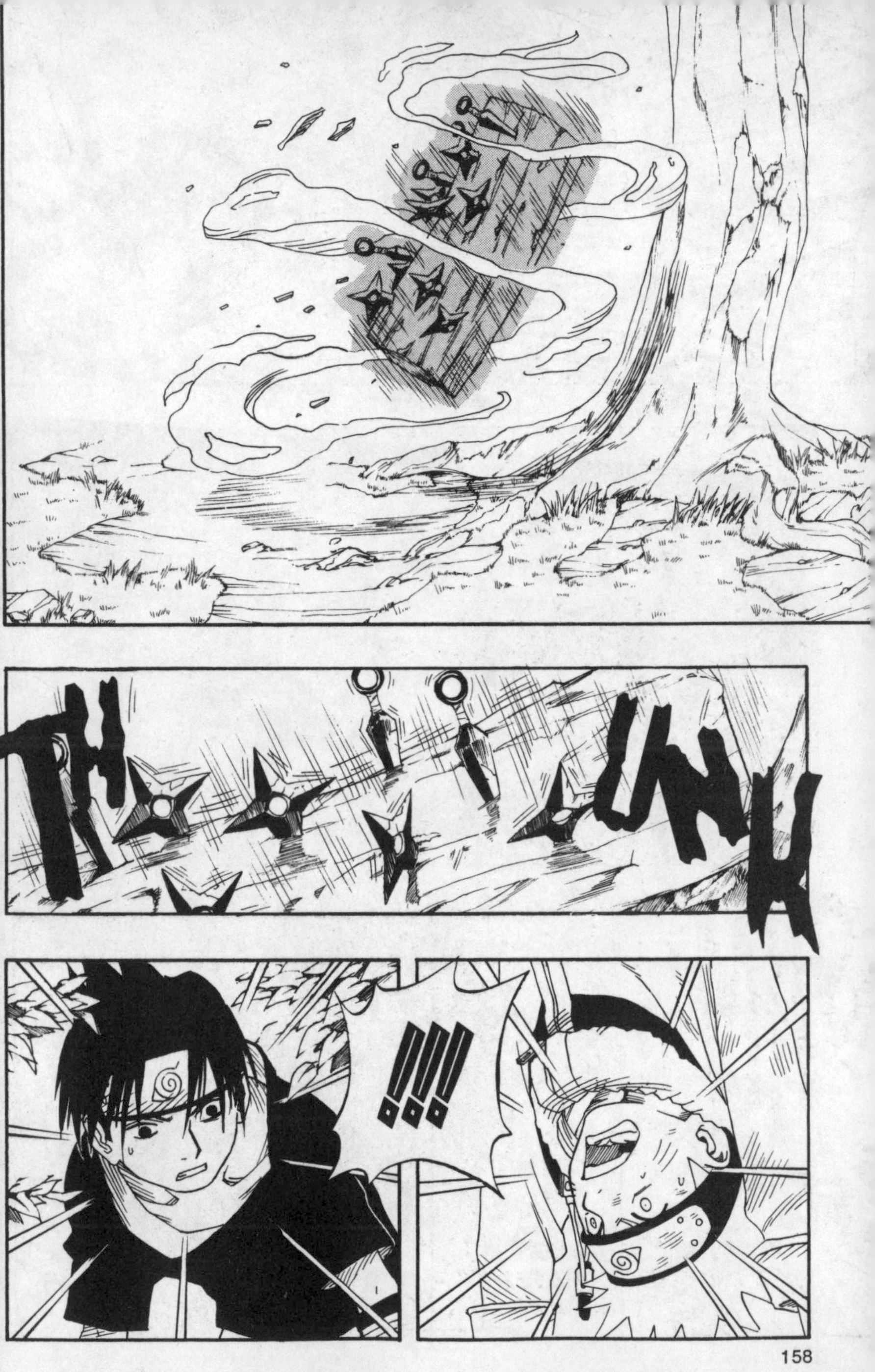
THUNK
!!!

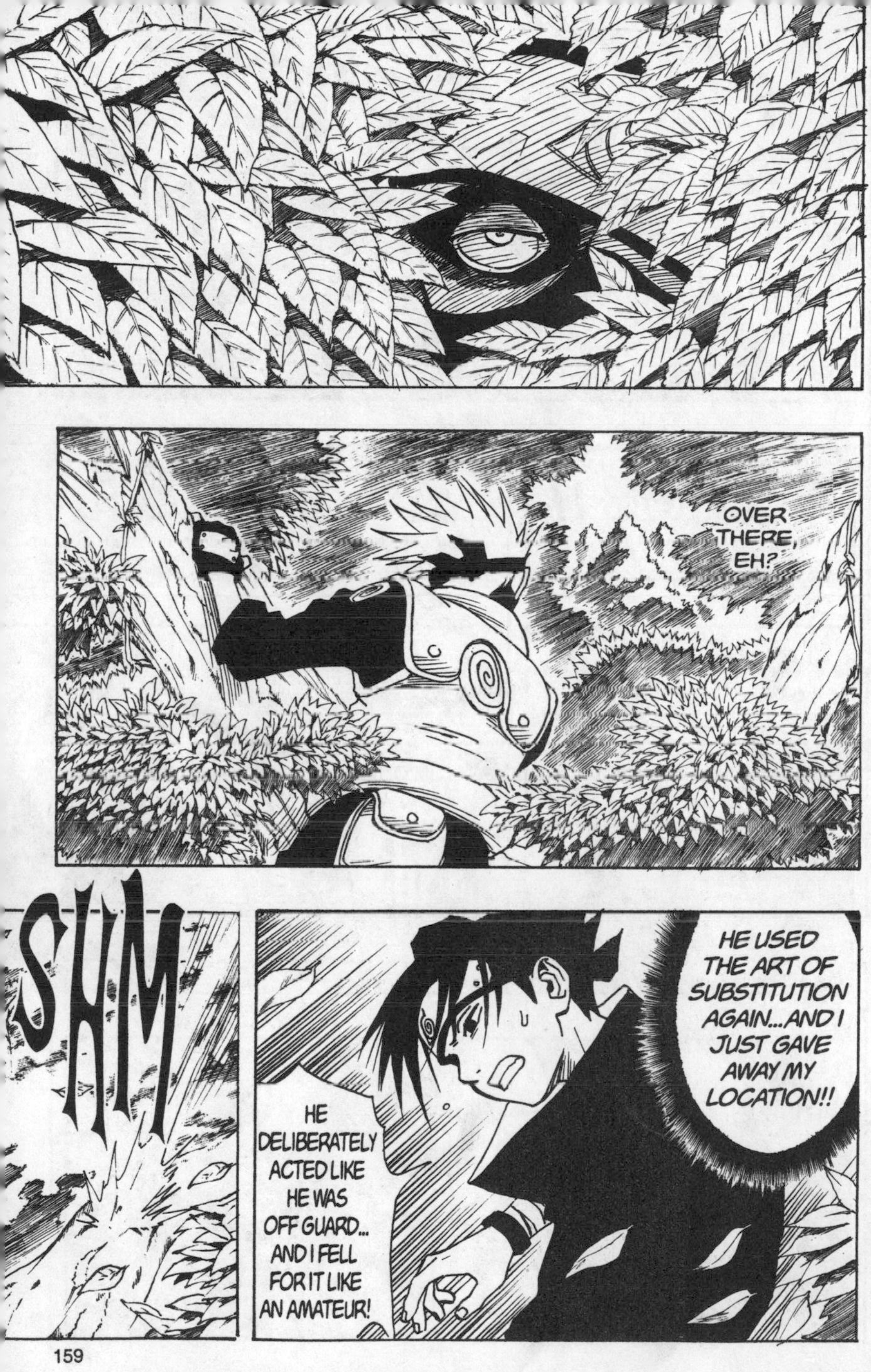
OVER THERE, EH?
HE USED THE ART OF SUBSTITUTION AGAIN...AND I JUST GAVE AWAY MY LOCATION!!
HE DELIBERATELY ACTED LIKE HE WAS OFF GUARD... AND I FELL FOR IT LIKE AN AMATEUR!
SHM

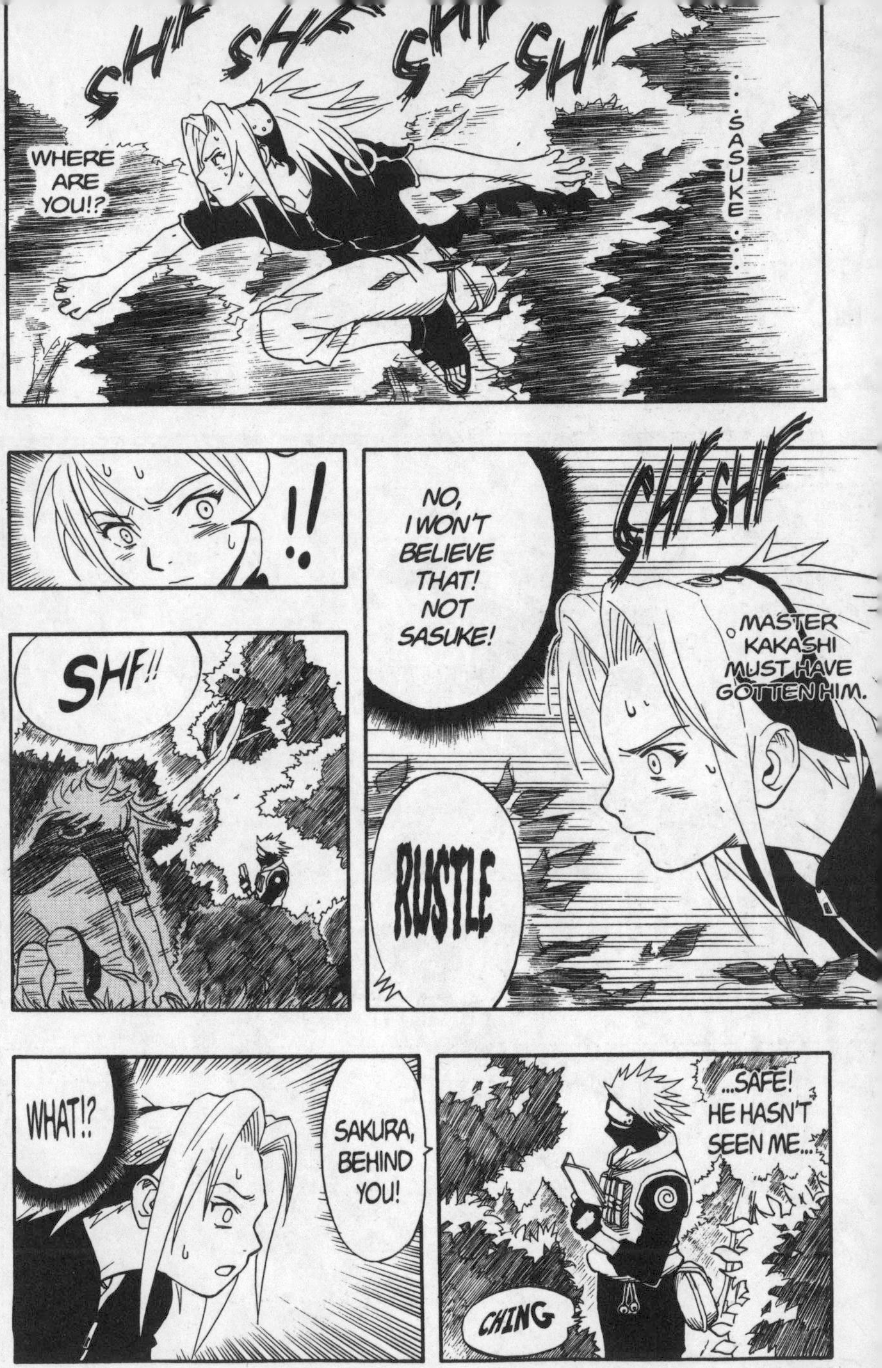
SHF SHF SHF SHF
...SASUKE...
WHERE ARE YOU!?
SHF SHF
MASTER KAKASHI MUST HAVE GOTTEN HIM.
NO, I WON'T BELIEVE THAT! NOT SASUKE!
RUSTLE
!!
SHF!!
...SAFE! HE HASN'T SEEN ME...
CHING
SAKURA, BEHIND YOU!
WHAT!?

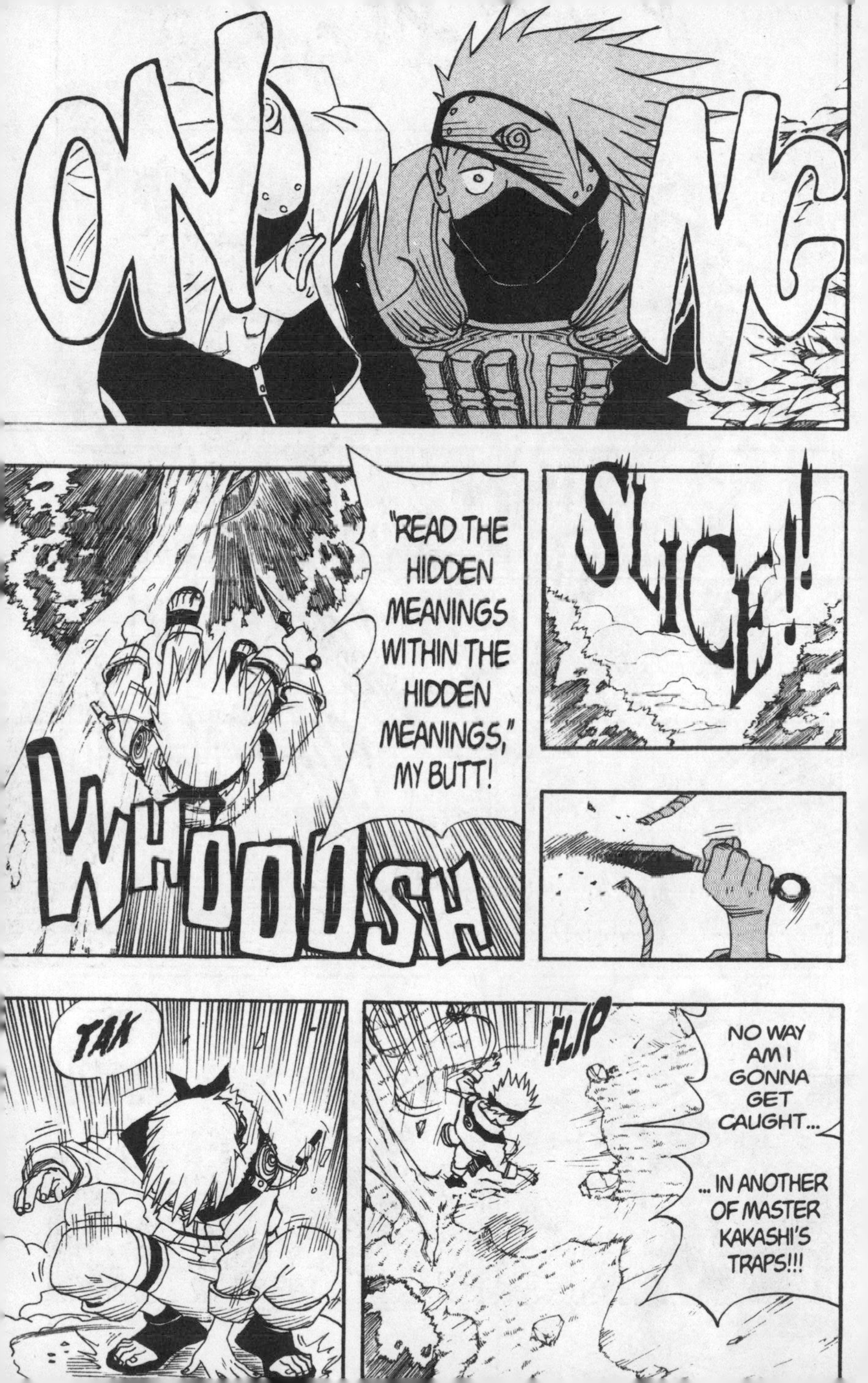
OW
NG
SLICE!!
"READ THE HIDDEN MEANINGS WITHIN THE HIDDEN MEANINGS," MY BUTT!
WHOOOSH
FLIP
NO WAY AM I GONNA GET CAUGHT...
...IN ANOTHER OF MASTER KAKASHI'S TRAPS!!!
TAK

READ THIS WAY

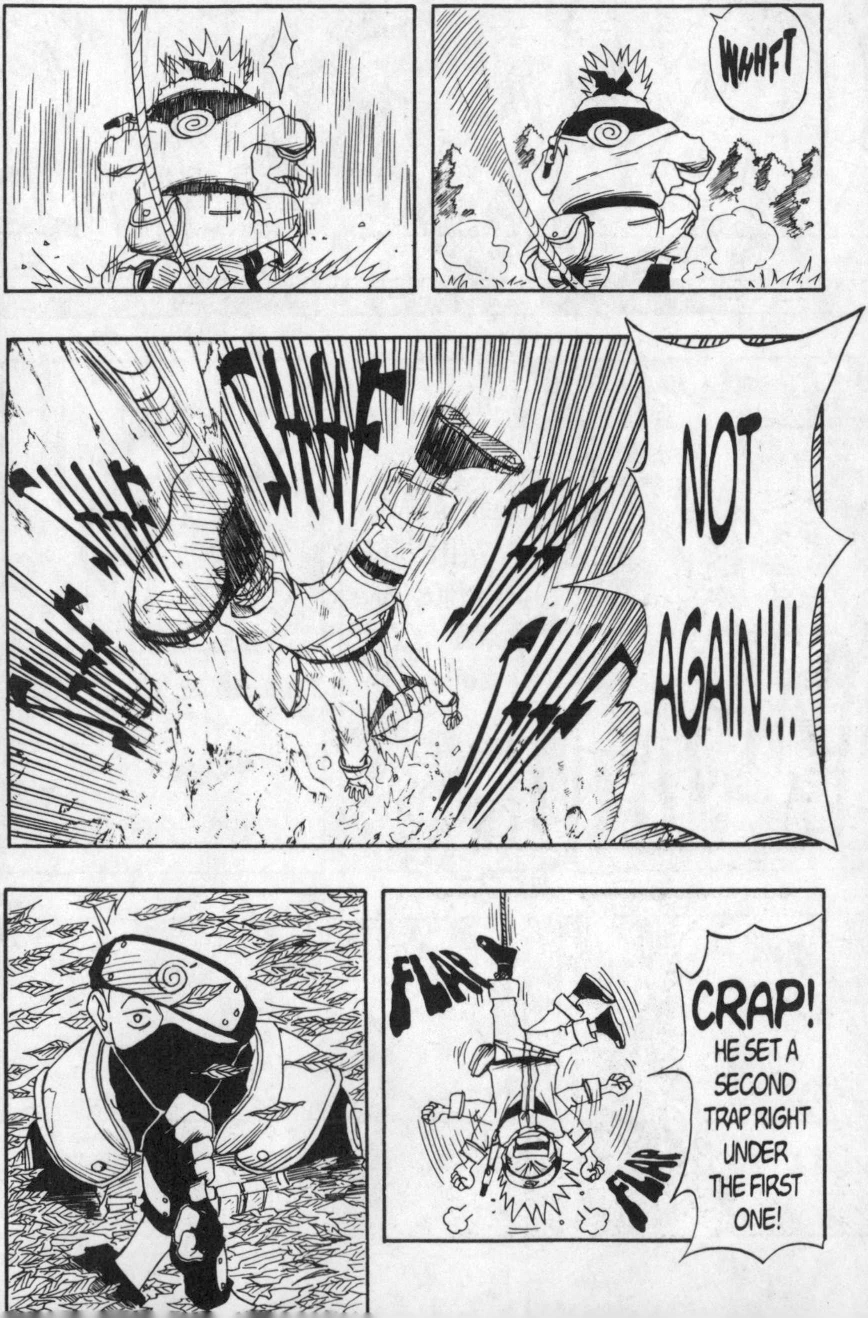
WHHFT
NOT AGAIN!!!
SHFF
SHHF
CRAP!
HE SET A SECOND TRAP RIGHT UNDER THE FIRST ONE!
FLAP
FLAP

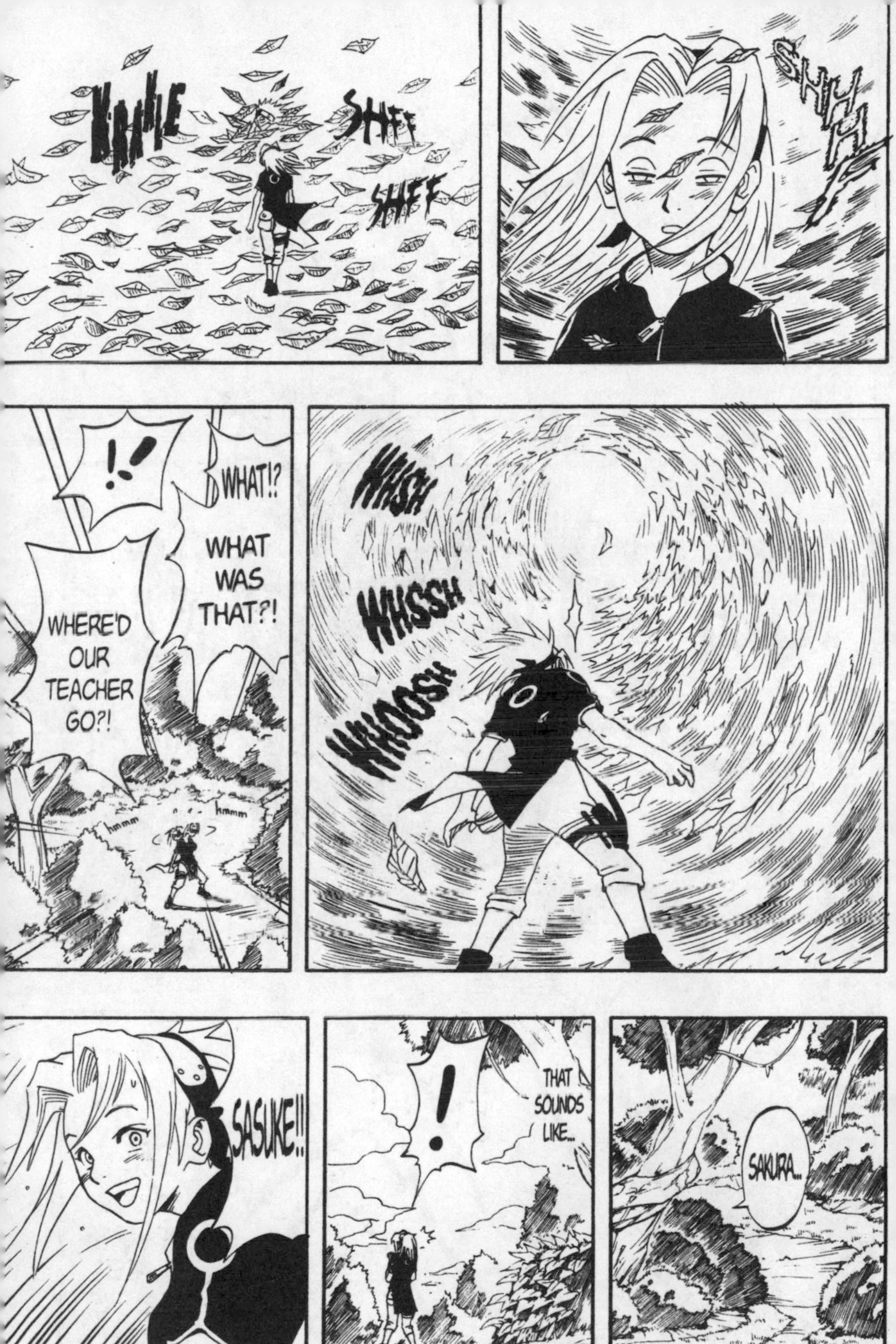
SHHHF
SHFF
SHFF
WHSH
WHSSH
WHOOSH
!!
WHAT!?
WHAT WAS THAT?!
WHERE'D OUR TEACHER GO?!
hmmm
hmmm
SAKURA...
!
THAT SOUNDS LIKE...
SASUKE!!

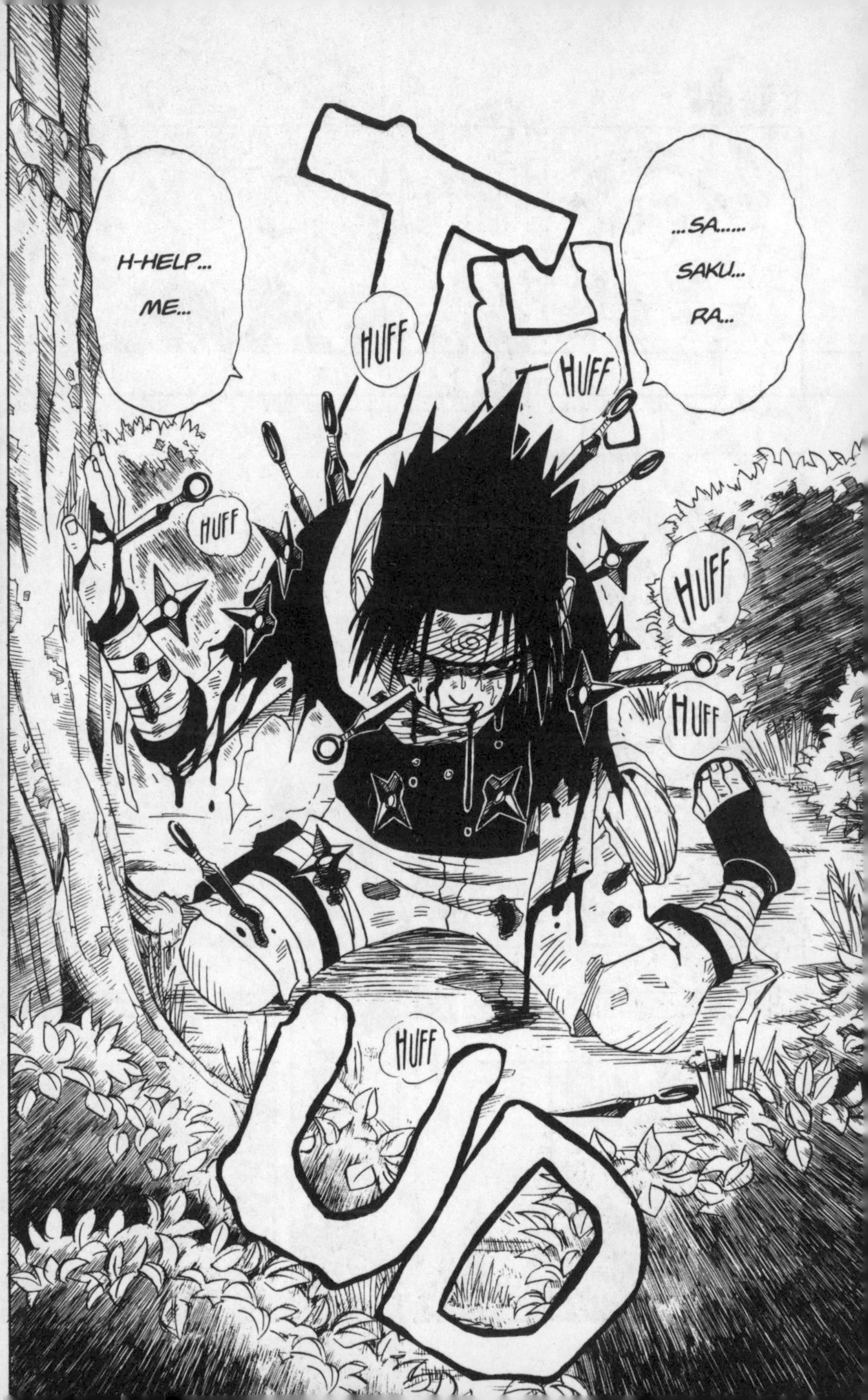
...SA...... SAKU... RA...
H-HELP... ME...
HUFF
HUFF
HUFF
HUFF
HUFF
HUFF

READ THIS WAY

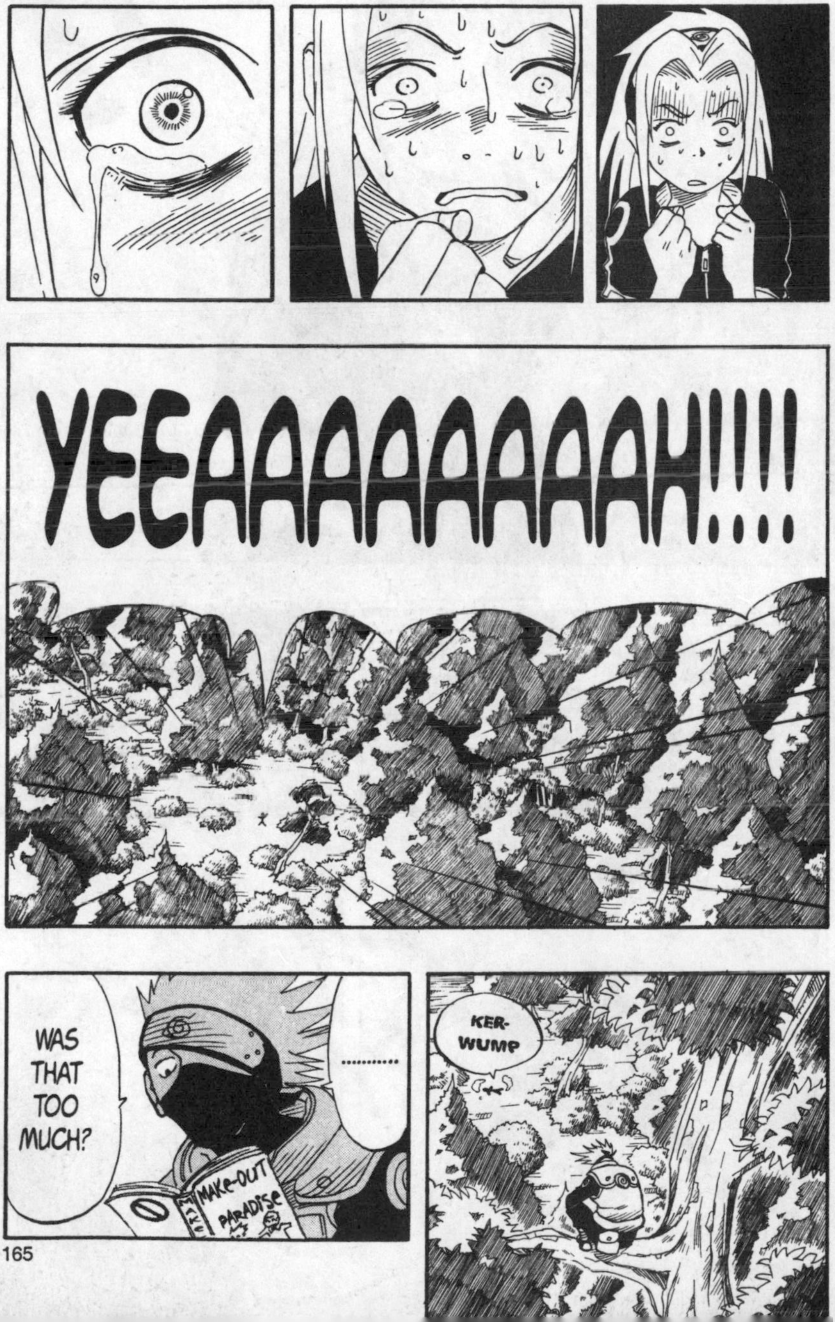
YEEAAAAAAAAH!!!!
KER-WUMP
....
WAS THAT TOO MUCH?
MAKE-OUT PARADISE

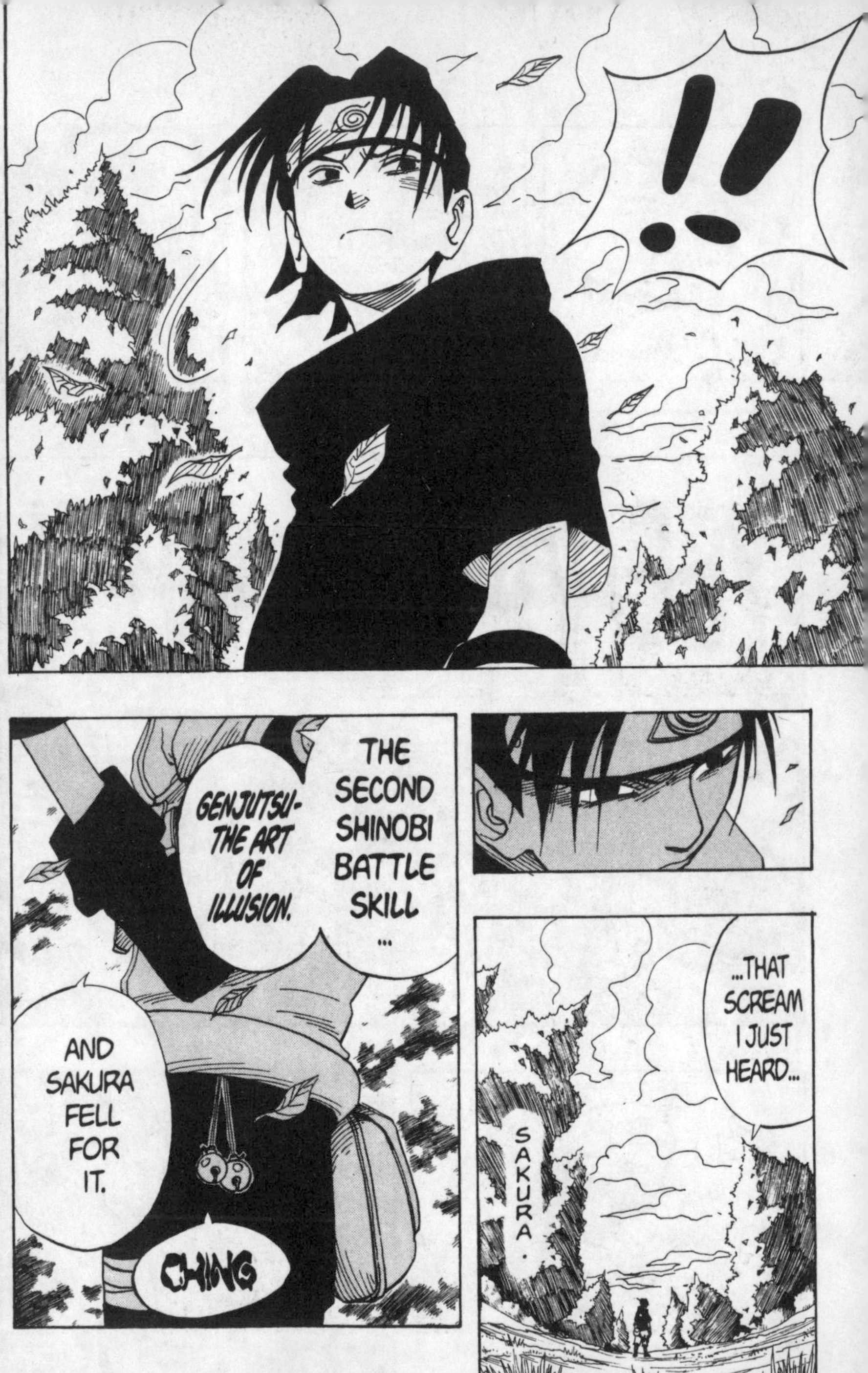
!!
...THAT SCREAM I JUST HEARD...
SAKURA.
THE SECOND SHINOBI BATTLE SKILL ...
GENJUTSU- THE ART OF ILLUSION.
AND SAKURA FELL FOR IT.
CHING

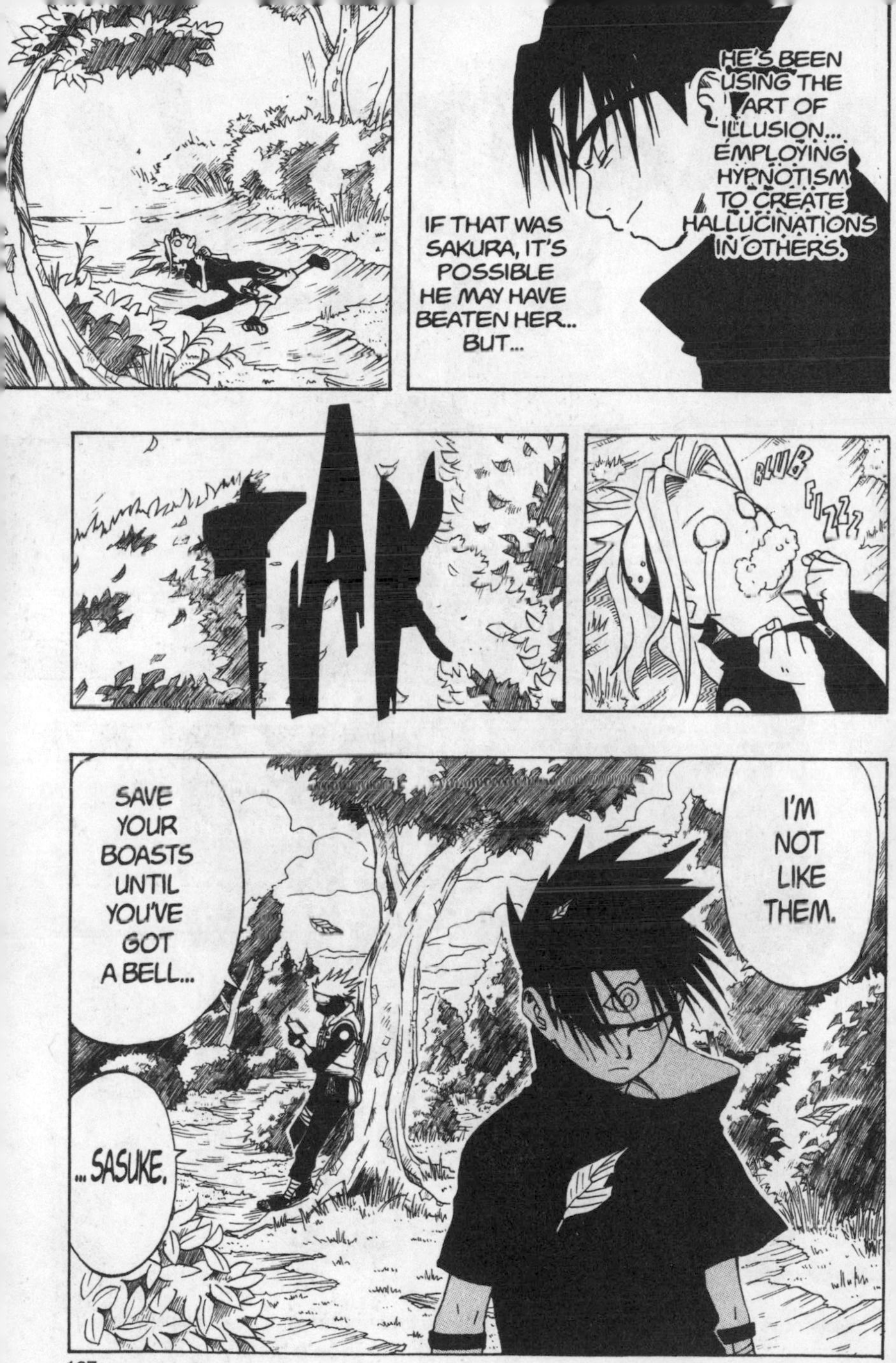
HE'S BEEN USING THE ART OF ILLUSION... EMPLOYING HYPNOTISM TO CREATE HALLUCINATIONS IN OTHERS.
IF THAT WAS SAKURA, IT'S POSSIBLE HE MAY HAVE BEATEN HER... BUT...
BLUB
FIZZZ
TAK
I'M NOT LIKE THEM.
SAVE YOUR BOASTS UNTIL YOU'VE GOT A BELL...
...SASUKE.

NARUTO STAFF

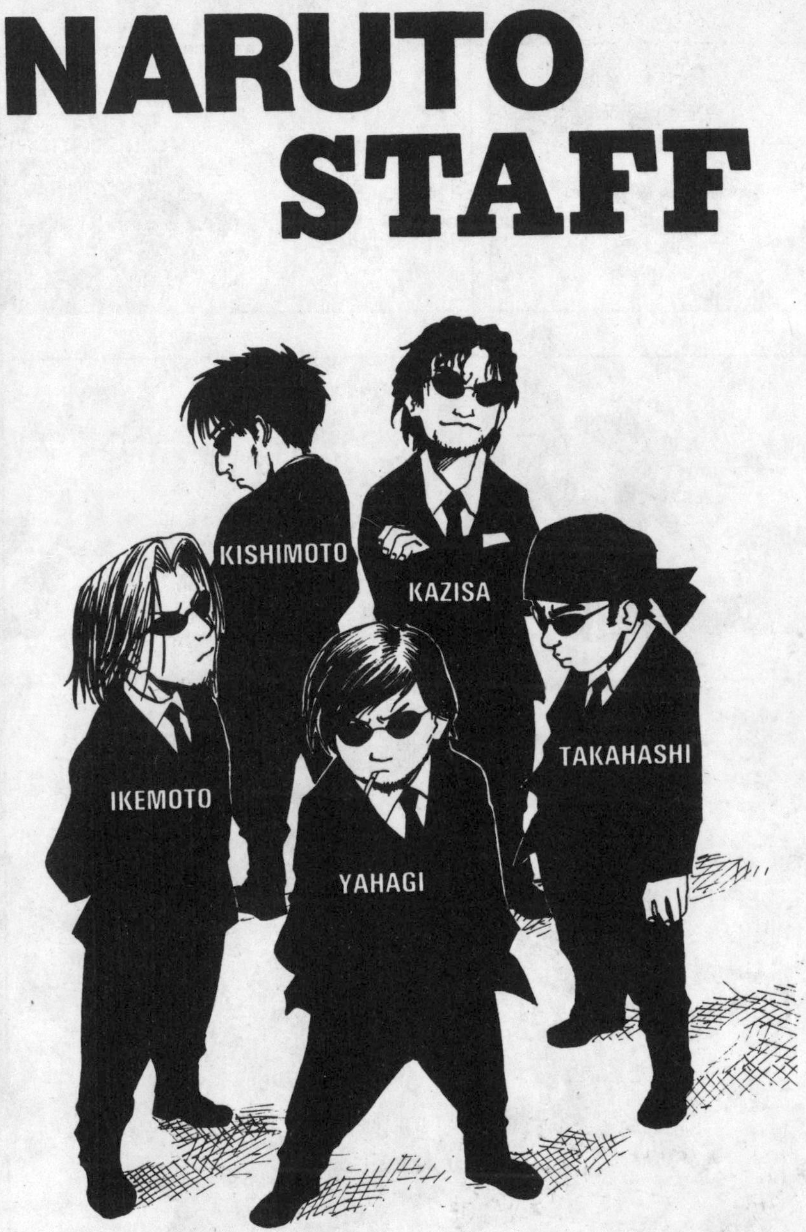
KISHIMOTO
KAZISA
TAKAHASHI
IKEMOTO
YAHAGI

Kishimoto and his assistants work together to create **Naruto** for the Japanese **Weekly Shonen Jump** magazine…20 pages a week!

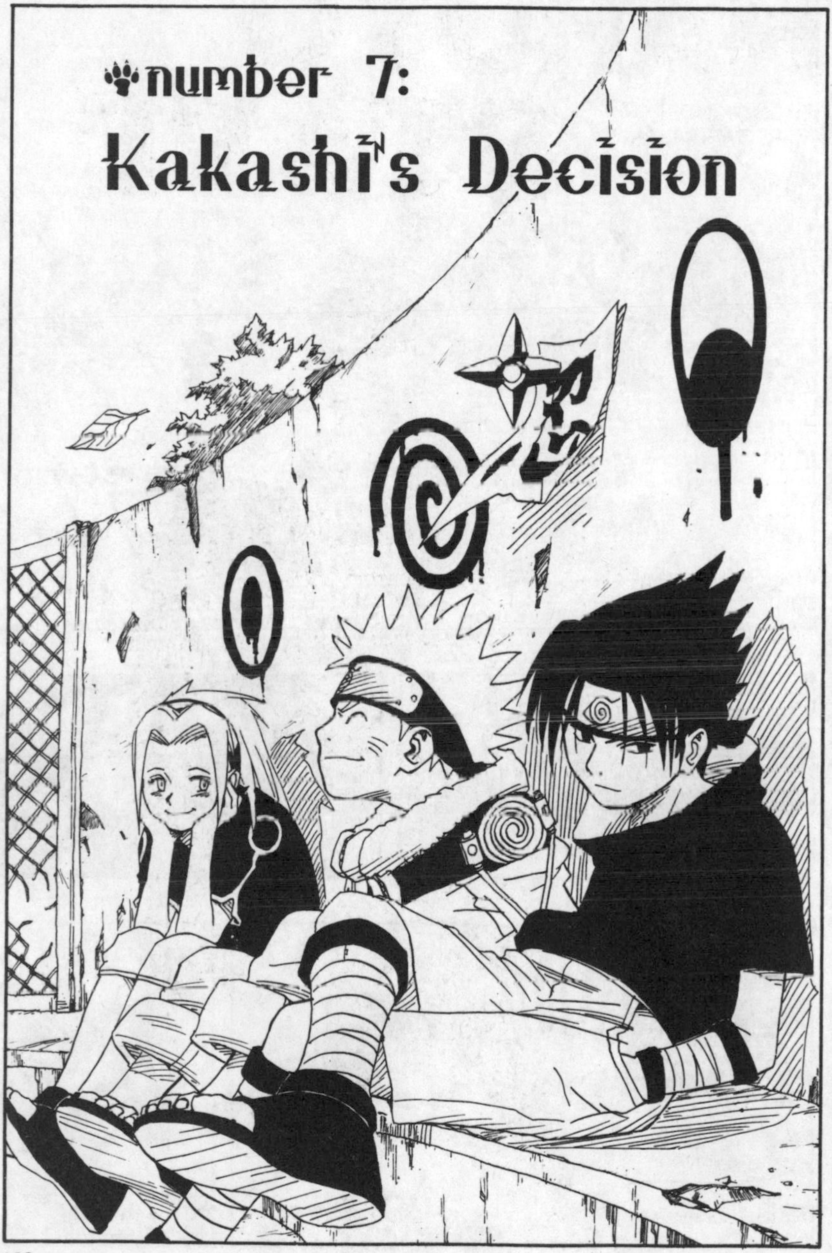
number 7:
Kakashi's Decision

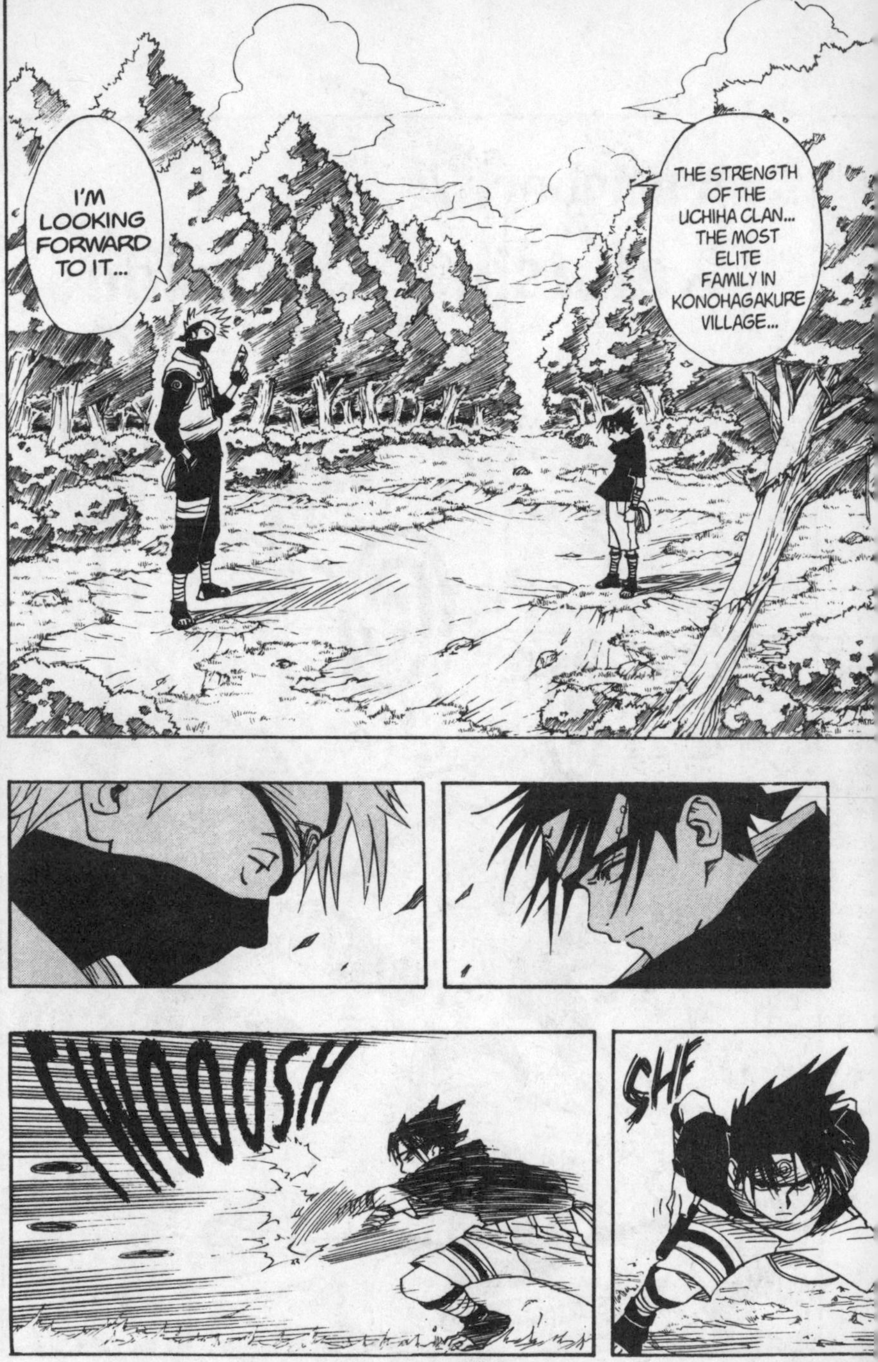
THE STRENGTH OF THE UCHIHA CLAN... THE MOST ELITE FAMILY IN KONOHAGAKURE VILLAGE...
I'M LOOKING FORWARD TO IT...
SHF
SWOOOSH

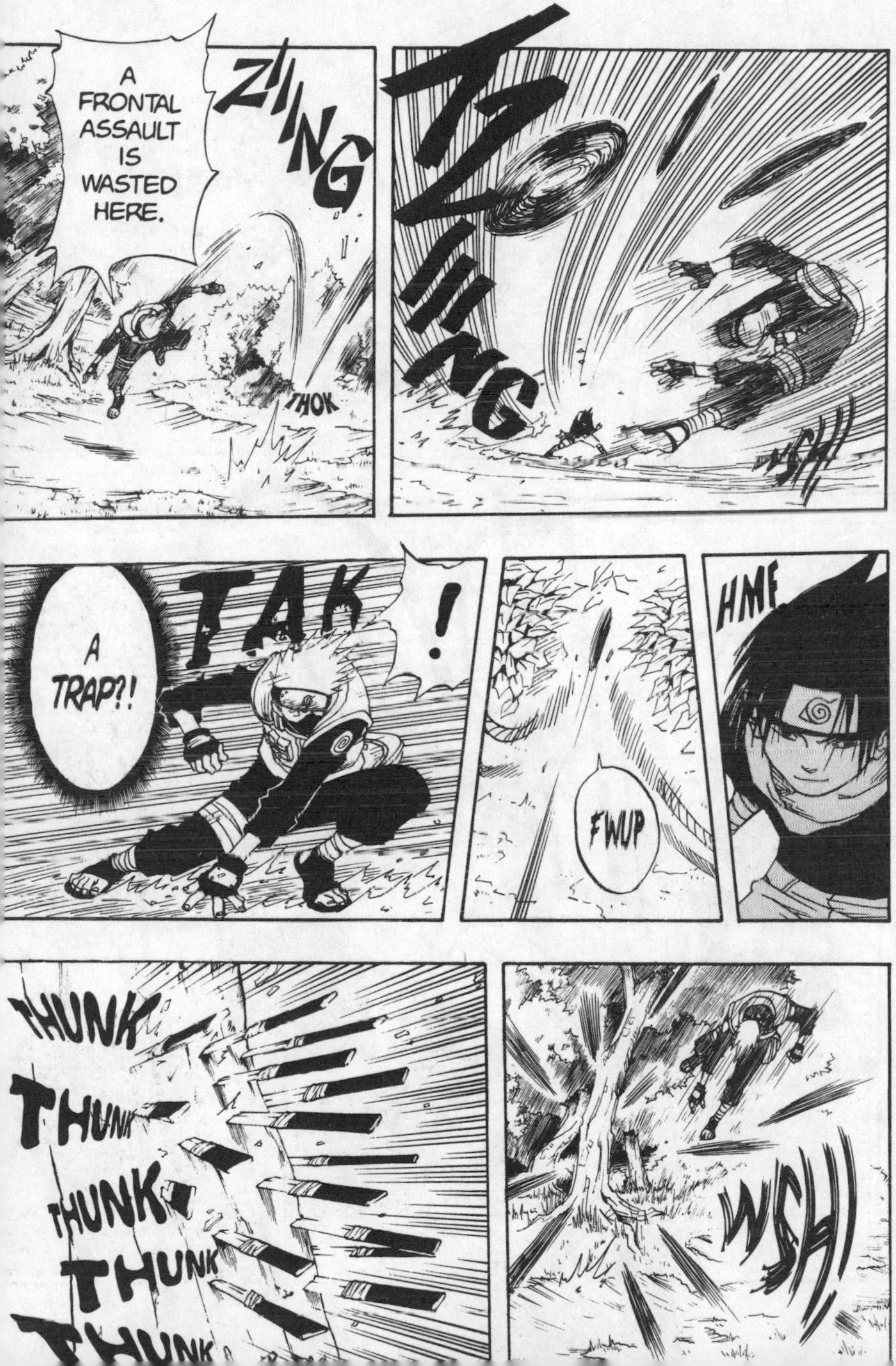
ZIIIING
WSH
ZIING
A FRONTAL ASSAULT IS WASTED HERE.
THOK
HMF
FWUP
TAK!
A TRAP?!
WSH
THUNK
THUNK
THUNK
THUNK
THUNK

READ THIS WAY

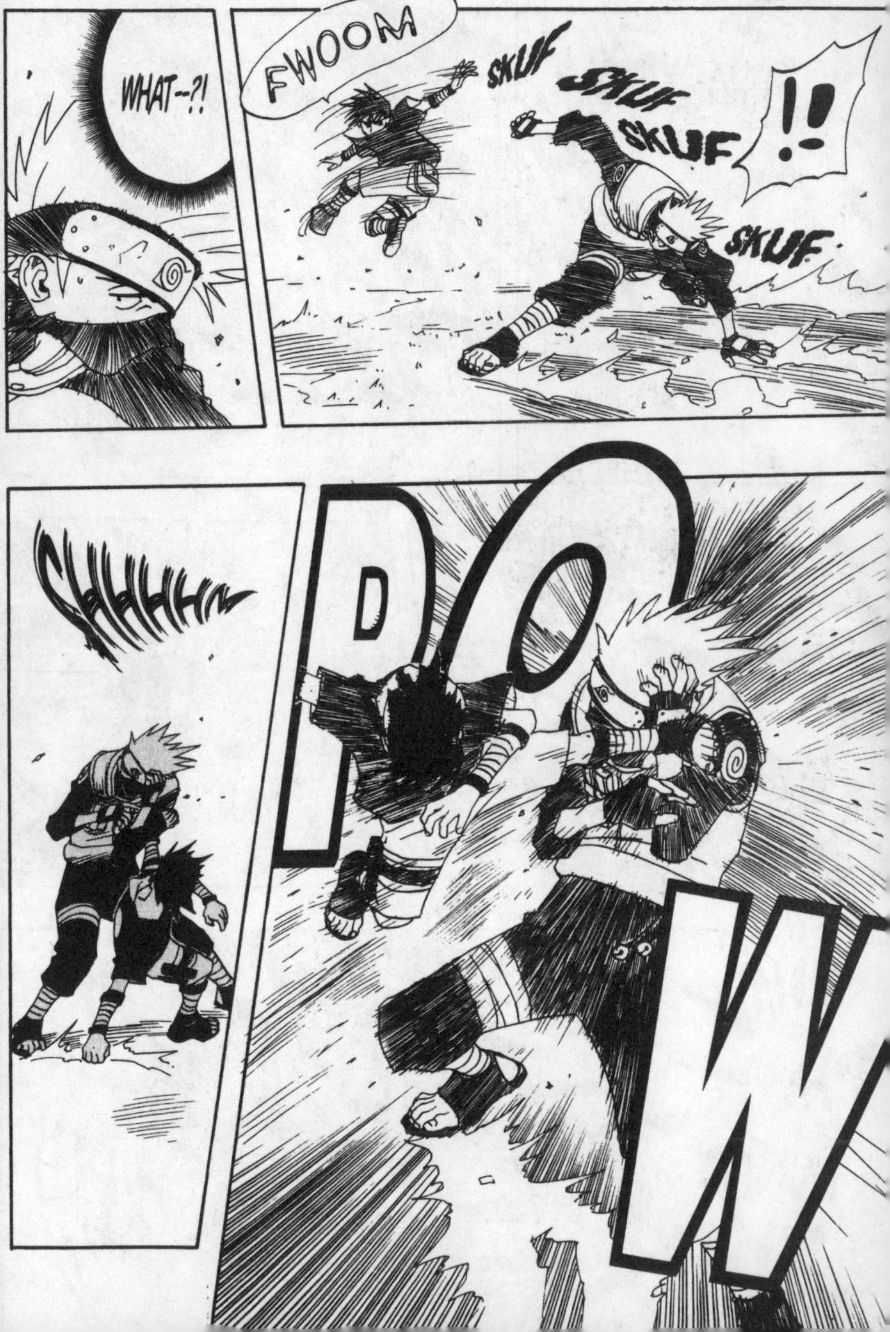
!!
SKUF
SKUF
SKUF
SKUF
FWOOM
WHAT--?!
POW

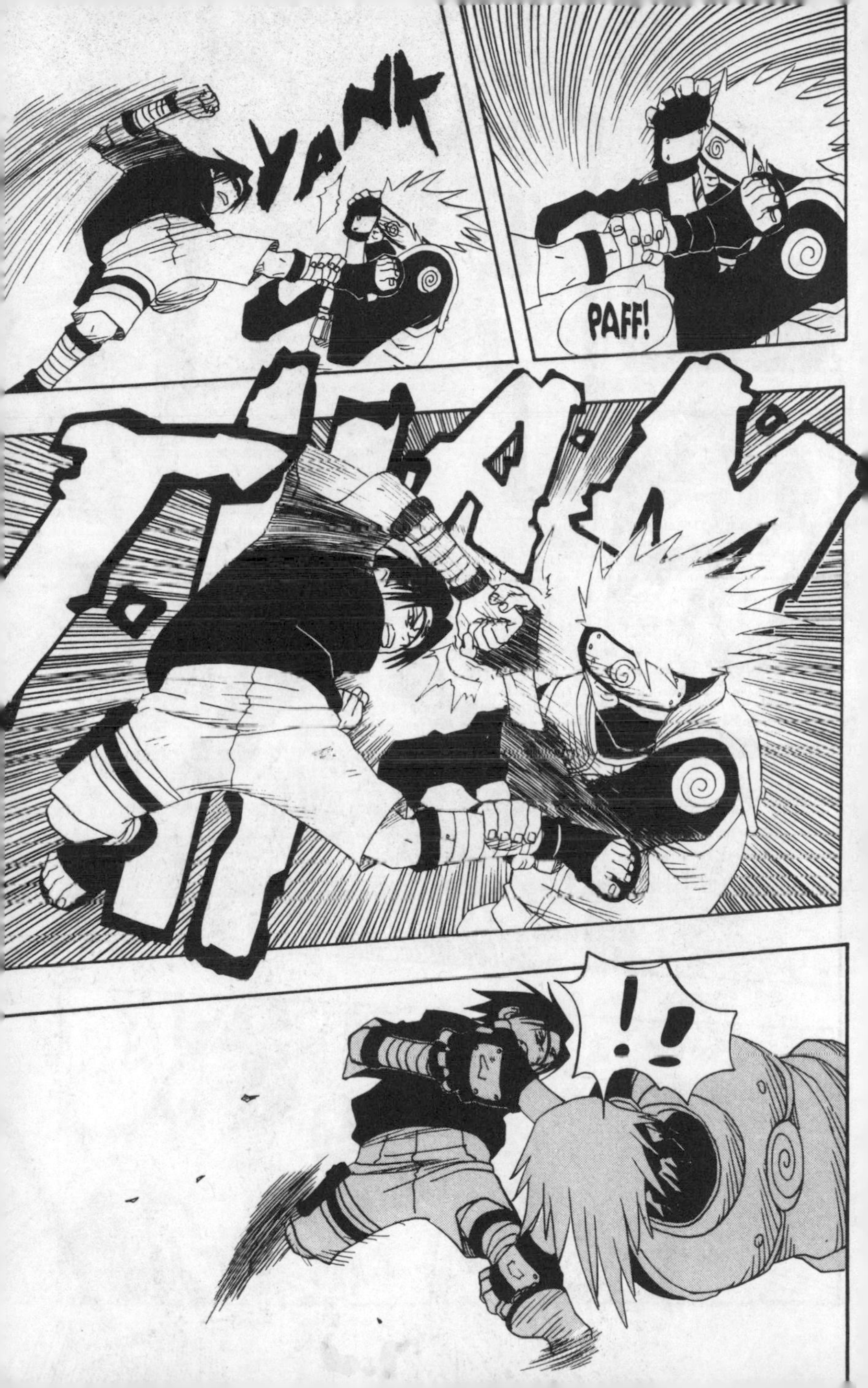
PAFF!
YANK
!!

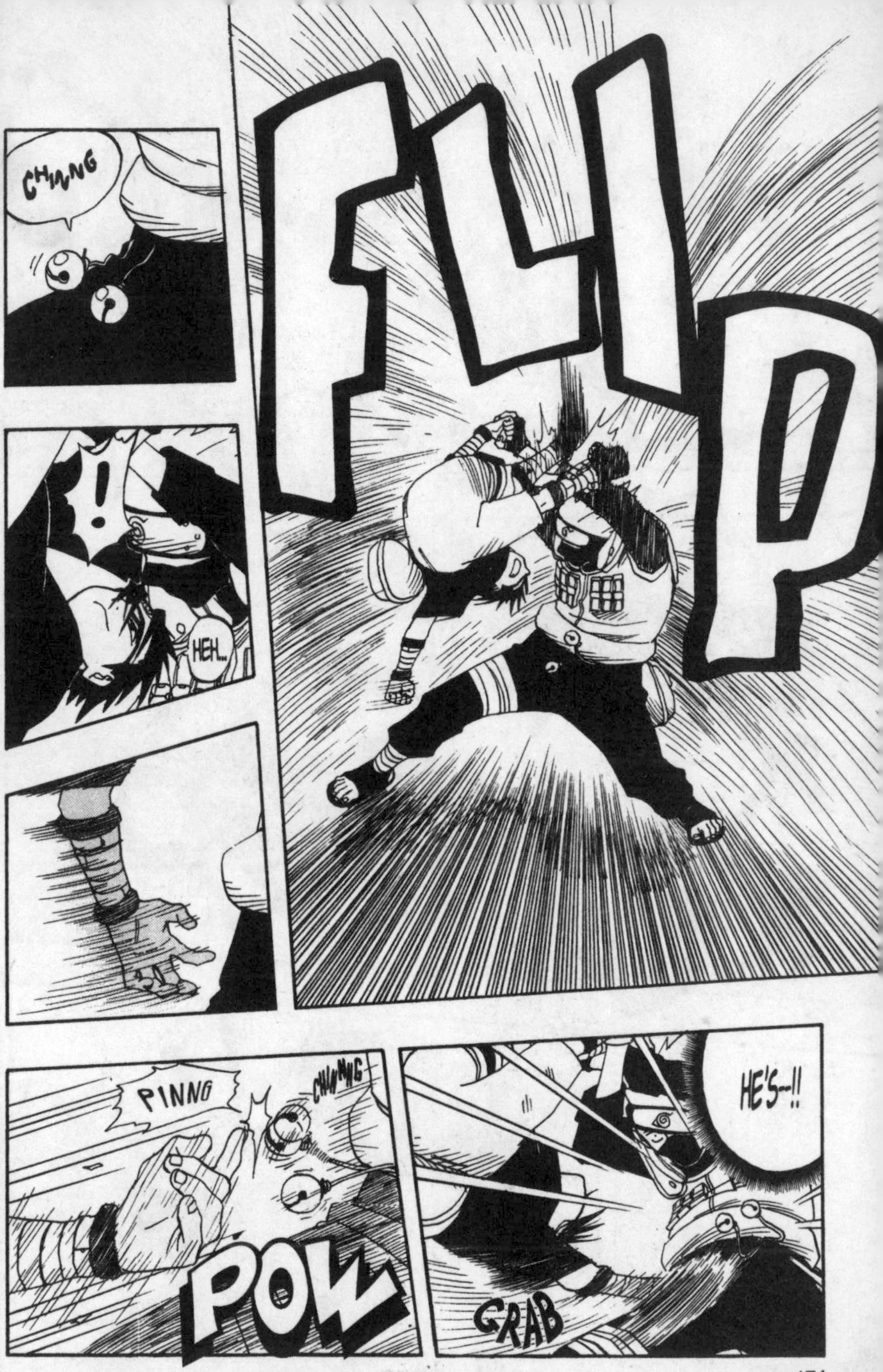

FLIP
CHINNG
!
HEH...
HE'S--!!
GRAB
PINNG
CHINNNG
POW

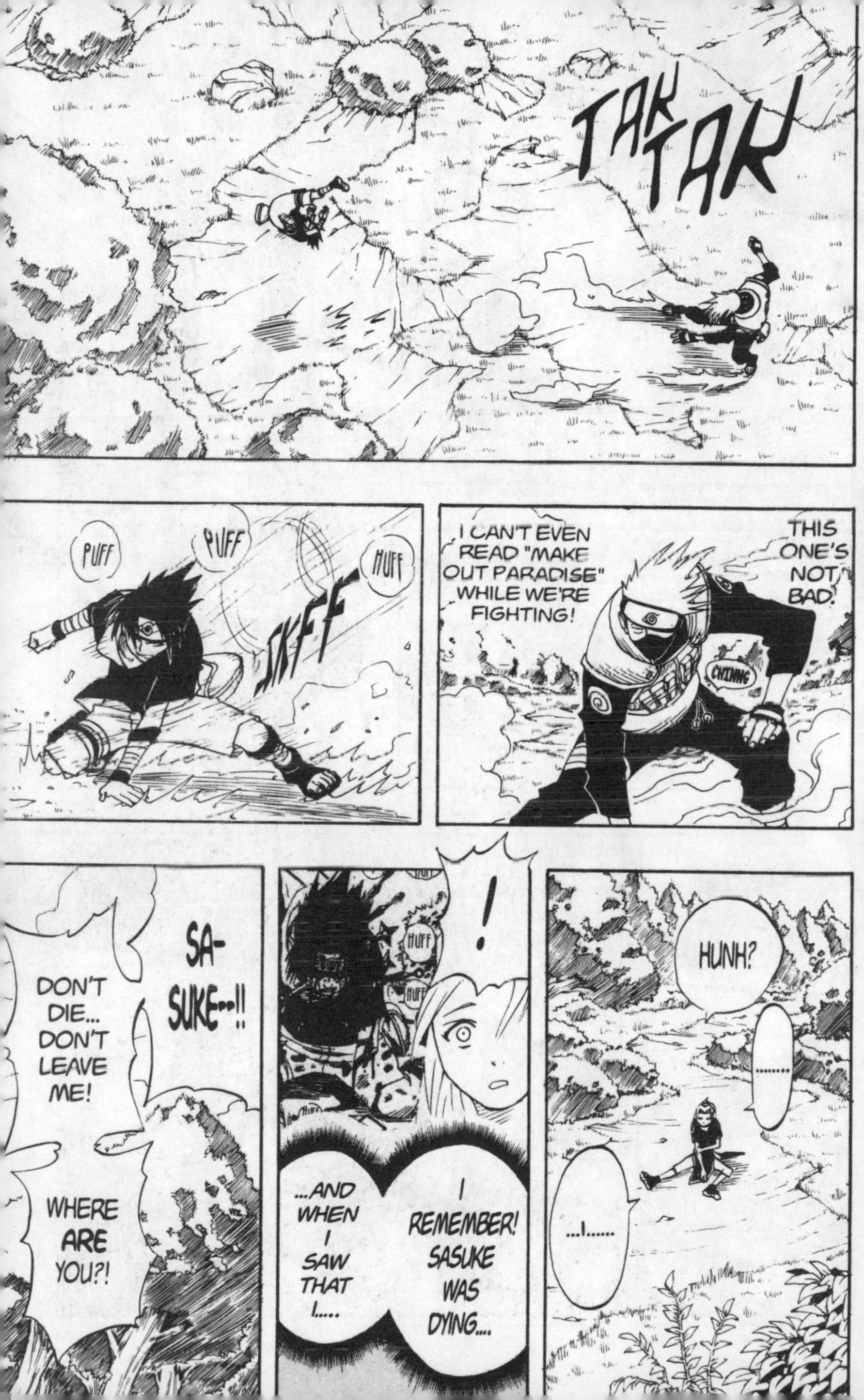
TAK TAK
THIS ONE'S NOT BAD.
I CAN'T EVEN READ "MAKE OUT PARADISE" WHILE WE'RE FIGHTING!
CHIINNG
PUFF
PUFF
HUFF
SKFF
HUNH?
....
...I......
!
HUFF
HUFF
HUFF
I REMEMBER! SASUKE WAS DYING...
...AND WHEN I SAW THAT I.....
SA-SUKE--!!
DON'T DIE... DON'T LEAVE ME!
WHERE ARE YOU?!

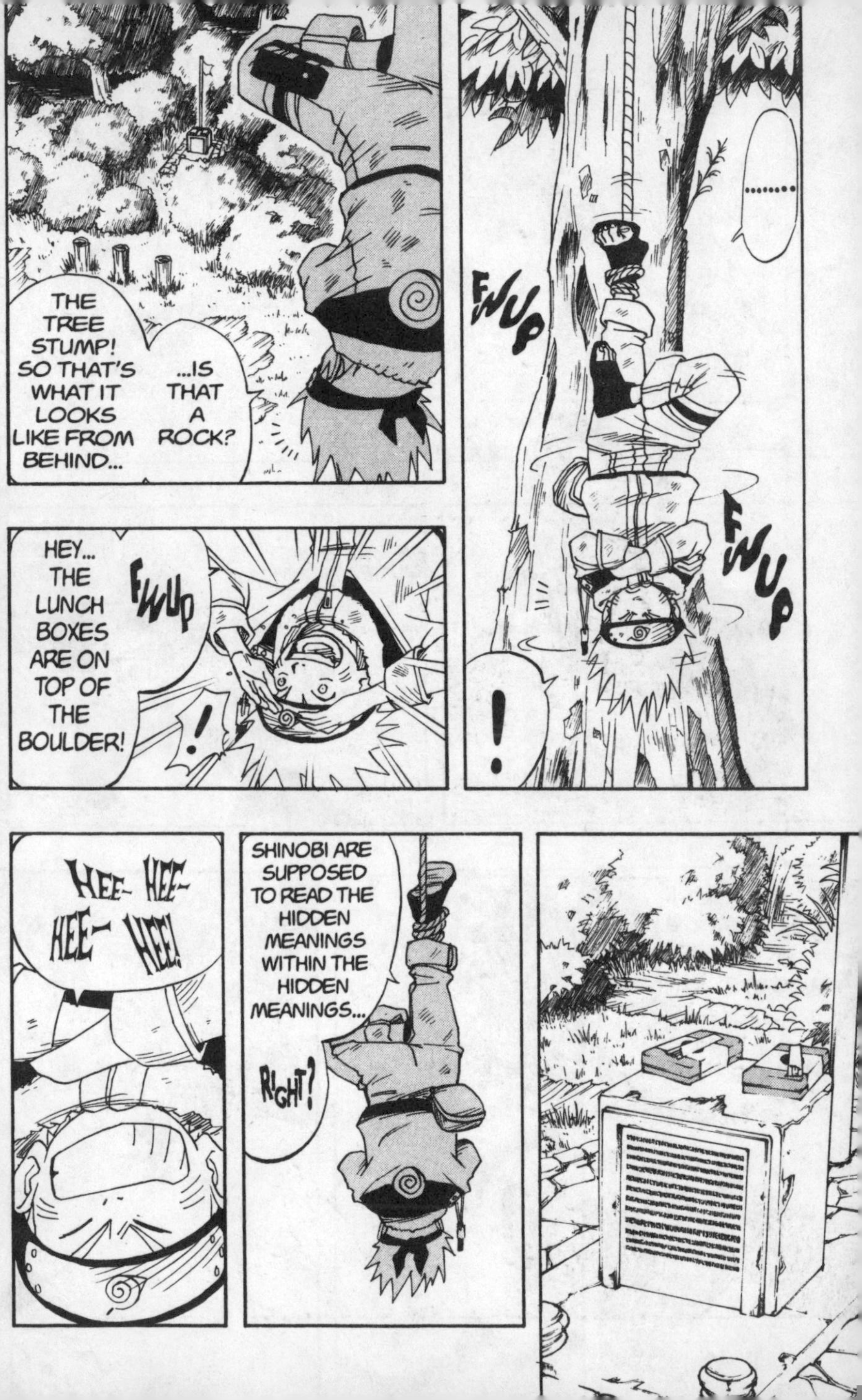

....
FWUP
FWUP
!
THE TREE STUMP! SO THAT'S WHAT IT LOOKS LIKE FROM BEHIND... ...IS THAT A ROCK?
HEY... THE LUNCH BOXES ARE ON TOP OF THE BOULDER!
FWUP
!
SHINOBI ARE SUPPOSED TO READ THE HIDDEN MEANINGS WITHIN THE HIDDEN MEANINGS...
RIGHT?
HEE- HEE- HEE- HEE!

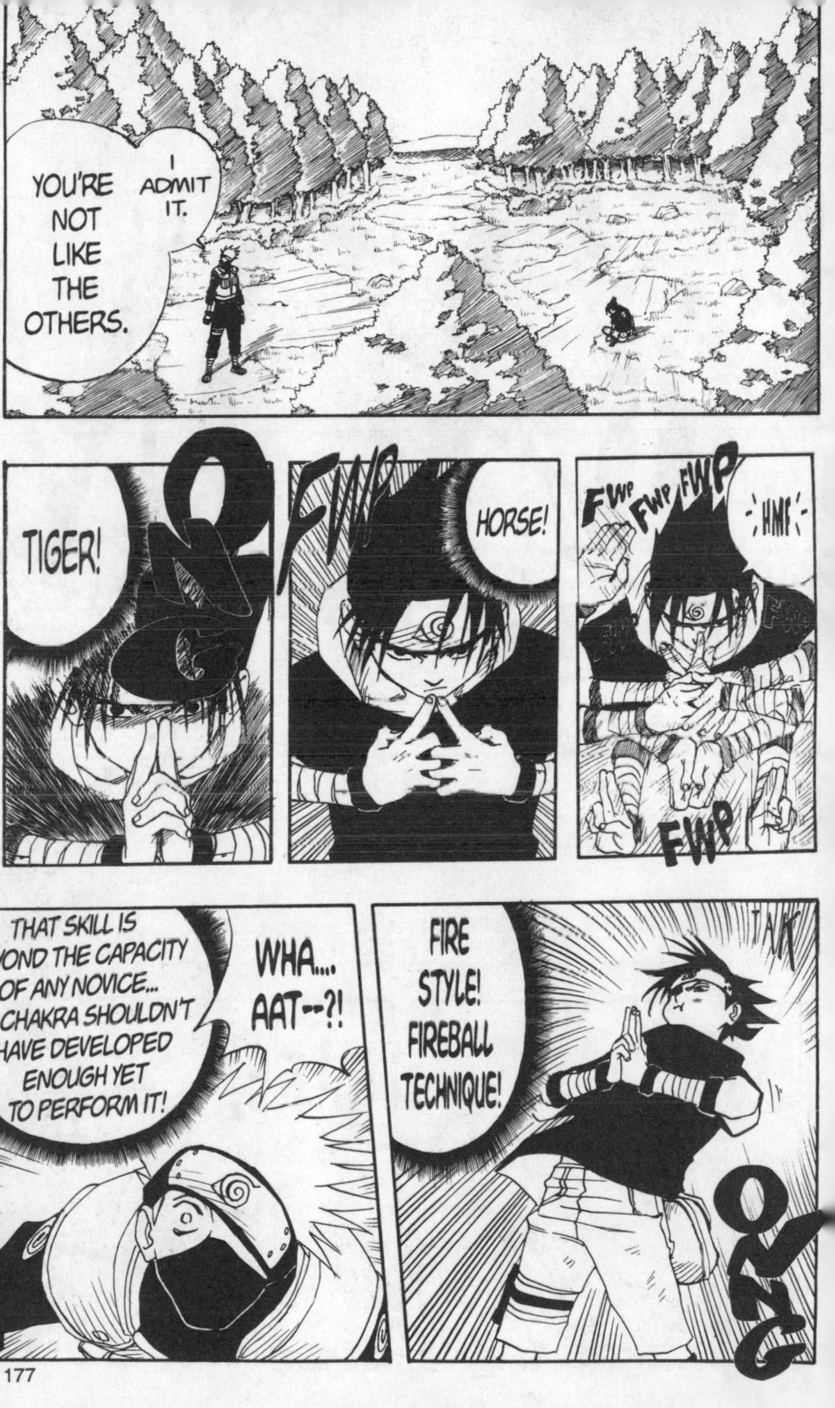
I ADMIT IT.
YOU'RE NOT LIKE THE OTHERS.
FWP FWP FWP
FWP
-HMF-
FWP
HORSE!
TIGER!
TAK
FIRE STYLE! FIREBALL TECHNIQUE!
ONG
WHA.... AAT--?!
THAT SKILL IS BEYOND THE CAPACITY OF ANY NOVICE... HIS CHAKRA SHOULDN'T HAVE DEVELOPED ENOUGH YET TO PERFORM IT!

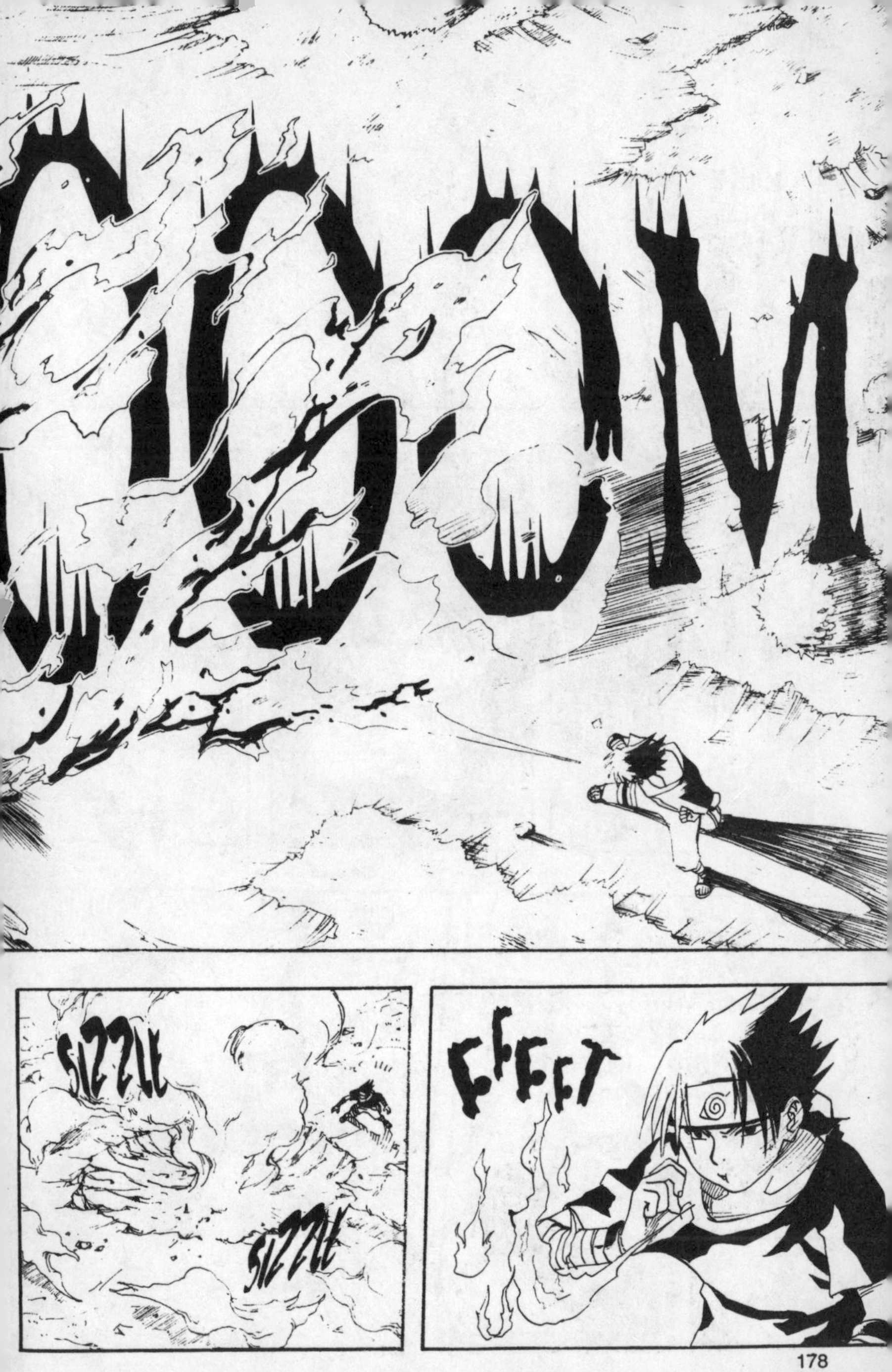
FFFT
SIZZLE
SIZZLE

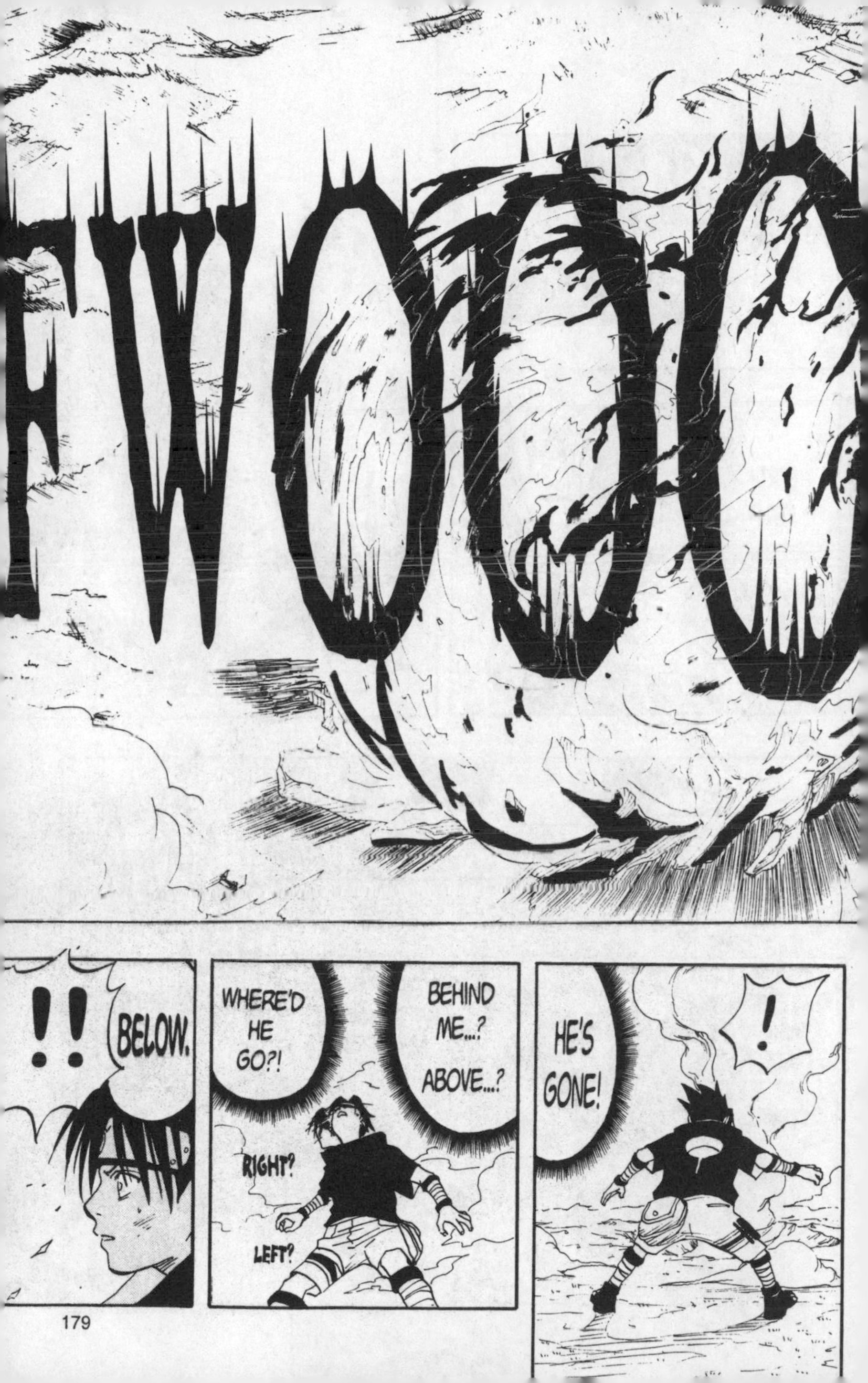
FWOOO
!
HE'S GONE!
BEHIND ME...? ABOVE...?
WHERE'D HE GO?!
RIGHT?
LEFT?
BELOW.
!!

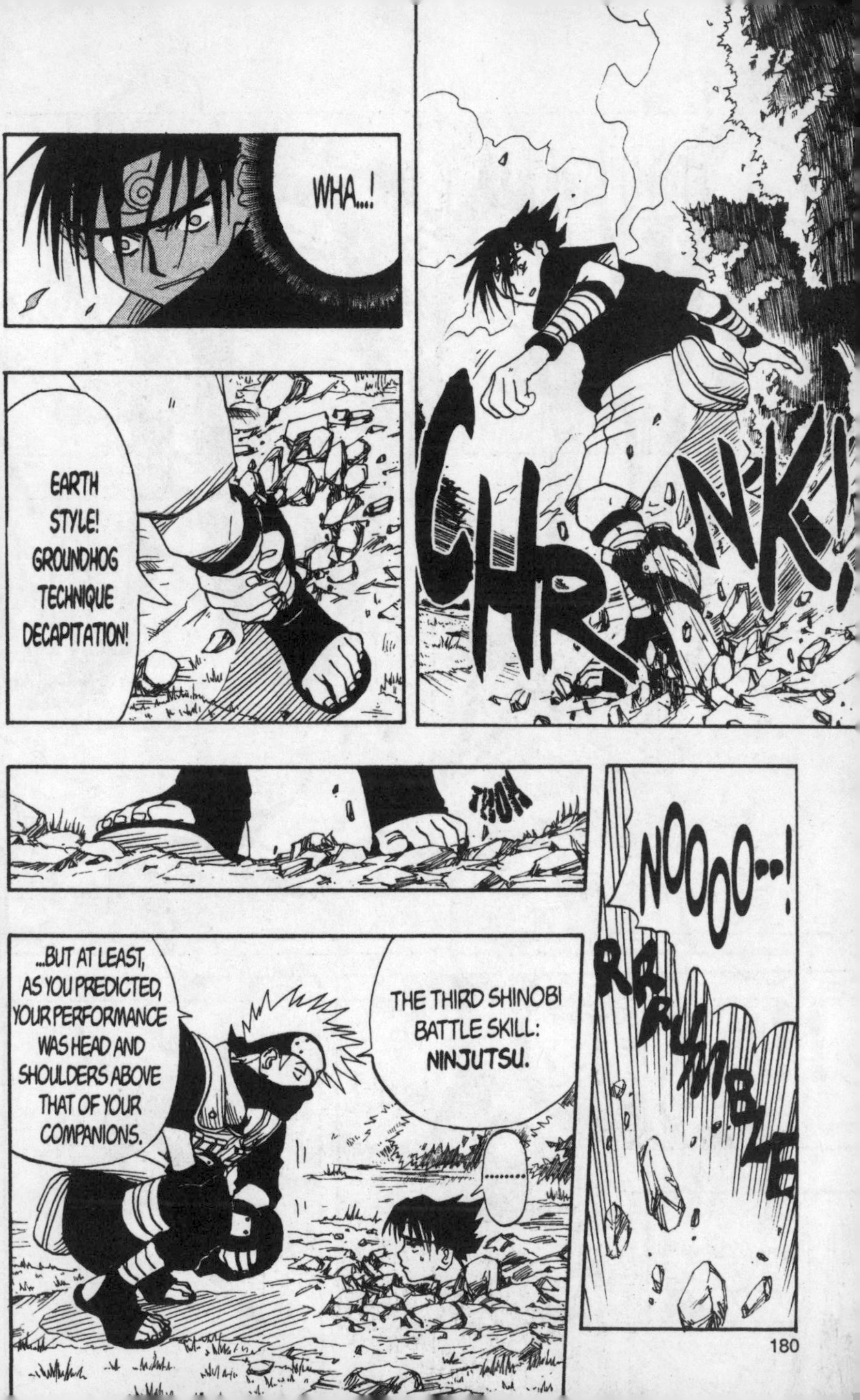
CHRNK!!
WHA...!
EARTH STYLE! GROUNDHOG TECHNIQUE DECAPITATION!
NOOOO--!
RRRUMBLE
THUH
THE THIRD SHINOBI BATTLE SKILL: NINJUTSU.
...BUT AT LEAST, AS YOU PREDICTED, YOUR PERFORMANCE WAS HEAD AND SHOULDERS ABOVE THAT OF YOUR COMPANIONS.
....

READ THIS WAY

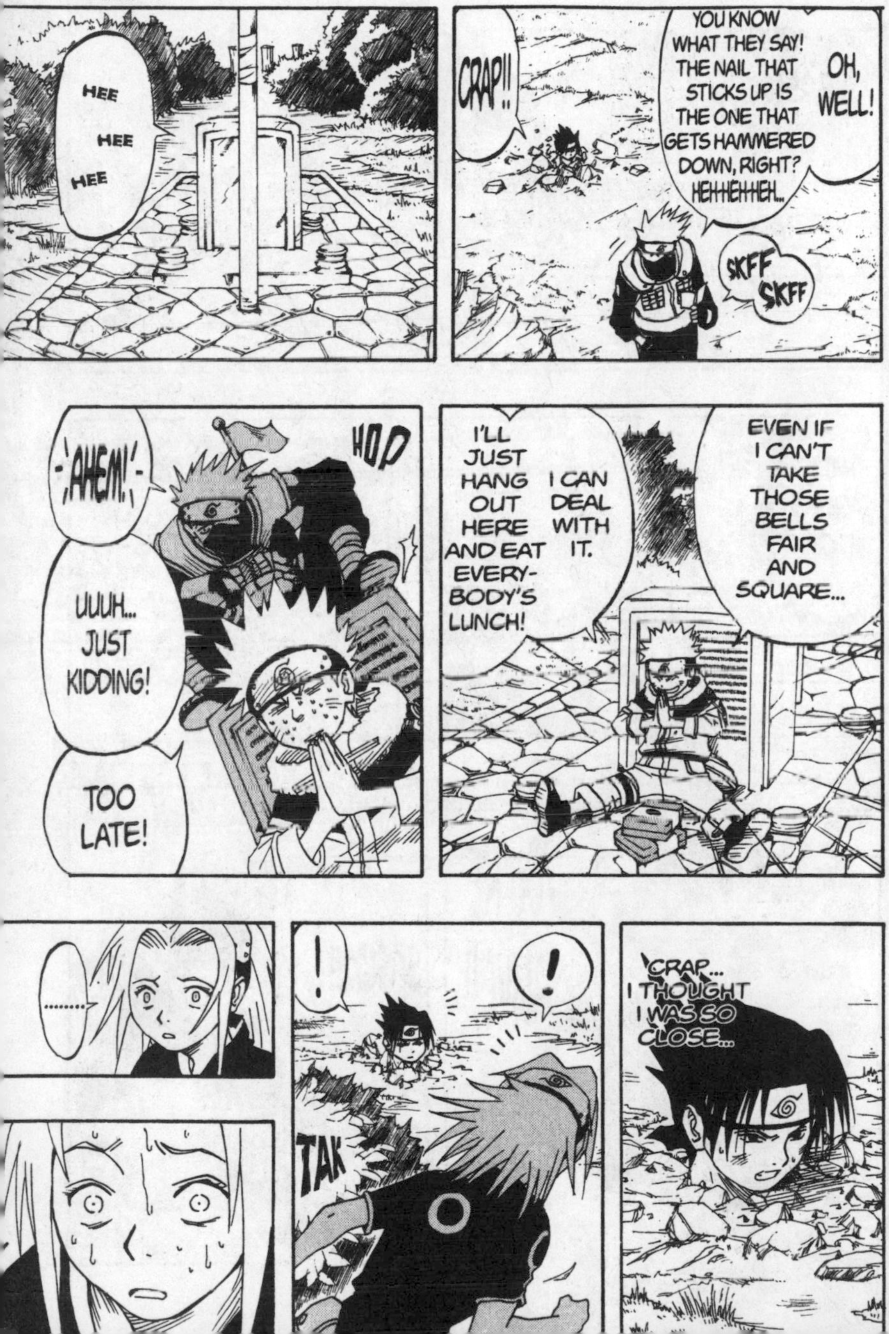
OH, WELL!
YOU KNOW WHAT THEY SAY! THE NAIL THAT STICKS UP IS THE ONE THAT GETS HAMMERED DOWN, RIGHT? HEH-HEH-HEH...
CRAP!!
SKFF SKFF
HEE HEE HEE
EVEN IF I CAN'T TAKE THOSE BELLS FAIR AND SQUARE...
I CAN DEAL WITH IT.
I'LL JUST HANG OUT HERE AND EAT EVERY-BODY'S LUNCH!
HOP
AHEM!
UUUH... JUST KIDDING!
TOO LATE!
CRAP... I THOUGHT I WAS SO CLOSE...
!
!
TAK
....

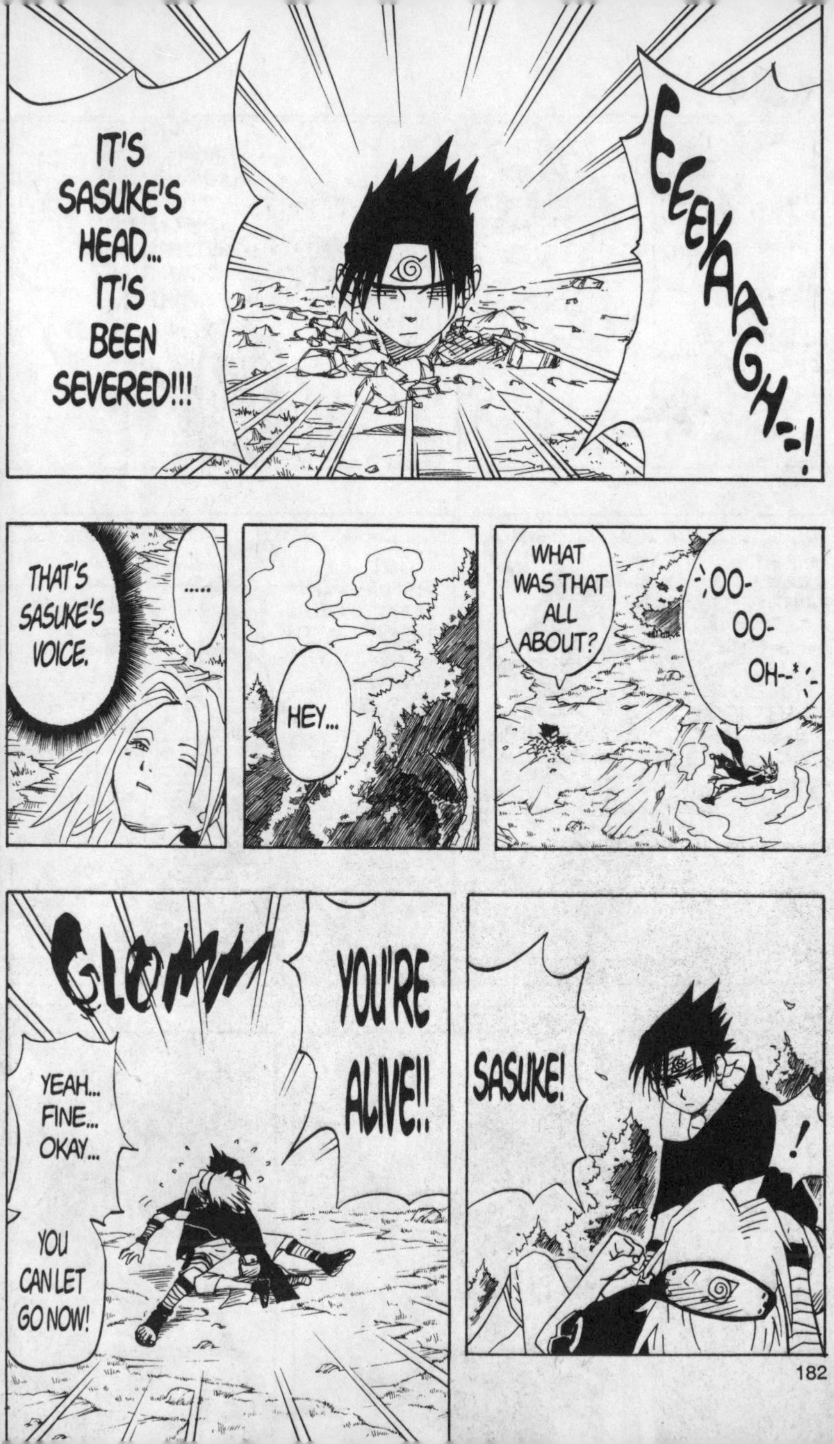
EEEYAAGH--!
IT'S SASUKE'S HEAD... IT'S BEEN SEVERED!!!
OO-OO-OH--*
WHAT WAS THAT ALL ABOUT?
HEY...
.....
THAT'S SASUKE'S VOICE.
!
SASUKE!
YOU'RE ALIVE!!
GLOMM
YEAH... FINE... OKAY...
YOU CAN LET GO NOW!

READ THIS WAY

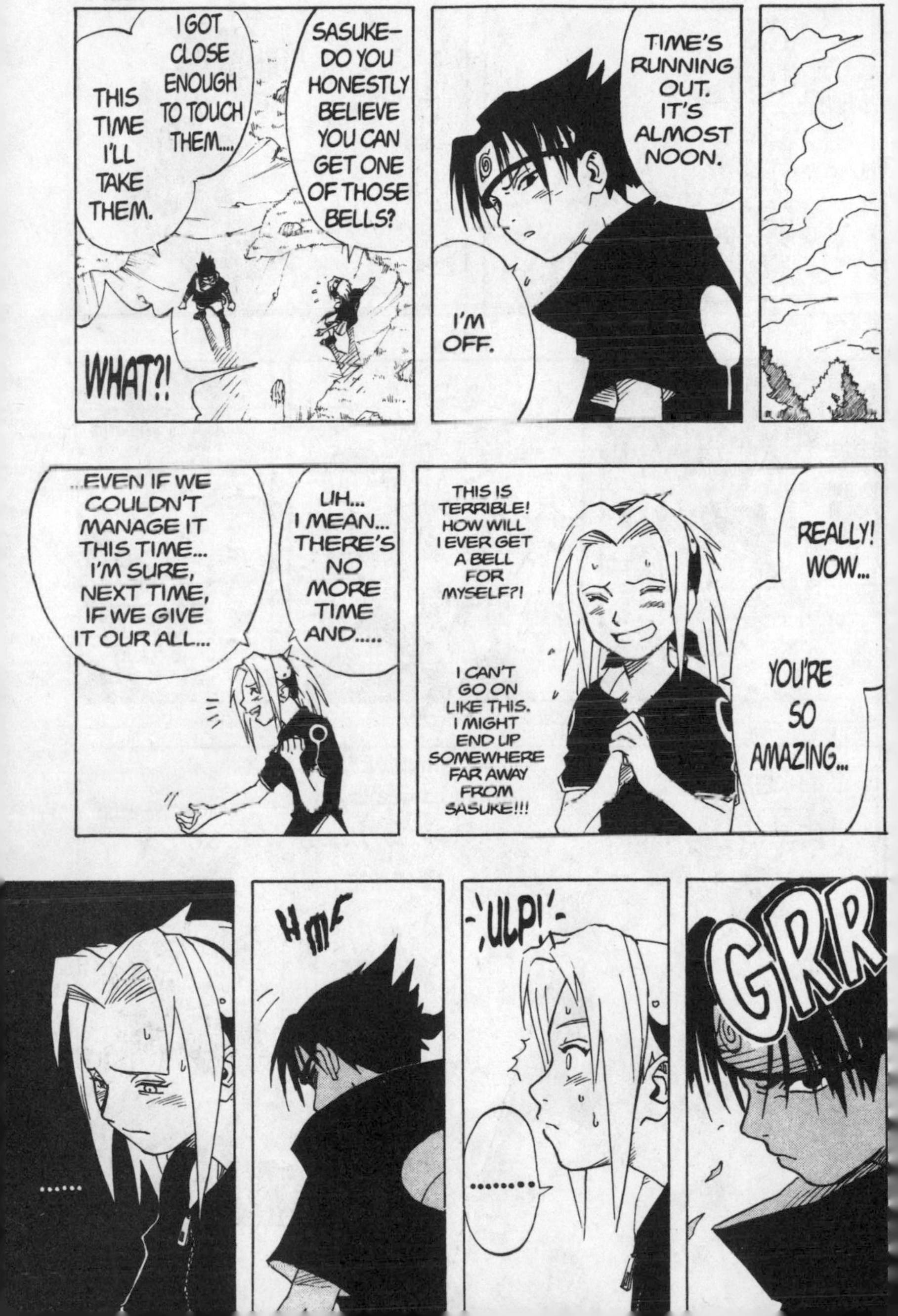
TIME'S RUNNING OUT. IT'S ALMOST NOON.
I'M OFF.
SASUKE— DO YOU HONESTLY BELIEVE YOU CAN GET ONE OF THOSE BELLS?
I GOT CLOSE ENOUGH TO TOUCH THEM....
THIS TIME I'LL TAKE THEM.
WHAT?!
REALLY! WOW...
YOU'RE SO AMAZING...
THIS IS TERRIBLE! HOW WILL I EVER GET A BELL FOR MYSELF?!
I CAN'T GO ON LIKE THIS. I MIGHT END UP SOMEWHERE FAR AWAY FROM SASUKE!!!
UH... I MEAN... THERE'S NO MORE TIME AND.....
...EVEN IF WE COULDN'T MANAGE IT THIS TIME... I'M SURE, NEXT TIME, IF WE GIVE IT OUR ALL...
GRR
ULP!
....
HMF
......

READ THIS WAY

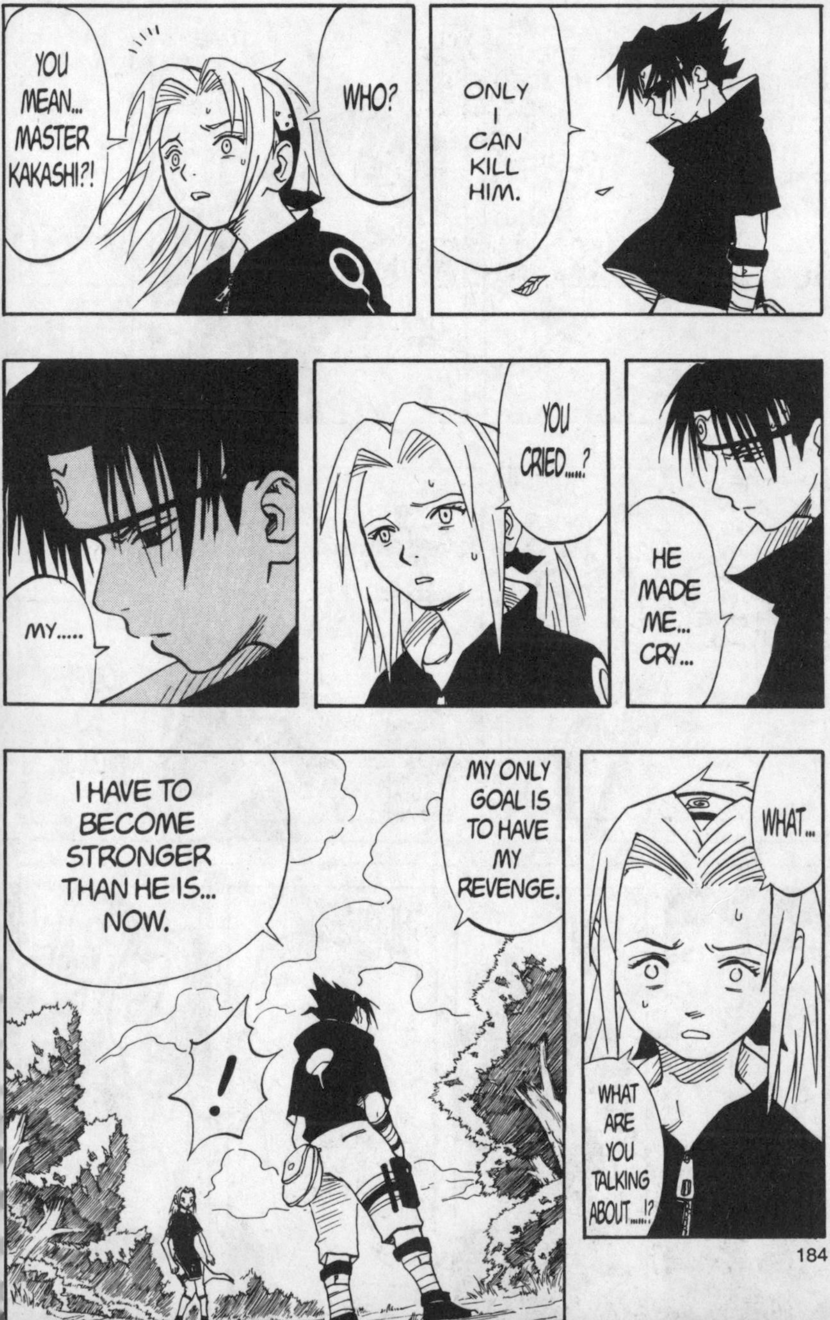
ONLY I CAN KILL HIM.
WHO?
YOU MEAN... MASTER KAKASHI?!
HE MADE ME... CRY...
YOU CRIED.....?
MY.....
WHAT...
WHAT ARE YOU TALKING ABOUT.....!?
MY ONLY GOAL IS TO HAVE MY REVENGE.
I HAVE TO BECOME STRONGER THAN HE IS... NOW.
!

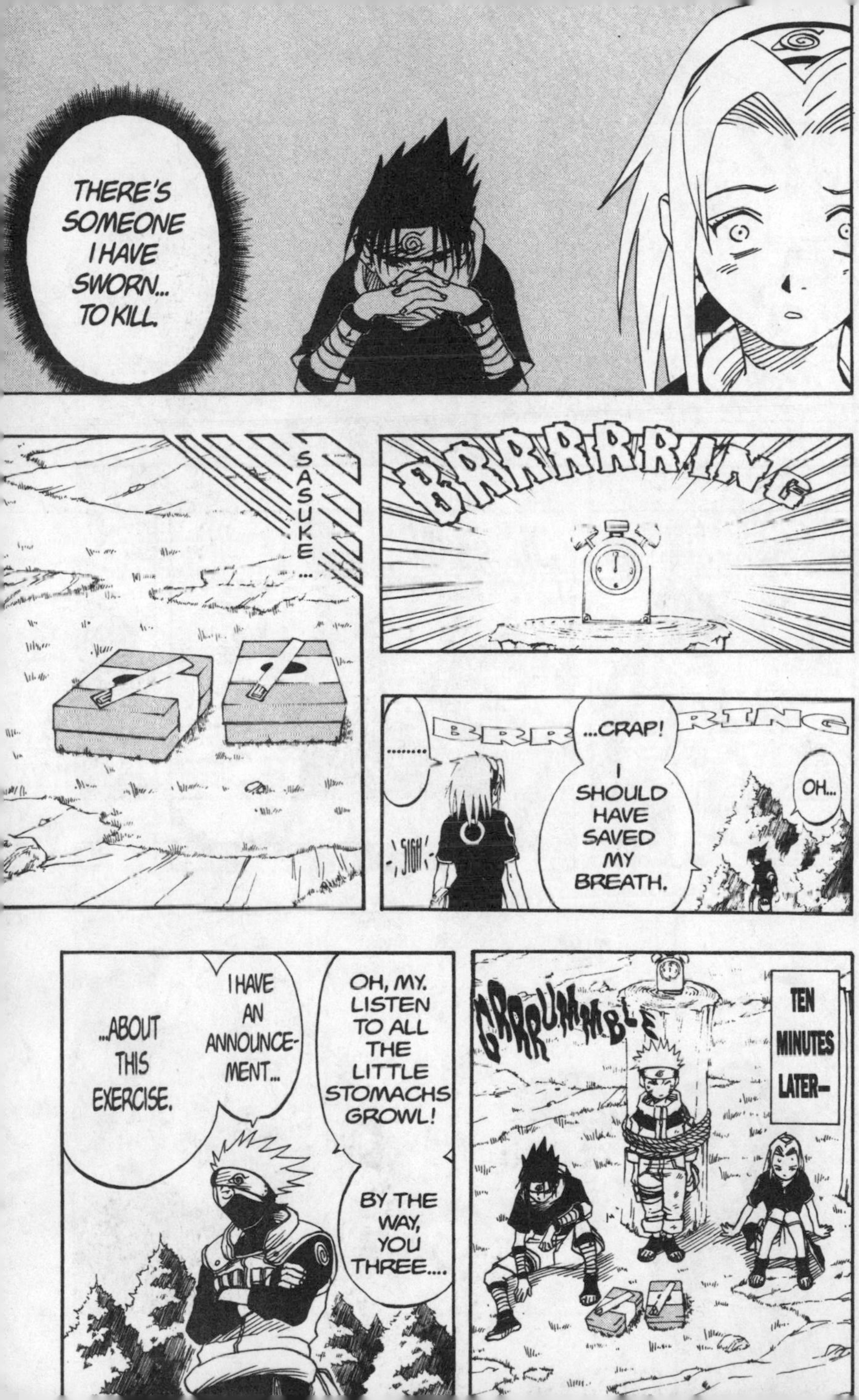
THERE'S SOMEONE I HAVE SWORN... TO KILL.
BRRRRRRING
BRR...RING
OH...
...CRAP! I SHOULD HAVE SAVED MY BREATH.
....
SIGH
SASUKE...
TEN MINUTES LATER—
GRRRUMMBLE
OH, MY. LISTEN TO ALL THE LITTLE STOMACHS GROWL!
BY THE WAY, YOU THREE....
I HAVE AN ANNOUNCEMENT...
...ABOUT THIS EXERCISE.

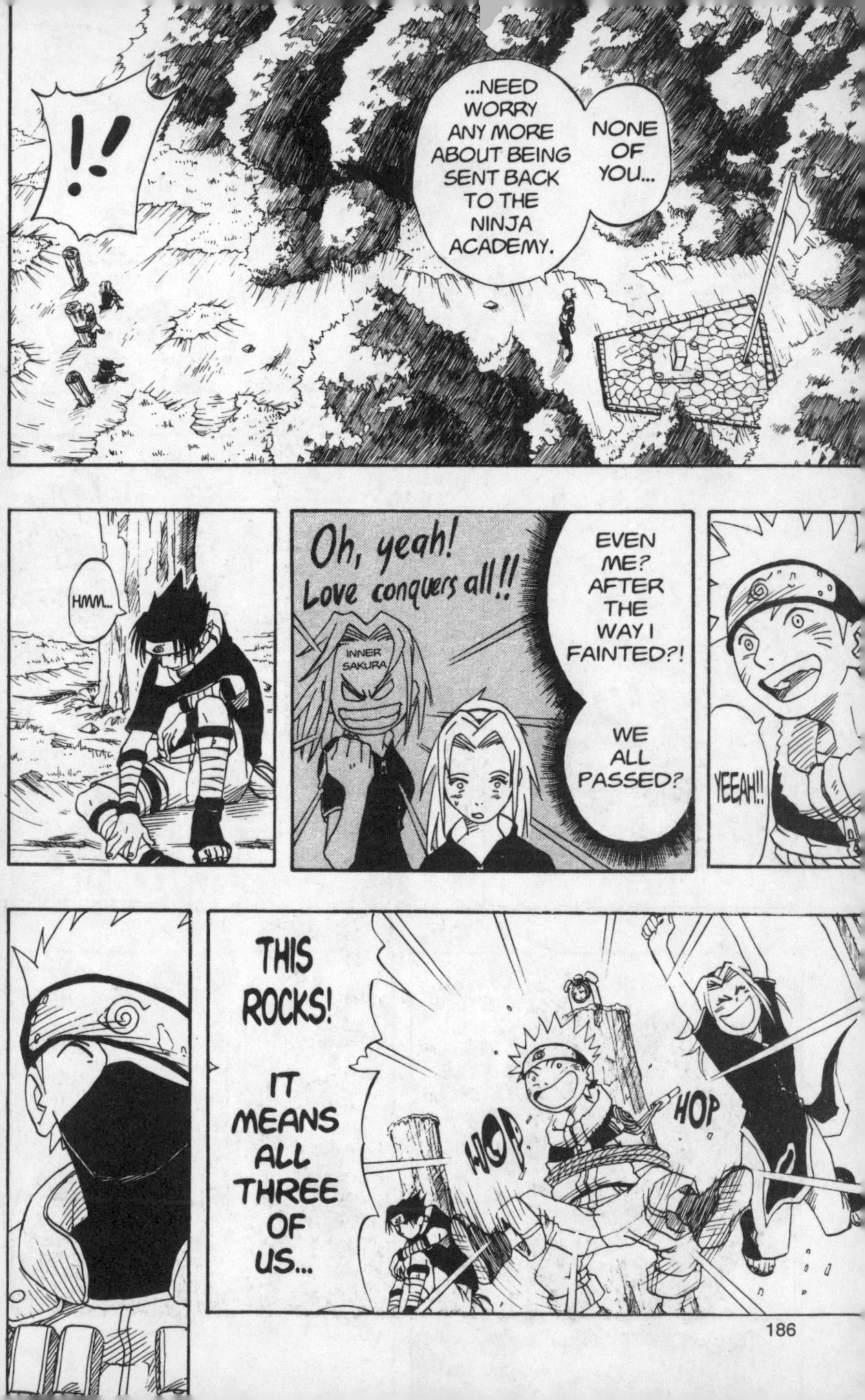
NONE OF YOU...
...NEED WORRY ANY MORE ABOUT BEING SENT BACK TO THE NINJA ACADEMY.
!!
YEEAH!!
EVEN ME? AFTER THE WAY I FAINTED?!
WE ALL PASSED?
Oh, yeah! Love conquers all!!
INNER SAKURA
HMM...
THIS ROCKS!
IT MEANS ALL THREE OF US...
HOP
HOP

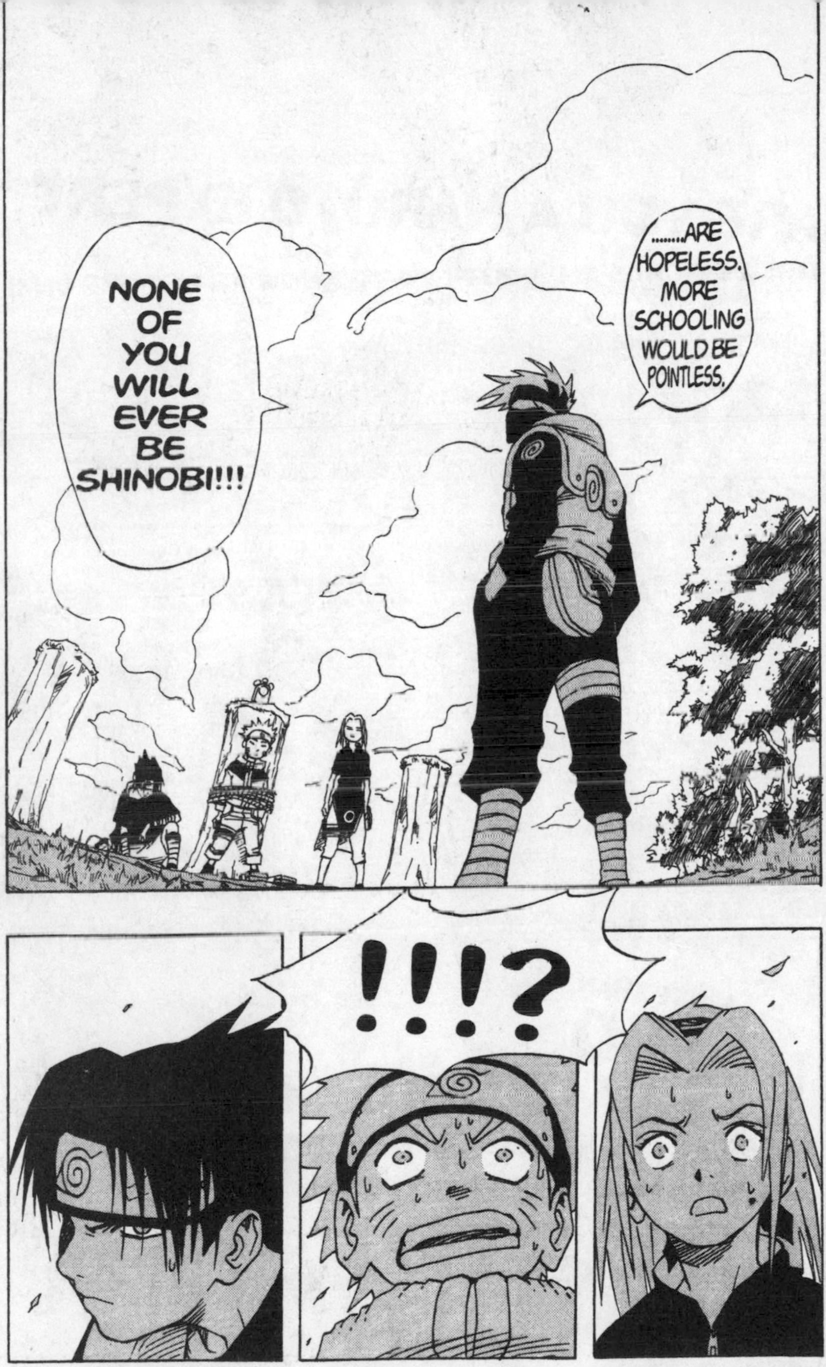

........ARE HOPELESS. MORE SCHOOLING WOULD BE POINTLESS.
NONE OF YOU WILL EVER BE SHINOBI!!!
!!!?

TO BE CONTINUED...

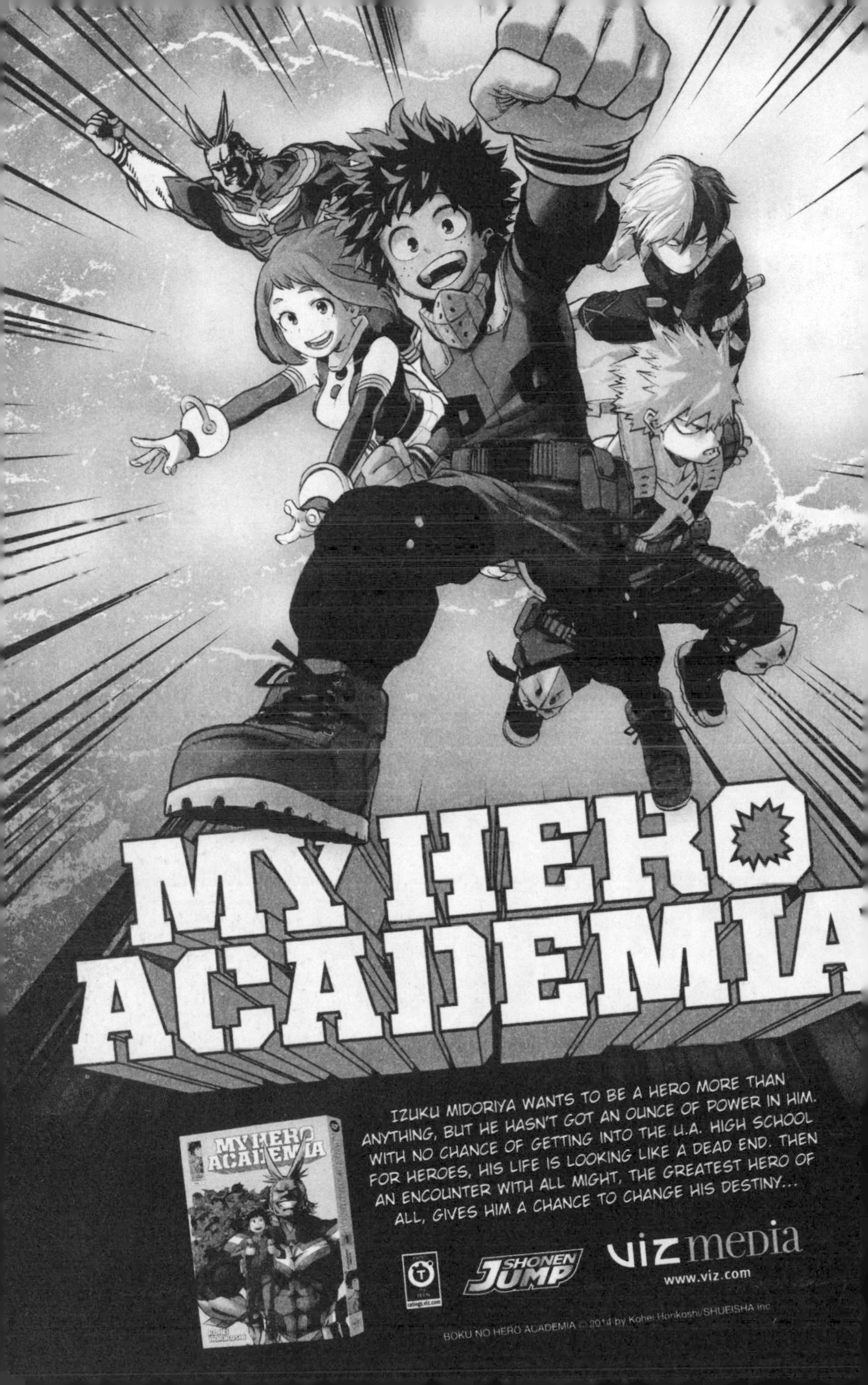
MY HERO ACADEMIA
IZUKU MIDORIYA WANTS TO BE A HERO MORE THAN ANYTHING, BUT HE HASN'T GOT AN OUNCE OF POWER IN HIM. WITH NO CHANCE OF GETTING INTO THE U.A. HIGH SCHOOL FOR HEROES, HIS LIFE IS LOOKING LIKE A DEAD END. THEN AN ENCOUNTER WITH ALL MIGHT, THE GREATEST HERO OF ALL, GIVES HIM A CHANCE TO CHANGE HIS DESTINY...
MY HERO ACADEMIA
KOHEI HORIKOSHI
SHONEN JUMP
viz media
www.viz.com
BOKU NO HERO ACADEMIA © 2014 by Kohei Horikoshi/SHUEISHA Inc.

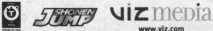